QUIET DIPLOMACY IN ACTION

Quiet Diplomacy in Action:

The OSCE High Commissioner on National Minorities

Edited by

Walter A. Kemp

KLUWER LAW INTERNATIONAL
THE HAGUE / LONDON / BOSTON

Published by:
Kluwer Law International
P.O. Box 85889, 2508 CN The Hague, The Netherlands
sales@kli.wkap.nl
http://www.kluwerlaw.com

Sold and Distributed in North, Central and South America by:
Kluwer Law International
101 Philip Drive, Norwell, MA 02061, USA
kluwerlaw@wkap.com

Sold and Distributed in all other countries by:
Kluwer Law International
Distribution Centre, P.O. Box 322, 3300 AH Dordrecht, The Netherlands

A CIP Catalogue record for this book is available from the Library of Congress

Printed on acid-free paper.

Photograph on p. ii ©Hof Filmproductions.
Cartoon on p. 138 ©P. Schrank, appeared in *The Economist*, 11 September 1999.
Photograph on p. 286 ©Walter Kemp.

ISBN 90-411-1651-6

Kluwer Law International incorporates the publishing programmes of Graham & Trotman Ltd, Kluwer Law and Taxation Publishers and Martinus Nijhoff Publishers

'Over the years, Mr. Van der Stoel has achieved something remarkable: a modicum of trust between would-be warring parties on many of the ragged edges of Europe. Dull he may be. But he has helped make the continent a safer place.'

The Economist, 11 September 1999

'Much conflict could also be prevented if the rich cultural diversity within so many of our states were considered as an asset, rather than a threat, and allowed to flourish accordingly.

This is why the quiet but effective work of your High Commissioner on National Minorities is so important.

All European states should heed his advice, and other continents would do well to adopt a similar mechanism.'

United Nations Secretary General, Kofi Annan,
OSCE Istanbul Summit, 18 November 1999

Contents

Preface

In his acceptance speech as the first High Commissioner on National Minorities of the Organization for Security and Co-operation in Europe (OSCE), Max van der Stoel observed that 'being the first in this newly created post, I will not be able to profit from the experience of my predecessors. In many ways I will have to explore a path which has not been trodden before – a path moreover, that might sometimes be quite slippery.' Van der Stoel not only kept his balance during his eight and one-half years as OSCE High Commissioner on National Minorities, but he blazed a trail that established the High Commissioner's role as an effective instrument of conflict prevention.

Because of the nature of his work, the High Commissioner's success lies in what did not happen: tensions resolved were crises averted. In order to achieve this, his mandate required quiet diplomacy. This fit well with Van der Stoel's sense of discretion. However, as a result, relatively little has been written about his work. This book attempts to shed light on an international actor who operated mainly in the shadows. It goes behind the scenes to discover and explain how quiet diplomacy works in action. While offering a more or less official account of the High Commissioner's work, it also provides an analysis of Van der Stoel's approach and activities. It retraces his path and outlines his methods and techniques in order to explain his contribution to preventive diplomacy.

Quiet Diplomacy in Action explains why the post of High Commissioner was created, the mandate, Van der Stoel's approach, his work in practice, his co-operation with and support from other OSCE and international bodies, and the recurrent themes and issues that he encountered in his work, including general recommendations he initiated and promoted. In addition, summaries are given of the situations in which he was engaged. This book provides a public record of the High Commissioner's activities from 1 January 1993 through early 2001. Major documents relating to national minorities in the OSCE context are included in an annex.

This book has been written in the framework of the ongoing activities of the High Commissioner's office, without prejudicing current engagements and endeavors. To respect the nature of quiet and co-operative diplomacy and to maintain the integrity of the High Commissioner's office, there remain matters of confidence relating to individuals and institutions which can not be breached.

Quiet Diplomacy in Action was written by Walter Kemp, a Senior Adviser to the High Commissioner, with the input of colleagues in the Office of the High Commissioner and in co-operation with Mr. Van der Stoel. Comments on earlier drafts were provided by four external experts who have first-hand experience with the High Commissioner's work: Jonathan Cohen (Programme Associate, Conciliation Resources), Steven Ratner (Professor of Law, University of Texas Law School), Anders Rönquist (Deputy Director, Division for European Security Policy, Swedish Ministry for Foreign Affairs) and Rob Zaagman (First Secretary, Permanent Mission of the Netherlands to the United Nations in New York). Generous support for the production of this book was provided by the Ford Foundation.

Our hope is that this book provides useful insights into a unique instrument of conflict prevention in order that the reader will better appreciate the importance of such work and profit from Van der Stoel's experience.

John Packer
Director
Office of the OSCE High Commissioner on National Minorities

Foreword by Michael Ignatieff

Everyone talks about conflict prevention. One of the few senior figures who actually does it is the High Commissioner on National Minorities of the Organization for Security and Co-operation in Europe (OSCE). Between 1993 and 2001, the first High Commissioner, Max van der Stoel of the Netherlands, shuttled between his base in The Hague and the 15 or so States that have (re)emerged since the collapse of the Communist Bloc, quietly persuading them to modify restrictive language laws, adapt electoral laws to ensure minority participation and enter into dialogue with disaffected minorities before disaffection escalated into conflict. He is not a Higher Commissioner for Minorities, and so he is not their advocate or champion. Sometimes, his role has been to persuade minorities to moderate demands that are bound to lead to trouble and to inch them unwillingly towards dialogue with States that are run by hostile ethnic majorities. Sometimes, his focus has been on State parties, trying to get leaders of new democracies to understand that democracy means something more than ethnic majority tyranny, and that long-term stability depends on the accommodation of minority rights claims.

There are new styles of conflict prevention – in which international NGO's and actors from civil society intervene directly with minorities and State representatives, using the latest in mediation techniques derived from social science and psychology. Being a diplomat of the old school, Max van der Stoel did conflict prevention the old-fashioned way. As these pages show, his modus operandi was quiet behind the scenes negotiation with foreign ministers and heads of State, followed up by formal exchanges of correspondence, accompanied by behind-closed-door meetings with recognized minority leaders. He dealt primarily with legitimated authorities, not with informal civil society groups, and his work focused at the highest political level, not in confidence building from the ground up, nor in direct mediation between communities in conflict. The focus of his work was minority rights legislation in the emerging States, and what marked Van der Stoel's work was minute attention to detail. In Latvia and Estonia, for example, he and his experts devoted eight years to negotiating the various language and citizenship laws bearing on the Russian minority, examining the draft legislation clause by clause and making suggestions to bring it up to international standards.

As this book reveals, sometimes he was successful. Threatened ethno-national conflicts in the Baltic States, which seemed imminent in 1993 and 1994, have receded. A possibly violent secession of the Crimea, which loomed on the horizon in 1993, has now been replaced by wary co-operation between Crimean and Ukrainian authorities. The High Commissioner did useful work calming down conflict over the establishment of an Albanian university in Macedonia in 1997. Throughout his period, he worked with the authorities in Slovakia, Romania and Hungary to prevent the treatment of the Hungarian minorities in Slovakia and Romania from erupting into conflict. So the High Commissioner's tale is the story of the dog that didn't bark. And Europe is stronger because these dogs did not bark.

Even when he was successful, it isn't always clear that he can claim the credit. Success in the Baltic States depended not just on him, but on the political imagination of Baltic leaders, the restraint of the Russians, and important political support for his initiatives from Nordic countries and other OSCE members. In any event, by personal temperament and by professional inclination, a good High Commissioner should not be in the business of claiming credit. He (or She) should be seen and not heard. If the others get the credit, especially local leaders, so much the better.

Sometimes – and Kosovo is the leading example – the High Commissioner's best efforts met with failure. To his credit, he realized on taking office in 1993 that Kosovo was a tinder-box, but the suspension of the Federal Republic of Yugoslavia by the OSCE made it difficult to get access to the province, and by the mid 1990's, Kosovar leaders refused to see him, on the grounds that they were not a national minority, but a nation, with a valid claim to external self-determination. In other areas of Europe, the Basque country and Northern Ireland, he was precluded from working, because of the reluctance of the State parties and because the contending groups had resorted to terror. In some cases – Georgia and Abkhazia – the gulf between the sides proved unbridgeable –

one insisting on territorial integrity, the other insisting on national self-determination. As *Quiet Diplomacy in Action* makes clear, the High Commissioner's type of conflict prevention works only when (a) State parties accept his presence, (b) minorities accept that they are minorities, (c) the conflict has not escalated into an overt struggle between a defense of territorial integrity and a demand for external self-determination, (d) terror has not been used on either side, and (e) both sides have clear interest in compliance with OSCE guidelines on minority rights.

The last point – that both sides must have an interest in compliance – deserves special attention. Why should emerging States, with difficult histories that foreigners may not understand, have any interest in submitting to the persistent, even unrelenting attention of the High Commissioner and his experts?

It is not enough to say that the European political climate has changed since 1991 and that all OSCE States now accept that their exercise of sovereignty is conditional upon minority rights observance. This simply asserts what has to be explained: why European States have found it in their interest to accept the human rights' oversight of the European convention, beginning in the 1950's, and how since 1991, newly emerging States have followed suit, accepting OSCE monitoring of their minority rights performance? Why don't they see such 'intervention' as an infringement of sovereignty, as an insult to their dignity as new States? It is easy to explain why minorities want the High Commissioner to visit their country and examine their grievances. They are usually the weaker party in any internal struggle for recognition, and they have a strong incentive to seek external attention, if not support, from an authoritative international body. The High Commissioner, in effect, provides them with important international validation and legitimacy in their struggle with domestic national authorities. So if this is the case, why should newly emerging States have any incentive whatever to co-operate with a process that may, in their eyes, only validate their internal opponents? Any successful strategy of conflict prevention has to improve the incentives, and set aside the disincentives, for States to allow their domestic problems to be 'internationalized'.

Van der Stoel certainly worked at setting aside the disincentives. The logic of quiet diplomacy is to reduce the costs for emerging States of complying with international advice. It isn't always easy for domestic political leaders, backed by ethnic majorities, to be seen to be listening to foreign advice on issues as sensitive as treatment of ethnic minorities. Van der Stoel understood these sensitivities and took particular care to be as nearly invisible as possible, in order to reduce the transaction costs for domestic leaders in adopting his advice. At other times, however, he made himself visible in the domestic political debates of these States, for example in Croatia, to lend his support to the claims of the minority side. At all times, however, he was sensitive to the risks of being visible and taking sides. Any conflict prevention strategy depends, essentially, on managing and maintaining the political consent of State representatives and minorities. The process must be secretive, so that the costs of concession and compromise, and the costs of appearing to do the bidding of foreigners, can be kept as low as possible to the local leaders.

So much for the disincentive side of the question. What incentives for co-operation did Van der Stoel have at his disposal? Newly emerging States need two things: resources and international legitimacy. The High Commissioner couldn't do very much about resources: he did not have the budget to fund textbooks in minority languages or signage in minority tongues, although he did use his influence to channel European and OSCE funding to these good causes. He was able to channel another crucial resource: drafting expertise, provided by his experts, to these newly emerging States. He could offer them 'best international practice' in minority rights legislation, and he could offer it free of charge. This was one incentive to co-operation, but it is clear that he lacks the resources to improve these incentives. Conflict prevention remains a worthy but impoverished orphan of international diplomacy. Van der Stoel remarked pointedly that the cost of one modern warplane would have funded his work for a decade. If the OSCE is serious about preventing conflict in Europe before it starts, it needs to give the High Commissioner the resources to improve the economic incentives for compliance.

The second overwhelming need of newly emerging States is international legitimacy. Eventually, this means membership in military alliances like NATO, economic organizations like the EU and security collectives like the OSCE. Van der Stoel understood that this need for international legitimacy and eventual membership constituted his chief point of political leverage in newly emerging States in the European area. Without having to make this point explicit, the High Commissioner served, in effect, as a crucial institutional gatekeeper, holding out the prospect of eventual integration into European security and economic institutions in return for compliance with international standards of minority rights protection. But this leverage can only retain legitimacy with emerging States if some of them do progress beyond the waiting rooms of Europe into full membership of her institutions. In effect, Van der Stoel's diplomacy depended, especially in the Baltic, on the expectation that one-day Europe would reciprocate if emerging States did what they were told on minority rights issues. The future stability of these States depends critically on whether Europe keeps the tacit promises that enabled Van der Stoel to be effective.

The larger lesson here is that successful conflict prevention depends on creating positive incentives for good behavior on the part of State parties and minority groups. Positive incentives are relatively easy to create when the body holding out the incentives is as rich and powerful as Europe has become. In this context, emerging States have good reasons to permit benign interventions of the kind that Van der Stoel pioneered. Elsewhere, in Africa and Asia where regional organizations are weaker, the available incentives for good behavior are weaker and the prospects of exporting the European model of conflict prevention pioneered by Van der Stoel are doubtful.

This book highlights a feature of European integration that has not received enough attention: the ability of strong transnational European institutions to offer incentives for good behavior to emerging States on Europe's periphery. Not all States respond to these incentives. Milosevic's Serbia is the classic example of a State that refused to 'internationalize' its minority rights problems, believing that they remained within the exclusive purview of the State. The consequences, both for Serbian minorities outside Serbia and for minorities within Serbia, have been catastrophic. The key fact that the High Commissioner's work makes clear is that the 'internationalization' of minority rights problems, at as early a stage as possible, by a reputable, impartial, quiet diplomat is the single most effective way to avoid the horror of ethnic conflict and war.

Michael Ignatieff is Director of the Carr Center for Human Rights Policy at the Kennedy School of Government, Harvard University.

PART ONE

CHAPTER ONE

Background and Origins

The 1975 Helsinki Final Act of the Conference on Security and Co-operation in Europe (CSCE) made an inextricable link between human rights and security. That link was a major catalyst in developing a comprehensive view of security that obliged CSCE participating States to respect human rights if they were to be treated as responsible partners in other issues like arms control. This linkage, and the process that it engendered, played an important part in eroding Communism and overcoming the division of Europe during the Cold War.

The profound changes of 1989 and 1990 led to equally significant changes in human rights norms and commitments. With the old bipolar confrontation giving way to a new spirit of co-operation, CSCE participating States became more progressive and normative in setting out commitments relating to human rights. This was most evident in the increasing intrusiveness of CSCE mechanisms, beginning with the adoption of the Human Dimension Mechanism at the Vienna Follow-Up Meeting in January 1989. This mechanism provided CSCE participating States, for the first time, with a permanently available instrument to address human dimension issues bilaterally and multilaterally.[1] It was also an implicit recognition of the fact that human rights questions had become a legitimate subject of discussion between participating States. Previously, Governments, particularly Communist ones, had invoked the principle of non-intervention in internal affairs (principle 6 of the Helsinki Final Act) to prevent probing questions into their human rights record.

Further steps were taken at the June 1990 Copenhagen meeting on the human

---

1 For more on this issue and the establishment of the post of High Commissioner on National Minorities see Rob Zaagman & Hannie Zaal, 'The CSCE High Commissioner on National Minorities: prehistory and negotiations', in Arie Bloed (ed.), *The Challenges of Change: the Helsinki Summit of the CSCE and its Aftermath*, (Dordrecht: Martinus Nijhoff Publishers, 1994), pp. 95–111.

dimension. In the most extensive listing of 'human dimension' commitments since the Helsinki Final Act, the Copenhagen Document sets out provisions designed to strengthen respect for, and enjoyment of, human rights and fundamental freedoms, to develop human contacts and to resolve issues of a related humanitarian character. Significantly, ten paragraphs concern the protection and promotion of the rights of persons belonging to national minorities (see Annex 1).

National minority issues also figured in the Charter of Paris for a New Europe, signed in November 1990. In it, the CSCE Heads of State or Government, recognizing democracy as 'the only system of government of our nations', affirmed that 'the ethnic, cultural, linguistic and religious identity of national minorities will be protected and that persons belonging to national minorities have the right freely to express, preserve and develop that identity without any discrimination and in full equality before the law'. They pledged that full respect for these and a wide range of human rights-related precepts would be 'the bedrock on which we will seek to construct the new Europe'.[2]

However, that bedrock was already cracking within months of the Paris Summit. In 1991, a number of crises rocked the CSCE area. Soviet special forces attacked government buildings in Riga and Vilnius in January and war escalated in Nagorno-Karabakh in April. Fighting broke out on three fronts between Croatia and Yugoslavia (around Vukovar, Krajina and Dalmatia) in the spring and Slovenia braced for attacks from Yugoslavia after declaring independence in June 1991. In Moldova, Government forces battled the Transdniestrian National Guard (supported by Cossacks and the former Soviet 14th Army), while trouble brewed in Georgia on a number of fronts; in South Ossetia, Abkhazia, and in opposition to President Zviad Gamsakhkurdia. One of the greatest threats to security in the CSCE area came in August 1991 with the attempted coup against Soviet President Mikhail Gorbachev.

Other more latent conflicts threatened to harm relations within and between CSCE participating States. Tensions were high between the Hungarian and Romanian populations in Transylvania. Questions were raised about the future of the Crimean peninsula after Ukraine voted for independence in December 1991. The independence referendum in the former Yugoslav Republic of Macedonia was boycotted by that country's Albanian minority. When independence

2 Charter of Paris for a New Europe (Paris 1990), p. 14.

was declared in September 1991, Greece took exception to the name 'Macedonia' and the use of certain national symbols. A trade boycott was introduced and bilateral relations between Greece and the 'former Yugoslav Republic of Macedonia' soured. Meanwhile, the situation in Kosovo smoldered while Bosnia and Herzegovina threatened to ignite.[3]

Most of these conflicts were intra- rather than inter-state in character and almost all related to ethnicity and nationalism. Their root causes varied. Some were power struggles over the void left by the collapse of Communism. Others resulted from the accentuation of identities which had been denied or suppressed under years of Communism. An increase in national consciousness was not necessarily a negative phenomenon, yet in many cases nationalism was a powerful mobilizing force for populist leaders who played on the restored pride yet uncertain futures of 'awakening' populations. Nationalist awakening by one group usually aroused a heightened sense of identity (and insecurity) in another – either a neighbouring state or a national minority. This almost invariably led to an increase in tensions.

In many countries in post-Communist transition, the challenges of change included dealing with the disappointment of the pace of economic growth and even disillusionment with democracy. As raised expectations were not fulfilled, social cleavages often provoked a backlash against minorities. This anger all too often manifested itself in attacks on migrant workers, Roma and Jews. Such discrimination, xenophobia and anti-Semitism were not limited to countries of the former Communist bloc. The era of confrontation and division in Europe may well have ended, but it was clear that a New World Order was a long way off.

In order to focus more attention on national minority issues, a meeting of experts was convened in Geneva in July 1991. For three weeks, experts from CSCE participating States discussed issues of national minorities and of the rights of persons belonging to them. Among the topics raised were national legislation, democratic institutions, international instruments, possible forms of co-operation, the implementation of the relevant CSCE commitments, and the scope for the improvement of relevant standards.[4] Representatives of the

---

3 For more detailed information on these conflicts see Sven Gunnar Simonsen (ed.), *Conflicts in the OSCE Area* (Oslo: International Peace Research Institute, 1997).

4 Report of the CSCE Meeting of Experts on National Minorities (Geneva 1991).

participating States also considered new measures aimed at improving the implementation of their commitments. However, there was no agreement on a definition of 'national minorities' or on whether they should be granted collective rights.[5]

Nevertheless, consensus slowly built around the need for an institutional response to ethnic and national conflicts. There was a growing realization among a number of States that the instrument to be developed would have to deal not only with states, but also with non-state actors, namely representatives of national minorities. After all, it was the quest of these non-state actors for recognition and rights that fuelled many of the ethnically charged intra-state conflicts.

Already at the Copenhagen meeting of June 1990 a proposal was introduced (by Sweden) to establish a CSCE Representative on National Minorities. Although this proposal did not go further than providing food for thought, it at least whet the appetite of a number of participating States which were in favour of more effective conflict prevention and crisis management mechanisms. For example, at the Geneva meeting, the United States proposed a mechanism which provided for the involvement of a good offices panel of three experts who would address problems regarding national minorities upon the initiative of the state concerned, while Austria, supported by the Czecho-Slovak Federal Republic, Hungary, Norway, Poland and Sweden, proposed the establishment of a CSCE rapporteur procedure to deal with questions relating to the human dimension of the CSCE, including those relating to national minorities.

Some of these ideas were refloated a few months later at the Moscow meeting of the conference on the human dimension, held between 10 September and 4 October 1991. There, participating States noted that 'in spite of the significant progress made, serious threats and violations of CSCE principles and provisions continue to exist and have a sobering effect on the assessment of the overall situation in Europe'. In particular, they deplored acts of discrimination, hostility and violence against persons or groups on national, ethnic or religious grounds. They therefore expressed the view that, 'for the full realization of their commitments relating to the human dimension, continued efforts are still required which should benefit substantially from the profound political changes that

---

5 Arie Bloed (ed.), *The Conference on Security and Co-operation in Europe: Analysis and Basic Documents, 1972–1993* (Dordrecht: Kluwer International Publishers, 1993), p. 98.

have occurred'.[6] This was a collective recognition of the fact that problems involving national minorities, if neglected, could develop into violent conflict that not only affected the lives of the individuals concerned, but could also destabilize a country and even regional security.

It was evident from the Moscow Document that the tendency of 'continued efforts' to combat this threat should be in the direction of greater outside involvement in the internal affairs of participating States. This was most noticeable in the revolutionary declaration made by the participating States in the Moscow Document that 'commitments undertaken in the field of the human dimension of the CSCE are matters of direct and legitimate concern to all participating States and do not belong exclusively to the internal affairs of the State concerned'.[7] This sentiment had been clearly implied in the Charter of the United Nations and subsequent international commitments. But this unequivocal reiteration was a sign of the times. Human rights were not only everybody's business, but states could now legitimately intervene in matters arising in another state if human rights were being violated.

Several practical proposals were made to implement this idea. One suggestion was to establish a procedure under which states would regularly report on measures taken at the national level concerning the protection and implementation of the rights of persons belonging to national minorities, on the basis of which the CSCE Committee of Senior Officials (at the time the main CSCE decision-making forum) would examine concrete situations and make recommendations to the Council of [Foreign] Ministers. Germany and the United Kingdom urged states to utilize the CSCE mechanisms in order to settle peacefully problems and conflicts arising out of national minority situations.

At the Moscow meeting, the human dimension mechanism, described in the Vienna Concluding Document of January 1989, was strengthened allowing for visits by experts to facilitate the resolution of a particular question or problem relating to the human dimension of the CSCE. Under this so-called Moscow Mechanism, States were obliged to co-operate with the mission. As well as working with representatives of the State during its visit, the mission was also

6 Document of the Moscow Meeting of the Conference on the Human Dimension of the CSCE (Moscow 1991), p. 29.

7 *Ibid.*

given the possibility to 'receive information in confidence from any individual, group or organization on questions it is addressing'.[8]

These initiatives highlighted the evolution of the CSCE's 'conference culture' towards a more operational approach: the CSCE was beginning to shift the emphasis of its work from broad-ranging diplomatic negotiation to fairly specific conflict prevention. The decisions taken at the Moscow meeting also demonstrated the realization of the need to deal with non-state actors and further developed the possibility of legitimate external involvement in the internal affairs of sovereign states on the basis of the common interest in security.

The deepening crisis in Yugoslavia and the threat of conflict in the former Soviet Union intensified the desire to combat ethnic conflict at an early stage. As one observer has noted, an instrument had to be designed to facilitate the role of the OSCE in managing change resulting from post-Communist transition – essentially to address the relationship between minorities and majorities as part of the political process in the broadest sense.[9]

The Netherlands, influenced by its experience of the European Community presidency which coincided with the conflagration of the Yugoslav crisis, was particularly concerned about the need for a European structure to prevent the recurrence of inter-ethnic conflict in the future. It saw the necessity of having an effective intermediary who could provide early warning and also intervene in order to reduce tensions before they erupted into armed conflict. As most conflict situations related to issues of ethnicity and nationalism, it seemed logical to gear this instrument to these minorities in particular. Accordingly, the Minister for Foreign Affairs of the Netherlands, Hans van den Broek, proposed that a High Commissioner on National Minorities (HCNM) be appointed within the framework of the CSCE. A proposal was formally introduced at the Helsinki Follow-Up meeting of April 1992.[10]

---

8 Document of the Moscow Meeting of the Conference on the Human Dimension of the CSCE, paragraph 6, p. 32.

9 John Packer, 'Conflict prevention by the OAU: the relevance of the OSCE High Commissioner on National Minorities', p. 285, in *African Yearbook on International Law* 4 (1996), pp. 279–91.

10 For more on the process see Rob Zaagman & Hannie Zaal, 'The CSCE High Commissioner on National Minorities: prehistory and negotiations', in Bloed 1994, pp. 95–111.

In making the proposal, the Head of the Dutch delegation, Ambassador Bert Veenendaal warned that 'the situation of national minorities is likely to become the cause, or a fertile environment, for several inter- or intra-state conflicts' and that 'this issue could develop into one of the most dangerous threats to stability and security in Europe'. He said that 'The Netherlands, and many other delegations with us, are of the opinion that the CSCE should acquire an operational capability to act immediately on national minority matters, and to assist contentious parties directly concerned, with independent, impartial advice and mediation at the earliest possible stage of a developing conflict'.[11]

Although all participating States agreed with the principle of establishing the post of High Commissioner on National Minorities, the devil, as usual, was in the details. Because ethnic and national minority issues are so sensitive insofar as they may raise questions of identity, culture, recognition, self-government and collective rights, some participating States were very cautious about the potential role of the High Commissioner. Besides, this was new ground and there were no precedents to refer to. As a result, the process of drafting the High Commissioner's mandate was protracted and difficult.

As some countries do not recognize national minorities (or at least certain groups of minorities), they did not wish to create any special rights, duties or institutions for particular sections of the population. Others stressed the importance of individual rather than collective rights and worried that the appointment of a High Commissioner on National Minorities would lead to the recognition of rights for groups who would push for a special status on the basis of language, nationality, religion or culture.

Some participating States with one or more sizeable minority populations within their borders were afraid that the High Commissioner would support the aspirations of these minorities against the interests of the government of the country concerned and that this would jeopardize the territorial integrity of their states. In other words, he would be a High Commissioner *for* National Minorities. A number of countries with minorities within their borders were concerned that the High Commissioner would be used by neighbouring countries (especially kin-States) to further their own national interests in adjoining countries (even to the point of irredentism) and that the High

11 Statement by Ambassador Veenendaal to the Helsinki Follow-up Meeting, 15 April 1992.

Commissioner would therefore contribute to the escalation rather than the resolution of tensions. Others feared that the appointment of an HCNM would prompt national minorities to make more and greater demands, on the assumption that they would be supported by the High Commissioner or at least attract the attention of the international community.

A very small group of countries (particularly the United Kingdom and Turkey), which were confronted with open violence, insisted that the High Commissioner should under no circumstances be involved in national minority issues where use was made of organized acts of terrorism. This view was opposed by countries that felt that such a formulation unjustly suggested a general relationship between national minorities and terrorism.[12]

A number of states concerned about the potential influence of émigré or diaspora interest groups thought it important to specify that if the High Commissioner decided to investigate a particular issue, he should only enter into contact with those parties directly involved in the tensions and living in the area affected.

The High Commissioner's level of independence was also hotly contested. One school of thought suggested that it was necessary to give the High Commissioner a considerable amount of independence and flexibility of action and that by working in relative confidentiality he would be more effective. Others, who already had reservations about what they regarded as the potential intrusiveness of the mandate, were uneasy about the lack of accountability of what they perceived could become a free-roaming and independent international official. CSCE purists raised reservations about the relationship of the High Commissioner to the rest of the organization.[13]

These doubts and reservations left their mark on the mandate of the High Commissioner on National Minorities which, like all OSCE decisions, was eventually taken by consensus.[14]

---

12 These points were made on the record in a number of interpretive statements. See Journal No. 50 of the 22nd Plenary of the Helsinki Follow-Up Meeting.

13 This section on reservations to the mandate and its drafting draws heavily on points made by Zaagman & Zaal, in Bloed 1994; and H. Zaal, 'The High Commissioner on National Minorities', *Helsinki Monitor* 3(4), (1992), pp. 33–7. Thanks is due to both for their comments on this chapter.

14 The only exception to the consensus rule is outlined in a decision of the Prague

The Mandate

The CSCE Heads of State or Government met at the Helsinki Summit on 9 and 10 July 1992 'to give impetus' to the CSCE process. In the Summit document they noted that 'the legacy of the past remains strong. We are faced with challenges and opportunities, but also with serious difficulties and disappointments'.[15] Many of the latter related to the inability to curb aggressive nationalism and cope with inter-ethnic conflict. In the early 1990s, Europe witnessed loss of life, human misery, gross violations of human rights and a refugee crisis on a scale that it had not seen since the Second World War. Whereas the 1990 Charter of Paris for a New Europe was brimming with optimism, in the Helsinki Document the Heads of State or Government were forced to admit that:

> 'Economic decline, social tension, aggressive nationalism, intolerance, xenophobia and ethnic conflicts threaten stability in the CSCE area. Gross violations of CSCE commitments in the field of human rights and fundamental freedoms, including those related to national minorities, pose a special threat to the peaceful development of society, in particular in new democracies.'[16]

The participating States therefore approved a programme to enhance their capabilities for concerted action and to intensify their co-operation for democracy, prosperity and equal rights of security. This included the development and strengthening of structures to ensure political management of crises and the creation of new instruments of conflict prevention and crisis management. The most important of these was the post of CSCE High Commissioner on National Minorities.

As noted above, a number of States had reservations about various aspects of the High Commissioner's mandate. But few questioned the need for the creation of an instrument for preventing inter-ethnic conflict. Conflicts in the former Yugoslavia and in several states which used to be part of the Soviet Union had

---

Ministerial Council of January 1992 that says that appropriate action can be taken without the consent of the state concerned in 'cases of clear, gross and uncorrected violation' of OSCE commitments. This is the so-called 'consensus minus one' principle.

15 CSCE Helsinki Document: the Challenges of Change (Helsinki 1992), p. 5.

16 *Ibid.*, p. 7.

made it clear by the early 1990s that intra-state conflicts could threaten the stability and prosperity of States and boil over into regional conflict. Such conflicts had to be addressed at an early stage.

Consenus on the mandate was reached by the Helsinki Summit. This was a major development in the CSCE's conflict prevention capabilities and a significant innovation for the protection of persons belonging to national minorities. The importance that participating States attached to the High Commissioner's position can be noted by the fact that the mandate is given a separate chapter (Chapter II) in the 1992 Helsinki Document immediately following the 'Strengthening of CSCE Institutions and Structures'. Significantly it was not introduced under Chapter VI as a human dimension instrument; it was a conflict prevention instrument.

This section will look at the mandate in theory. Subsequent chapters will look at its application in practice. One will note significant differences between theory and practice.

The mandate of the High Commissioner, as elaborated in the Helsinki Summit document (see Annex 3), is

> 'to provide "early warning", and as appropriate, "early action" at the earliest possible stage in regard to tensions involving national minority issues which have not yet developed beyond an early warning stage, but, in the judgment of the High Commissioner, have the potential to develop into a conflict within the CSCE area, affecting peace, stability or relations between participating States, requiring the attention of and action by the [Ministerial] Council or the CSO [Committee of Senior Officials, now Senior Council].'[17]

According to the mandate, the High Commissioner's role is 'to assess at the earliest possible stage the role of the parties directly concerned, the nature of the tensions and recent developments therein and, where possible, the potential

---

17 *Ibid.*, p. 9 paragraph 3 of Section II 'CSCE High Commissioner on National Minorities' (hereafter referred to as II). The Committee of Senior Officials was established by the 1990 Charter of Paris to meet at the level of political directors to prepare the work and implement the decisions of the Ministerial Council and – between sessions of the Ministerial Council – to oversee, manage and co-ordinate OSCE affairs. It was subsequently changed to the Senior Council and in 1997 meetings became very rare and its tasks were taken over by the Reinforced Permanent Council.

consequences for peace and stability within the CSCE area'.[18] To do this, the High Commissioner may collect and retrieve information regarding national minorities 'from any source'[19] including media and non-governmental organizations with the exception of 'any person or organization which practises or publicly condones terrorism or violence' (hereafter referred to as paragraph 25).[20]

The High Commissioner can also receive specific reports from parties regarding developments concerning national minority issues. These include reports on violations of OSCE commitments with respect to national minorities as well as other violations in the context of national minority issues. The 'parties directly concerned' (as opposed to émigré representatives) who may provide such reports and with whom the High Commissioner may seek to communicate in person during a visit to a participating State include the governments of participating States (including, if appropriate, regional and local authorities in areas which national minorities reside), and representatives of associations, non-governmental organizations, religious and other groups of national minorities directly concerned in the area of tension, which are authorized by the persons belonging to those national minorities to represent them.[21]

The mandate authorizes the High Commissioner to pay visits (or 'a visit' as it says) to any participating State and communicate in person (subject to the provisions of paragraph 25 regarding terrorism which are explained below) with parties directly concerned to obtain first-hand information about the situation of national minorities.[22] Various mechanisms, mainly the Moscow Mechanism, had foreseen the possibility of sending missions to inspect the situation in a participating State. However, under these mechanisms it was only the participating States which were competent to initiate such visits or decide on them. With the establishment of the High Commissioner on National Minorities, intrusiveness had reached a stage in which a non-State entity could independently decide to visit a State – even without the formal consent of the State concerned.[23]

---

18 II, para. 16.

19 II, para. 23.

20 II, para. 25.

21 II, para. 26, 26a & 26b.

22 II, para. 11c.

23 Zaagman & Zaal, in Bloed 1994, p. 116.

This was an operational embodiment of the idea noted earlier (first expressed in the Moscow Document) that 'issues concerning national minorities, as well as compliance with international obligations and commitments concerning the rights of persons belonging to them, are matters of legitimate international concern and consequently do not constitute exclusively an internal affair of the respective State'.[24] This was revolutionary for not only was the invocation of sovereignty as an argument to prevent the consideration of human rights as a matter of international concern no longer valid, OSCE states now agreed – by consensus – on a mechanism that could legitimately allow others to become engaged in their 'internal' affairs.

As part of his conditions of travel, the High Commissioner is obliged by his mandate to submit to the participating State concerned specific information regarding the intended purpose of a prospective visit.[25] He must also consult the Chairman-in-Office (the Foreign Minister of whichever country holds the one-year revolving Chairmanship of the OSCE).[26] In turn, the State(s) concerned are obliged to consult with the High Commissioner on the objectives of the trip.[27] During the High Commissioner's visits, 'the State concerned will facilitate free travel and communication of the High Commissioner subject to the provisions of paragraph 25'. If the State concerned does not allow the High Commissioner to enter the country and to travel and communicate freely, 'the High Commissioner will so inform the CSO'.[28]

For such visits, the High Commissioner may decide 'to request assistance from not more than three experts with relevant expertise in specific matters on which brief, specialized investigation and advice are required'.[29]

On his visits, the High Commissioner may (subject to the provision of paragraph 25 concerning terrorism) 'consult the parties involved, and may receive information in confidence from any individual, group or organization directly concerned with the questions the High Commissioner is addressing'; he is

24 Report of the CSCE Meeting of Experts on National Minorities (Geneva 1991), p. 4.

25 II, para. 27.

26 II, para. 17.

27 II, para. 27.

28 II, para. 28.

29 II, para. 31–4.

expected to respect the confidential nature of the information that he receives.[30] Where appropriate, he may also 'promote dialogue, confidence and co-operation' between the parties directly involved.[31]

After a visit to a participating State, the High Commissioner is obliged to provide strictly confidential reports to the Chairman-in-Office. No other reporting was foreseen.[32]

Because the mandate was attempting to draw up guidelines for a voyage into uncharted waters, some of its elements were rather formalistic and now seem outdated. As will be seen in Chapter 4, practical working methods have given nuances to certain sections of the mandate and stretched others. Strictly speaking, pursuant to paragraph 19 the High Commissioner, after terminating his involvement in a particular situation, should report to the Chairman-in-Office on his findings, results and conclusions. Within a period of one month, the Chairman-in-Office will consult, in confidence, on the findings, results and conclusions, with the participating State(s) concerned and may also consult more widely. Thereafter the report, together with possible comments, will be transmitted to the CSO.[33] As will be noted below, the way this worked in practice was considerably different.

The provisions for early warning in the mandate are also very formalistic. According to paragraphs 13 and 14, if, on the basis of exchanges of communications and contacts with relevant parties, the High Commissioner concludes that there is a *prima facie* risk of potential conflict, he or she may issue an early warning, which will be communicated promptly by the Chairman-in-Office to the CSO. The Chairman-in-Office will include this early warning in the next meeting of the CSCE at which time the High Commissioner has an opportunity to explain the reasons for raising the alarm.[34]

In the mandate, the transition from early warning to early action is also rigidly structured. Paragraph 16 notes that 'the High Commissioner may recommend that he/she be authorized to enter into further contact and closer

30 II, para. 29.

31 II, para. 12.

32 II, para. 18.

33 II, para. 19.

34 II, para. 13 & 14.

consultation with the parties concerned with a view to possible solutions, according to a mandate to be decided by the CSO'. In practice, most of the High Commissioner's activities have concerned early action – and in a way that has been far more subtle and operational than the method foreseen by the mandate. The High Commissioner's approach and methods will be described in Chapters 3 and 4.

There is also an 'exit strategy' (or escape clause) contained in the mandate that says 'should the High Commissioner conclude that the situation is escalating into a conflict, or if the High Commissioner deems that [his] scope for action . . . is exhausted, the High Commissioner shall, through the Chairman-in-Office, so inform the CSO'.[35] In Van der Stoel's over eight years as High Commissioner, this strategy was never employed.

Some limitations are built into the mandate. For example, 'the High Commissioner will not consider national minority issues occurring in the State of which the High Commissioner is a national or a resident, or involving a national minority to which the High Commissioner belongs, only if all parties directly involved agree, including the State concerned.'[36]

More significantly, the mandate states that 'the High Commissioner will not consider national minority issues in situations involving organized acts of terrorism'[37] and, in the oft-cited paragraph 25, that he 'will not communicate with and will not acknowledge communications from any person or organization which practices or publicly condones terrorism or violence'. The implication is that violence should never be a solution, neither for groups in a State nor for the State itself. This is explicitly stated in paragraph 26 of the human dimension chapter of the Helsinki Document which says participating States 'will address national minority issues in a constructive manner, by peaceful means and through dialogue among all parties concerned on the basis of [O]SCE principles and commitments'.

The High Commissioner's mandate is also designed so that he will not consider individual cases. Paragraph 5c states explicitly that the High Commissioner will not consider violations of CSCE commitments with regard to an individual person belonging to a national minority.

35 II, para. 20.

36 II, para. 5a.

37 II, para. 5b.

There is also an implication in the mandate that the High Commissioner should not re-invent the wheel. Paragraph 6 states that 'in considering a situation, the High Commissioner will take fully into account the availability of democratic means and international instruments to respond to it, and their utilization by the parties involved'. In other words, his involvement should have some added value. He was also theoretically expected to draw on the facilities of the Office for Democratic Institutions and Human Rights (ODIHR). This stemmed from the fact that in the early 1990s CSCE participating States were wary of creating a large bureaucracy and therefore wanted to keep the size and costs of CSCE institutions to a minimum. He was therefore supposed to draw on existing resources instead of requesting new ones. This never occurred in practice. Instead, he was soon given a separate budget within the overall OSCE budget.

As noted earlier, the High Commissioner may go wherever he wants and communicate with whomever he wants, with few restrictions. In doing so, he is expected 'to work in confidence and will act independently of all parties involved in the tensions'.[38] The High Commissioner's confidential approach will be explained in the next chapter.

This independence is kept in check by accountability to OSCE bodies and institutions. According to the mandate, the High Commissioner is appointed by the (Ministerial) Council[39] and acts under the aegis of the Committee of Senior Officials (CSO).[40]

According to the mandate, the CSO can request and provide a mandate for the High Commissioner to become involved in a particular national minority issue.[41] It could also decide on a mandate for early action.[42] However, the High Commissioner's mandate was carefully formulated to avoid any indication that the CSO can give instructions to the High Commissioner or that it can overrule him.[43] The main interaction between the High Commissioner and the CSO is

38 II, para. 4.

39 II, para. 9.

40 II, para. 2.

41 II, para. 7.

42 II, para. 16.

43 Zaagman & Zaal, in Bloed 1994, p. 120. See also II, paragraphs 21 and 22 of the mandate.

anticipated during times of crisis.[44] The High Commissioner must communicate early warning to the CSO (through the Chairman-in-Office). He is also obliged to report to the CSO on the termination of his role in a particular situation.[45] The way that this relationship evolved will be examined in Chapter 5.

According to the mandate, the High Commissioner's main point of contact within the OSCE is the Chairman-in-Office. He or she is the person to whom the High Commissioner reports before and after his visits,[46] to whom the High Commissioner would give an early warning[47] and to whom the High Commissioner reports that he has completed or exhausted his activities.[48]

The Appointment of Van der Stoel

The mandate states that the High Commissioner should be 'an eminent international personality with long-standing experience from whom an impartial performance of the function may be expected'.[49] Because the mandate draws so heavily on the judgement, experience, and political and diplomatic sense of the appointed personality, it is clear that the acquired reputation and the personal traits of the prospective candidate are vitally important.[50]

The Netherlands put forward Max van der Stoel as a candidate at the 16th Committee of Senior Officials meeting which took place in Prague between 16 and 18 September 1992. He fit the desired profile and had the necessary political and moral authority to take on the job.

Born in 1924, by 1992 Van der Stoel was a senior statesman with a long and distinguished career. He was twice Minister for Foreign Affairs of the Netherlands (1973–1977 and 1981–1982). He was elected to the Upper House of Parliament in 1960 and maintained his seat for three years. He became a member of the lower house in 1963 and remained a member until 1981. He was a member of

44 II, para. 13.

45 II, para. 19 & 20.

46 II, para. 17 & 18.

47 II, para. 13.

48 II, para. 19 & 20.

49 II, para. 8.

50 Packer 1996a, p. 288.

the European Parliament (1971–1973) and a member of the North Atlantic Assembly (1968–1973, 1978–1981) as well as a Member of the Council of Europe Consultative Assembly (where he was Rapporteur on Greece during the colonels crisis) and a member of the WEU Assembly between 1967 and 1972. He served as Permanent Representative of the Netherlands to the United Nations between 1983 and 1986 and in 1992 was appointed by the UN Commission on Human Rights as Special Rapporteur on Iraq (a post which he held until the end of 1999). He was familiar with the work of the CSCE as Foreign Minister during the Helsinki consultations from 1973 to 1975, as Chairman of the Netherlands Helsinki Committee for several years, and as head of delegation for the Netherlands during the CSCE conferences on the human dimension in Paris, Copenhagen and Moscow.

Van der Stoel was officially appointed (for a period of three years) at the Ministerial Council in Stockholm on 15 December 1992. He was re-appointed to a second three-year term in 1995 and was extended for an exceptional one-year term in 1998. When no consensus was reached on his successor in 1999, he was asked by the Heads of State or Government at the Istanbul Summit in December 1999 to continue for another year. The Ministerial Council of November 2000 extended his appointment 'as an exceptional measure' until 30 June 2001. He was succeeded by Rolf Ekens of Sweden.

As there was no precedent for the High Commissioner's position, Van der Stoel had to start from scratch. In his acceptance speech he said that 'preventive diplomacy adds a new element to the classic methods of diplomacy; it opens new possibilities for creativity and imagination, but on the other hand, . . . because there is relatively little experience in this field, there is also the need to move cautiously in order to avoid pitfalls'.[51] The way that Van der Stoel did this will be examined in the next five chapters.

Van der Stoel also had to start from scratch in setting up an office. The budget for the first year was approximately $400,000. A small office in The Hague, with second-hand furniture and computers, was provided by the Dutch Government and began operation in early 1993. The Dutch Government seconded a personal adviser to the High Commissioner and two advisers were seconded by Sweden and Poland. They were assisted by one secretary. To bolster

---

51 Acceptance Speech to the Stockholm Meeting of the Council of Ministers of Foreign Affairs of the CSCE, 15 December 1992, Stockholm, Sweden.

the High Commissioner's limited resources, a Foundation on Inter-Ethnic Relations was set up in 1993. In the spring of 1994, two more advisers were recruited. Two administrative assistants joined the staff one year later. These were modest beginnings for an office that would play an important role in reducing inter-ethnic conflict in the OSCE area.

CHAPTER TWO

The High Commissioner's Approach to Conflict Prevention

Although the mandate of the High Commissioner is very specific in several regards, it is very general in others. Basic terms like 'national minorities' are left undefined and there are few guidelines on important points like how the High Commissioner should promote dialogue, confidence and co-operation between the parties and on what basis he would interpret a situation as a *prima facie* risk of potential conflict. As the instrument of a High Commissioner on National Minorities was unique and the scope of his involvement unprecedented, it was left to Van der Stoel to define his approach to conflict prevention.

The way that Van der Stoel interpreted his mandate evolved over his eight-year period as High Commissioner on National Minorities. Although he did not start with a 'grand idea',[1] from the beginning his approach was characterized by a number of features: independence, co-operation, impartiality, incrementalism, persistence, confidentiality, trust and credibility. He regarded his role as that of a political instrument, while grounding his work in international standards (including legal instruments), particularly those relating to human rights. This approach defined his views on national minorities and nationalism, and shaped his methods of preventive diplomacy and early warning.

The High Commissioner in the OSCE Security Context

The High Commissioner on National Minorities is part of the OSCE's comprehensive view of security. In this context, the protection and promotion of human rights and fundamental freedoms, along with economic and environmental co-operation, are considered to be just as important for the maintenance

1 See page 16 of interview with Van der Stoel, in Wolfgang Zellner & Falk Lange (eds.), *Peace and Stability through Human Rights: Speeches by the OSCE High Commissioner on National Minorities.* (Baden-Baden: Nomos, 1999).

of peace and stability as politico-military issues. These various elements of security are interdependent and complement each other. They are also all based on common principles.

The High Commissioner's work touches on many aspects of security from human rights and 'identity' issues to highly political questions concerning the territorial integrity of states and the affect of inter-ethnic relations on the cohesion of governments and states. This is why Van der Stoel often stressed that he is not an instrument of the human dimension. A former adviser to the High Commissioner was unequivocal in stating this opinion saying, 'the HCNM is a conflict prevention instrument and is not intended to be an instrument of the human dimension nor, indeed, does he protect the rights of persons belonging to national minorities, either as individuals or as groups'.[2]

As noted in Chapter 1, the impetus for the creation of the post of the High Commissioner was to address security issues, particularly in the context of conflict prevention. As a result, the emphasis of the High Commissioner's mandate is on early warning, and it was elaborated in discussions on politico-military aspects of security rather than the 'human dimension'.

In September 1993 Van der Stoel explained that 'preventing ethnic conflict requires that the net be thrown wider than the human dimension. Minority questions are so intimately connected to issues which go to the heart of the existence of states that an approach based exclusively on the human rights aspects would be incomplete and therefore insufficient'.[3]

However, because of the OSCE's comprehensive view of security, the politico-military and human dimensions are linked. As the 1991 Geneva document emphasizes, 'human rights and fundamental freedoms are the basis for the protection and promotion of rights of persons belonging to national minorities.'[4] Van der Stoel acknowledged this connection on a number of occasions saying, for example, that 'full respect for human rights, a working democracy and the existence of the rule of law, are the best guarantees for a positive situation for national minorities. It is my experience that problems in inter-ethnic relations

---

2 Zaagman, in Bloed 1994, pp. 140 & 127.

3 Intervention at the Human Dimension Implementation Meeting, Warsaw 28–29 September 1993.

4 Report of the CSCE Meeting of Experts on National Minorities (Geneva 1991), p. 3.

very often go hand in hand with problems in the human dimension in general'.[5] On another occasion he noted that

> 'the protection of minorities is centered on the protection and promotion of the human rights of persons belonging to national minorities. If these rights are respected in a democratic political framework based on the rule of law, then all citizens, regardless of ethnicity, language or religion, will have the opportunity and the equal right to freely express and pursue their legitimate interests and aspirations. This entails the fostering of inter-ethnic integration which can build harmonious and stable societies and resolve or manage the sources of conflict.'[6]

This is a process that the High Commissioner was actively involved in.

A Political Instrument

To understand Van der Stoel's approach to conflict prevention it is important to realize that he regarded his position to be that of a political instrument. In 1999, reflecting on six years as High Commissioner he wrote: 'I understand my tasks as High Commissioner on National Minorities as being framed in political terms and the tools in my hands as being essentially tailored to deal with political issues'.[7]

He mainly considered national minority issues in the context of how they affected intra- and inter-State relations. Although, as will be explained below, Van der Stoel framed many of his recommendations in the context of international standards, in the first instance he usually considered issues (like culture, history, language, and education) in relation to how they affected political processes within and between OSCE participating States. In keeping with his

5 OSCE Human Dimension Implementation meeting, November 1997. See also his speech at the London School of Economics, 19 October 1999, entitled 'Human Rights, the Prevention of Conflict and the International Protection of Minorities: a Contemporary Paradigm for Contemporary Challenges'.

6 Speech at the London School of Economics, 19 October 1999.

7 Max van der Stoel, 'Reflections on the Role of the OSCE High Commissioner on National Minorities as an Instrument of Conflict Prevention', *OSZE Jahrbuch* (Baden-Baden: Nomos, 1999).

mandate, he felt that it was incumbent on him to intervene – as a political actor, an 'interested' third party – in those situations that he regarded as potentially destabilizing to OSCE participating States by advocating achievable and durable solutions.

It is hard to pigeon-hole his type of involvement as his position and mandate are unique. He is not a mediator because he tries to prevent conflicts rather than solve them. He is not a classic facilitator because he is not necessarily trying to bring two sides to the bargaining table. Nor is he strictly an envoy of the OSCE because, although acting on behalf of and with the support of the OSCE, he is not coming to a particular situation with an OSCE agenda; he is very much responsible for shaping the agenda and then reporting back to the Chairman-in-Office and participating States. An apt description of his role is that of nonpartisan adviser who fulfills several functions simultaneously: adviser, negotiator, and intermediary.[8]

Most of the issues that the High Commissioner dealt with arose in political processes. They concerned decision-making, policy and law-making, the strategies and internal dynamics of political parties, the politics of coalition Government, the workings of Parliament, and diplomacy (both bilateral and multi-lateral). In order to have insights into these processes and to act effectively when dealing with them, the High Commissioner must have considerable political acumen. This was foreseen to some extent in the mandate when it cited the need for 'an eminent international personality with long-standing relevant experience'. Van der Stoel set the mould that the 'long-standing relevant experience' should include political experience. With his political, diplomatic and legal background, he knew where the levers of powers were and how to pull them. A great deal of this was instinctive; he had a nose for sniffing out what was behind issues and an eye for reading the motivation of political actors. Furthermore, the longer he held office, the more familiar he was with the individuals and issues that he was engaged with.

In the cases that he dealt with Van der Stoel sought pragmatic solutions

---

8 Diana Chigas, 'Preventive diplomacy and the Organization for Security and Co-operation in Europe: creating incentives for dialogue and co-operation', in Abram Chayes & Antonia H. Chayes (eds.), *Preventing Conflict in the Post-Communist World. Mobilizing Internationanl and Regional Organizations.* (Washington: Brookings Institution, 1996), p. 31.

based on what was politically possible. This required a sound knowledge of the political context in which decisions would have to be made (and implemented) and an ability to affect change in that environment. Van der Stoel's track record in this regard will be examined in Chapter 6.

International Standards

While seeing himself as a political instrument, Van der Stoel also interpreted his role as having a solid basis in international standards. He once remarked that 'my blueprints are OSCE principles and commitments and international legal norms and standards'.[9] This was particularly evident in his recommendations, both oral and written, which often reminded countries of applicable international standards.

In his work, the High Commissioner greatly relied on established standards. These included politically binding OSCE commitments together with international legal obligations arising from the United Nations, the Council of Europe, bilateral treaties or other sources. These were seen as the basic standards that States should adhere to. At the same time, Van der Stoel would often remind States that 'it should be borne in mind that the relevant international obligations and commitments constitute international minimum standards. It would be contrary to their spirit and intent to interpret these obligations and commitments in a restrictive manner'.[10] The High Commissioner also invoked the relevant domestic law of the States in which he was engaged.

As one observer, Steven Ratner, has put it, Van der Stoel can be considered as a 'normative intermediary' – 'an agent dispatched by a norm-concerned community with the authority and tools to communicate norms and persuade states to comply with them'.[11] In Van der Stoel's words, the challenge is to explain to the parties 'The logic and possibility of internalizing and applying the norms under discussion. The key is to move from the abstract to the concrete, to get States to take measures – legal and political – to create the types of conditions

---

9 Van der Stoel, 1999a, p. 429.

10 See for example the *Hague Recommendations Regarding the Education Rights of National Minorities*, October 1996, paragraph 3 (in Annex 4).

11 Steve Ratner, 'Does International Law Matter in Preventing Ethnic Conflict?', *New York University Journal of International Law and Politics*, 32(3) (spring 2000) p. 668.

foreseen in the standards concerning minorities'.[12] The OSCE did not create his position for the purpose of implementing norms concerning minorities, but as Ratner points out:

> 'He has invoked and interpreted them constantly at all stages of discussion, especially if one party is seeking to ignore them or mischaracterize them. He has proposed solutions in which states specifically acknowledge duties to undertake behavior required or at least encouraged by the norms. And he has used a variety of strategies to support outcomes consistent with norms and to oppose policies not consistent with them. In short, he uses norms to achieve solutions, and he seeks solutions consistent with norms.'[13]

Beyond this function, it proved useful for Van der Stoel to be able to refer, in his dialogue and recommendations, to established standards freely undertaken by the State concerned; this saved him from accusations of arbitrariness and furnished him with a possible solution on the basis of already prescribed norms and rules agreed by the State.[14] He was also careful to be consistent in his argumentation and recommendations so that he would not be accused of double standards. In this vein, he sometimes invoked the policies of other states in the OSCE area by way of comparison.

It should be noted, however, that although the High Commissioner sought consistency, he did not follow a policy of uniformity. Nor did he bow to pressure for reciprocity, for example when a state demanded that its kin in a neighbouring country be treated in the same way as minorities in its own country (an argument made by Slovak President Vladimir Mečiar concerning Slovak minorities in Hungary or Albanian President Sali Berisha concerning people of Albanian ethnicity in Greece). Although standards are universal, the situations in respective countries are not. Therefore, although the approach and issues may have been

---

12 'The Relevance of International Standards for the Protection of Minorities', speech at the International Bar Association Human Rights Instititute Showcase Programme, Amsterdam, 20 September 2000.

13 *Ibid.*, p. 622.

14 John Packer, 'The OSCE High Commissioner on National Minorities', in G. Alfredsson *et al.* (eds.) *Human Rights Monitoring Procedures: A Textbook on How to Petition and Lobby International Organisations*; Festschrift für Jakob Müller (The Hague: Kluwer Law International, 2001), p. 641.

similar from country to country, in every individual case Van der Stoel had to take into account the political context in which the standards were to be applied. As he once remarked, 'the implementation of international norms and standards is essential for the protection of the identity of minorities, but will often not be sufficient to ensure an adequate solution to the specific problems with which a particular minority has to cope'.[15]

In many cases the High Commissioner made recommendations on the drafting of legislation concerning (or affecting) the protection of persons belonging to national minorities. This often concerned legislation on language, education, or citizenship. As Van der Stoel's reputation for fairness and expertise grew, States began to look to his office to assess whether their legislation conformed to international standards. By providing expertise, and by giving accurate and useful assessments, the High Commissioner came to be seen as an important standard-bearer regarding compliance with international standards in the field of minority rights protection. This not only enhanced his status, but in some situations gave him a type of 'gate-keeper' role vis-à-vis entry criteria for the European Union (according to the 1993 Copenhagen criteria) and for other Euro-Atlantic organizations. Furthermore, the stronger his authority on national minority issues grew, the more states drew on his expertise (or at least could not ignore his advice) as they knew that his support could affect the perception of their country's policy towards national minorities. They discovered that working with him at an early stage was more productive than being criticized by him later on. As will be explained in greater detail in Chapter 5, this gave him considerable leverage when making, and monitoring the implementation of, recommendations.

There was also a strong underlying moral tenor to Van der Stoel's approach. His recommendations and statements are characterized by a highly principled style and are based on fairness, consistency and justice. This is, perhaps, a reflection of personal convictions which were formed as a result of witnessing over half a century of turbulent European history, beginning with the German occupation of the Netherlands when he was a teenager, seeing first-hand the Communist takeover of Czechoslovakia as a student in 1948, confronting the Greek colonels as Rapporteur on Greece for the Consultative Assembly of the

---

15 Report to the OSCE Implementation Meeting on Human Dimension Issues, (Warsaw 2 October 1995).

Council of Europe in the late 1960s, meeting East European dissidents as Foreign Minister of the Netherlands in the 1970s and 80s, and dealing with the excesses of post-Communist nationalism, first as the head of the Netherlands delegation during CSCE Human Dimension meetings and ultimately as OSCE High Commissioner on National Minorities in the 1990s. As an elder statesman and one of the longest-serving high-ranking officials of any international organization, Van der Stoel spoke with conviction and was listened to with respect. He knew better than most that 'where there is injustice, there is insecurity and this in time gives rise to instability and ultimately threats to peace'.[16]

In the second half of his term as High Commissioner on National Minorities, Van der Stoel became increasingly involved in the clarification of standards. On three separate occasions he commissioned a group of international experts to draw up recommendations on issues which he felt deserved further elucidation and interpretation. These recommendations, described in detail in Chapter 5, concerned minority education rights (1996), minority language rights (1998) and the effective participation of minorities in public life (1999).

His motivation for doing so was to clarify the content and application of minority rights in a straightforward way, particularly for the use of policy- and law-makers. Experience had shown him that certain recurrent issues and themes relating to the legal protection of persons belonging to national minorities required further clarity. This was symptomatic of the relatively limited attention given to national minority issues in international and domestic law or in international organizations until the position of OSCE High Commissioner on National Minorities was created in December 1992. It is worth noting, for example, that the term 'national minorities' is seldom defined in international legal instruments.[17]

---

16 'Peace and justice, power and principle: from Nuremburg to The Hague', Statement of Van der Stoel on 'Punishing war crimes in the Former Yugoslavia: a critical juncture for the international community', pp. 334–40, *The Finnish Yearbook of International Law* VII (The Hague: Martinus Nijhoff Publishers, 1996). Based on a statement made at the Institute for Human Rights, Åbo Akademi University, Finland, 14–15 June 1996.

17 John Packer, 'Problems in defining minorities', in D. Fortrell & B. Bowring (eds.), *Minority and Group Rights in the New Millennium.* (The Hague: Kluwer Law International, 1997) pp. 223-274.

Perception of National Minorities and Nationalism

The term 'national minority' is also not defined in the High Commissioner's mandate. As one observer has pointed out, 'this problem of terminology derives partly from difficulties that the mandate's framers had in choosing proper labels to describe practices and procedures that had not yet been operationalized, either within the CSCE or elsewhere among international organizations'.[18] However, this is not something that preoccupied Van der Stoel. Indeed, the absence of a definition afforded him considerable flexibility in the types of groups and cases that he could deal with. His opinion on defining national minorities was already evident in his acceptance speech of 12 December 1992 when he said: 'I wonder whether there is a need for it. It seems to me preferable to proceed pragmatically'.[19] On another occasion he said 'I want to point out that definitions, as important as they are for legal clarity, are not essential for getting on with the job of pragmatically trying to prevent conflicts between groups'.[20]

Van der Stoel's perception was that 'within the [O]SCE framework, the existence of a minority is a question of fact and not definition'.[21] He based this interpretation on paragraph 32 of the Copenhagen Document that says: 'To belong to a national minority is a matter of a person's individual choice.' This view was echoed in an article written for the *OSZE Jahrbuch* in 1998 when he wrote: 'the question of who belongs to a minority can be determined only by the subjective feelings of its members.'

This subjective analysis is reflected in Van der Stoel's own views on national minorities. He once quipped that 'even though I may not have a definition of what constitutes a minority, I would dare to say that I know a minority when I

18 Konrad Huber, 'Averting inter-ethnic conflict: an analysis of the CSCE High Commissioner on National Minorities in Estonia, January–June 1993', p. 24. See also Packer 1997.

19 Acceptance speech at the meeting of the Council of Ministers of Foreign Affairs of the CSCE, Stockholm, 15 December 1992.

20 'The Relevance of International Standards for the Protection of Minorities', speech at the International Bar Association Human Rights Instititute Showcase Programme, Amsterdam, 20 September 2000.

21 Speech at Leiden, 25 June 1993, 'International Response to Ethnic Conflicts'.

see one'. This remark, which is often taken out of context, was followed by two rather more objective interpretations of what constitutes a minority: 'First of all, a minority is a group with linguistic, ethnic or cultural characteristics which distinguish it from the majority. Secondly, a minority is a group which usually not only seeks to maintain its identity but also tries to give stronger expression to that identity'.[22]

Although nationalism, as a term, is not in the High Commissioner's mandate, Van der Stoel had clear views on what it is and how it should be confronted. With his pragmatic and instrumentalist approach, Van der Stoel regarded nationalism as an extension or motor of politics. He did not see it as a primordial force. He often said that 'so-called ethnic conflicts are not inevitable. Although ethnic groups may have a centuries-old history of difficult mutual relations, conflicts between such groups very often have more immediate political causes. This becomes apparent if one considers that most communities co-exist in relative harmony, interacting, interrelating, and often intermingling'.[23] Also he did not regard nationalism as necessarily malign. It could be a noble force, for example as a positive expression of a people defending their collective interests in the face of aggression. Van der Stoel saw nothing wrong with love of one's country; he was a patriotic Dutchman. Rather, the problem as he saw it was when one's national pride manifests itself at the expense of the rights of others. This is why he was careful to make a distinction between nationalism and aggressive or excessive nationalism. He also made a distinction between civic and ethnic nationalism, the latter which was often invoked at the expense of the equal rights of individuals, especially those of the minority.[24]

Van der Stoel's view was that inter-ethnic tensions and conflicts were very often the result of competing interests over resources, power or prestige: 'Evidently, they indicate a failure of one or both sides to realize and value shared

22 Intervention at the Human Dimension seminar, Warsaw, 24 May 1993.

23 See for example speech at Utrecht University on 19 September 1994.

24 See for example his address at the International Conference on Human Rights of the Visegrad 4 Countries (Bratislava 10 December 1999). His ideas on civic and ethnic nationalism drew, in part, on the work of Michael Ignatieff. See for example *Blood and Belonging: Journeys into the New Nationalism.* (London: BBC Books, Chatto &Windus, 1993.)

interests'.[25] He regarded the mobilization and manipulation of ethnic and national identity as a function of élite politics. It was his experience that 'threats to identity – whether real or imagined – are often accentuated in order to promote narrow interests'.[26] He once wrote that: 'To my mind, most ethnic conflicts are not "natural" or "inevitable" occurrences, even in the wake of dissolving multi-ethnic and multi-national state structures. Ethnic conflicts are the result of extremist politics, as well as the basis for future rehearsals of political extremism'.[27] In this environment, moderates are either forced aside or must re-invent themselves in more extremist terms.

This tendency towards extremism is particularly evident, and dangerous, during periods of transition and insecurity when there is a pervasive uncertainty about the functioning of basic societal structures such as the economy and the political system. As Van der Stoel once observed, 'during such times, leaders, both elected and unelected, may perceive the potential for popular support by pursuing or advocating policies aimed at the restitution or enhancement of a national identity'.[28] This can be evident in post-conflict as well as pre-conflict situations. As he once explained, 'Even if violence has come to an end, very often the underlying causes which led to the conflict have not been removed. In situations in which the threshold between non-violence and violence has already been crossed before, renewed armed clashes are not unlikely'.[29] Such excessive nationalism is often at the expense of minorities, either because they are perceived as a threat, an historical enemy, or a soft target.[30]

---

25 'Human Rights, the Prevention of Conflict and the International Protection of Minorities: a Contemporary Paradigm for Contemporary Challenges', speech at the London School of Economics, London 19 October 1999.

26 *Ibid.*

27 Presentation delivered (on his behalf) to a seminar in Saskatoon, Canada on 'International Response to Ethnic Conflicts: Focusing on Prevention', 6 March 1993. See also 'Preventive Diplomacy in the Situation of Ethnic Tensions: the Role of the CSCE High Commissioner on National Minorities', Bonn 27 January 1994.

28 Saskatoon speech 6 March 1993.

29 Keynote speech to the CSCE Seminar on Early Warning and Preventive Diplomacy, Warsaw, 19 January 1994.

30 'Early Warning and Early Action: Preventing Inter-Ethnic Conflict'. Speech to the Royal Institute of International Relations, London 9 July 1999.

Of course malign nationalism is not a one-way street. Nationalism among minority groups is often perceived as a threat by the majority population.[31] Whatever the origin of the excessive manifestations of nationalism, they can precipitate a malign spiral of distrust which can, in turn, cause tensions within and between communities and states and ultimately lead to violence. Van der Stoel often remarked that 'to my mind, malign nationalism remains one of the biggest dangers to European security'.[32] Indeed, towards the end of his term as High Commissioner on National Minorities, almost every public pronouncement contained a clarion call against excessive nationalism. For example, in a speech at the London School of Economics in October 1999 he said:

> 'We must fight against extreme nationalism in all its manifestations, whether political or popular. At the political level, we must forthrightly reject the arguments and language invoked by . . . irresponsible and dangerous leaders . . . At the popular level, we must establish regimes to protect against it, including strengthening the rule of law but also building tolerant and understanding societies . . . to achieve this aim requires a major shift in thinking, supported with sufficient resources and political will. This century, even this past decade, has provided us with enough examples of what happens if we do not prevent inter-ethnic conflict.'[33]

In a speech in Bratislava in December 1999 he said:

> 'I think that it is fair to say that one of the defining characteristics of the 20th century was the impact of excessive nationalism and the clash between the principles of sovereignty and self-determination. Wars have been fought in defence of these principles; states have been created and broken up in their name; ideologies have been driven by them; and millions of people have been expelled or killed either fighting for, or being victimized by, nationalistic or ethnically-based ideals'.[34]

---

31 *Ibid.*

32 *Ibid.*

33 LSE speech 19 October 1999.

34 Address at the International Conference on Human Rights of the Visegrad 4 Countries, Bratislava, 10 December 1999.

However, as he pointed out, nationalism is man-made and can be prevented by mankind.[35]

Philosophy of Early Warning and Preventive Diplomacy

Since outbreaks of ethnic conflicts are not inevitable and are largely preventable, the key is to head them off at an early stage. As Van der Stoel once stated, 'the logic of preventive diplomacy is simple. Timely and effective action can help to avert a costly crisis'.[36] Successful preventive diplomacy can also foster long-term stability.

On several occasions, Van der Stoel used the analogy of 'fire fighting' to describe the usual course of crisis management in international affairs: in peace-keeping or peace enforcement operations, NATO or the United Nations are referred to as the fire brigade, trying to put out the flames of war. As he explained in a speech to the Royal Institute of International Affairs in London in July 1999, 'the role of my office is to prevent fires caused by inter-ethnic tensions from breaking out in the first place. If there are signs of smoke, my job is to address the situation and try to put it out or, if that fails, to raise the alarm'.[37]

Earlier in his period as High Commissioner he said that 'early warning should provide the relevant [O]SCE bodies with information about escalatory developments . . . far enough in advance in order for them to react in a timely and effective manner, if possible still leaving them time to employ preventive diplomacy and non-coercive and non-military preventive measures'. He noted that 'this also includes the "tripwire function" of early warning and preventive diplomacy, meaning that the [O]SCE will be alerted whenever developments threaten to escalate beyond a level at which the "preventive diplomat" would still be able to contain them with the means at his disposal'. Preventive diplomacy 'should contain particular disputes and threats and prevent them from escalating into armed conflict'.[38] Although originally foreseen as an instrument of conflict prevention, Van der Stoel not only tried to contain disputes, but also to address

35 *Ibid.*

36 Speech to the Royal Institute of International Affairs, 9 July 1999.

37 *Ibid.*

38 Speech to a seminar on early warning and conflict prevention, Warsaw January 1994.

the reasons why disputes broke out in the first place (the 'root causes'). In this respect he looked at the earliest phase of the conflict cycle, not only to prevent crises from developing into conflicts but also with a longer-term perspective of fostering integrated and peaceful societies.

The means at Van der Stoel's disposal and the way that he used them will be the focus of the next chapter. However, in terms of his general approach it is worth noting that Van der Stoel's emphasis was on effective preventive action in the hope of reducing the need for activating the formal early warning 'trip wire' mechanism. As he put it in an interview with the *Financial Times*, 'My job is to issue early warnings to avoid action, and to take action to avoid early warnings'.[39]

His approach can be characterized by several key words: independence, co-operation, impartiality, confidentiality, incrementalism, persistence, trust and confidence. These elements defined Van der Stoel's style of quiet diplomacy in action.

Independence

As noted in the discussion on the mandate in Chapter 1, the involvement by the High Commissioner in a particular situation does not require the approval of the Senior or Permanent Council or the State concerned.[40] This gives him unprecedented room for maneuver. Firstly, it is crucial in the timing of the High Commissioner's involvement. Not being reliant on decisions made by consensus-based negotiating bodies, the High Commissioner can move quickly and independently. It also affects his relations with his interlocutors. Although he is the instrument of an international organization (which is comprised of sovereign states), he is neither the advocate of OSCE States, nor the defender of minorities. As his mandate explicitly states, he works 'independently of all

39 Quentin Peel, 'OSCE minorities chief aims for early action', *Financial Times* (19 May 2000), p. 3.

40 Based in Vienna, the Permanent Council is the regular body for political consultation and decision-making on all issues pertinent to the OSCE and is responsible for the day-to-day business of the Organization. The Senior Council was a body that met only occasionally and at the level of political director. Since 1997 its function has been replaced by the Reinforced Permanent Council.

parties directly involved in the tensions'.

This level of independence was unprecedented. As Van der Stoel observed towards the end of his term in office, 'when one looks back at this, one wonders whether, if the mandate would have to be negotiated now in 1999, the Commissioner would have that degree of freedom'.[41]

That being said, the High Commissioner is accountable to the Organization that he represents. His work is based on OSCE principles and commitments and he relies on the participating States for political support and credibility. As he said in his acceptance speech (and later reconfirmed on a number of occasions) 'I am convinced that even the most talented High Commissioner would fail if he would not be able to count on the support of CSCE member states'.[42]

This is particularly important when he presents his reports and recommendations. The participating States can give collective support for his work and provide the necessary backing to encourage their implementation. He also needs the confidence and co-operation of the states that he is dealing with. This not only facilitates his work, but helps to ensure that his specific initiatives will find success.

Co-operation

In keeping with the fact that the OSCE is a co-operative security organization, the High Commissioner took a co-operative approach in his work. This approach was characterized by a non-confrontational and non-coercive attitude towards the parties involved. That is not to suggest that Van der Stoel was passive – on the contrary. Indeed, he was considered by some of his interlocutors to be 'annoying' in his tenacity. What the co-operative approach implies is that the High Commissioner will seek to work with the parties to find solutions to tensions involving national minority issues. As one observer has remarked, such an approach is 'concerned less with using power than with using persuasion as a means of inducing changes of policy, less with judging compliance with legal obligations than with generating practical decisions, and less with formality than with acting with the flexibility needed to address the situation at hand and

---

41 As cited in Zellner & Lange 1999, p. 13.

42 Acceptance speech to the Stockholm Meeting of the Council of Ministers of Foreign Affairs of the CSCE, Stockholm 15 December 1992.

as a facilitator and adviser over the long term'.[43] This was manifested in his deportment during visits and the spirit of his recommendations.

He was aware that sometimes his involvement was seen as a stigmatization against a state. But as he once explained 'it would be wrong to assume that the simple fact of my involvement in these situations does already constitute an implied criticism of the governments concerned. Let me stress again that in my eyes getting involved only means an acknowledgement that these states have to cope with particularly delicate and difficult minority problems'.[44]

A typical example of Van der Stoel's co-operative approach can be noted in a letter he sent to the Foreign Minister of Kazakhstan in April 1994. In it he wrote:

> 'Next week I hope to begin my visit to your country. Permit me to assure you that I am coming as a friend with an open mind and without preconceived ideas. I am especially eager to learn as much as possible about the way you try to achieve a harmonious inter-ethnic society and about the problems you are encountering in trying to achieve this aim. Perhaps it can be of some interest for your Government to learn about the difficulties other CSCE Governments are encountering in their efforts to solve similar problems.'[45]

As he said in an address to the Netherlands Institute for International Relations in 1994,

> 'by declaring the legitimacy of international concern for human rights and minority questions, the CSCE community has assumed as its responsibility the burden of supporting individual CSCE States which cannot by themselves solve the problems which are confronting them. It is not enough to monitor developments and admonish states when they are not doing well – a positive commitment is also called for.'[46]

---

43 Chigas 1996, p. 63.

44 Report to the OSCE Implementation Meeting on Human Dimension Issues, Warsaw 2 October 1995.

45 Letter to Mr Tuleutai Suleimenov, Minister for Foreign Affairs of the Republic of Kazakhstan, 11 April 1994, CSCE Communication no. 26/94.

46 Speech at the Netherlands Institute of International Relations, The Hague during a seminar on 'Conflict and Development: Causes, Effects and Remedies', 24 March 1994.

The High Commissioner is an example of that positive commitment. He tries to help the parties to find common ground, he assists them in solving their problems and he encourages them to look for ways of dealing with issues in a way that benefits all members of society. The goal of his involvement is not only to de-fuse a crisis, but also to catalyze a process of exchange and co-operation between the parties, leading to concrete steps to de-escalate tensions and to address underlying issues. As Van der Stoel has described it,

> 'the nature of the High Commissioner's involvement is such that he offers his advice and assistance. In this process he might express criticism, to States and minorities alike, but he certainly is not out to condemn parties to a conflict. The involvement of the High Commissioner should therefore never be seen as stigmatizing, but rather as a sign of solidarity, by the OSCE community, to its members who are facing certain difficulties.'[47]

This reflects Van der Stoel's basic conviction that in the vast majority of cases durable progress depends on the willingness of the authorities in question to co-operate, and that co-operation and compromise cannot be forced upon the parties – although he may appeal to their enlightened self-interest.[48] After all, the key is for the parties to internalize his advice and implement it over the long term, rather than merely appeasing him (and by extension the international community) in the short term.

The example of co-operative security is something that he tried to communicate to governments and minorities. Simply put, he co-operated with the parties in order to encourage them to co-operate with each other. As he noted in an address to the 1997 Human Dimension Implementation Review Meeting,

> 'durable solutions to minority problems are only possible if there is a sufficient measure of good will and consent on the part of all parties involved. As an impartial third party, it is my aim to propose such solutions and to bring the parties to a consensus, on the basis of convincing arguments. Coercion would certainly never have a lasting positive effect. In other words: if solutions are

47 OSCE Human Dimension Implementation Meeting, Warsaw November 1997.

48 Rob Zaagman, *Conflict Prevention in the Baltic States: the High Commissioner on National Minorities in Estonia, Latvia and Lithuania*, European Centre for Minority Issues monograph 1 (Flensburg, 1999), p. 10.

found, it is essentially because parties themselves want a solution, but require some advice or assistance in getting there.'[49]

This sentiment was often evident in the High Commissioner's recommendations. Illustrative of this is a passage from a letter which Van der Stoel addressed to the Latvian Foreign Minister in April 1993 in which he wrote: 'I hope that the ideas that I am submitting to you – inspired as they are by the various CSCE documents to which Latvia, together with all other CSCE participating States, has subscribed – can contribute to the promotion of harmony and dialogue between the various population groups in your country'.[50] Some of the techniques that he used to promote harmony and dialogue will be examined in Chapter 3.

Impartiality

In view of the sensitive issues with which he was called upon to deal, the High Commissioner could not afford to be identified with one party or another. Van der Stoel's approach was to listen to all parties' concerns and draw his own conclusions. As noted earlier, the High Commissioner is not an instrument for the protection of minorities or a sort of international ombudsman who acts on their behalf. He is the High Commissioner *on* rather than *for* national minorities. At the same time, despite the fact that he is an instrument of a multilateral organization, he is not a pawn of OSCE States. In short, he seeks to be impartial.

Very often parties to a conflict have entrenched positions and therefore find it hard to either see things in a different way or, even if the political will is there, to find some common ground with their opponent in order to overcome long-standing differences. The impartiality of the High Commissioner means that he is sufficiently distanced from an issue to be able to give objective and well-informed advice.

At the same time he is close enough to the situation to have an insider's perspective. As a result, the High Commissioner's role has been aptly described

49 Address to the OSCE Human Dimension Implementation Meeting, Warsaw November 1997.

50 Letter to Foreign Minister of Latvia Andrejevs, 6 April 1993, CSCE Communication no. 124/93.

as that of an 'insider third party'. As Diana Chigas explains,

> 'the role combines some of the basic characteristics of traditional mediation by international organizations with those of an 'insider' to the conflict working for change from within the governmental and political processes in the state concerned, and in some cases actually becoming part of the governing process. It maintains two essential characteristics of an outside mediator of the conflict: impartiality and lack of vested interests in the substantive issues at stake. This allows the third party to move easily back and forth among the parties. The 'insider third party' role also maintains the traditional function of the international organization as watchdog and monitor of the conflict, while ensuring transparency and providing an impartial analysis of the situation, as well as exerting by its very presence pressure on the government to modify its behaviour.'[51]

For example, if international standards, to which OSCE participating States have committed themselves, were not met, the High Commissioner would ask the Government concerned to change its policy, by reminding it that stability and conflict prevention are, as a rule, best served by ensuring full rights to the persons belonging to a minority. At the same time, he cautioned national minorities about the repercussions of their actions and reminded them that they have duties as well as rights. This was not a question of passing judgement on one side or the other. It was a co-operative approach designed to deal with the tensions emerging from disputes about compliance and to facilitate the parties' finding a just and workable process to deal with those issues. To summarize, he used his insider knowledge and contacts with his outsider objectivity and influence to help parties find solutions that were in their best interests, or at least the interest of inter-ethnic accommodation.

Van der Stoel's impartiality was sometimes questioned. He was accused, particularly in the context of his involvement in Latvia and Estonia, as being a puppet of the State (against the minorities) by one side, or an ill-informed agent of a foreign power interested in 'bashing' the Government by the other. Indeed, in many instances his job was a thankless one where he was disliked by both sides. Governments sometimes saw him as an advocate of minority positions whereas those same minorities felt that he insufficently defended their views.

---

51 Chigas 1996, p. 49.

Xan Smiley of *The Economist* described the High Commissioner's role as that of a prefect in a run-down boys school: 'The prefect's main job is to stop big boys bullying little ones, and to stop boys of all sizes from fighting among themselves. He is not allowed to use his own fists . . . He is, perforce, a bit of a swot, a bit of a sneak, and a bit of a prig. Nobody likes him much'.[52]

Van der Stoel usually brushed criticism off, but he sometimes confronted it head-on. For example in a letter to Foreign Minister Juri Luik of Estonia in March 1994 he wrote:

> 'Regrettably, in the public discussion in your country, there have been complaints that I am acting as an advocate of one population group. I was glad to note, that your Government has a better understanding of my role, the essence of which is in my view to help, in a strictly objective way, in finding solutions that can contribute to inter-ethnic harmony in your country.'[53]

He knew that he got under the skin of some nationalists in countries where he was active. But he did not mind. As he once said:

> 'I am not going to hide from you that, in trying to [remove the danger of inter-ethnic conflict and to promote inter-ethnic harmony] I am making enemies. But I also have to add that these enemies are almost invariably extreme nationalists. I think this is inevitable. I would even feel that I would not perform my task properly if they would not object to my activities and views. These nationalists are not interested in promoting inter-ethnic harmony – they prefer to stir up ethnic hatred.'[54]

However, impartiality is not the same thing as sitting on the fence. One can be impartial without being neutral. As Van der Stoel once explained, having an independent position and not being identified with the parties in a dispute

---

52 *The Economist*, 'Max van der Stoel, minority man', vol. 352(8136) (11–17 September 1999), p. 36.

53 Letter to Juri Luik, Minister for Foreign Affairs of Estonia, 9 March 1994, CSCE Communication 20/94.

54 Speech by the High Commissioner to the OSCE Parliamentary Session, Stockholm 5 July 1996.

'does not preclude me from finding credible and meritorious various positions held by one or other of the parties. Indeed, though I seek to reduce tensions by reconciling conflicting positions, I may well have to discern the better of competing claims that are mutually exclusive in substance'.[55] At first glance this may seem like a contradiction for it suggests that his impartiality allows him to take sides. But the point is that he makes an assessment on the basis of international standards and therefore while he does make judgments, they are partial in favour of OSCE and other international commitments rather than the political interests of one or another of the parties. It is worth recalling Ratner's description of the High Commissioner as a 'normative intermediary' and how this was combined with his attributes as a political and diplomatic instrument of conflict prevention.

Confidentiality

In the spirit of his mandate, Van der Stoel usually operated in a confidential way. His meetings were restricted, he seldom talked to the press, his recommendations were kept out of the public domain for a considerable length of time, and his reports to the Chairman-in-Office were strictly confidential. This quiet diplomacy was one of the secrets of Van der Stoel's success.

However, at the same time, his willingness to stay out of the limelight gave him a low public profile and was interpreted by many as awkwardness or the result of a colourless personality. Because he kept his cards close to his chest, his public persona was seen as stiff and even boring – he did not give much away. As *The Economist* put it: 'Van der Stoel . . . with his heavy spectacles and slightly lugubrious, stolid manner is stunningly unglamourous'.[56] When asked once why he had such an enigmatic and seemingly dull image, Van der Stoel replied: 'As a public personality you have to be careful, certainly when you are skating on thin ice. In the last years I have done nothing else but skate on thin ice, and on all sides there are people who would not mind if I fell through the ice. So that explains perhaps why I give this impression of a sphinx, of a very reserved,

55 Max van der Stoel, 'The role of the OSCE High Commissioner in conflict prevention', in C.A. Croker *et al.*, *Herding Cats: Multiparty Mediation in a Complex World* (Washington DC: United States Institute for Peace, 1999), p. 71.

56 *The Economist*, 11–17 September 1999, p. 36.

maybe even cool personality'.[57]

Van der Stoel's work was seldom the focus of media attention. Although he would have appreciated more publicity about the importance of conflict prevention, in most cases he did not actively court the press. Indeed, he saw his job as trying to avoid creating headlines. As he once remarked, 'as [OSCE] High Commissioner on National Minorities, my job is to prevent conflict, or at least conflicts concerning persons belonging to national minorities. In my line of work, no news is good news'.[58]

The confidential approach was evident in all phases of the High Commissioner's work. Before Van der Stoel would get involved in a situation, he would quietly confer with the Government involved in order to give an unambiguous explanation of his intentions and mandate. This was designed to alleviate any feelings of suspicion or stigmatization that governments may have felt by having the High Commissioner involved in what are usually highly sensitive matters.

During visits and consultations, Van der Stoel kept the dialogue low-key, even if it was at the highest political level. As will be noted in Chapter 4 when looking at Van der Stoel's use of the press, when he did go public it was usually for calculated reasons. Experience showed the tendency of both sides in a conflict to use every word stated publicly by the High Commissioner to its own advantage. Therefore, Van der Stoel said very little on the record. This not only avoided sensationalization and/or misinterpretation of sensitive issues, it also helped to build confidence between Van der Stoel and the parties. They were more inclined to trust him and speak candidly to him if they knew that their remarks were being made in confidence. This confidentiality bred confidence. This was vital for as he once explained, 'because my engagement in a particular country is a gradual process that usually requires follow-up, I regard it as important that the confidence and trust of my interlocutors is maintained over a long period of time'.[59]

Confidential meetings allowed the parties to open up to the High Commissioner, and to each other. If they knew that they would not be subject to external

---

57 Interview between Van der Stoel and Michael Ignatieff, 7 October 1999.

58 'Early Warning and Early Action: Preventing Inter-Ethnic Conflict', Speech to the Royal Institute of International Relations, 9 July 1999.

59 Max van der Stoel, 1999a, p. 430.

pressures or would not be seen to be climbing down from entrenched positions, they were usually willing to consider issues and solutions which would be less politically palatable if they were discussed under public scrutiny. Asked once if he thought this type of quiet diplomacy was out of touch with the way that international relations were conducted in the late 20th century, Van der Stoel replied that he tried to pursue a course of quiet diplomacy 'plus'. In other words, he tried to remain confidential as long as possible, but he would not hesitate to mobilize others to take up the cause if he was unsuccessful.[60]

Incrementalism and Persistence

The High Commissioner advocated a step-by-step approach in his work. As the challenges that he faced were usually rather great, he was realistic in his assessment of what was achievable. While conscious of the long-term perspective, he advocated short-term measures that could put in place mechanisms, frameworks and legal provisions for the protection of persons belonging to national minorities. In his interaction with the parties and his efforts to get the parties to interact with each other, he was concerned with the process as much as the substantive issues. In most cases the aim was to come up with workable steps to keep the process moving forward. The ultimate prize may have been a long way off, but the point was to move away from crisis. As he once remarked, 'Immediate de-escalation of a situation can only be a first step in the process of reconciling the interests of the parties concerned. The goal is to start, maintain and enhance a process of exchanges of views and co-operation between the parties, leading to concrete steps which would de-escalate tensions and, if possible, address underlying issues'.[61]

Developing appropriate structures for the protection of minority rights and the integration of national minorities into society (particularly public life) is a process which requires a great deal of time and effort. Whereas minorities (especially those without political representation) often advocate ambitious agendas, Governments frequently argue that minority issues are either a low priority or too expensive. In the cases that he dealt with, Van der Stoel encouraged

60 Interview between Van der Stoel and Michael Ignatieff, 7 October 1999.

61 Remarks to a Seminar on Conflict Development: Causes, Effects and Remedies, Netherlands Institute of International Relations, The Hague, 24 March 1994.

both sides to move away from their maximalist positions by advocating a gradual process of change. He tried to highlight the merits of compromise and reconciliation. He often cautioned parties that a maximalist approach would meet maximum opposition. When one side felt that it had too much to lose or had given away too much, Van der Stoel reminded them that the process is a long one that requires give and take on both sides. Because he was conscious of the process in its political context, he tried to balance the concerns of both parties by sometimes encouraging Governments to stretch the bounds of the possible, while cautioning minorities to keep their demands within the realm of the probable. In that sense, he was less concerned with producing a comprehensive settlement as he was with 'ripening' a situation to the point that parties would deal with contentious issues in a constructive and co-operative manner.[62]

This incremental approach was also evident from the High Commissioner's recommendations and travels. They were seldom a 'one off': One recommendation or visit built on the previous one. This is examined in greater detail in the next chapter.

Once the High Commissioner became engaged in a particular situation he usually saw it through. That is not to say that he 'solved' every issue that he was engaged in, rather he would keep the dossier open until he was satisfied that the possibility of inter-ethnic conflict had passed (or the scope for his action had become too limited). The fact that Van der Stoel was High Commissioner for more than eight years meant that he had long-term involvement in a number of OSCE participating States. His view was that passage of a law or the creation of an institution relating to national minorities is an important first step, but the real proof of a country's commitment to the protection of the rights of persons belonging to national minorities is in the implementation of good laws and policies. The High Commissioner was therefore persistent in following through on his recommendations by making repeat visits to countries in which he was engaged. Indeed, in some countries he was infamous for his perseverance. But his view was that this engagement was essential for long-term security. As he once observed, 'building confidence between communities and ensuring legal and political frameworks for protecting minority rights cannot be achieved

62 See Chigas 1996, p. 29.

overnight. It requires steady, continuous and constructive engagement. We should not take our eye off an issue just because it is no longer in the news. Rather, we should re-enforce fragile relationships and strengthen processes precisely so that they avoid making headlines.'[63] The High Commissioner's persistence increased the credibility of his recommendations and ensured that appropriate follow-up was taken by the Governments of the states that he was dealing with, and the OSCE as a whole.[64]

Trust and Credibility

Through his independent, co-operative, impartial, confidential and incremental approach, Van der Stoel built up trust and credibility and was able to develop good working relations with the parties that he was involved with. Frequent travel put him touch with the latest developments and familiarized him with the individuals concerned. As a result, he was up to date with the issues and knew most of his interlocutors personally. They may not have liked the fact that he was involved in a particular situation and they may have disagreed with some of his recommendations, but they at least respected the fact that he was mandated to do so and that his words and actions carried considerable weight. This not only stemmed from the fact that the High Commissioner is an instrument of the OSCE, but, as importantly, from the realization that Van der Stoel's approach and methods achieved results. An illustrative example comes from Latvia where the outgoing President, Guntis Ulmanis, said to Van der Stoel during his visit to Riga on 25 May 1999: 'We have both quarreled and co-operated, but overall your contribution to Latvia has been a positive one'. In another example, in December 1999, Deputy Prime Minister of the Slovak Republic, Pal Csaky said '. . . inasmuch as a positive solution to inter-ethnic matters . . . means support for the process of democratization of the country, I am convinced that Slovak democracy as such can be grateful to the High

63 'Preventing Ethnic Conflicts: Lessons and Prospects', Address to an international conference on Preventing Ethnic Conflict in Central-Eastern Europe, Warsaw 6 November 2000.

64 D. Chigas, 'Bridging the gap between theory and practise: the CSCE High Commissioner on National Minorities', *Helsinki Monitor* 5(3) (1994), p. 37.

Commissioner'.[65] By looking closer at some of the tools and techniques that he employed, one can get an idea of the work of the High Commissioner in practice.

65 Remarks by Pal Csaky at the Max van der Stoel Symposium, Stockholm, 3 December 1999.

CHAPTER THREE

The High Commissioner in Practice

The High Commissioner's mandate allowed for a considerable amount of flexibility. But while it offered general guidelines on how the High Commissioner should operate and what he should aim to achieve, it was short on specifics as to how the mandate should be implemented. There was no ready-made toolbox of techniques and instruments from which the High Commissioner could pluck ideas and methods on how to deal with particular issues and crises. Instead, using the approach described in Chapter 2, Van der Stoel adapted to the situations at hand and gradually developed several 'best practices'. This chapter will go behind the scenes to explain the tools and techniques developed and used by Van der Stoel during his eight years as High Commissioner. It will explore his methods of early action and early warning and thereby illustrate how conflict prevention and quiet diplomacy can work in practice. Although indications will be made as to how these techniques evolved, the chapter will take a subject-oriented rather than a chronological approach. Specific country analyses are provided in Chapter 6.

Collecting Information

Early warning and early action depend on reliable information. Information gathering and analysis are therefore fundamental to the effectiveness of the High Commissioner.

According to his mandate, the High Commissioner may collect and retrieve information regarding national minorities 'from any source' with the exception of 'any person or organization which practices or publicly condones terrorism or violence'.[1] The High Commissioner and his advisers spend a great deal of their time collecting and analyzing information from wire services, the Internet

1 See paragraphs 23a and 25 of the mandate.

and other media, experts, secondary sources (like journals and reports[2]), and non-governmental organizations. Contacts with OSCE missions, regular participation in OSCE meetings and the receipt of information from partner organizations and through internal OSCE channels also enriched the High Commissioner's views.

Because the High Commissioner tries to be involved at the earliest possible stage, 'inside' contacts, for example within ministries and political parties, are particularly important, especially in fast-breaking situations: information from secondary sources may sometimes come too late to be effective. People who are close to, or involved in, the action are able to provide valuable insights into pertinent issues as well as the views of the key players. This information (properly weighed) allows the High Commissioner and his staff to be one step ahead of – or at least up to date with – developments which could lead to inter-ethnic tensions.

Collecting and analyzing information is an ongoing process. But there comes a point when the passive analysis of information leads to the active involvement of the High Commissioner. What is the basis for this transition?

Why, Where, and When to Become Involved?

As noted in Chapter 1, the High Commissioner's mandate is to provide early warning and early action in tensions involving national minority issues which, 'in the judgement of the High Commissioner', have the potential to develop into a conflict within the OSCE area. This is subjective and leaves much to the discretion of the High Commissioner.

Issues concerning persons belonging to national minorities are prevalent in many OSCE countries, but it is the degree to which these problems affect security that interests the High Commissioner. As he once explained, it was not his job to deal with all minroty-related situations: 'I am not dealing with Samis in Scandinavia or with the Sorbs or Danes in Germany or the Frisians in Holland, not because these minorities do not have problems but simply because there is little reason to believe their problems will lead to international

---

2 For example, Van der Stoel daily received classified cables from the Dutch Foreign Ministry.

tensions'.[3] Van der Stoel's approach was to weigh the information available to him and determine whether it contained indicators of potential conflict. There was no checklist of warning signs that he consulted, nor did the job's mandate indicate specific conditions for involvement. Thus, it was often Van der Stoel's experience and political intuition (together with the advice of his staff) that formed the basis of a decision to intervene.

Two main factors on which he weighed his decision to become engaged in a particular situation were the extent to which his involvement was needed and the degree to which it would have a positive impact. As he told a workshop in Skopje in October 1996:

> 'Sometimes I am asked: on what basis do you select the countries on which you concentrate your activities? Why have you selected this group of 10 and why not any of the remaining 44 OSCE states? The answer is rather simple. Though the list may, depending on circumstances, be expanded, I am presently active in these 10 states because it is my view that they face especially difficult and complicated minority questions and because it is my hope that my office can be of some help in coping with them.'[4]

There was a limit to how many crises he could deal with at the same time.

Another of the High Commissioner's rules of thumb was that his involvement should have added value. In some cases (for example in Bosnia and Herzegovina or Cyprus) where there were already a number of international actors involved, Van der Stoel felt that the usefulness of his additional input would be limited. Similarly, in some cases, the High Commissioner decided to be involved, but only to the extent of referring the issue to another OSCE institution or international organization.[5] A notable example is his work on Roma issues where he

---

3 'Minorities, Human Rights and the International Community', speech to a conference in Strausberg, Germany, 7 July 1995.

4 Presentation to a workshop on 'An Agenda for Preventive Diplomacy', Skopje 18 October 1996.

5 Stefan Vassilev, 'The HCNM approach to conflict prevention', *Helsinki Monitor* 10(3) (1999), p. 140. It is worth noting that a Senior Council Meeting devoted to the OSCE's prospective role in Bosnia-Herzegovina and other areas of South-Eastern Europe which took place on 27 October 1995 called for the active involvement of the High Commissioner and the ODIHR. Furthermore in a decision taken by the

passed the torch to the OSCE's Office for Democratic Institutions and Human Rights.

In some situations the High Commissioner felt that his involvement, however discrete, could exacerbate rather than ameliorate the situation by encouraging one or another of the parties to exploit outside attention for support of extreme positions. Becoming involved might have highlighted a crisis that was still latent, and/or legitimize the position of radicals who may have been seeking to internationalize a crisis instead of working constructively with their Government. There were other situations (for example Chechnya and Dagestan) where the structures of civil society were so tenuous that the High Commissioner's room for maneuver and potential effectiveness would have been limited. One could also argue that Van der Stoel was a political realist to the extent that he only became involved in situations where he felt that he could exert some leverage.[6] As noted in Chapter 1, due to the restraints of the mandate, there are also some cases in which the High Commissioner can not become involved, most notably situations involving organized acts of terrorism. This exclusion in his mandate provides the answer to the often-asked question as to why he was never involved in the Basque, Kurdish or Northern Ireland situations.

In addition to situations where the High Commissioner chose to become engaged, there were occasions when he was asked by others to address specific issues. Such requests can (and have) come from OSCE negotiating bodies like the Committee of Senior Officials (as was the case, for example, on follow-up visits to Estonia, the former Yugoslav Republic of Macedonia and Ukraine), or by invitation of a representative or Head of State (visits to Romania 1993, Ukraine 1994, Moldova 1995, Georgia 1997 and the Federal Republic of Yugoslavia in November 2000). In 1993 the Chairman-in-Office requested Van der Stoel to study the problems of the Roma and their relevance to the mandate of the

---

OSCE Ministerial Council on 'OSCE Action for Peace, Democracy and Stability in Bosnia and Herzegovina' (Decision no. 1 of 8 December 1995), the High Commissioner and the ODIHR were invited 'to contribute to the implementation of this decision in accordance with their mandates and experience'.

6 See Jonathan Cohen, *Conflict Prevention Instruments in the Organization for Security and Co-operation in Europe: an Assessment of Capacities* (The Hague: Netherlands Institute of International Relations, 1999), p. 120.

High Commissioner.

Satisfied that a situation fell within his mandate and that actions were both required and opportune,[7] the High Commissioner carefully considered the timing of each of his visits. He usually subscribed to the philosophy of 'the sooner, the better', although he was careful to plan the dates of his visits to maximize their impact. Sometimes events developed in such a way that he considered it most prudent to wait. At other times, he felt that his presence could act as a catalyst in moving a process forward. In short he went when he felt that the time was ripe.

Obviously when a crisis was imminent the High Commissioner could not afford to wait. In a few cases he rushed to the scene of a brewing conflict in order to head off the eruption of violence. For example, in July 1993 he went to Estonia to undertake shuttle diplomacy between the Government and the Russian-speaking minority over a crisis sparked by the call for a referendum on 'national-territorial autonomy' by the Russophone-dominated city councils of Narva and Sillamae. On two occasions (February 1995 and July 1997) Van der Stoel flew at short notice to the former Yugoslav Republic of Macedonia when riots threatened to trigger a worsening of inter-ethnic relations.[8] However, such examples of short-term crisis management are the exception rather than the rule. In most cases he was not dealing with 'hot' conflicts and was able to make a more calculated decision concerning the timing and scope of his involvement.

In his acceptance speech Van der Stoel said that 'in my view, the best course to follow is, on the one hand, to avoid rushing to an area at the slightest sign of possible tension, but, on the other hand, not to wait to take the initiative for a visit until the atmosphere has become so heated that efforts to reduce tensions and to promote dialogue might no longer have a useful effect'.[9] As he once explained, the advantage of becoming involved at an early stage is that 'bargaining positions have generally not yet hardened, and the parties may still have considerable interest in peaceful solutions, particularly at the earliest stages of

7 Cohen 1999, pp. 60–61.

8 These incidents are analyzed in greater detail in Chapter 6.

9 Stockholm Acceptance Speech, 15 December 1992.

friction. The cycle of violence and revenge has not yet taken hold'.[10] Conversely, 'the later one gets in, the more difficult it is to stop the escalation process because by then more emotions, more passions, more prestige are involved, sweeping aside rational considerations'.[11]

Visits and Travel

Once the High Commissioner decided that he would like to visit a particular country, he informed the respective foreign minister of his intentions and requested meetings with a number of officials. Although the High Commissioner did not need the approval of the Government of the State concerned, he is an instrument of co-operative security and therefore sought the co-operation of the governments with which he worked. This co-operation, which was almost always forthcoming,[12] facilitated the arrangement of meetings and created an atmosphere of trust that generated a positive working environment during visits.

Official meetings were arranged by the foreign ministry of the country to which the High Commissioner was going to visit. Van der Stoel almost always met with the foreign minister. Depending on the subjects to be discussed and the gravity of the issues, other meetings could also include the head of state, ministers, members of parliament and/or the upper house, and representatives of government committees or other bodies. It is worth noting that it was the High Commissioner, rather than the host Governments, who set the programme. In order to gain as wide a spectrum of opinion as possible, the High Commissioner also usually organized meetings with opposition figures, non-governmental organizations and representatives of the minority community. In these cases he usually sought out moderate representatives. He saw to it that these meetings were not attended by government officials. He also sometimes met

---

10 Speech on 'Preventive Diplomacy in Situations of Ethnic Tensions: the Role of the CSCE High Commissioner on National Minorities', Bonn 27 January 1994.

11 Speech at Strausberg, 1995.

12 Turkey was a notable exception. For more see Chapter 6. On some visits to Slovakia (under Mečiar) and Estonia the governments were not particularly co-operative, but they did not deny him access. However, as Personal Representative of the Chairman-in-Office for Kosovo his effectiveness was severly limited by the refusal of the Milosevic government to grant him a visa.

with representatives of the international community based in the country that he was visiting.

Sometimes Van der Stoel thought it best to have a meeting outside the country that he was dealing with. This allowed him to meet on neutral ground or on 'his own turf' as it were. In this way he could control the setting, the agenda, and the inter-play of the parties. For example, just after the Slovak parliamentary elections of September 1998, Van der Stoel met with a number of Slovak political leaders in Hainburg, Austria (close to the Slovak border) to raise specific concerns about the minority policy of the previous Mečiar government and to make a number of recommendations concerning national minority issues. In May 1995 and March 1996 the High Commissioner organized round-tables in neutral locations (Locarno, Switzerland and Noordwijk, the Netherlands) to cool off the heated dialogue between Kyiv and Simferopol over the status of Crimea and to try to find common ground among the parties on contentious constitutional issues. As Personal Representative of the Chairman-in-Office dealing with Kosovo,[13] he held consultations with a number of Kosovar leaders and Serb experts on Kosovo in Dürnstein, Austria. He also often had informal consultations on the margins of OSCE or international meetings and sometimes hosted meetings in his office in The Hague.[14]

Visits served several purposes. Firstly, they were an invaluable opportunity for gathering information. They were the best way of fulfilling paragraph 16 of the High Commissioner's mandate, namely 'to assess at the earliest possible stage the role of the parties directly concerned, the nature of the tensions and

13 For more on this role, which was separate from yet indirectly related to his role as High Commissioner on National Minorities, see Chapter 6.

14 For example: in November 1997 he met with leaders of the Albanian Party of Democratic Prosperity in his office to discuss developments concerning inter-ethnic relations in the former Yugoslav Republic of Macedonia; he was visited by Latvian Foreign Minister Valdis Birkavs in April 1999 to discuss the State Language Law; together with representatives of the Council of Europe and the European Commission he met with a Slovak Government delegation to break the deadlock over the law on minority languages in April 1999; and in July 1999 he met with the leaders of the Hungarian Coalition Party who requested a meeting in The Hague to explain their views on the law on minority languages and the state of inter-ethnic relations in Slovakia.

recent developments therein and, where possible, the potential consequences for peace and stability within the OSCE area'. The High Commissioner heard first-hand from the main actors what their concerns were and had an opportunity to pose questions and discuss the issues with them. This direct exposure to the situation not only allowed him to familiarize himself with the main players and issues, it also built contacts and provided insights that gave him indispensable credibility in devising and following up on his recommendations.[15]

Secondly his visits had a symbolic and indicative function. The very fact that the High Commissioner went to a particular country suggested that he was aware of inter-ethnic tensions there and he felt that they deserved his attention. This was for better or for worse. On the one hand, it reassured the parties (particularly the minorities) that their situation was being followed by the international community. On the other hand, some of his interlocutors (usually the host government) were sometimes not overly enthusiastic about the attention of the international community, particularly if the High Commissioner made repeat visits. As already discussed, in order to reduce this feeling of stigmatization and to avoid any sensationalism that his visit could provoke, Van der Stoel, to the extent possible, operated in confidentiality.

Van der Stoel also built confidence by being a good listener. As conflicts may stem in part from misunderstandings, lack of communication or disillusionment, it was important for the High Commissioner's interlocutors to feel that they had been heard and understood.[16] At the same time, visits afforded the High Commissioner the opportunity to explain and make clear his role and possible contribution. As one of his advisers has noted, 'the most effective role of the Commissioner is one of close confident with international leverage'.[17]

This leads to the third point, namely that visits played an educative role. Van der Stoel made the parties aware that he was the High Commissioner *on* and

---

15 Huber 1994, p. 16.

16 For more analysis on this and other aspects of the High Commissioner's work see Conflict Management Group, 'Methods and strategies in conflict prevention', Report by an Expert Consultation in Connection with the Activities of the CSCE High Commissioner on National Minorities, 2–3 December 1993, *Working Paper Series* (Cambridge, MA 1994).

17 Stefan Vassilev, 'The HCNM approach to conflict prevention', *Helsinki Monitor* 10(3) (1999), p. 54.

not *for* National Minorities and was therefore neither a defender of the State nor an advocate of minorities. He reminded States of their international commitments in regard to the protection of the rights of persons belonging to national minorities, and made national minorities aware of their rights and obligations. This could also include a cautionary function. He tried to help the parties understand the results of unilateral actions, including the eventual international repercussions. These could include the effect that decisions could have on relations with international financial institutions, membership in international organizations, or how excessive demands do not enjoy the support of the international community.[18]

This raises the fourth and, arguably most important, element of the High Commissioner's visits, namely (pursuant to paragraph 12 of his mandate) to 'promote dialogue, confidence and co-operation' between the parties directly involved. This element of the High Commissioner's work evolved far beyond the expectations of the mandate.[19] Van der Stoel's effective diplomacy during, and as a follow-up to, visits was one of the main reasons why he came to be seen as an active and effective instrument of preventive diplomacy.

Paragraph 12 of the mandate, which says that during his visits the High Commissioner may, where appropriate, promote dialogue, confidence and co-operation between the parties, appears under the heading of 'early warning'. As discussed in Chapter 1, the mandate foresaw a very formalistic transition from early warning to early action. In practice, Van der Stoel turned this interpretation on its head. By making full use of paragraph 12, he, in effect, took early action through his visits, thereby pre-empting the need for formal provisions of early warning.

The High Commissioner used his visits to try to help the parties to come up with solutions that are both politically possible and in line with international standards. Of course this cannot be accomplished during one visit. Therefore follow-up was a key component of the High Commissioner's work. This too went beyond the mandate which says that the High Commissioner will be able to pay 'a visit' to any participating State.[20] Van der Stoel discovered that the effective implementation of his mandate required an ongoing involvement in

---

18 *Ibid.*, p. 55.

19 Zaagman, in Bloed 1994, p. 162.

20 II para. 11c.

most situations. Indeed, he visited some countries up to five times a year. As he was engaged in approximately ten countries at the same time (not to mention regular trips to the Permanent Council and participation in international conferences), this meant that he was usually on the road for some 150 days a year. He was, quite literally, the flying Dutchman.[21]

Very little information was released about the High Commissioner's visits. A strictly confidential report was sent to the Chairman-in-Office and a very brief synopsis of the High Commissioner's activities was included in the monthly *OSCE Newsletter*. Some information on the High Commissioner's activities was also available on the OSCE website. OSCE delegations in the Permanent Council were regularly briefed on the High Commissioner's activities. But beyond that, the High Commissioner's work was shrouded by a veil of secrecy.

Recommendations

During his visits (and other consultations for example in telephone conversations with key players), Van der Stoel often made oral recommendations. But most recommendations were written, usually in the form of a follow-up letter to the Foreign Minister of the state that he had just visited. Most of the High Commissioner's recommendations are available on the HCNM section of the OSCE website at www.osce.org. It should be noted that the High Commissioner did not issue formal recommendations to the minorities that he was in contact with.[22]

Although not provided for in the reporting procedures outlined in the mandate, written recommendations evolved into one of the main tools of the High Commissioner. Van der Stoel's original impulse was more or less to repeat in written form what he had tried to convey to the persons with whom he had spoken during his visit and to complete this by suggesting specific steps. This

21 Van der Stoel always managed to travel with only carry-on luggage – a practice which was also adhered to by his advisers.

22 There have been, however, occasions when he has asked the Government to forward his recommendations to minority representatives. For example, when making recommendations on the status of Crimea he often asked the Foreign Minister of Ukraine to forward a copy of his recommendations to the Parliament of the Autonomous Republic of Crimea.

process was aided by a period of reflection after a visit that allowed him (in consultation with his advisers) to put all of his discussions into context. Writing down his recommendations meant that his views were on the record. He soon discovered that by having his recommendations in written form he could win greater backing from OSCE participating States, particularly through the Committee of Senior Officials (and later the Permanent Council).[23]

In his letters, the High Commissioner provided his analysis of the situation – taking into account all the legitimate interests in play – and offered his specific recommendations for its resolution. The recommendations tended to be precise and detailed in substantive terms rather than making a general commentary. They provided an informal means to convey insights and suggestions without commiting the parties to detailed legal negotiations nor threatening them with sanctions in the event of non-compliance.[24] The recommendations are 'food for thought' usually prepared in a way that is digestible to the Government to which they are addressed; 'they are formulated in a way that builds incentives for positive action by the government with respect to its relations with national minorities'.[25]

The High Commissioner used the recommendations to spell out his concerns with regard to issues that were either the matter of existing tensions or, in his opinion, could develop in that direction. This sometimes involved putting issues on the table that the Government may have wanted to avoid.

Points made in the recommendations usually referred to specific policies and administrative practices. The High Commissioner commented on them in relation to relevant domestic law (particularly constitutional provisions) and international standards. But he did not look at the issues in a legalistic vacuum. Before making recommendations he considered a range of issues (e.g. economic, cultural, historical, social, systemic) the most important of which was the political context surrounding state-minority relations. The issues examined frequently realted to domestic legislation, language usage, mechanisms for dialogue and participation, education and citizenship, as well as policy approaches (many of these issues are discussed in greater detail in Chapter 5). In examining specific

---

23 See Zellner & Lange (eds.) 1999, p. 17.

24 Cohen 1999, p. 64.

25 Chigas 1996, p. 34.

issues Van der Stoel generally suggested options for governments to consider. In this way they were designed to aid policy makers in developing feasible policy responses and to provide a framework in which governments and minorities could address general and specific legal, policy, institutional and process issues.[26]

The tone of the letters was usually constructive and cordial. The recommendations were diplomatically phrased, not seeking to apportion blame but rather to make constructive contributions to an analysis of sensitive issues. An illustrative example is a letter from the High Commissioner to the Minister for Foreign Affairs of the former Yugoslav Republic of Macedonia, Stevo Crvenkovski dated 1 November 1993. On presenting his recommendations Van der Stoel said 'I hope you will consider them in the way I intended them to be: as an effort to contribute to the thought process in your Government regarding the ways and methods to be followed in order to cope with the complicated questions which a multi-ethnic country has to face'.[27]

Recommendations also had a cautionary function. They could be used to make states aware that the ratification of international instruments is itself not an adequate means of ensuring compliance with the duties they establish. Recommendations could serve to point out to states where and how they were failing to live up to international standards and to explain the repercussions that this could have. Such warnings were usually couched in terms that explained why a Government should reflect on a particular course of action and why changing that course of action could be of benefit both to the Government and to society as a whole.

After an official letter was sent, it was usually the case that the Foreign Minister would reply. The practice developed that following relatively soon after receiving a response, the High Commissioner shared the correspondence with the Permanent Council. The circulation of the correspondence to OSCE delegations, at the initiative of the Chairman-in-Office, allowed the OSCE community to become acquainted with the High Commissioner's concerns regarding the security situation in those countries in which the High Commissioner was active.

---

26 Cohen 1999, p. 64.

27 Letter to Stevo Crvenkovski, Minister for Foreign Affairs of the former Yugoslav Republic of Macedonia, 1 November 1993, CSCE Communication no. 305/93.

As such they can be regarded as an informal early warning mechanism.[28] This also put peer pressure on the State concerned to follow-up on the points raised in the correspondence. It was much more difficult for a Government to dismiss the High Commissioner's recommendations once they had become known to all OSCE participating States.

Initially, the recommendations were withheld from the public. This practice afforded the parties adequate time without public scrutiny in which to act in good-faith.[29] In this way, confidentiality was maintained (often for months) during which time quiet diplomatic activities could be pursued and the State to which the recommendations were addressed had time to consider, react to, and, very often, implement the High Commissioner's recommendations. Ultimately most exchanges were made public with a view to enabling all interested parties (in particular, the representatives of minorities and the affected general public) to know exactly the opinions and recommendations of the High Commissioner as an impartial and independent actor together with the opinions and positions of the Government vis-à-vis those of the High Commissioner. This was usually done through a decision by the Permanent Council in which the exchange of letters became officially regarded as an OSCE document. This process eventually became less formal and after a period of time official correspondence was simply released into the public domain some time after the High Commissioner reported on their contents to the Permanent Council.

Van der Stoel originally feared that his recommendations would simply be filed and left to collect dust on a shelf. Afterall, they are not legally binding and there exists no enforcement mechanism. The degree to which they are implemented is entirely at the discretion of the recipient state. However, the High Commissioner, OSCE missions and the political bodies of the OSCE informally monitored the extent to which recommendations influenced policy within the States at which they were directed.[30] If the High Commissioner felt that his recommendations were not being sufficiently implemented, he would follow-up (either with a further letter or visit) and/or ask sympathetic OSCE States or partner organizations to approach the Government with the same message. Recommendations therefore were, and are, stimulants of an ongoing process

---

28 Cohen 1999, p. 64.

29 Packer 1996a, p. 288.

30 Cohen 1999, p. 64.

rather than dead letters. Furthermore, it has been argued that their cumulative effect has been to create a soft jurisprudence of international standards vis-à-vis national minority issues.[31]

Lobbying and Contacts with 'Kin States'

Implementation of the High Commissioner's recommendations takes time and sometimes the response of Governments is grudging. As already noted, Van der Stoel occasionaly sought outside support for his recommendations. The fact that he felt the need to do so indicates that although his recommendations were intended as a co-operative instrument, they were not always perceived as such.[32]

The High Commissioner lobbied support for his recommendations through regular briefings in the Permanent Council in Vienna, through informal discussions with influential delegations in Vienna, and through visits to, or communication with, capitals. The aim was to win general support for his work, and, when necessary, to inform governments on his positions vis-à-vis particular states and issues. Once the High Commissioner's office became an established institution, there was an increasing interest by participating States to meet with Van der Stoel to discuss issues of mutual interest. Exchange of information, and sometimes lobbying, went both ways.

Van der Stoel maintained open channels with kin-States of minority communities that he was engaged in. For example, he kept in close contact with the Hungarian Government concerning issues relating to the Hungarian minorities in Romania, Slovakia and the Federal Republic of Yugoslavia or with the Russian Government, for example, on developments in Latvia, Estonia, Ukraine and Kazakhstan. This gave him a clearer idea of the dynamics between the minority and the kin-State and how this could affect relations between the kin-State and the State in which the minority lives. Such visits were especially revealing after a change in government.

In other cases, he contacted the kin-State in order to encourage it and/or the

---

31 See John Packer, 'Making International Law Matter in Preventing Ethnic Conflict: A Practitioner's Perspective', *New York Journal of International Law and Politics*, 32(3) (2000) p. 717.

32 Cohen 1999, p. 65.

kin-minority to be more moderate. In such cases his goal was not only to calm down inter-ethnic tensions within the country concerned, but also to contribute to the improvement of bilateral relations between the country with a disgruntled minority and that minority's kin-State. This was particularly important with the Russian Federation and its relations with Latvia and Estonia (and to a lesser extent Kazakhstan and Ukraine) over the treatment of Russian minorities in those countries.[33] The High Commissioner made a number of visits to the Russian Federation[34] to explain his activities, to learn the Russian view on specific minority issues, and, when a situation was tense, to urge the Government to exercise restraint. He did the same in Budapest when relations soured between Hungary and Slovakia and Hungary and Romania. In 1993 and 1994 he visited Greece several times when tensions were high between Greece and Albania concerning the Greek minority in Albania.[35] In all of these cases, the High Commissioner had usually already been in direct contact with minority representatives, but as these minorities usually look to their kin-State for support, he felt that it was necessary to be in contact with the kin-State as well.

In some cases the High Commissioner encouraged the kin-State and the State where the minority lives to engage in a dialogue about the duty of a State to respect and foster the identity of a minority on the one hand and the duty of persons belonging to a national minority to be loyal to the State on the other.

---

33 For example on 2 April 1998 the High Commissioner wrote to Minister of Foreign Affairs Yevgeniy Primakov calling for moderation of Moscow's views regarding the debates over the Citizenship Law and Language Law in Latvia. He said that 'I am afraid that any statement of your Government linking normalisation of relations between Russia and Latvia to the implementation of my Recommendations might not promote the chances of their acceptance. It is my firm conviction that, if such a policy is adopted, a considerable group of members of the Latvian Parliament, who are now in favour of their implementation, would then consider it a matter of pride to oppose them. I also fear that sanctions, official or unofficial, could have a similar effect. I therefore express the hope that you and your Government do not take such a step.'

34 He visited the Russian Federation in the spring of 1993, March 1994, October 1994, June 1995, February 1997, November 1998 and February 2000.

35 He visited Greece in July 1993, November 1993, August 1994, October 1994 and, in relation to other matters, October 1999.

While such a dialogue is not always free of tension, it can bring positive results. Indeed, the very process can often be an important confidence-building exercise. Sometimes this process can result in the signing of a bilateral treaty of good neighbourliness and friendly relations which confirms existing borders, guarantees the protection of minorities and which may include mechanisms for periodic consultations and opportunities for an exchange of views on minority matters. Such treaties can promote a more relaxed attitude on the part of the government of a state with a minority, while at the same time providing reassurances to the kin-State that the rights and identities of kindred minorities will be protected.[36] Van der Stoel acted a catalyst in the conclusion of a Basic Treaty between Romania and Hungary (signed on 16 September 1996).[37]

However, it should be borne in mind that such treaties cannot ensure specific solutions to specific minority problems: such problems have to be resolved within states on the basis of their commitment to international norms and principles. Furthermore, it is worth noting that the minority population may be more radical than the kin-State and its demands may not reflect the position of the kin-State's Government. In this respect, the kin-State may be hesitant about jeopardizing otherwise good relations with its neighbour in which case bilateral treaties will not solve the problem. Conversely, a kin-State may be more hard-line than the minority which can make life difficult for the minority and can complicate bilateral relations.[38]

---

36 For more on this subject see Arie Bloed & Pieter van Dijk (eds.), *Protection of Minority Rights Through Bilateral Treaties: the Case of Central and Eastern Europe* (The Hague: Kluwer Law International, 1999) and Kinga Gal, *Bilateral Agreements in Central and Eastern Europe: a New Inter-State Framework for Minority Protection?*, European Centre for Minority Issues Working Paper no. 4 (Flensburg).

37 For an analysis of the High Commissioner's involvement in ironing our differences between Romania and Hungary in the drafting of the Treaty, see Van der Stoel, 'The role of the OSCE High Commissioner in conflict prevention', in Croker *et al.* 1999, pp. 76–7.

38 See also Van der Stoel's remarks on this topic at the Rome meeting of the Council of Ministers for Foreign Affairs of the CSCE, 30 November 1993.

Suggesting Procedural Ways Out

In his analyses, recommendations and visits the High Commissioner paid particular attention to political processes including the drafting of legislation, voting procedures, the timing and wording of political pronouncements, and inter-party or inter-coalition politics. This is often where decisions are made, promises kept or broken, and tensions ameliorated or exacerbated.

Very often it is the process as much as the issues themselves that causes difficulties among the parties. Bad faith in procedural issues can have a knock-on effect that erodes trust and poisons political relationships. When the issues involved concern minorities, the result can lead to inter-ethnic tensions. Conversely, reciprocal good will, compromise and pragmatic politics can build confidence between parties – and by extension the people that they represent – and instill faith in the political system. As a result, Van der Stoel paid a great deal of attention to the political process.

It is usually the case that by the time the High Commissioner became involved in a legislative issue, the law in question was already before Parliament.[39] It may not yet have become controversial, but it was on the table and therefore already the subject of debate. As the law progressed through Parliament, the High Commissioner kept abreast of developments and, as appropriate, made recommendations.

Some of the types of procedural recommendations that the High Commissioner made included amending legislation, delaying a vote, or requesting the President to send the law back to Parliament.

There were a number of cases in which the High Commissioner, either through his written recommendations or those of a group of experts, suggested amendments to a law. After becoming aware of the position of the parties, he usually tried to propose politically feasible solutions that were in line with international standards. Examples include the drafting of a minority language law in Slovakia in 1999, state language laws in Latvia and Estonia in 1998 and 1999, and a law on higher education in Macedonia in 1999/2000. In these cases, the High Commissioner sent experts from his office to work with parliamentary committees and other groups involved in drafting the legislation

39 There are examples when Van der Stoel was involved in drafting a law before it was submitted to Parliament, for example the Citizenship Law in Latvia in 1998.

and, in the cases of Latvia and Slovakia, also led a team of experts from his office, the European Commission and the Council of Europe to offer advice.

In some cases, for example when debates on a law were protracted or a parliamentary session was coming to an end, the High Commissioner would urge the Government to accelerate the drafting and decision-making process. This was, for example, the case with the Law on Education in Romania in 1999 and the Law on Minority Languages in Slovakia in 1999. But there were also occasions when Van der Stoel suggested that a vote should be delayed. This allowed time for reflection and further consultations with the aim of increasing the chances of favourably amending a law.

This did not always work and there were times when a Parliament ignored Van der Stoel's recommendations and approved a law in final reading. When this occurred Van der Stoel sometimes felt that it was necessary to appeal to the President (depending on the constitutional system) to send the law in question back to Parliament on the grounds that the law was unconstitutional or in contradiction to international standards to which the State is a party. For example, in 1994 Van der Stoel was successful in convincing President Ulmanis of Latvia to send the Citizenship Law back to Parliament. In July 1999, after an appeal by the High Commissioner, Ulmanis' successor, President Vike-Freiberga, sent back the controversial Language Law. In Estonia in 1993 the High Commissioner was able to convince President Lennart Meri to send back the Law on Aliens to Parliament for further changes on the basis of certain objections made by the OSCE and the Council of Europe. In the spring of 1996 President Meri sent back to Parliament a law on local elections which did not, in the analysis of the High Commissioner, meet international standards. In another example, this time in Slovakia, in February 1996 President Michal Kovac sent back to Parliament proposed amendments to the penal code which Van der Stoel considered draconian. In all cases the legislation was subsequently amended.

There were, however, situations when the High Commissioner was frustrated and could not make any headway. In such cases he worked towards amending the law at a later stage (under a more receptive Government) or proposed that the Government introduce other legislation that would fill loopholes concerning the protection of persons belonging to national minorities in existing legislation (for example in Slovakia where a law on minority language use was introduced by the Dzurinda Government as a counter-balance to the Law on State Language). Where this failed he worked to highlight the extent to which the

Government was out of step with international standards and sought to bring outside pressure to bear.

In his confidential discussions, Van der Stoel stressed to his interlocutors (particularly disillusioned ones) the importance of the political process and their involvement in it. This was especially the case when minority parties (for example the Hungarian parties in Slovakia and Romania) lost faith in their coalition partners. When a particular tack was not working, he suggested to the minorities that they re-package their proposals. For example, he stressed that instead of framing their demands in culture-specific ways they could promote their needs in the context of issues for which broader based support could be found in the society at large, for example issues like administrative reform, decentralization and increasing of the powers of local self-government.

Occasionally the High Commissioner cautioned Governments that abuse of the political process, for example not creating the proper conditions for meaningful political discourse and participation, could cause individuals or parties to seek recourse in unconstitutional methods. That is not to say that Governments should bow to every minority demand, but that showing a certain amount of flexibility and sensitivity is good governance.

In his consultations, especially those concerning political procedure, Van der Stoel tried to point out to the parties that a gain by one side should not be seen as a loss for the other. He tried to help the disputants to explore options to de-escalate tensions and/or develop frameworks for co-operation in which the needs of both sides were addressed and met. He tried to demonstrate that mutual accommodation is not a zero-sum option and that diversity can be satisfactorily integrated. In this respect, his very involvement in a situation offered a procedural way out for one or another of the parties. One side (usually the Government) could accept their commitments under international (and often national) law by portraying such acceptance as acceding to Van der Stoel's recommendations rather than caving into the demands of the other party. In this respect he played a key face-saving role.[40]

As noted in Chapter 2, Van der Stoel frequently stressed to all parties that a step-by-step approach is the most realistic. Particularly in societies undergoing profound change, the issues at stake are often so thoroughgoing and fundamental

40 See Ratner 2000, p. 680.

that their full realization takes time – and could significantly change the whole fabric of society. Laws concerning language, education, and citizenship almost inevitably trigger wider debates over national identity. Because of the significance of the questions being discussed and the sensitivities that they aroused, Van der Stoel often pointed out to the parties that it was only possible to reach partial agreement on some major issues. A notable example was his suggestion on how to break the constitutional deadlock on the status of Crimea within Ukraine. In 1996 he recommended that instead of waiting for consensus on all articles of the proposed legislation, the Ukrainian Parliament should approve those sections of the Crimean Constitution (which were indeed the vast majority) that respected the Constitution and laws of Ukraine. In this and other cases, a gradual approach proved effective in creating conditions for further negotiation while preventing further escalation of the conflict. The goal was to keep the process tractable and to keep it moving.

In terms of stimulating this process, the High Commissioner acted as a type of conscience, a guide, a catalyst, and an instrument of sober second thought. His immediate aim was to assist parties in overcoming contentious issues. The ultimate objective was to create conditions that enabled the parties themselves to deal with conflicting interests and values over time. An important aspect of both of these was to initiate and maintain dialogue.

Initiating and Maintaining Dialogue

There are two types of dialogue that the High Commissioner tried to initiate: dialogue between himself and the parties, and dialogue between the Government and minority representatives. Establishing dialogue between himself and the parties has already been explained in Chapter 2 when looking at the High Commissioner's approach. As is noted later in this chapter, it was very often up to his advisers before and after visits to make sure that the channels of communication remained open and that the High Commissioner kept in contact with all parties that could enrich his understanding of a particular situation. If these channels dried up or if the High Commissioner was insufficiently informed, his effectiveness and credibility would have been reduced. It was therefore important to maintain dialogue with as many partners as possible, even (or perhaps especially) with Governments or minority representatives who did not see eye to eye with him.

Initiating and maintaining dialogue between the parties was a much greater challenge. The mandate explicitly assigns the promotion of dialogue between parties to the High Commissioner.[41] Van der Stoel's general philosophy on the importance of dialogue as a means of conflict prevention and integrating diversity will be analyzed in Chapter 5. This section will focus on the techniques that he used to get the parties to communicate with each other.

His usual approach was not to mediate a dialogue, but rather to create the conditions, frameworks and impetus for the parties to initiate and maintain their own dialogue. The aim was to help the parties to help themselves. This took different forms: using dialogue as a process to enhance mutual understanding; facilitating dialogue with regard to specific contentious issues; and promoting mechanisms which advance dialogue in a more institutional way.[42]

Concerning the promotion of dialogue as a process to enhance mutual understanding, the main aim of the High Commissioner was to get the parties to attack the problem and not each other. Problems often stem from a lack of communication. This is sometimes because the Government may not recognize a minority group. At other times – particularly in a highly charged nationalistic environment – it may not be politically prudent for a Government to be seen entering into dialogue with a minority. Free of any political constraints, the High Commissioner is ideally suited to provide a channel through which dialogue may be facilitated. That is not to suggest that he is a conduit, rather he can make clear the respective views of the parties to each other and look for common ground on which direct contacts can begin.

This is particularly important during times of crisis. Although the High Commissioner is an instrument of conflict prevention, there are times when he is involved in crisis management. Usually in such situations dialogue has broken down – restoring it becomes one of the High Commissioner's priorities. For example, in the summer of 1993 during a crisis in Estonia he was able, through shuttle diplomacy, to win assurances from the Estonian Government and representatives of the Russophone minority that both would engage in dialogue and seek to resolve their outstanding differences. In the spring of 1995 he acted

41 See paragraph 12 of the mandate 'The High Commissioner may . . . where appropriate promote dialogue, confidence and co-operation' between the parties.

42 Cohen 1999, p. 69.

as a vital channel of communication through which Kyiv and Simferopol could maintain a dialogue over the crisis in Crimea.

In the former Yugoslav Republic of Macedonia (fYROM), the High Commissioner regarded the lack of dialogue as a symptom of a general lack of communication and understanding between the Albanian and Macedonian communities. The corollary of this is that more effective mechanisms for inter-ethnic dialogue can be part of the solution. To kick-start this process, in the fYROM and elsewhere, the High Commissioner sometimes organized round-tables, seminars, or conferences either on his own initiative, or under the banner of the Foundation on Inter-Ethnic Relations. (For specific examples see Chapter 6.)

It must be said, however, that even when there are frequent and direct contacts, the lines of communication or the means of communicating the message may be poor. It may also occur, either intentionally or by accident, that the message becomes distorted. As one observer has put it, 'The nature of the situations in which the High Commissioner is engaged in is such that there is rarely a complete absence of communication between the parties, but there is often an absence of constructive dialogue'.[43] There are occasions, particularly during the drafting of legislation, that positions become entrenched and even coalition partners may cease to communicate effectively. In such cases the discrete and objective involvement of the High Commissioner as an 'insider third party' can give the parties a sounding board, offer them a new and informed perspective on contentious issues and suggest procedural ways out. This was the case in Slovakia and Romania in 1999 and 2000 when Hungarian parties, which were part of the Governments, fell out with their coalition partners over issues of language rights and education. In these and other cases the High Commissioner tried to break down misunderstandings or disagreements over major issues by stressing the need to 'be specific'. Behind closed doors, the parties were encouraged to 'unpack' the problems, to strip away the political rhetoric and hyperbole and to identify the underlying issues. By getting the parties to clarify their positions in this way, it often emerged that they were not seeking the radical positions that they sometimes proclaimed in public statements. It also helped to show where there was common ground and where there were significant differences. In this way, the High Commissioner could help to demonstrate the compatibility of

43 Cohen 1999, p. 47.

underlying interests and needs and isolate the issues of dispute.

The very process of dialogue can be a confidence-building process. Parties interact, they articulate their fears, needs and aspirations and hear those of the other side. In this way dialogue is an opportunity to positively transform the relationship between the parties. This was evident in round-tables in Locarno and Noordwijk organized by the High Commissioner in 1995 and 1996 when Ukrainian and Crimean representatives had an opportunity to air and resolve many differences face to face. It was also the case in two seminars on the Meshketian Turks held in The Hague and Vienna in 1998 and 1999. The same can be said for a seminar held in Locarno in December 1996 which provided an opportunity for dialogue on inter-ethnic relations in Kazakhstan, particularly as regards the status of the Cossacks. In many of these cases, before the seminars or round tables, communication had been mainly limited to (often inflammatory) public statements that added to rather than abetted disagreements over fundamental issues.

While dialogue can be useful in preventing the acute escalation of tensions, it should also be part of a more permanent process that permits the government and minorities to address their ongoing relationship and deal with the root causes of tensions.[44] The High Commissioner therefore stressed that integrating diversity and building representative democracy require institutional mechanisms which make dialogue a routine process. These mechanisms do not eliminate the possibility of conflict, but they provide a more structured means of discussion and can usually contain disagreements within a representative, accountable and transparent framework. Although they do not preclude the need for outside involvement, such institutional structures or bodies usually allow for parties to flesh out answers to their own problems. As Van der Stoel once described it: 'I encourage States to take care of their own problems and to develop institutions, legislation and mechanisms to pre-empt the types of crises which would necessitate my involvement'.[45]

---

44 Chigas 1994, p. 30.

45 'Early Warning and Early Action: Preventing Inter-Ethnic Conflict', Speech to the Royal Institute of International Relations, London 9 July 1999.

Minority Representation and Participation

Dialogue and participation are therefore inextricably linked. Dialogue, properly channeled, is a form of participation: in order to be effective, participation requires dialogue. Van der Stoel often noted that effective participation by national minorities in public life is an essential component of a peaceful society. Through effective participation in decision-making processes and bodies, representatives of minorities have the possibility to present their views to the authorities, which can help the authorities to understand minorities' concerns and take these into account when developing policies. At the same time the authorities are offered a platform to explain their policies and intentions. This can contribute to a more co-operative and less confrontational situation.

One way to ensure minority representation and participation is to have minorities as part of the Government. This is the case in Slovakia and Romania where Hungarian parties are part of the Government coalition or in the former Yugoslav Republic of Macedonia where a party representing the Albanian minority is part of the Government. Van der Stoel has noted that 'the electoral system should facilitate minority representation and influence'.[46] For example, in Ukraine the High Commissioner supported a guaranteed quota of seats for the Crimean Tatars in the Autonomous Republic of Crimea. He also often raised the point with the Hungarian Government that pursuant to an Act on the Rights of National and Ethnic Minorities (1993) minorities have the right to be represented in the National Assembly.

Such arrangements are, however, the exception rather than the rule. Van der Stoel therefore stressed that 'states should ensure that opportunities exist for minorities to have an effective voice at the level of central government, including through special arrangements as necessary'.[47] This can include a Government department relating to minority issues (as in Albania, Slovakia and Romania), a Plenipotentiary for specific minority issues (for example on the Roma in Slovakia), or an Ombudsman or Commissioner on Ethnic and Human Rights issues (as in a number of countries including Latvia, Kazakhstan and Kyrgyzstan). Such arrangements also apply to regional and local levels of government, for example the Joint Council of Municipalities in Eastern Slavonia, Croatia which

46 *Ibid.*

47 *Ibid.*

gives Serbs a voice in issues that concern them.

Van der Stoel urged States to establish and make full use of advisory or consultative bodies within appropriate institutional frameworks to serve as channels for dialogue between governmental authorities and national minorities. Often these bodies are Consultative Councils (like the Consultative Council on Nationalities in Latvia, the Council for Inter-Ethnic Relations in fYROM, Councils for National Minorities in Romania and the Czech Republic, the Advisory Government Council on National Minorities and Ethnic Groups in the Slovak Republic, the Assembly of Peoples of Kazakhstan, the Assembly of Peoples of Kyrgyzstan and Roma councils in a number of countries), which are usually under the auspices of the President. The goal of all such bodies is to be able to raise issues with decision-makers, prepare recommendations, formulate legislative and other proposals, and monitor and provide views on proposed governmental decisions that affect minorities.

Establishing such bodies is not enough. The High Commissioner was wary of Governments that set up bodies that were either insufficiently funded, only superficially consulted and/or packed with 'safe' minority representatives. He therefore stressed that minority bodies must be functional and effective. They should be 'genuine in their intentions and meaningful in their endeavours; without this they will represent nothing more than window dressing or tokenism'.[48]

On some occasions he encouraged the use of round-tables. As noted above, this more *ad hoc* format is useful during crisis situations or as a way of involving outside experts to provide input to a process that has foundered. They are akin to problem-solving workshops structured to allow a free-flowing dialogue around a series of pressing issues, under the chairmanship of the High Commissioner.[49] This was the case in Ukraine over the issue of Crimea and in Kazakhstan concerning inter-ethnic relations (particularly the Cossacks). Such round-tables can usually kick-start a process which then becomes more regular. They also allow important personal exchanges to take place and relationships to begin or develop among competing political leaders.

---

48 Address by the High Commissioner to the Supplementary Human Dimension Meeting on Roma and Sinti Issues, Vienna 6 September 1999, p. 4.

49 Cohen 1999, p. 69.

The goal of all of these institutions is to create opportunities to manage issues, not necessarily to solve problems. In a structured, inclusive, transparent and accountable process of consultation, trust and respect can be built up and a constructive climate of confidence can be maintained. This promotes a pattern of co-operative inter-action.

Leverage: Sticks and Carrots

In order to get his point across, Van der Stoel relied a great deal on his status, the authority of his office, and the force of reason. Sometimes these were not enough. One could argue that anything more would be unnecessary as the High Commissioner is an instrument of co-operative security. As one observer has put it, as a 'normative intermediary' he needed to provide a roadmap as much as carrots and sticks.[50] As Diana Chigas notes in looking at the diminishing relevance of 'solutions':

> 'Traditional methods for dealing with human rights compliance issues through confrontation, pressure and advocacy will frequently only exacerbate conflict, while traditional strategies for international mediation of conflicts, with their emphasis on "carrots" and "sticks" to induce settlements, are inadequate to deal with long-term psychological, social, economic, and political problems at the root of ethno-national conflicts'.[51]

This is certainly true of most of the work that that the High Commissioner was often involved in. However, there were occasions when the parties had to be cajoled and the strength of argument and quiet diplomacy needed to be re-enforced.

Usually Van der Stoel was able to avoid such situations. By clarifying the costs of failure to co-operate with the High Commissioner and by giving a concurrent, clear opportunity to do something to avoid them, he was often able to provide an effective disincentive for further escalation. Similarly, by spelling out the potential advantages of a certain course of action and providing ideas on how to proceed in that direction, he could facilitate a positive resolution of outstanding differences. But sometimes sticks and carrots were needed. He

---

50 Ratner 2000, p. 679.

51 Chigas 1996, pp. 28–9.

once admitted that those that he possessed were limited, and that he would not mind having slightly juicier carrots and slightly bigger sticks.[52]

One technique for increasing pressure was to 'go public', or threaten to do so. The knowledge that the High Commissioner's criticisms would reach the public domain played a role in convincing governments to change their ways, especially as they were aware that his assessments were carefully studied by the European Commission and Union. This 'speaking softly but carrying a big stick' is what he sometimes described as quiet diplomacy 'plus'.

Another 'stick' was to warn states of the potential reaction of the international community to a proposed policy, or indeed to rally the international community against an errant state. This was made credible by the fact that the High Commissioner had the backing of OSCE participating States and partner organizations. As Van der Stoel noted in a speech to the Royal Institute for International Affairs in July 1999, 'I may have small teeth and few carrots, but I am mandated by 55 States acting as part of a wider framework of European security organizations'.[53] OSCE participating States, who are regularly kept abreast of his activities and recommendations, were usually supportive. In fact, they often followed up his recommendations in bilateral contacts, through making demarches, strong public statements on his behalf or through other channels.

As will be discussed in greater detail in the next chapter, the High Commissioner could also usually count on the support of, and exert pressure through, or with, the European Union and/or the Council of Europe. As the protection of persons belonging to national minorities is a consideration for EU accession, the High Commissioner was able to use his links with the European Commission and EU Presidency to great effect. This leverage was crucial in affecting changes in Slovakia (particularly in regard to the law on minority languages), and in Latvia and Estonia (regarding language laws) in 1999. Indeed, Van der Stoel's criticisms of the Mečiar Government's treatment of minorities played a role in keeping Slovakia out of the first group of accession countries in 1997. As the Council of Europe and the High Commissioner had similar concerns regarding the respect for the rights of persons belonging to national minorities, they often delivered the same basic message. This common front was stronger than the

52 Interview between Van der Stoel and Michael Ignatieff, 7 October 1999.

53 'Early Warning and Early Action: Preventing Inter-Ethnic Conflict', Speech at the Royal Institute of International Affairs, 9 July 1999.

two bodies speaking individually.

'Carrots' often included official support for a Government policy. Because protecting the rights of persons belonging to national minorities is a prerequisite for being accepted as a member of major European institutions (particularly the European Union), having the support of the High Commissioner is seen as an important seal of approval for states. In countries where Van der Stoel was engaged, it was therefore in the interest of the countries concerned to demonstrate that they had addressed the concerns raised in his recommendations. Another more concrete incentive was facilitation of direct financial or economic assistance, through, for example, donor conferences, specific internationally funded projects or 'tension-reducing projects'.

Tension-Reducing Projects

Van der Stoel concluded through his experience that, in terms of conflict prevention, small steps at an early stage can be useful in preventing bigger problems later on. In the same way that the accumulation of small problems can have significant negative consequences, small-scale and focused assistance can have large-scale and long-term positive results.

Some problems of inter-ethnic relations may be rooted in competition for scarce jobs, resources or economic benefits, unequal development, status or prestige, or the persistence of basic human needs. In many of these situations, the governmental authorities genuinely lack sufficient resources to respond adequately to a problem. As a result, the non-resolution of socio-economic problems sometimes exacerbates underlying ethnic tensions. This has been evident in Crimea (with the Crimean Tatars), with the Roma in a number of countries, with the Russian speakers in Narva, Estonia and with the Albanian minority in the former Yugoslav Republic of Macedonia.

In such cases the High Commissioner tried to draw the attention of the international community to the problem in order to work with the Government(s) involved in finding solutions. Examples of the former include two donor conferences on Crimea, and efforts to raise money for a principally Albanian-language University in the former Yugoslav Republic of Macedonia.

In other cases, he took the initiative to develop projects to address specific issues which, in his opinion, could improve inter-ethnic relations. These can be regarded as tension-reducing projects.

Examples of tension-reducing projects include training of public officials (in Macedonia and Romania), information campaigns in Latvia and Estonia (explaining citizenship to minorities), language courses in the State language for minorities in Latvia and Moldova, publishing school textbooks (in Uzbek and Kyrgyz) in Kyrgyzstan, the establishment of a 'catch up' transition year programme for ethnic Albanian students in the former Yugoslav Republic of Macedonia, providing legal assistance to Serb returnees in Knin (Croatia) and the development of home schools in Ukraine (to educate Crimean Tatars in the absence of appropriate school facilities). The goal of these projects is to fill a niche that is not being filled by the Government or the international community – a niche which can play a practical role in addressing root causes of conflict. The projects are designed to satisfy specific (and often basic) needs, to encourage people to work together, and to underline the importance of common interests and a common future. They also serve to heighten awareness of the issues and to get the ball rolling among wealthier donors to continue to be engaged with the projects in the future. Many of these projects were carried out with the assistance of the Foundation on Inter-Ethnic Relations which was established by the High Commissioner in 1993. (The work of the Foundation is explained in greater detail in Chapter 5.)

The Role of Advisers

One seldom refers to 'the Office' of the High Commissioner, rather solely to the High Commissioner. To some extent, this was a reflection of the style of Van der Stoel. He was the main focus of attention and took a very 'hands on' approach to his work. He travelled to the countries which he was engaged in, drafted his own recommendations and gave personal attention to all substantive issues. He followed developments in all countries for which he had dossiers, he seldom took a day off, and was sometimes personally involved in the most minute details concerning the daily activity of the office . . . when he was in the office. As already noted, the High Commissioner spent at least half of his time on the road (or in the air). Furthermore, the fact that Van der Stoel was the first High Commissioner and held the post for eight years meant that he was personally associated with the post. He knew (and had defined) the position and had a long memory of the individuals and issues that he had been involved with.

Nevertheless, Van der Stoel did not work alone. He relied on a small group of advisers. As he once modestly remarked, a conductor is only as good as his orchestra.[54] Because of the frequent travel and sheer volume of material that had to be systematically analyzed, Van der Stoel could not possibly keep up to date with all concurrent developments. More often than not, two or three situations required his attention at the same time – and four or five others needed to be regularly checked up on. Keeping the High Commissioner up-to-date and well informed is the main role of his advisers. In 1993 Van der Stoel started with two advisers (both seconded – one from the Netherlands and one from Sweden) who were soon joined by a third (seconded from Poland). The office eventually grew to four advisers, a personal adviser (seconded by the Netherlands from 1993 to 1999 and Norway in 2000), two legal advisers and four administrative personnel. The position of Director was added in 2000. When the Foundation on Inter-Ethnic Relations was amalgamated with the Office in 2000, the staff rose by four more members (to a total of sixteen).

In line with OSCE recruiting policy, the High Commissioner tried to have advisers from as wide a geographical representation as possible. Over the years employees of the office have been from Bosnia-Herzegovina, Bulgaria, Canada, Czech Republic, France, Germany, Ireland, Kyrgyzstan, the Netherlands, Norway, Poland, Sweden, Switzerland, the United Kingdom and the United States.

Generally speaking, advisers cover specific regional areas or countries, i.e. the Baltic States, South-Eastern Europe, Central Europe, Caucasus and Central Asia. They are usually hired on the basis of their knowledge of a particular region (including language skills), their knowledge of the OSCE, and experience with national minority-related issues. Most have had a diplomatic background and/or relevant experience in international law, political science (international relations), or with a non-governmental organization.

The main tasks of advisers include: collecting information; planning the High Commissioner's visits and travelling with him; giving advice (particularly on the background to particular situations, the profiles and roles of key individuals, the dynamics of ongoing political processes and the content and timing of possible interventions); drafting recommendations, speechs and articles; writing internal memoranda and reports (either as background, on a specific evolving issue, or as a follow-up to a visit or event); contributing to

---

54 Remarks after receiving a Knighthood of the House Order of the Golden Lion of Nassau, The Hague, 31 August 1999.

conferences and seminars; and liaising with useful contacts. The latter task is arguably one of the most important for it provides the advisers, and by extension the High Commissioner, with useful insights into evolving situations, Government positions or reactions (e.g. to his recommendations), and the views of minority representatives. Advisers therefore spend a great deal of their time developing and cultivating contacts with OSCE missions, representatives of OSCE States located in The Hague, Vienna and/or capitals, as well as liaising with other inter-governmental organizations, non-governmental organizations and minority representatives.

The High Commissioner's personal adviser attends to the administration of the office (on the instructions of the High Commissioner), gives general advice on policy matters and often travels with the High Commissioner. He is also the main point of contact for relations with other OSCE institutions and the permanent delegations of OSCE participating States in Vienna.

Since 1995, the High Commissioner has increasingly drawn on the advice of legal experts. A legal adviser was hired in September 1995, and was joined by a junior legal adviser in May 1997. Upon the request of the High Commissioner, the legal advisers assess the compatibility of domestic policy, law and practice with applicable international standards, comparative constitutional law and jurisprudence and other relevant domestic law. They also advise the High Commissioner on alternative solutions to specific conflicts which may be satisfactory to the parties and remain compatible with international standards.

In 2000 the position of Director was created for the purpose of providing co-ordination and ensuring consistency in the legal and political advice, together with the project activities, of the office.

The Use of Experts

Van der Stoel was sometimes assisted by experts, but not to the extent anticipated by the mandate. The mandate includes six articles on the 'High Commissioner and involvement of experts' (as compared to four on early warning). The provisions state that 'the High Commissioner may decide to request the assistance from not more than three experts with relevant expertise in specific matters on which brief, specialized investigation and advice are required'.[55] According to the mandate, the experts will only visit a participating State at the same time

55 Paragraph 31 of the High Commissioner's mandate.

as the High Commissioner.[56]

In the first two years of the High Commissioner's mandate, expert teams visited Slovakia, Hungary, Albania and Ukraine, sometimes on his behalf and sometimes with him. Particularly in the case of the teams that went to Slovakia and Hungary, the observations and recommendations of the experts were useful in providing the High Commissioner with insights into ways of resolving the contentious inter-ethnic issues. They also gave symbolic clout to the High Commissioner's recommendation; the observations were not solely his own, they were those of, or backed up by, international experts. Although experts were occasionally asked for advice on specific international standards, for background information on certain issues, and for opinions on draft recommendations, the practise of involving them in visits of the High Commissioner faded after the last visit of the Team of Experts to Hungary in May 1996. After that, experts only travelled with the High Commissioner on rare occasions (for example on some trips to Central Asia). Notable exceptions were two major education-related projects in Romania and the former Yugoslav Republic of Macedonia (fYROM). Because there was no in-house expertise on these issues, the High Commissioner drew on international experts. Three experts travelled with the High Commissioner in the winter of 1999 and spring of 2000 as part of a team to make recommendations on developing the concept of multi-culturalism at Babes-Bolyai University in Cluj-Napoca, Romania. Two experts travelled with him to fYROM on a number of occasions in 2000 to give advice on the development of an Albanian language institute of higher education.

One reason why experts were not more frequently used can perhaps be attributed to the fact that the drafters of the mandate probably did not count on Van der Stoel travelling as much as he did. Being so personally involved in all activities, Van der Stoel seldom saw any added value in engaging the services of experts. Furthermore, the mandate made no mention of the use of advisers. As the number of advisers slowly grew, Van der Stoel could draw on in-house expertise to make exploratory trips, to prepare his visits or to gather information.

Van der Stoel also established built-in expertise by setting up the Foundation on Inter-Ethnic Relations in 1993. As described in greater detail in Chapter 4, the Foundation worked hand-in-glove with his office on a wide range of projects and often organized seminars and round-tables to which international experts

56 II, para. 33.

were invited. Most significantly, on three occasions, Van der Stoel drew on the advice of international experts to draft comprehensive recommendations on issues which he had recurrently encountered in a number of States. These resulted in the so-called Hague (1996), Oslo (1998) and Lund (1999) recommendations on education rights and national minorities, linguistic rights and national minorities and the participation of minorities in public life respectively. In each case the recommendations were drawn up by approximately twenty international experts after a series of consultations facilitated by the Foundation on Inter-Ethnic Relations. Depending on the issue discussed, the experts included jurists specializing in international law, linguists, educationalists, policy analysts, and advocates specializing in the situations and needs of minorities. Experts were also instrumental in drafting the *Report on the Linguistic Rights of Persons Belonging to National Minorities in the OSCE Area*, published in March 1999 and the *Report on the Situation of Roma and Sinti in the OSCE Area* published in April 2000. When further outside expertise was required, Van der Stoel would usually draw on information available in OSCE missions, or experts from partner organizations like the Council of Europe or the European Commission. On a number of occasions, particularly in 1998 and 1999, the High Commissioner's office, the Council of Europe and the European Commission made joint missions (i.e. to Estonia, Latvia and Slovakia) to provide expert advice on legislation. These joint visits were as symbolic as they were substantive, for by demonstrating the support of the Council of Europe and the European Commission for his recommendations, the High Commissioner gained considerable political clout and leverage.

The Media and Public Statements

Van der Stoel seldom talked to the media, but when he did it was usually done tactfully and tactically. As discussed in Chapter 1, the High Commissioner usually operated confidentially in an effort to avoid sensationalizing issues or creating misunderstandings that could exacerbate rather than ameliorate tensions. As a result, Van der Stoel's general policy was to avoid extensive, or perhaps one should say substantive, contacts with the media, limiting himself to general comments on the importance of reasonableness and dialogue.[57]

---

57 Chigas 1994, p. 35.

There were times when Van der Stoel considered public statements to be beneficial to his work. He made use of such statements as a confidence-building measure, as an expression of support for a particular action, as a way of getting ideas or recommendations on the record and as a means of clarification. On some occasions he also used the press in order to get his message out to the public at large rather than just the usual circle of high-level officials with whom he was in contact.

On several occasions, particularly during crises, the High Commissioner made carefully prepared and sometimes lengthy press statements. For example, during a time of heightened tension between the Russophone minority of Estonia – particularly in the northeast of the country – and the Estonian Government, the High Commissioner issued a public statement in which he listed assurances that he had received from both parties. The statement of 12 July 1993 was instrumental in spelling out commitments that had been made and steps that would be taken to normalize relations.[58] The fact that the assurances had been given orally to the High Commissioner yet written down in his statement meant that there was now a public document to which the High Commissioner, the parties and others could refer when seeking to find common ground in the future. On this and other occasions the publication of positive informal commitments and assurances given to him by the parties served both to clarify public misperceptions about the Government's or minority's intentions, and to create public pressure for the parties to keep their promises.[59] Another example of using the press for confidence-building came on a visit by Van der Stoel to Vukovar in January 1997 during which he took the unusual step of appealing to the Serb population to take part in the upcoming elections and to stay in Croatia.

Sometimes Van der Stoel used public statements as an expression of public support for a Government. This was usually the case in situations where he had been actively involved in an ongoing matter (for example the drafting of an important piece of legislation) and/or had previously been critical of the Government's handling of the issue. In the spring and summer of 1998, he made a series of statements in support of the Latvian Government. These included statements on the abolition of the 'window system' of naturalization

58 For more see the section on Estonia in Chapter 6.

59 Chigas 1994, p. 26.

(on 20 April), a statement on adoption of an amendment to the law on citizenship (on 23 June) and then a press release on 5 October expressing support for the decision confirming the amendments to the citizenship law which were made in the referendum of 3 October. Similarly, on 9 December 1998 he issued a press release in which he warmly welcomed the adoption by the Estonian Parliament of a law extending citizenship to the children of stateless parents. Another example can be seen in a statement issued on 15 July 1999 in which the High Commissioner praised the Latvian President on her decision to return the Law on the State Language to Parliament. As was his custom, Van der Stoel used the statement to give words of encouragement for further progress and to urge the parties to find a political compromise that would also be in line with international standards.[60] A few days later on 19 July 1999 he issued a statement on Slovakia in a similar vein in which he welcomed the restoration of the use of minority languages in official communications. As the High Commissioner had been closely involved in giving advice (and criticism) on drafts of the law and as its approval was seen as overcoming a major hurdle for Slovakia's accession to the European Union, his views were seen as an important signal. This was also the case when he welcomed the adoption of the State Language Law by the Latvian Parliament on 9 December 1999.

In some cases Van der Stoel calculated that it was better to make recommendations on the record rather than through his usual method of confidential correspondence. This was often the case in highly time-sensitive situations. For example, on 13 July 1997, he issued a statement from Skopje calling for calm after visiting the scene of inter-ethnic riots in Gostivar and Tetovo. For the sake of transparency, he also issued a longer report on his meetings and observations. Also in connection to the former Yugoslav Republic of Macedonia, the High Commissioner issued a lengthy statement on 6 November 1998 in which he made a number of recommendations. In it he explained his reasons for 'going public':

> 'Now that the parliamentary elections have taken place and a new government has to be formed, the political discussion will concentrate on the best ways to ensure security, stabilty and economic progress of the country in the next few years. Undoubtedly, the promotion of harmonious inter-ethnic relations

60 Statement by the High Commissioner of 15 July 1999.

> will be one of the most important subjects which have to be discussed. I have therefore decided to choose this moment to formulate . . . recommendations regarding those subjects which I should like to bring to the attention of the President of the Republic, the leaders of political parties and to the general public.'[61]

A similar tactic was employed in Romania in September 1998 when he issued a press release on his views concerning a multi-cultural university. The statement came at a time when fundamental disagreements over the issue threatened to break up the Government coalition.

Some press statements fulfilled more than one function. For example, a statement issued on 1 September 1995 concerning education in Romania allowed the High Commissioner to explain international standards, it was a confidence-building measure in so far as it made public a number of clarifications and explanations that Van der Stoel had received from the Government (during his visit to Romania between 28 and 31 August) and it allowed him to make some supportive statements and recommendations on the record.[62]

There were a few occasions when Van der Stoel issued press statements for the sake of clarification. These occurred either when his remarks had been misconstrued (as in the case of Romania in 1998[63]), or when he thought it prudent to provide clarification of interpretations of international standards which had been taken out of context. An example of the latter was a press statement issued on 24 August 1999 in which he gave an opinion on the discussion in Greece regarding the question of national minorities. This, and similar remarks on the record during a visit to Turkey in April 2000, was a way of injecting ideas into an on-going debate without becoming formally engaged in a situation.

Outside of these official statements, Van der Stoel had limited contact with the press. His view was that 'in my line of work no news is good news'. He once remarked 'if a crisis is averted – especially at an early stage – nothing

---

61 Statement by the High Commissioner, 9 November 1998.

62 See the statement by the OSCE High Commissioner on National Minorities on the occasion of his mission to Romania on 28–31 August 1995, 1 September 1995.

63 See the statement issued on 11 September 1998 on teaching in the language of national minorities at State Universities in Romania.

"newsworthy" has occurred. And yet, for the people this is the best possible outcome.'[64] Of course this point should be nuanced slightly. It did occasionally irritate Van der Stoel that the mainstream media did not give conflict prevention more attention. In that respect, in the last two years of his period as High Commissioner he tried to raise the public profile of his office. However, concerning most of his daily activities, he thought that publicity would be unhelpful.

'Ringing the Bell' and an 'Exit Strategy'

To some extent, Van der Stoel perceived the need to ring the alarm bell as a sign of failure. He was also concerned that drawing too much attention to a potential crisis would heighten the sense of tension and thereby hasten rather than reduce the outbreak of violence. Similarly, he wanted to avoid the perception of crying wolf too often. He once said: 'If I would have to issue an early warning notice, it means that I would not be able to fulfill the most essential of my tasks which is to prevent the matter from getting out of hand.'[65] As noted earlier, he therefore tried to use more informal means of early warning in order to raise the alarm. Indeed, he only rang the bell once and that was in regard to the situation in fYROM when, on 12 May 1999, he raised the alarm over the possible repercussions on inter-ethnic relations of the large influx of Kosovar Albanian refugees into Macedonia.

In the Macedonian case the situation soon became less acute as many of the refugees returned to Kosovo. However, had the situation escalated, the High Commissioner may have had to pass the torch to a different OSCE institution or other international organizations better suited to crisis management. This is the type of 'exit strategy' foreseen in the mandate. As discussed in Chapter 1, he should disengage himself from a situation when he reaches the limits of his possible contribution, either due to the limitations of the mandate, a significant shift of developments, or exhaustion of the means and resources available to his office. At this point he approaches other OSCE institutions or international

64 'Early Warning and Early Action: Preventing Inter-Ethnic Conflict', Speech to the Royal Institute of International Affairs, 9 July 1999.

65 Keynote Address to the CSCE Human Dimension Seminar, Warsaw 24 May 1993.

organizations, offering his accumulated knowledge of, and experience with, the situation and his assistance, if required.[66] The implication is that the situation has passed from conflict prevention to crisis management.

The second type of exit strategy is used when the issues which could have led to inter-ethnic tensions are resolved. The most important responsibility of the High Commissioner at this stage is to further assist the implementation process through developing and implementing special stabilizing measures that will provide for the self-sustainability of the process.[67] The goal is to encourage States to take care of their own problems and to develop institutions, legislation and mechanisms to pre-empt the types of crisis which would necessitate his involvement. Of course, it is hard to establish when this has taken place. But what usually happened was that as a situation improved, the High Commissioner no longer needed to visit the country in question. He continued to monitor developments there, but it slipped down his agenda. Ultimately, his goal is to put himself out of business, but that is not likely in the near future. As he once observed: 'Perhaps there will come a day when the OSCE area no longer needs a High Commissioner on National Minorities. As recent developments continue to demonstrate, however, there is still a long way to go before we can feel safe that a new "Kosovo" will not reappear'.[68]

---

66 Vassilev 1999, p. 56.

67 *Ibid.*

68 Van der Stoel, 1999a, p. 441.

CHAPTER FOUR

Co-operation and Support

Van der Stoel, despite his energy and skills as a diplomat, would have been considerably less effective without the co-operation and support of OSCE institutions, OSCE participating States, and international governmental and non-governmental organizations. This chapter will explain the links that bolstered the High Commissioner and look at how these relationships worked in both theory and practice.

Relations with OSCE Negotiating Bodies

Political support from OSCE participating States was important for the High Commissioner as it gave his office heightened credibility. Indeed, as he himself admitted, he would not have been able to properly function without it.[1] The highest level of support for the High Commissioner came from OSCE Heads of State or Government. At the 1996 Lisbon Summit, for example, they pledged that

> 'as an important contribution to security we reaffirm our determination to fully respect and implement all our commitments relating to the rights of persons belonging to national minorities. We reaffirm our will to co-operate fully with the High Commissioner on National Minorities. We are ready to respond to any participating State seeking solutions to minority issues on its territory.'[2]

Support was also usually expressed in decisions of Ministerial Council

1 Van der Stoel, 1999a, p. 430.

2 Lisbon Declaration on a Common and Comprehensive Security Model for Europe for the Twenty-First Century, point 10.

meetings.[3] For example, during the Rome Ministerial of December 1993 Foreign Ministers of OSCE participating States encouraged the High Commissioner in his work and 'stressed the importance of participating States co-operating fully with the High Commissioner and supporting follow-up and implementation of his recommendations'.[4] Indeed, it became almost a cliché for official documents, from meetings where the work of the High Commissioner was discussed, to refer to the fact that all participating States 'expressed appreciation for his efforts and reiterated its full support for the continuation of his efforts'.[5] The very fact that he was re-appointed so often was proof of that.

The High Commissioner's main focus of co-operation and support was to have been the Committee of Senior Officials (later the Senior Council). As noted in Chapter 2, his mandate is strewn with references to the Committee of Senior Officials or CSO. The High Commissioner is appointed on the recommendation of the CSO, he is to act under its aegis, he is supposed to bring potential threats to security to the attention of the CSO, if he is denied access to a participating State he is to inform the CSO, he is obliged to explain to the CSO the reasons for issuing an early warning, and his involvement in certain situations can be requested and mandated by the CSO. Furthermore, the CSO is to be informed after the High Commissioner terminates his involvement in a particular country, if the situation is escalating into a conflict, or if he deems that the scope for his action is exhausted. According to paragraph 21 of the mandate, 'should the CSO become involved in a particular issue, the High Commissioner will provide information and, on request, advice to the CSO, or to any other institution or organization which the CSO may invite, in accordance with Chapter III of [the Helsinki Document 1992][6], to take action with regard to the tensions or conflict.' The High Commissioner is also mandated to report

---

3 The Ministerial Council officially appoints the High Commissioner. The High Commissioner gives an address to the Ministerial Council.

4 Chapter III of the Document of the Rome Ministerial Meeting (1 December 1993).

5 This formulation was common-place, see as one example Journal no. 3 of the 27th CSO meeting of 15 June 1994.

6 Chapter III of the 1992 Helsinki Document relates to 'Early Warning, Conflict Prevention and Crisis Management (including Fact-finding and Rapporteur Missions and CSCE Peacekeeping), Peaceful Settlement of Disputes'.

on his activities at OSCE implementation meetings on Human Dimension issues.

This is the theory. The practise was quite different. Of course Van der Stoel was reliant on the support and co-operation of the Committee of Senior Officials from the beginning. That gave him his legitimacy and the backing of the participating States. But as the CSO met only a few times a year and the High Commissioner was operational from day one, he needed a relatively free reign to carry out his activities effectively. Van der Stoel was given considerable latitude and nobody complained since he did not abuse his independence. The relationship between the High Commissioner and the CSO therefore became one in which the High Commissioner would periodically report on his activities to the CSO which in turn would take note and basically say 'carry on, keep up the good work'.

When national minority issues were discussed by the CSO (in addition to regular reports by the High Commissioner to the CSO), the formal provisions foreseen in the mandate for involving the High Commissioner were not followed to the letter. According to paragraph 7 of the High Commissioner's mandate, 'when a particular national minority issue has been brought to the attention of the CSO, the involvement of the High Commissioner will require a request and specific mandate from the CSO'.[7] This seldom occurred. During a crisis in Estonia in the summer of 1993, the CSO expressed concern over problems related to inter-ethnic relations in Estonia and in bilateral relations between Estonia and Russia. It invited the High Commissioner 'to respond promptly, on behalf of the CSCE, to the request by the President of Estonia for an expert opinion from the CSCE on the law on the status of aliens'.[8] The use of the verb 'to invite' is a reflection of the great measure of independence that the High Commissioner enjoyed in relation to the CSO.[9] In another example, in the spring of 1994 the issue of Crimea was on the agenda of a series of CSO meetings. On 15 June 1994 the High Commissioner reported on his observations from a recent trip to the region; the initial exchange of letters between the High Commissioner and the Foreign Minister were also made public at that time.

---

7 Zaagman, in Bloed 1994, p. 170.

8 22nd CSO Journal no. 2, annex 2, 30 June 1993.

9 Zaagman 1994, p. 170.

Among the points made in a statement released at the end of the meeting was simply that the CSO 'supported the continued activities of the CSCE High Commissioner on National Minorities in Ukraine'.[10] As one observer has noted, one can hardly interpret these types of formulations as the 'request and specific mandate' required pursuant to paragraph 7 of the High Commissioner's mandate. Indeed, it is remarkable that the CSO gave the High Commissioner more or less *carte blanche*.[11]

CSO meetings became less frequent and less substantive as the Permanent Committee, established in late 1993 and renamed Permanent Council in December 1994, became the regular body for consultation and decision-making. Formal meetings of the Permanent Council (PC) were held weekly and informal meetings were also held on a regular basis. This was part of an overall process of institutionalization which resulted in the conversion of the Conference on Security and Co-operation in Europe (which had been quite literally a series of meetings and conferences since 1972) into the Organization for Security and Co-operation in Europe in December 1994.[12]

Now that meetings of the participating States had become more routine and almost all participating States were represented at the level of ambassador in Vienna, contacts between the High Commissioner and political bodies of the participating States became more frequent than initially foreseen when the mandate was drafted in 1992. The practice developed that the High Commissioner regularly briefed the Permanent Council – usually once every two months – and his recommendations were circulated to OSCE delegations based in Vienna. This type of on-going inter-action reduced the need for formal early warning as participating States were constantly kept abreast of the High Commissioner's work and developments in countries where he was active.

The Permanent Council also proved to be a useful forum for following up on the High Commissioner's recommendations. In the PC, participating States

---

10 27th CSO, Journal No. 3, annex 2.

11 Zaagman 1994, p. 171.

12 For more background on this process of institutionalization see Walter Kemp, *The OSCE in a New Context*, Discussion Paper no. 64 (London: Royal Institute of International Affairs, 1996), and Victor-Yves Ghebali, *L'OSCE dans l'Europe post-communiste, 1990–1996* (Brussels: Bruylant, 1996).

often took up points raised by the High Commissioner. It was often the case that a State or States would express support for the High Commissioner's recommendations, criticize another state for failing to live up to its commitments, or take the floor to defend its policies relating to inter-ethnic relations.

Supportive decisions of the Permanent Council increased the leverage of the High Commissioner vis-à-vis specific states. Indeed, his effectiveness would have been limited without it. As he once remarked:

> 'I am always very grateful for the strong and continued support that my activities receive from so many of the [Permanent Council's] members. This support is indispensable for the continuation of these activities, as it is proof of the commitment of the OSCE community to conflict prevention in the field of minorities. Without this commitment, the actions of the High Commissioner would not amount to much more than the efforts of one man operating in isolation and would therefore probably be of very little significance.'[13]

A representative example of the type of explicit yet broad support that he often received can be seen in a decision taken by the Permanent Council in January 1995. In it the Permanent Council,

> Notes with appreciation the report by the High Commissioner on National Minorities on his most recent visit to the former Yugoslav Republic of Macedonia and the conclusions and recommendations contained therein;
>
> Commends the Government of the former Yugoslav Republic of Macedonia for its close co-operation with the High Commissioner on National Minorities;
>
> Encourages the Government of the former Yugoslav Republic of Macedonia to implement those recommendations;
>
> Reiterates its full support for the continuation of the activities of the High Commissioner.[14]

---

13 Statement at the OSCE Review Meeting in Vienna, 4 November 1996.

14 Decision no. 5 of the 3rd Plenary meeting of the Permanent Council (12 January 1995).

Participation in Permanent Council meetings furnished the High Commissioner with the opportunity to consult delegations, 'thereby joining the process of consultations and lobbying that lubricates the OSCE'.[15] On trips to Vienna, he usually met with ambassadors of the major power brokers in the OSCE – the European Union, the Russian Federation and the United States. He also often met with representatives of States in which he was active and delegations that may have had an interest in one or another of his projects or recommendations. Perhaps most importantly, during visits to the Permanent Council the High Commissioner's main point of contact was the Chairman-in-Office.

Relations with the Chairman-in-Office

The Chairman-in-Office is vested with overall responsibility for executive action in the OSCE and the co-ordination of its activities.[16] As a result, it is important that the High Commissioner has a good working relationship with the Chairmanship. This requires a good rapport between the High Commissioner and the Foreign Minister of the country that holds the chair (which changes annually),[17] regular communication between the High Commissioner and the Representative of the Chairman-in-Office in Vienna (who chairs meetings of the Permanent Council),[18] and good working relations between the respective staffs of the High Commissioner's office and the Chairman-in-Office's team.

In theory and practice the High Commissioner is accountable to the Chairman-in-Office. Although all aspects of the relationship between the High Commissioner and the Chairman-in-Office which are outlined in the mandate were not always followed to the letter, the spirit of co-operation that was foreseen was usually in evidence.

---

15 Cohen 1999, p. 53.

16 See OSCE Handbook 1999, pp. 29–30.

17 Countries that held the Chairmanship during Van der Stoel's more than eight years as High Commissioner were Sweden 1993, Italy 1994, Hungary 1995, Switzerland 1996, Denmark 1997, Poland 1998, Norway 1999, Austria 2000 and Romania 2001.

18 On policy questions the High Commissioner contacted the Chairman-in-Office directly. On operative questions he would contact the head of the Chairmanship's OSCE Co-ordination Unit, and for questions concerning decisions in the Permanent Council he liaised with the Representative of the Chairman-in-Office in Vienna.

The High Commissioner is supposed to consult the Chairman-in-Office prior to travelling to a particular country.[19] One of the reasons behind this provision in the mandate was that on the basis of indications from the High Commissioner, the Chairman-in-Office would consult, in confidence, with the participating States concerned (and others as necessary). This procedure was seldom followed. Van der Stoel usually conferred with the Chairman-in-Office before he made a visit to a country during a crisis situation or before his first visit to a country. He also sometimes asked the Chairman's view on whether or not he should become involved in certain situations (for example Chechnya and Dagestan). However, for the most part he seldom consulted the Chairmanship before travelling. This was partly due to the fact that he travelled so often, but mainly because the Chairmanship was aware – and supportive – of his range of activities. In most cases Van der Stoel himself was in contact with the States concerned and if he anticipated any difficulties he would raise them with the Chairmanship.

In accordance with the mandate, Van der Stoel submited strictly confidential reports to the Chairman-in-Office after a visit to an OSCE State. These reports, usually two or three pages long, provided the Chairman with an overview of the visit, a synopsis of the current situation, insights into the positions of the key players and parties, and a candid assessment of the current political environment. He usually provided background information on his confidential discussions (including a list of his interlocators), an explanation of his recommendations and how they had been received by the Government, as well as his conclusions and plans for further action. He would also sometimes flag issues which he felt deserved the attention of the Chairman-in-Office. Unlike his recommendations that were diplomatically phrased and carefully formulated, the High Commissioner's strictly confidential reports were a frank and unpolished assessment of the situation as Van der Stoel saw it. This was, in a way, another form of early warning, although one that was exclusively restricted to the Chairman-in-Office.[20]

In addition to contacts through strictly confidential reports, correspondence, and meetings at the Permanent Council (and on the margins of other OSCE meetings), the High Commissioner was also in contact with the Chairman-in-

---

19 Mandate of the High Commissioner, para. 17.

20 As a courtesy, copies were also sent to the Secretary General.

Office through Troika meetings. The OSCE Troika is made up of the past, present and future Chairmen-in-Office and meets at regular intervals. Senior OSCE officials also take part. Troika meetings review the major issues facing the Organization and try to ensure that there is a common approach among all arms of the OSCE.

The Chairman-in-Office is the Organization's most senior official. This position provides the Chairman with numerous contacts and valuable information about a wide range of issues. For the High Commissioner, this is useful for through the Chairman he can rally support for his recommendations, he can become better aware of the dynamics within the Permanent Council, and he can get feedback on security issues that the Chairmanship may have a global perspective on. In theory, the Chairman-in-Office could have reined in Van der Stoel if he was too outspoken or if it looked as though his recommendations did not have sufficient support. In practise, Van der Stoel was never brought to heel by the Chairman-in-Office. Rather, he was given full support in his work.[21] As he once observed, 'I think that they could afford to leave me so much freedom because they knew that I kept them informed about what I was doing'.[22]

Generally speaking, relations between Van der Stoel and the Chairman-in-Office were good. Foreign Minister Margaretha af Ugglas of Sweden, was the first Chairperson-in-Office with whom Van der Stoel co-operated and their level of co-operation was probably the closest of any thereafter. This stemmed in large measure from the fact that during 1993, the year of the Swedish Chairmanship, most of the High Commissioner's activities were focused on the Baltic States, particularly Latvia and Estonia (where Sweden had foreign policy interests

---

21 The exception was in Van der Stoel's position as Personal Representative of the Chairman-in-Office for Kosovo. When Polish Foreign Minister, Bronislaw Geremek (who was Chairman-in-Office in 1998) responded favourably to a proposal of the Contact Group to appoint Felipe Gonzales as Personal Representative of the OSCE Chairman-in-Office for all of the Federal Republic of Yugoslavia, including Kosovo, Van der Stoel felt that his role, especially the contacts that he had established, was being ignored. He therefore tendered his resignation as Personal Representative for Kosovo (which was accepted). The incident soured relations between Van der Stoel and the Polish Chairmanship.

22 See interview in Zellner & Lange 1999, p. 20.

and with which Sweden had good relations). It was also due to the fact that this was Van der Stoel's first year as High Commissioner, he had yet to imprint his stature on the job, and he was learning as he went. He once referred to this first year as a 'joint venture' with the Swedes. Sweden, both through the OSCE Chair and in its bilateral relations with its Baltic neighbours, played a key role in rallying public support for his work and recommendations and diplomatically twisting arms behind-the-scenes.

The relationship with the Swiss Chairmanship in 1996 was also very good. This was due to good personal relations with many key members in the Swiss Chairmanship, but also because the Swiss gave considerable operational and financial support to the work of the High Commissioner's office.

Relations with the Norwegian Chair were also close. The Chairman-in-Office, Norwegian Foreign Minister Knut Vollebaek, backed up the High Commissioner when fifteen members of the Estonian Parliament accused Van der Stoel of having a destabilizing effect on their country.[23] Van der Stoel also had frequent contact with the Chairmanship when he issued an early warning on the situation in the former Yugoslav Republic of Macedonia on 12 May 1999. Mr Vollebaek sent a letter to all participating States on 27 May noting the extraordinary step 'which must be given an appropriate response'. He urged participating States to respond 'quickly and positively' to his warning 'so that the situation can be improved'.[24] He also asked Van der Stoel to continue to follow the situation and to report back to the Permanent Council, which he did on 4 June. In the autumn of 1999 there were occasional discussions between the High Commissioner and members of the Norwegian Chairmanship concerning the lack of consensus on a successor for Van der Stoel, and the possibility of him staying on for another year.

Relations with OSCE Institutions and Field Activities

Except for his accountability to the OSCE political bodies and the Chairman-in-Office, Van der Stoel acted independently. At the beginning, this was due to the fact that his office was more or less a self-contained unit. Established in The

23 See page 148.

24 Letter from Knut Vollebaek, Minister for Foreign Affairs of Norway, to Ministers of Foreign Affairs of the OSCE Participating States, 27 May 1999.

Hague in 1993, the office received most of its support (including two seconded personnel) from the Dutch foreign ministry and most of his administrative staff were Dutch nationals. This slowly changed in 1995 as the staff became more international and more links were established with the rapidly growing OSCE institutions and field activities. Nevertheless, under Van der Stoel, the support from the Dutch Government remained strong. This is reflected in a decision of the Oslo Ministerial meeting of December 1998 which accepted with gratitude the commitment of the Netherlands to continue providing the HCNM with premises in The Hague (up to and including 2004) and its readiness to renovate, enlarge and refurbish them.[25]

In 1993 the OSCE still had few central institutions. The Secretariat was still in its infancy in Prague; it was only established in Vienna in late 1993.[26] Even then it was a relatively limited operation until 1995. Later, when the Secretariat grew and assumed more responsibilities for the overall administration of the Organization, the High Commissioner continued to run the office according to his own imperatives. 'His way' had worked since 1993 and he was resistant to change. Besides, it was his impression that there was very little that he needed from the Secretariat in terms of operational support. Unlike almost all other OSCE institutions, the High Commissioner's office did not expand significantly and it was centred around the individual work of the High Commissioner. As long as the High Commissioner's methods were successful, no pressure was exerted on him to change.

It is worth noting that the relationship between the High Commissioner and the Secretary General was never explicitly defined in any OSCE document, except for references to the fact that the Secretary General is responsible for the management of OSCE structures and institutions. Although this sometimes caused petty squabbles over the position of the respective offices on the organizational chart, it had little bearing on the day-to-day relationship between the High Commissioner's office and the Secretariat. Van der Stoel was grateful for the support of Ambassador Wilhelm Höynck of Germany who was the first

---

25 Decision No. 6, Ministerial Council in Oslo (3 December 1998).

26 The Secretariat was officially established through a decision of the 24th CSO meeting which took place in Rome on 29 November 1993 although a skeleton staff (including the Secretary General) had already been operating in Vienna since the spring of 1993 to support the CSO Vienna Group.

Secretary General of the CSCE/OSCE between June 1993 and June 1996. On Höynck's retirement Van der Stoel thanked him for his 'constant support' saying 'my task would have been much heavier without it'. Höynck, who was an old CSCE-hand with a long and distinguished career, often acted as a confidant to Van der Stoel, particularly concerning procedural discussions in OSCE negotiating bodies. In a letter to Höynck on the latter's departure from the position of Secretary General, Van der Stoel told him that: 'I have often profited from your ingenuity in finding solutions for problems for which I did not see a way out'.[27] Relations with Höynck's sucessors, Giancarlo Aragona and Jan Kubiš, were also good, particularly with Kubiš who Van der Stoel had known since the latter's involvement in the Czechoslovak Chairmanship of the CSCE in 1992 and subsequently as Director of the Conflict Prevention Centre.

Van der Stoel had limited but friendly contacts with other OSCE institutions. There were a few common initiatives with the Office for Democratic Institutions and Human Rights (ODIHR) located in Warsaw. For example, they co-operated on establishing Ombudsman offices in Kazakhstan and Kyrgyzstan, they co-organized and co-hosted the Locarno conference on 'Governance and Participation: Integrating Diversity' in October 1998, and there was general co-operation on issues of common interest in Ukraine. There was also close co-operation with the OSCE/ODIHR office in Montenegro. For some ODIHR election reports the High Commissioner's office was asked to provide a critique of legislation effecting elections and the participatory rights of minorities, and the two institutions co-operated closely in elaborating guidelines to enhance the effective participation of minorities in political decision-making through electoral processes.[28] There was also close contact on Roma issues. However, co-operation could have been even closer if things had turned out as originally proposed in 1992. At one point it was envisioned that the office of the High Commissioner would be established in Warsaw.[29] Although

27 Private letter to Ambassador Wilhem Höynck, Secterary General of the OSCE, 7 June 1996.

28 See The Guidelines to Assist National Minority Participation in the Electoral Process, ODIHR, Warsaw, January 2001.

29 Ironically this was a suggestion of the Netherlands Government. See non-paper of 14 September 1992.

this never materialized, the High Commissioner's mandate foresees that the High Commissioner 'will draw upon the facilities of the ODIHR in Warsaw'[30] and indicates that the budget for the HCNM will be determined at the ODIHR.[31] This idea proved unwieldy and was soon discontinued. So too was the provision in the High Commissioner's mandate that experts for missions with the High Commissioner would be taken from a resource list maintained by the ODIHR.[32]

The High Commissioner's office had a number of regular contacts with OSCE missions and other field operations. In countries where he was actively engaged, missions gave him a valuable set of eyes and ears and were helpful in assisting with his visits and following up on his recommendations. This was particularly the case in Latvia, Estonia, Ukraine and the former Yugoslav Republic of Macedonia where there was frequent information exchange. He also developed good working relations with the Central Asia Liaison Office in Tashkent. In Georgia, the High Commissioner worked with the OSCE Mission on the issue of the Meshketian Turks. In Moldova, the High Commissioner co-organized a seminar on the Hague and Oslo Recommendations with the OSCE Mission in May 2000. In Albania, most of Van der Stoel's work was completed by the time the OSCE Presence in Albania was established in March 1997. In Croatia, he was active before a mission was in place and was actually instrumental in pushing for the establishment of a mission. Van der Stoel worked in close co-operation with the mission after it began operations in July 1996. A number of common projects were initiated, for example his office began to review the compatibility of the country's legislation in respect to minority protection. However, after its mandate was expanded in 1997 to look at the two-way return of refugees and the protection of persons belonging to national minorities, there was considerable overlap and the High Commissioner reduced his level of activity.

Co-operation with International Organizations

The High Commissioner co-operated with a range of international organizations. Co-operation was particularly close with parts of the United Nations

30 Para. 10 of the mandate.

31 Para. 37 of the mandate.

32 Para. 35 of the mandate.

and its agencies, the European Commission and the Council of Europe.

Because the OSCE is a regional arrangement of the United Nations under Chapter VIII of the Charter, links between the OSCE and the UN are well established. For example, the High Commissioner occasionally took part in co-ordination meetings between the UN and various organizations including the OSCE. There were close contacts with relevant UN agencies. There was good co-operation between the High Commissioner's office and the United Nations High Commissioner for Refugees (UNHCR). Both share a commitment and interest in the prevention of ethnic tensions leading to instability, conflict and displacement. For example the two (together with the International Organization of Migration) worked together on addressing the citizenship problems of formerly deported peoples in Crimea, particularly the question of Crimean Tatars and the problems that they faced in emigrating from Central Asia and integrating into Ukrainian life. They also made a joint mission to Krasnordarski Krai in the Russian Federation from 15 to 18 December 1998 to make a closer examination of the plight of the Meshketian Turks. The aim of the mission, which was a follow-up to a meeting on the Meshketian Turks which the two co-organized in The Hague in September 1998, was to collect information for a draft plan of action to be discussed during the International Meeting on the Meshketian Turks scheduled for March 1999 in Vienna. It was also designed to send a signal to the governments concerned on the importance attached by the international organizations to a peaceful solution of the Meshketian Turks issue. The High Commissioner also supported UNHCR's efforts in assisting children to learn Moldovan in the Latin script in Transdniestria.

In Croatia, the High Commissioner supported the work of the United Nations Transitional Administration in Eastern Slavonia (UNTAES), particularly the two-way return of refugees and the protection of persons belonging to national minorities. In Crimea and Central Asia the High Commissioner's office co-operated closely with the United Nations Development Programme (UNDP). In Ukraine, the UNDP runs a number of 'home schools' which provide education for children in Tatar settlements. This programme was developed in co-operation with the High Commissioner's office. The UNDP was also a key player in two donor conferences organized by the High Commissioner to raise international awareness and funding to assist the Ukrainian Government in coping with the humanitarian crisis faced by the returning Tatars. The High Commissioner's office also worked closely with the UNDP and the United

Nations High Commissioner for Human Rights on the establishment of Ombudsman offices in Kazakhstan and Krygyzstan. In the former Yugoslav Republic of Macedonia the two kept in contact on the development of programmes relating to the alleviation of inter-ethnic tensions through resolving education issues. The High Commissioner also supported UNDP efforts to promote teaching of the state language to non-native speakers in Latvia and Moldova. In addition to these specific projects, there were also regular consultations with the UNDP on a range of issues concerning the use of development assistance to foster security and integration.

A similar approach was taken with the World Bank and, to a lesser degree, the European Bank for Reconstruction and Development. The High Commissioner encouraged these institutions to target funding where it could facilitate an improvement in inter-ethnic relations and to delay or withdraw funding to countries that did not live up to international standards concerning the protection of persons belonging to national minorities.

The High Commissioner's main partners for co-operation and support were the Council of Europe and the European Commission. Because the Council of Europe and the OSCE share similar aims and membership, the two co-operate on issues relating to democracy-building and respect for human rights, particularly as regards the protection of persons belonging to national minorities. At the political level, a point of contact was the so-called '2+2' meetings where the respective heads of the two organizations met to discuss issues of common concern. The High Commissioner, or a representative of his office, was a regular participant in these meetings. He also had frequent contacts with the Council of Europe's Director of Political Affairs which allowed the two to co-ordinate strategy and tactics and to ensure that they were sending the same signal. There were also regular contacts between the High Commissioner's advisers (particularly the legal advisers) and the minority section of the Directorate of Human Rights. In this way, the High Commissioner's office and the Council of Europe were able to identify issues of common interest, consult on the analysis of current issues and confer on the compatibility of legislation with international standards. The latter point was particularly important since some of the most important standards affecting OSCE participating States in regard to minorities are set by the Council of Europe. Chief among these is the Framework Convention on the Protection of National Minorities (which is based on the OSCE's 1990 Copenhagen Document) which was opened for signature on 1 February 1995 and entered into force on 1 February 1998. It has become a cornerstone for the protection of the rights of persons belonging to national minorities particularly as regards language, education and participatory rights. In his recommendations, the High Commissioner frequently referred to the Framework Convention. Supporting arguments were also made with reference to the jurisprudence of the Council of Europe's Court of Human Rights, in applying the European Convention on Human Rights. The High Commissioner's office also conferred closely with the European Commission for Democracy through Law (Venice Commission) which provides useful assessments and advice on comparative European constitutional law and practice, including its compatibility with Council of Europe standards. He was sometimes asked by the Venice Commission to give his assessment on countries with which he was engaged. Van der Stoel occasionally invited legal experts from the Council of Europe to join delegations from his office in visits to, e.g., Latvia, Estonia and Slovakia. In addition to its substantive value, this held improtant symbolic value as it showed that the OSCE and Council of Europe had a unified position.

A similar approach was taken with the European Commission. As with the Council of Europe, it was important for the High Commissioner's office and the Commission to be sending the same message. This had reciprocal benefits for both bodies. On the one hand, because the protection of human rights (including the rights of minorities) is part of EC Law and the Commission has limited expertise in monitoring compliance with human rights in non-European Union member countries, it benefitted from the advice of the High Commissioner's office in forming its assessments of the minority policies of countries seeking EU accession. At the same time, having the ear of the EC enabled Van der Stoel to gain powerful backing for his recommendations.

Co-operation between the High Commissioner's office and the European Commission was particularly close at times when the EC prepared its opinion on possible future members. At such times, and during the drafting of progress reports on potential accession members, notes were compared on the general situation of minorities in a particular country, the approximation of laws (particularly language and election laws) and the extent to which they adhered to international standards. For example, Van der Stoel's negative assessment of the Mečiar Government's minority policy was a contributing factor for Slovakia to be sent to the back of the queue of potential EU members in 1996.

Van der Stoel was able to use the Commission for carrots as well as sticks. In a few instances, for example concerning language training in Latvia and Estonia, he urged the Commission to support specific minority-related projects.

The Role of NGOs

The High Commissioner's office had relations with non-governmental organizations, but only to a limited extent. The usual practice was to use NGOs as a source of background information on human rights, international law, nationalism, conflict prevention, security policy and developments in specific countries. But they were an under-utilized resource and there was no systematic networking or information gathering save for the receipt of information via periodicals, the internet or participation in seminars. However, good personal contacts were maintained between some staff of the High Commissioner's office and a few specialized NGOs (such as Minority Rights Group and the European Centre for Minority Issues) along with NGOs in countries where the High Commissioner was active. There were also good contacts with Nordic institutes for human rights with which collaborative endeavours were undertaken over the years (particularly organized consultations with groups of experts).

Experts from NGOs were sometimes asked to participate in target-oriented seminars and specific projects. Local NGOs were sometimes engaged in organizing these seminars or in helping to collect information on specific situations. But these were the exception rather than the rule.

The Foundation on Inter-Ethnic Relations

The one exception was the Foundation on Inter-Ethnic Relations (FIER), an NGO which was established in The Hague on Van der Stoel's initiative in 1993. The Foundation was a rather unique creation, unlike almost any other non-governmental organization. On the one hand it had an independent legal and financial status and followed its own working methods. It was governed by a private Board of Directors (to which Van der Stoel was a Special Adviser) and was supported by funding from OSCE States, international organizations and private funders. But on the other hand it was located in the same building as the High Commissioner's office, there was close co-operation between the staff of the High Commissioner's office and the Foundation, and its very *raison d'etre* was to serve the High Commissioner in order to enhance his effectiveness.

Indeed, it is fair to say that FIER took no substantive decisions without Van der Stoel's authorization.

As the FIER generated income through various private and state funders, it provided the High Commissioner with flexibility (and indeed basic resources) in the funding of projects and initiatives which were additional to the running costs of the High Commissioner's activities.

The two offices worked hand in glove, although the High Commissioner's office was always the lead party. The Foundation played a support role, acting as an implementing agency for the High Commissioner's projects. The FIER's interpretation of the relationship was that the High Commissioner 'confronts ethnic problems and addresses them at the highest levels' whereas FIER 'addresses these inter-ethnic disputes by involving the local or regional parties to the conflictive situations in active projects as agreed upon by governmental and non-governmental parties, majority and minority representations'.[33] It would be more accurate to add 'as instructed by the High Commissioner'.

At the beginning, its focus was on research, expert consultations, publications and in-country projects. One of its main functions was to provide an inter-face between the High Commissioner and the broader community of non-governmental actors promoting conflict prevention.[34] Research focused on comparative analyses of various minority situations across the OSCE area in order to better understand points of contention and 'best practises' for dealing with them. Some of the specific issues that it focused on were improving minority education, institutional mechanisms for promoting dialogue, and the role of autonomy arrangements.

The Foundation's work was not strictly analytical. It also carried out a wide range of in-country projects that were aimed at assisting government officials and minority representatives to jointly consider constructive policy options and to strengthen the institutional capacity for avoiding ethnic conflict.[35] For

---

33 Introduction to FIER Annual Report 1997.

34 Cohen, 'Zusammenarbeit im Bereich der Konfliktpravention: Die Stiftung fur Interethnische Beziehungen under der Hohe Kommissar fur Nationale Minderheiten der OSZE – eine Fallstudie', in *Friedenspolitik der Zivilgesellschaft* (Münster: agenda Verlag, 1998), p. 215.

35 The Foundation on Inter-Ethnic Relations, Year Report 1999, p. 5.

example the Foundation worked to improve the effectiveness of the Presidential Roundtable for Minorities in Estonia, the Assembly of the Peoples of Kazakhstan, and the Assembly of the People of Kyrgyzstan. A main feature of this process was to organize round-tables, seminars and workshops to bring government and minority representatives together to consider constructive approaches to inter-ethnic issues and, quite simply, to facilitate dialogue. The Foundation also worked with existing councils in a number of countries and organized training seminars with the aim of increasing council participants' knowledge of international minority rights standards and their familiarity with practical approaches to minority policy in other countries.

The focus of the Foundation's work gradually shifted to capacity-building and tension-reducing projects. For example, in 1996 a project was initiated to familiarize Albanian police officers with democratic policing (particularly dealing with inter-ethnic relations). Similar projects were carried out in the former Yugoslav Republic of Macedonia and Romania. In Kyrgyzstan, a programme was initiated to train officials in public administration dealing specifically with inter-ethnic issues. A similar project was organized for Macedonian officials. A specific training programme was also established for employees of the Department for the Protection of National Minorities in Romania. Perhaps the most ambitious project of this type was in Croatia where the Foundation worked with the (Serb) Joint Council of Municipalities to provide expert training on representing, advocating for, and advising on the needs and rights of the Serb minority community in the former UNTAES region. The Foundation was also instrumental in a 'home school' project in the Autonomous Republic of Crimea, aimed at providing educational opportunities to children in Crimean Tatar settlements where there were no schools.[36]

In a unique project, the Foundation set up, and supported, a legal aid centre in Knin, Croatia specifically geared to deal with housing and property problems. The aim was to try to reconcile, in a very concrete way, concerns (mostly of the Serb minority) over property issues which resulted from the dislocation of populations in the area because of the war.

In Kyrgyzstan the Foundation worked with the Government to monitor and analyze inter-ethnic relations. The result was a sociological survey on the ethnic situation in South Kyrgyzstan, a seminar 'On the Administration of Inter-Ethnic

---

36 Cohen 1998, p. 217.

Relations in Local and Regional Government' and an on-going project (in co-operation with a local NGO) monitoring inter-ethnic relations in the southern Kyrgyz oblasts of Osh and Jalal-Abad. A similar project was subsequently initiated in Kazakhstan.

On the theme of improving minority education, the Foundation undertook a pilot project in the former Yugoslav Republic of Macedonia in 1995 to evaluate the possibilities for promoting government-minority co-operation in the field of education and for developing appropriate curricular and teaching materials for minority education. A similar project was undertaken in Albania. Also in the fYROM, the Foundation developed a 'Transition Year' programme for ethnic Albanian students to increase their proportion of representation at the university level. The programme concentrated on providing an intensive exam preparation course in three subjects (Biology, Mathematics and Sociology) in the Macedonian language for Albanian secondary school students to improve their chances of enrolling in higher education institutions in Macedonia. The Foundation also closely tracked developments related to minority education in Romania and, in 1995, organized a seminar on 'Educational Opportunities for Minorities'. Another round-table on higher education in Romania was organized in Snagov, Romania in February 1998.

The Foundation was also instrumental in organizing seminars on deported peoples of the former Soviet Union (on issues concerning the Crimean Tatars and the Meshketian Turks).

Some projects were thematic rather than country-oriented. In November 1995 the Foundation, on the request of the High Commissioner, organized an international expert consultation on the subject of the education rights of national minorities. Other meetings followed, leading to the finalization of the *Hague Recommendations Regarding the Education Rights of National Minorities.* On the same model, two international expert consultations took place in Oslo in October 1996. During these meetings, a small group of internationally recognized experts finalized *Recommendations on the Linguistic Rights of National Minorities*, also known as the Oslo Recommendations. The third such set of recommendations grew out of a seminar co-organized by the Foundation in Locarno, Switzerland in October 1998 on issues of minority participation in governance. Following on from this meeting, a group of eighteen international experts met in a series of meetings (the last one in Lund, Sweden) and drew up the so-called *Lund Recommendations on the Effective Participation of National*

Minorities in Public Life, which were published in September 1999. The Foundation published all three sets of recommendations in English and a number of other languages (Croatian, Estonian, Hungarian, Latvian, Romanian, Russian, Serbian, Slovak, and Ukrainian). The Foundation then organized a number of seminars in States where the High Commissioner was engaged in order to explain the recommendations and to discuss their applicability in those States.

These recommendations were the main publications of the Foundation, but not the only ones. As the High Commissioner's office did not have a public information section, the Foundation played an important role in responding to enquiries spreading the word about the High Commissioner and his activities. In another vein, the Foundation produced information to support activities that the High Commissioner was involved in. For example, in 1996 and 1997, it published a brochure (in Estonian and Russian) to facilitate the process of acquiring Estonian citizenship. The brochure provided information regarding the citizenship process and gave helpful information to applicants taking the citizenship exam. A similar project was carried out in Latvia in 1997.

In light of changing circumstances, at the end of 1999 the Foundation was dissolved and its activities were incorporated into the office of the High Commissioner and are now carried on by the office's Project Unit.

CHAPTER FIVE

Recurrent Themes and Issues

In the course of his work, Van der Stoel came across a number of themes and issues that have repeatedly been the cause of inter-ethnic tensions. The recurrence of these themes and issues allowed him to develop certain consistent approaches which guided his activities during his tenure as High Commissioner. Whereas Chapter 4 looked at his specific methods, this chapter will concentrate on the bigger picture of how he tried to address questions of identity, dialogue, participation, citizenship, language, education and resources and how all of these relate to the over-arching theme of integrating diversity in multi-ethnic States. This chapter takes a thematic approach to explain the problems that he encountered and the possible solutions that he advanced with respect to national minority issues.[1] It can be considered as a catalogue of 'lessons learned', an indication of the types of problems relating to national minority issues and food for thought on how to cope with nationalism. (Please note that where examples are cited, more details are usually available in Chapter 6 which makes a country-by-country analysis of the situations in which the High Commissioner has been involved.)

Integrating Diversity

A theme to all of Van der Stoel's work as High Commissioner on National Minorities was the need to integrate ethnic or cultural diversity in the same State. It was only developed as a paradigm towards the end of his period as High Commissioner (particularly through the Locarno Conference of 1998 and

1 The categorization used is based on John Packer, 'The OSCE High Commissioner on National Minorities', in G. Alfredsson *et al.* (eds.) *Human Rights Monitoring Procedures: A Textbook on How to Petition and Lobby International Organisations*, Festschrift für Jakob Müller (The Hague: Kluwer Law International, 2001), pp.632-647.

the subsequent Lund Recommendations of 1999), but the undercurrents were there from the beginning.

Integration is quite different from forced assimilation where a minority is absorbed by the majority, loses its identity, and disappears as a recognizable group. Integration assumes instead that the distinctive identity of the minority can be maintained, while, at the same time, the minority should be part of the society at large. In this paradigm, preserving and promoting the rights of persons belonging to national minorities does not threaten the integrity of the State, while the integrity of the State does not hinder the flourishing of national minorities. Rather than being a zero-sum equation, the minority and the majority can find an accommodation that enriches all of society. Van der Stoel summarized the problem as follows:

> 'As few modern societies are ethnically homogenous, this means integrating minorities into society. Integration cannot occur if whole groups of persons remain excluded from being a legitimate and recognized part of the community in which they live, and on which they must depend for the enjoyment of their rights. The need for integrating diversity should therefore be one of the main lessons that we take from the 20th century. Attempts to peacefully or violently create ethnically "pure" nation-states have largely failed. In cases where a nation and a state are virtually congruent, the majority still usually has to come to terms with minorities in their midst. In short, multi-ethnic society is a reality which one cannot "solve".'[2]

As a result, integrating diversity is a fundamental aspect of both conflict prevention and respect for minority rights. It is not only a function of international law, it is also good governance. As United Nations Secretary General Kofi Annan said in his speech at the OSCE Istanbul Summit of December 1999, 'Much conflict could also be prevented if the rich cultural diversity within so many of our states were considered as an asset, rather than a threat, and allowed to flourish accordingly'.[3]

The first step towards integrating diversity must be recognition of the plurality

---

2 Speech in Bratislava, Slovak Republic, 10 December 1999.

3 Speech by UN Secretary General Kofi Annan at the OSCE Istanbul Summit, 18 November 1999.

of communities and interests within the state. This means an official acknowledgement of the existence of minorities and therefore of diversity within the State. This is not a legal step; it should be a recognition of fact. It is not up to the State unilaterally to make a determination as to the existence of a minority. This is a matter to be determined on the basis of objective criteria, first and foremost the individual choice of the persons concerned. As paragraph 32 of the Copenhagen Document notes: 'To belong to a national minority is a matter of a person's individual choice and no disadvantage may arise from the exercise of such choice'.[4]

Clearing this hurdle is often the most difficult step for a government to take. Even when they do acknowledge the existence of national minorities in their country, governments are sometimes concerned about giving too much away. Van der Stoel confronted this point head-on when he declared: 'the impression that I have is that some participating States, in living up to their commitments in regard to the protection of persons belonging to national minorities, worry that they are building a Trojan Horse from which the minority will jump out in a few years and make even further demands to the detriment of the integrity of the state as a whole'.[5] He stressed that states should not hold the view that in satisfying their commitments vis-à-vis national minorities they are either bestowing something on minorities or giving something away. To support his argument, on this and other occasions, he often cited the second part of paragraph 32 of the Copenhagen Document which says that: 'Persons belonging to national minorities have the right freely to express, preserve and develop their ethnic, cultural, linguistic or religious identity and to maintain and develop their culture in all its aspects, free of any attempts at assimilation against their will'.[6] This should not be considered detrimental to the State. Rather integrating diversity should be regarded as being in the best interests of the State. He made this point clearly in a statement issued on 6 November 1998 in connection with the controversy over the question of an Albanian university in the former Yugoslav Republic of Macedonia. He said:

---

4 Document of the Copenhagen Meeting of the Conference on the Human Dimension of the CSCE 1990, para. 32.

5 Speech at the OSCE Review Conference Vienna, 20 September 1999.

6 Copenhagen Document 1990, para. 32.

'I want to emphasize that it would be wrong to consider any concession to a minority as a weakening of the state. It ought not to be forgotten that meeting wishes of a minority within the constitutional framework of a unitary state might even strengthen the state, because the removal of major sources of its dissatisfaction will strengthen the willingness of a minority to identify with the state.'[7]

To promote integration, Van der Stoel stressed the importance of recognizing, protecting, and promoting the identity of minorities, creating the possibility for effective dialogue between the minority and majority communities, allowing for the effective participation of minorities in public life, and being sensitive and responsive to the linguistic and educational needs of minorities. All of these issues are described in greater detail below.

The failure to effectively integrate diversity can cause frustration, breed resentment and arouse feelings of alienation within the minority community.[8] This may lead minorities to take matters into their own hands and/or seek the support of their kin-State, possibly resulting in inter-ethnic tensions and even the disintegration of the State. When taken to such extremes, the argument between the minority and majority can become polarized between secession and the protection of the sovereignty and territorial integrity of the State. Van der Stoel described this clash of apparently mutually exclusive positions as a defining feature of the twentieth century and warned that 'the negative impact of malign nationalism and the inability to satisfy the aspirations of minorities without violently breaking up States will be with us well into the next century unless we come up with new ways of integrating diversity and developing more effective means of protecting the rights of persons belonging to national minorities'.[9]

As already noted, one way of heading off this problem is to address issues

---

7 Statement of the High Commissioner, 6 November 1998.

8 See p. 9 of 'The Role and Importance of Integrating Diversity', Address by Van der Stoel at the Conference on 'Governance and Participation: Integrating Diversity', Locarno, Switzerland 18 October 1998.

9 'Human Rights, the Prevention of Conflict and the International Protection of Minorities: a Contemporary Paradigm for Contemporary Challenges', speech at the London School of Economics, 19 October 1999.

(like dialogue, participation, education and language issues) at an early stage so that the very existence of the State does not become the issue. When issues of autonomy and secession did arise, it was a virtual maxim for Van der Stoel to seek solutions within existing States rather than creating new ones. As he once explained:

> 'secession is seldom a viable option for achieving lasting peace, security and prosperity. Although it should not be ruled out, it is not a panacea for protecting national identity. The creation of new States leads to the creation of new minorities and the proliferation of fragile mini-States. It is also usually a violent affair: we have witnessed few Velvet Divorces. Secession breeds secession: what's good for one minority is good for another. Where territorial units are ethnically defined, the congruence of nation and State may encourage separatism, thereby breaking down multi-ethnic and multi-cultural societies and strengthening the politics of difference. Moreover, I submit that ethnically pure territorial units are a myth, and efforts to achieve them are conflict causing and fraught with serious violations of human rights.'[10]

To achieve a synthesis between conflicting demands for self-determination and maintenance of the territorial integrity of the State, Van der Stoel advocated self-governance and 'internal self-determination'.[11] He stressed that 'such autonomies should not be confused with separatism since they rely upon common understandings and shared institutions of rule of law, respect for human rights, common security and destiny'.[12] He pointed out that there was an under-utilized tool box of ideas concerning various forms of self-government that could satisfy the needs of minorities without risking the break-up of States. Notable in this regard were the possibilities laid out in the *Lund Recommendations on the Effective Participation of National Minorities in Public Life* which were drawn up by a group of international experts at his request in 1998/99.

A common misperception is that self-governance means external self-determination. Self-determination relates to the status of territory and therefore raises

10 *Ibid.*

11 For an explanation of the concept of internal self-determination see Patrick Thornberry, *International Law and the Rights of Minorities* (Oxford: Clarendon and Oxford University Press, 1992), pp. 215–17.

12 Speech at the LSE, 19 October 1999.

fears of secession. Thus it can be confusing when one refers to territorial arrangements of self-governance that do not espouse self-determination. To clarify, the idea is that although a system can remain integrated, certain legislative and executive functions can be shifted from the central to the regional or even local level. As the Lund Recommendations suggest, 'drawing on the principle of subsidiarity, States should favorably consider [a] territorial devolution of powers, including specific functions of self-government, particularly where it would improve the opportunities of minorities to exercise authority over matters affecting them'.[13] These self-governance arrangements should be established by law.[14] The idea is that by allowing national minorities to have a measure of control over affairs which directly affect them, they will be able to protect and promote their interests and identities without jeopardizing the stability and integrity of the State in which they live. This so-called 'internal self-determination' can balance the seemingly antithetical concepts of (external) self-determination and the maintenance of the territorial integrity of States. Of course, the key is to strike a balance between functions to be undertaken by the central authorities and those to be carried out by regional or autonomous authorities. This often leads to considerable political wrangling, particularly in highly centralized States such as those undergoing post-Communist transition.

'Internal' self-determination can also have a non-territorial character (sometimes referred to as personal, cultural or extra-territorial autonomy). This type of autonomy or self-governance is useful when the minority population is widely dispersed within a state. This relates to the right of national minorities to, *inter alia*, use (and receive official recognition of) their names in the minority language, to determine curricula for teaching of their minority languages and cultures, and the right to determine and enjoy their own symbols and other forms of cultural expression.

The subtleties of these arrangements are sometimes lost on the parties. Too often, any discussion of decentralization or autonomy is seen by governments as the beginning of a slippery slope towards external self-determination. Sometimes the expressions used by minorities when discussing 'self-determination' or 'autonomy' or the signals that they send when discussing their aims do little

13 The Lund Recommendations on the Effective Participation of Minorities in Public Life, 1999, para. 19

14 *Ibid.*, para. 22

to assuage government concerns or the fears of the majority population.

Although the Copenhagen Document mentions that one of the possible means for protecting and creating conditions for the promotion of the ethnic, cultural, linguistic and religious identity of certain national minorities could be to establish 'appropriate local or autonomous administrations corresponding to the specific local or autonomous circumstances of such minorities',[15] it does not commit governments to establish such autonomous administrations. It should also be borne in mind that paragraph 37 of the Copenhagen Document makes it clear that none of the commitments mentioned in the Copenhagen Document may be interpreted as implying a right to engage in any activity or any action in contravention of the principle of the territorial integrity of States.[16] Van der Stoel was careful to avoid advocating territorial autonomy (for example, in the case of Vojvodina). The one exception was his support for the Autonomous Republic of Crimea. His usual position was that even though the Copenhagen Document mentions territorial autonomy as an option, minorities have to take into account that such a demand would probably meet maximum resistance, while many if not most of their needs could be satisfied by other means.

Developing this argument further, Van der Stoel cautioned that 'external' self-determination through secession is fraught with the potential for conflict. Firstly, a minority may be spread out over a wide area, living with persons belonging to other groups. In such cases there is not a compact spatial dimension to the ethnic identity, and achieving one would cause considerable dislocation for all parties concerned. Secondly, redrawing borders on the basis of ethnic homogeneity could open a Pandora's box of claims and counter-claims which could accentuate national exclusivity (and more abhorrent practices like 'ethnic cleansing') rather than multi-ethnic Statehood, and lead to non-viable and unstable fragmentation.

> 'So do not expect from me any proposals for changing borders in order to facilitate the solution of minority questions . . . Firstly, I have yet to meet any government which is ready to consider border changes, even secondary ones

---

15 Copenhagen Document, 1990, para. 35.

16 This point was made in a statement by the High Commissioner on 23 August 1999 in reference to confusion over the terms of the Copenhagen Document and fears about self-determination in relation to national minorities in Greece.

> . . . The second reason is that whatever way one draws borders, especially in Central or Eastern Europe, it is never possible to draw them in such a way that there will be no minorities.'[17]

He has noted that there are few 'quick-fixes' when it comes to minority issues,

> 'least of all through secession, irredentism, or other formulas involving even minor border changes. Wherever the border is drawn, there will almost always be different ethnic groups living together. They will have to learn to live harmoniously with one another. State sovereignty for each group is thus not a cure-all; it might instead lead to greater ethnic tensions and regional instability.'[18]

At the same time, he noted that maintaining territorial integrity should not be a justification for the rejection or suppression of minority rights. This could provoke the very sense of threat that arouses national consciousness in the first place. It would create a dissatisfied minority with a grudge against the government and could lead to the antithesis of the type of prerequisites that are necessary to foster inter-ethnic harmony. Thus, protecting the rights of persons belonging to national minorities is not only required by international law, it is good governance and effective conflict prevention.

To summarize, integrating diversity should not be regarded as compromising the identity or integrity of either the minority or the majority community. On the one hand, it should be borne in mind that the preservation of a culture does not require a territorial expression: the concepts of nation and State do not have to be congruous. Similarly, the promotion of a minority culture should not be regarded as a threat to the majority culture: accommodation can be reached within the multi-ethnic or multi-cultural State. The challenge for the State is to build upon values which are inclusive rather than exclusive, to protect individual rights and to promote a social ethos of equality, mutual respect and

---

17 Speech in Strausberg, Germany, 7 July 1995.

18 'Controlling Ethnic Tensions: the Experience of the CSCE High Commissioner on National Minorities', Remarks at the Annual Conference of the European Research Centre on Migration and Ethnic Relations, Utrecht University, 19 September 1994.

participation.[19] The State should also create the legal space and the institutions and mechanisms that can allow minorities to maintain and develop their identities. For their part, national minorities must recognize that they share a common destiny and common interests with the majority of the State within which they live.

In this process, perceptions are important. Integrating diversity has to be seen to be beneficial to both sides. As Van der Stoel once described it:

> 'a minority must be able to perceive that there are legitimate opportunities for maintaining and developing its distinctive identity and for participating in the economic, social, and political life of the country. The majority group must see that no dangers, but instead some benefits, arise from the expression of cultural differences and the full participation of all citizens in society, governance and the economy.'[20]

Citizenship

If solutions to various inter-ethnic problems are to be sought as much as possible within the framework of the State, then national minorities must feel that they are full and equal members of that State. To start with, they must be citizens. This entitles them to exercise the rights that go with citizenship, while obliging them to act as responsible citizens.

Citizenship figured in many of the situations that Van der Stoel was involved in. In some cases, for example in Estonia and Latvia where there is a high percentage of 'stateless' persons, it was the dominant issue.

In Latvia and Estonia, and other States where population transfers during the Soviet period dramatically tilted the demographic balance, Van der Stoel was sensitive to the concerns of the newly independent Governments in their efforts to redress historic grievances. However, at the same time, he stressed the importance of establishing citizenship rather than ethnicity as the basis of the State. Although his office was created after the constitutions of most States in

---

19 Max van der Stoel, 'Minorities in transition', *War Report* 48 (Jan/Feb 1997), p. 17.

20 'Early Response to Ethnic Conflicts: Focusing on Prevention', Address to the Parliamentary Assembly of the CSCE, Helsinki, 8 July 1993.

post-Communist transition were re-written, he tried to ensure that the constitutional and legislative efforts by the majority to reassert their national identity after years of communism did not infringe on the rights of persons belonging to national minorities. In Latvia and Estonia the Governments did not grant automatic citizenship to those people, or their descendants, who had settled in the country during the Soviet period. This created a great deal of insecurity for the large numbers of non-ethnic Latvians and Estonians who did not qualify for the citizenship criteria set up by the newly independent Governments in Riga and Tallinn. Van der Stoel, while sensitive to the grievance felt by the Balts because of their illegal annexation by the Soviet Union and resultant forty-five years of Russification, battled long and hard with the Governments over their proposals to restrict the number of new citizens, their resistance to granting citizenship to children of Stateless parents, problems relating to difficult citizenship tests, and the slow pace of naturalization.[21] In Kazakhstan and Kyrgyzstan he encountered the opposite problem. There the Governments were concerned about the steady stream of Russians and Ukrainians (and to a lesser extent Germans in Kazakhstan) who were leaving their newly independent republics. The High Commissioner therefore worked with the Governments to stem the tide by coming up with a formula that granted virtually automatic citizenship to Russians wanting to leave in the hope that they would stay in the knowledge that they had the option to use their Russian citizenship should the need arise in the future. Van der Stoel was also able to help in easing the process of acquiring citizenship for Crimean Tatars who wanted to return to Ukraine from Central Asia (particularly Uzbekistan), or who had already returned but had yet to obtain Ukrainian citizenship as they wished to.

In these and other cases, Van der Stoel stressed that equal access to and enjoyment of citizenship is required to reduce feelings of inferiority and to create the basis for equitable inter-cultural integration. Citizenship is both a statement of belonging and a basis for the enjoyment of certain rights, human, political and economic.[22] Van der Stoel therefore regarded working with governments to create conditions of equality before the law for all citizens (regardless of ethnicity) as one of his most important tasks.

---

21 See Chapter 6 and also Zaagman 1999, pp. 37–48.

22 Packer 2001, p. 8.

This required treading a fine line between the general development of civil society for all citizens, and the specific protection of the rights of persons belonging to national minorities. This gets back to the overall theme of integrating diversity. The starting point is that all persons should enjoy the same basic human rights without discrimination and in full equality before the law. However, because certain ethnic groups are in the minority they sometimes need special protection for their rights. Because, by definition, minorities are numerically inferior, they require special rights in addition to all other universal human rights. These rights should not privilege persons belonging to national minorities, but act to ensure respect for their dignity, in particular their identity. The Copenhagen Document, for example, says that OSCE participating States 'will adopt, where necessary, special measures for the purposes of ensuring to persons belonging to national minorities full equality with the other citizens in the exercise and enjoyment of human rights and fundamental freedoms'.[23] Of course, the other side of the argument, often used by nationalists of the majority population, is that minorities should not receive special treatment at the expense of the majority population. This brings up contentious and often heated debates about the legitimacy of interests, especially how they are reflected in legislation (and even the constitution). The High Commissioner therefore often found himself in the delicate position of trying to seek a balance between the interests and rights of the majority and minority communities.

Van der Stoel's starting point when trying to achieve such a balance was to insist on the need for civic rather than ethnic nationalism. His philosophy was that national identity, whether that of the minority or the majority, should not be accentuated at the expense of human rights and fundamental freedoms. Rather, a distinction should be made between the nation (or the *ethnie*) and the State. He once observed that 'if there is a civic rather than an ethnic nationalism, then feelings of loyalty will have more scope to prevail over any tendency towards separatism'.[24] Civic nationalism is based on allegiance to the State which therefore requires citizenship and measures to treat all citizens equally. Ideally, members of minorities should feel that they belong not only to their particular ethnic or linguistic community, but also that they share and value an important sense of belonging to the wider polity. To build up this sense of civic nationalism, both

---

23 Copenhagen Document, 1990, para. 31.

24 Van der Stoel 1997, p. 16.

the minority and the majority have to realize that 'the notion that the state can serve only the interests of one ethnic or cultural group is antiquated. It is essential that all parties recognize that a state does not have to be ethnically homogeneous to survive'.[25] As he once observed,

> 'this requires us to move beyond [the traditional concept of the nation-state espoused since the 1648 Treaty of] Westphalia, the myth of the nation-State, towards integrated societies within and between States. Building on our common interests and shared values, we can find a new way to accommodate varying and often multiple identities in our multi-ethnic states and world. We must change our notion of the State from the antiquated idea of the nation-State protecting the so-called 'State-forming nation' into a new system and ideal where States, individually and collectively, protect and facilitate the diverse interests of all citizens on the basis of equality.'[26]

Putting this idea into practice requires a type of social contract.

The first half of the contract is for the State to create opportunities for prospective citizens to be naturalized. This requires an acceptance by the Government, and the majority population as a whole, that the minority is there to stay and should therefore be accommodated: otherwise fear of the fifth column will create the fifth column. The Government's half of the social contract also requires it to live up to its commitments as regards the protection of persons belonging to national minorities, namely 'to protect the ethnic, cultural, linguistic and religious identity of national minorities on [its] territory and create conditions for the promotion of that identity'.[27] In its policies the State should observe non-discrimination on grounds of belonging to a minority. Furthermore, the State should make efforts to promote tolerance, mutual acceptance, and non-discrimination in society. In both of these cases 'equality in fact' should accompany 'equality in law'. These two standards help to prevent certain groups from feeling like second-class citizens.

The second half of the contract is that minorities must realize that citizenship brings with it obligations as well as entitlements. Van der Stoel often cautioned

---

25 Address to the OSCE Parliamentary Assembly, Ottawa, 4 July 1995.

26 Speech at the LSE, 19 October 1999.

27 Copenhagen Document, 1990, para. 33.

minority representatives that, on the one hand, they have the right to reject assimilation and to insist on the right to express their identity in various fields, but, on the other hand, they live in a State where persons belonging to the majority also have rights. He therefore encouraged them to use (and not to abuse) appropriate means to preserve and develop their language, culture, religion and traditions without this leading to discrimination against persons belonging to the majority.

Citizenship therefore relates very closely to the idea of integrating diversity. One assumes certain responsibilities by becoming a citizen of a State. At the same time, by doing so, one enjoys the protection of the State that allows for the full enjoyment of one's rights and the realization of one's identity. In this way, a balance is achieved between the rights of the individual and the obligations of the citizen. All of this gets back to the fact that peace and stability are, as a rule, best served by ensuring that persons belonging to national minorities can effectively enjoy their rights. If the State shows loyalty to persons belonging to national minorities, it can expect loyalty in return from those persons who will have a stake in the stability and well-being of that State. This can lead to a more integrated and harmonious society and prevent the rise of inter-ethnic tensions.

This, of course, is the archetype of a harmonious society and it is seldom realized, even in the most advanced democracies. Nevertheless, as Van der Stoel once remarked, 'because it is the kind of society that we want to build, it is the model that we espouse when holding States accountable for their actions'.[28] This is the type of model that Van der Stoel advocated in almost all of the situations that he dealt with.

However, even in such an archetypal civil society one's quest for self-realization is not diminished. But that's the point. The integrative State merely sets the framework in which one can develop one's identity. It sets the parameters for a type of code of conduct through which individuals can inter-relate in a governable system (legislation, mechanisms of protection and dispute resolution, etc.) and fully realize their potential. In the end, the extent to which that system is harmonious depends on its ability to accommodate competing identities while defending and promoting common interests. As Van der Stoel put it: 'diversity and pluralism must be accepted and seen as potential sources of strength

28 Speech at the LSE, 19 October 1999.

rather than as weaknesses or threats. Diversity is a fact and can enrich collective human experience. Pluralism offers a conceptual framework through which to understand and accommodate diversity'.[29]

Identity

Identity is a basic defining element of all individuals and groups. It also goes to the heart of nationalism. National characteristics like language, common history, symbols, and culture are defining elements of one's identity. They also provide a bond to a community of people defined by the same references and sentiments; a community which because of this sameness has a sense of collective consciousness. Individually and collectively, people try to protect and promote their national identity because that identity is seen as an essential part of their existence and way of life. Similarly, a threat to the elements that define one's identity is seen as a threat to one's identity both individually and collectively as 'the nation'. It is such threats to identity that often trigger inter-ethnic tensions. As the High Commissioner noted in a speech in 1999, 'in many cases that I have encountered, political debates become issues of identity as either the minority or majority community feels that their way of life is threatened by "the other".'[30]

Identity is a rather nebulous concept, which helps to explain why it can be so easily manipulated. Furthermore, it is subjective as identifying with a particular group is self-defining. It should also be borne in mind that individuals can identify themselves in numerous ways in addition to their identity as members of a national group. In other words, they can have multiple identities. All of these factors can make identity a difficult concept to come to terms with. That being said, the component parts of national identity can be broken down and analyzed. By better understanding these elements, efforts can be made to prevent policy issues from blowing up into more emotive questions of nationalism.

In dealing with specific situations, Van der Stoel tried to be sensitive to the historic, symbolic and/or demographic factors that influenced the views of the parties. As he was aware that these questions of identity closely relate to dignity, he stressed the need for governments to respect the identities of their citizens.

---

29 Address at the International Conference on Human Rights of the Visegrad 4 Countries, Bratislava, 10 December 1999.

30 Speech at the Royal Institute of International Affairs, London, 9 July 1999.

This need is acknowledged in paragraph 33 of the Copenhagen Document which obliges OSCE States to 'protect the ethnic, cultural, linguistic and religious identity of national minorities on their territory and create conditions for the promotion of that identity'.[31] States therefore have to protect *and* promote minority identities. The idea is that by creating the legal space for the development of cultural identity, the State can accommodate an untold and enriching diversity.[32]

But disputes seldom arise over questions of 'identity' *per se.* It has been Van der Stoel's experience that although questions of identity can help to explain the context of a dispute, or can be used as the umbrella under which an eclectic range of issues is clustered, in themselves they are seldom the crux of the problem. Even if they were, they could not be tackled as an abstract whole. In fact, looking at the issues abstractly is often part of the problem as it perpetuates stereotypes and makes unhelpful generalizations. Van der Stoel's view was that a minority or even a majority may be concerned about the protection of its identity, but this is usually in relation (often in reaction) to a particular issue or set of issues. Therefore, instead of entering into a general discussion about the role of a minority in a specific society, Van der Stoel concentrated on the fundamental issues in dispute. This approach was consistent with his instrumentalist view of nationalism. He regarded nationalism as more of a means than an end. In that respect he sought to understand why one or another of the parties appealed to nationalist sentiment, why it felt threatened, what it hoped to achieve by arousing national consciousness, and why such appeals found popular resonance. He therefore took a 'root causes' approach, not in the sense that he tried to redress historical grievances, rather in the sense that he tried to strip away romanticized nationalist rhetoric and symbolism to get to the bottom of the underlying contentious issues. As this chapter will demonstrate, these issues usually concern political participation, citizenship, language, education, culture, or resource allocation.

By getting down to brass tacks, Van der Stoel was usually able to get the parties to 'be specific' – to set aside questions of identity and focus on questions

---

31 Copenhagen Document, 1990, para. 33.

32 See p. 5 of the speech by the High Commissioner entitled 'The Role and Importance of Integrating Diversity' given at the Conference 'Governance and Participation: Integrating Diversity', Locarno Switzerland, 18 October 1998.

of substance. It was his experience that these substantive questions are intrinsically related to identity (i.e. language, education, culture), but by focusing the discussion on policy, legislation, human rights and government practice, the parties could frame their concerns in a subject-oriented rather than national(ist)-oriented way and one which would hopefully allow them to better put their views (and those of the other side) into perspective, and therefore resolve their differences in a co-operative and pragmatic way.

Dialogue

One way of dispelling misperceptions and building trust is to encourage dialogue. It is the first step in getting the parties to communicate directly, to articulate their concerns, and to seek co-operative and constructive solutions to their problems. It is therefore important to have adequate structures for dialogue between the government and minorities. Even if dialogue will not lead to full agreement on the issues at hand, the exchange of views in itself can help to create a better understanding of the problems and concerns of the other side and to lower walls of mutual suspicion. It allows the parties to speak to each other around the same table instead of about each other through the media.

As discussed in Chapter 3, the bodies established to facilitate dialogue should have meaningful competencies. If not, they may not only be ineffectual but counter-productive. Participants must feel that there is some real value in their dialogue and that their views will contribute to a concrete outcome, or at least the advancement of a larger process. Participants should come in good faith and be willing to engage in an exchange of views.

Dialogue between the Government and the minority is seldom limited to a single issue. It also usually develops over a period of time. As a result, in some cases it is appropriate to institutionalize the process by setting up a council or round-table at which the authorities and representatives of the minorities can discuss specific problems together. In other cases, an independent governmental body, such as an ombudsman or a special ministry, can serve to receive and respond to complaints by minorities.

In his work, Van der Stoel promoted the development of structures for dialogue and the establishment of other instruments of democratic discussion. He advocated that conclusions reached at such forums should be submitted to the authorities in the form of recommendations which could, with time, become an integral part of policy-making in these countries. The development of these institutions and processes of dialogue can demonstrate, on the one hand, that the authorities are willing to listen to minorities' concerns and, on the other hand, that minorities are willing to participate in the political life of the country in which they live.

Participation

The theme of effective participation was a centre-piece of Van der Stoel's work and an undertone of many of his recommendations. In order to focus more attention on the subject, a conference was held in Locarno, Switzerland in October 1998 entitled 'Governance and Participation: Integrating Diversity'. As a follow-up to this conference, the High Commissioner requested a group of international experts to draft a set of recommendations on 'The Effective Participation of Minorities on Public Life' (also known as the Lund Recommendations).[33] (See Annex 6.)

The Lund Recommendations, finalized in September 1999, are based on the premise that 'effective participation of national minorities in public life is an essential component of a peaceful and democratic society'.[34] The idea is that pluralism, multiculturalism, and an inclusive response to diversity can all strengthen the fabric of society. This is why, broadly speaking, the High Commissioner encouraged open and peaceful processes of social integration which accommodate difference through choice drawing on creative solutions and alternatives which are consistent with human rights standards.

The underlying assumption is that integration through participation is an important element in forging links of mutual loyalty between the majority and minority communities within the State, and in giving minorities input to processes which directly effect them. It also improves overall governance for if minorities feel that they have a stake in society, if they have input into discussion and decision-making bodies, if they have avenues of appeal, and if they feel that their identities are being protected and promoted, the chances of inter-

---

33 For the background to the Lund Recommendations, see John Packer 'The Origin and Nature of the Lund Recommendations on the Effective Participation of National Minorities in Public Life', *Helsinki Monitor* 11(4) (2000), pp. 29-45.

34 Lund Recommendations, point 1.

ethnic tensions arising will be significantly decreased.

Good and effective democratic governance implies that the persons affected should be involved in the process of decision-making, at least in the form of consultative participation. This kind of participation can significantly enhance the level of identification by members of a minority with the state in which they live. Van der Stoel stressed that it is especially important that draft legislation relating to minorities has adequate input from the effected parties before being presented to parliament. This helps to avoid trouble later on. Of course, it follows that laws have to be implemented and not merely codified. The High Commissioner spent a great deal of time following up on recommendations that he had made concerning the adaptation of domestic legislative frameworks to international standards.

Representation is also vital. The Lund Recommendations note that 'States should ensure that opportunities exist for minorities to have an effective voice at the level of central government, including through special arrangements as necessary'. They may include forms of guaranteed participation in the legislative process, representation of minorities in high office, mechanisms to ensure that minorities interests are considered within relevant ministries as well as special measures for minority participation in the civil service as well as the provisions of public services in the languages of the national minorities.[35] This also relates to minorities in the public service, for example the police force. In some cases (for example with the Roma or the Albanian minority in the former Yugoslav Republic of Macedonia) the High Commissioner recommended a policy of affirmative action to make up for the under-representation of minorities in sensitive positions like the police force.

The point is also made in the Lund Recommendations that 'the electoral system should facilitate minority representation and influence'. For example 'States shall guarantee the right of persons belonging to national minorities to take part in the conduct of public affairs, including the right to vote and stand for office without discrimination'.[36]

Another recommendation, as discussed in Chapter 4, is that States should establish advisory or consultative bodies within appropriate institutional frame-

35 See Lund Recommendations, point 6.

36 See Lund Recommendations, point 7.

works to serve as channels for dialogue between governmental authorities and national minorities. These bodies should be able to raise issues with decision-makers, prepare recommendations, formulate legislative and other proposals, monitor developments and provide views on proposed governmental actions which may affect minorities. The Lund Recommendations also note the importance of channels of communication for the prevention of conflict and dispute resolution.[37]

Van der Stoel often stressed that dialogue and participation should not be limited to the national level. Many minority issues are local issues and should be tackled at the regional or local level. In cases where decision-making is highly centralized, minority concerns are often under-represented. In such cases the High Commissioner sometimes advocated decentralization either territorially, for instance in the form of devolution of authority through local self-government, or through distribution of limited powers of jurisdiction on a 'personal' or cultural minority basis. One can note that dialogue and participation are closely inter-related and both are fundamental elements of integrating diversity.

Language

Because language is usually a defining element of a national group (especially in Europe), it is not surprising that language issues figured in a number of situations in which the High Commissioner was engaged. Van der Stoel's view on the issue was that 'because of the centrality of language to ethnic identity, the process of ensuring the linguistic rights of minorities is critical to the advancement of minority rights overall and human rights generally'.[38]

Most language disputes that the High Commissioner was engaged in dealt with the right of persons belonging to national minorities to use their language in the public sphere. In a number of cases, especially in Slovakia, Moldova, Latvia and Estonia, the High Commissioner tried to stress to the Government that efforts to strengthen the State language – which he sympathized with – should not come at the expense or the detriment of minority languages. This is consistent with the 1990 Copenhagen Document which obliges States to protect

37 Lund Recommendations, point 24.

38 Report on the Linguistic Rights of Persons Belonging to National Minorities in the OSCE Area, March 1999, p. 39

and promote the linguistic identity of national minorities on their territory.[39] Paragraph 34 explictly states:

> 'The participating States will endeavour to ensure that persons belonging to national minorities, notwithstanding the need to learn the official language or languages of the State concerned, have adequate opportunities for instruction of their mother tongue or in the mother tongue, as well as, wherever possible and necessary, for its use before public authorities, in conformity with applicable national legislation.'

This is easier said than done since governments, especially in small States, see the official or State language (often designated as such in the Constitution) as a central feature of the majority community's identity and therefore feel obliged to defend its primacy. Furthermore States in post-Communist transition often stressed the need to strengthen the State language in order to redress the effects of Russification. On the other hand, as minorities also see the use of their language as essential to the preservation of their culture, any threat to their language is seen as a threat to their existence. As Van der Stoel put it: 'Majorities feel that too much protection for minority languages will create a Tower of Babel in their midst, while minorities fear that strengthening the State language will lead to linguistic assimilation.'[40]

In Slovakia, for example, major disputes arose between the Hungarian minority and the Mečiar Governments between 1993 and 1998 on issues such as improved teaching of minority languages, the use of minority languages in official communications, the registration of Hungarian names in Hungarian, the publication of school certificates in both the State and minority languages, and the use of minority languages in topographical and other markings. The situation became particularly acute after the adoption of a new State Language Law in November 1995. This new law created a legal vacuum as far as the use of minority languages in official contacts was concerned as it stated that the rights of minorities would be addressed in a subsequent law (for which there was no draft until 1999), yet, in effect, prescribed certain limitations on the use of minority languages. It also fell short of international standards in several regards.

39 Copenhagen Document, 1990, para 33.

40 Speech on 'Integrating Diversity in a Multi-ethnic Region: Promoting Peace and Security in South Eastern Europe', Portorož, Slovenia, 16 March 2000.

Initiatives designed to allow experts to assist in the drafting of a complementary minority language law did not come to fruition under the Mečiar Government even though Van der Stoel cautioned the Government on several occasions that compliance with international standards was an important consideration for developing closer relations with the European and international communities.

In October 1998 the new Slovak Government, which included Hungarian representatives, immediately started to implement a number of the High Commissioner's recommendations, including those relating to minority language use. The most important of these was the commitment of the Government to introduce a new law on minority languages. However, because of differences between the predominantly ethnic Slovak and Hungarian parties in the coalition, drafting of the law was held up by discussions over issues concerning the use of minority languages in official communications and university entrance exams, and the threshold percentage of persons belonging to a national minority needed in order for a community to provide minority language services (10% or 20%). Eventually a compromise solution was worked out, with the advice of the High Commissioner's office together with the Council of Europe and the European Commission, that created new opportunities for the use of minority languages, especially in official communications. However, even after the law was approved, Slovak nationalists warned of creeping 'Magyarization' and called for a referendum to overturn the law while the Hungarian parties argued that the law did not go far enough.

In Latvia and Estonia the High Commissioner stressed the need to promote the knowledge of the State language among the minority population, especially in relation to language teaching. He felt that this was important since a language test was part of the application process for citizenship, but also in terms of encouraging the integration of national minorities into society as a whole.[41]

At the same time he stressed that the State Language Law, in both countries, should not interfere into the private sphere. Similar arguments were made in Moldova during his visit of May 2000.[42] He suggested that intrusions into the private sphere (for example imposing a duty to use the State language in all institutions, enterprises, organizations, businesses, catering establishments,

41 See Zaagman 1999, p. 40.

42 See his speech on 'The Linguistic and Education Rights of National Minorities and their Application in Moldova', Chisinau, 18 May 2000.

meetings, and conferences in the country) would not only curtail human rights and international commitments to which the States are bound (for example the International Covenant on Civil and Political Rights and the European Convention on Human Rights), but would also be very difficult to implement, 'entailing considerable disruption in a range of personal and business affairs'.[43] In the case of Latvia he argued that the State Language Law, as it was drafted between 1997 and 1999, 'would, in various provisions and to varying degrees, violate the freedoms of expression, association and assembly, the right of privacy (including correspondence), the norms of international labour law, and the freedom of choice in private enterprise'.[44] He also argued that it would discourage investment in the country. He suggested that the best way to restore the Latvian language after years of Sovietization (basically Russification) while protecting the rights of persons belonging to national minorities would be 'to adopt a relatively general State Language Law mainly prescribing its use in the public sphere and establishing the legal basis for institutions of language promotion. With regard to permissible interferences in the private sphere, these should be prescribed at each place and in detail by specific legislative reform'.[45]

Because language issues were both recurrent and contentious in a number of countries that the High Commissioner was involved in, during the summer of 1996 Van der Stoel asked the Foundation on Inter-Ethnic Relations to request a number of internationally recognized experts to draw up recommendations on the linguistic rights of national minorities. The aim was 'to provide a useful reference for the development of State policies and laws which will contribute to an effective implementation of the language rights of persons belonging to national minorities, especially in the public sphere'.[46] The result was the so-called *Oslo Recommendations Regarding the Linguistic Rights of National Minorities* issued in February 1998. The recommendations cover a number of situations including linguistic rights in relation to names, religion, community life and non-governmental organizations, the media, economic life, administrative

43 Letter to Mr Valdis Birkavs, Minister for Foreign Affairs of Latvia (13 April 1999).

44 *Ibid.*

45 *Ibid.*

46 Introduction to *The Oslo Recommendations Regarding the Linguistic Rights of National Minorities* (February 1998).

authorities and public services, independent national institutions, the judicial authorities and the deprivation of liberty (see Annex 5).

Also in 1996 the High Commissioner sent a questionnaire to all OSCE participating States concerning the linguistic rights of persons belonging to national minorities in their countries. The idea was that through the official replies to the questionnaire, the extent of common practices and the variety of existing approaches to the protection of the linguistic rights of persons belonging to national minorities would be revealed and conclusions could be drawn.[47] The questions asked of the participating States sought information on four fundamental aspects of linguistic rights: the status of particular languages in the State; the extent of the rights of, and possibilities for, persons belonging to national minorities to use their language with administrative and judicial authorities of the State; the role of minority languages in the educational curriculum; and access for persons belonging to national minorities to public media in their language. Particular emphasis was put on practices relating to education because, in the words of the High Commissioner, 'education is fundamental to maintenance not only of linguistic proficiency, but also maintenance of identity'.[48]

What followed was a two-year comparative study on the linguistic rights of persons belonging to national minorities. A *Report on the Linguistic Rights of Persons Belonging to National Minorities in the OSCE Area* was issued in March 1999. Among its conclusions was that States need to be better aware of the content of international standards, that more legal protection for minority linguistic rights was needed in some countries, and that more communication between governments and minorities was needed to assess genuine needs of persons belonging to national minorities. A number of other specific recommendations were made including the desirability of extending some form of status or recognition to non-official languages in States that have an official language, the need for resources to facilitate the use of minority languages in official communications, the need for improvements in the teaching of and in minority languages, and the need for more courses in minority languages and about minority cultures. Importantly, the replies received from OSCE participating States also indicated

47 Foreward to the *Report on the Linguistic Rights of Persons Belonging to National Minorities in the OSCE Area* (March 1999).

48 *Ibid.*

the variety of practices already existing in the OSCE area, from which different States could draw inspiration in responding to situations within their own State.

Education

Education is a vital element in the preservation and development of the identity of persons belonging to national minorities. It is a central means of forming and transmitting identity within a cultural group, particularly as regards language, history and culture. As a result, debates over education often become the battleground for broader questions of identity.

Because education was a recurring issue faced by the High Commissioner, in the autumn of 1995 he requested the Foundation on Inter-Ethnic Relations to consult a small group of internationally recognized experts with a view to receiving their recommendations on an appropriate and coherent application of minority education rights in the OSCE region. The resultant *Hague Recommendations Regarding the Education Rights of National Minorities* encourage States to approach minority education rights in a proactive manner (sse Annex 4). They note that 'where required, special measures should be adopted by States to actively implement minority language education rights to the maximum of their available resources, individually and through international assistance and co-operation, especially economic and technical'.[49]

In the situations that the High Commissioner dealt with, it was usually the case that disputes centred around questions of curriculum, language teaching, control over minority education, and tertiary education.

Because education is an important means of socialization within the State but also a primary instrument for a minority's cultural reproduction, curriculum is often a contentious issue between minorities and the State. This is especially the case in subjects relating to language, history and culture. Where possible, the High Commissioner encouraged the development of alternative textbooks to offer teachers wider possibilities to develop the curriculum. In one case, in Kyrgyzstan, he personally intervened to assist with the development of textbooks for the Uzbek minority. Concerning the core curriculum, he encouraged governments to develop materials that reflect the views of all groups in society (and not only the majority view) and to raise awareness from an early age on the need for

---

49 *Hague Recommendations Regarding the Education Rights of National Minorities*, para. 4.

tolerance and understanding of other cultures. For example, he emphasized the need for greater understanding of the Roma by non-Roma students. The Hague Recommendations echoed this point saying:

> 'State educational authorities should ensure that the general compulsory curriculum includes the teaching of histories, cultures and traditions of their respective national minorities. Encouraging members of the majority to learn the languages of the national minorities living within the States would contribute to the strengthening of tolerance and multiculturalism within the State.'[50]

Because of the importance of language as a means of communication and a carrier of culture, the issue of language teaching is one that the High Commissioner often encountered. The Hague Recommendations note that

> 'the right of persons belonging to national minorities to maintain their identity can only be fully realized if they acquire a proper knowledge of their mother tongue during the educational process. At the same time, persons belonging to national minorities have a responsibility to integrate into the wider national society through the acquisition of a proper knowledge of the State language.'[51]

Minorities often complained to the High Commissioner that they felt left out on one or both counts. On the one hand, they (for example the Greek minority in Albania, the Albanian minority in the former Yugoslav Republic of Macedonia, or the Hungarian minority in Slovakia) sometimes criticized the lack of State-funded facilities to train teachers who could offer instruction in minority languages. They complained that their children did not have enough opportunities to be educated in their mother tongue. At the same time, they often raised concerns about the lack of teachers (or at least quality teachers) to teach the State language. This was not only a problem in schools (for example in Hungarian schools in Slovakia, or Roma schools throughout Central and Eastern Europe), but also at the level of adults who had difficulties becoming integrated into society because of their lack of knowledge of the State language. In the latter case, particularly in Latvia, Estonia and Moldova, the High Commissioner recommended that the Government open language training centres. He also

---

50 *Ibid.*, para. 19.

51 *Ibid.*, para. 1.

encouraged States to train more teachers to teach both the minority and the State language. As this can be expensive, Van der Stoel sought funding from OSCE participating States to support these activities.

Control over education was a recurrent issue in situations that the High Commissioner was engaged in. His usual rule of thumb was to advocate local solutions to local problems. He therefore encouraged States to consider decentralization of educational authorities to allow schools to better reflect and respond to local needs. This sentiment is echoed in the Hague Recommendations that note: 'States should create conditions enabling institutions which are representative of members of the national minorities in question to participate, in a meaningful way, in the development and implementation of policies and programmes related to minority education'.[52] This type of approach lends itself to more flexibility and the possibility of imaginative solutions to difficult problems. For example, in Ukraine the High Commissioner was able to work with the Ukrainian Government, representatives of the Crimean Tatars and international partners (particularly the United Nations Development Programme) to develop 'home schools' to address the problem faced by Tatar children who live in widely dispersed settlements away from mainstream schools. In Albania, he proposed that a certain amount of flexibility be shown towards Greek children in communities where ethnic Greeks make up a significant proportion of the population. Compromises were proposed on questions of class size, the introduction of a school bus system to bus pupils to minority schools, and allowing for children of mixed marriages to have a certain amount of choice concerning the language on instruction.

Questions of control often relate to questions of funding. States are often resistant to the creation of separate institutions for minority education, and if they do allow them they usually argue that such institutions should be privately funded. Minorities, on the other hand, argue that because they are tax payers the state should fund their schools and universities. Nowhere is this argument more heated than over the question of minority education at the tertiary level.

The Hague Recommendations say that 'persons belonging to national minorities should have access to tertiary education in their own language when they have demonstrated the need for it and when their numerical strength

---

52 *Ibid.*, para. 5.

justifies it'.[53] This is a contentious issue. As culture (particularly history and language) is the essence of identity, the teaching of that culture is an integral, indeed defining, element of a nation's identity and a guarantor of its survival. Because the university is the highest level of education, it becomes the locus of symbolic power and an embodiment of the national ideal. Therefore, even where the minority represents a significant percentage of the population, central governments which are worried about the disintegration of the State are hesitant to allow for the creation of minority universities.

The High Commissioner encountered this problem in the former Yugoslav Republic of Macedonia (fYROM) and in Romania. In both cases the minority community became mobilized around the question of a minority university to the extent that the Government's resistance to their demands strained inter-ethnic tensions. In the fYROM, the decision of radical elements within the Albanian community to set up an 'Albanian University' in Tetovo (without the consent of the authorities) was done in such a way that it reaffirmed the Government's worst fears about the intentions of the Albanian community to develop their own (parallel) institutions outside the framework of national legislation. The High Commissioner worked with the parties for several years to find a compromise solution to this thorny issue. Common understanding was reached on the possibility of establishing an Albanian-language university, but constitutional limitations necessitated that it be established as a private institution with Government support. In Romania, the question of a Hungarian University in Transylvania was a frequent demand of the minority community. Several proposals were made including setting up a private university, establishing a university with Hungarian and German lines of study (the so-called Petofi-Schiller University) or developing the concept of multi-culturalism at Babes-Bolyai University in Cluj-Napoca. In the end, a new Law on Education was passed in the summer of 1999 that allowed for the further development of the concept of multi-culturalism. The High Commissioner, together with a team of experts, visited Cluj-Napoca several times during the winter of 1999/2000 to see how the law could be implemented at Babes-Bolyai University. The law also created the possibility for the development of a private Hungarian university. In both the Macedonian and Romanian cases (indeed on all educational issues) the High Commissioner tried to focus the discussion on the issues of educational

---

53 *Ibid*, para. 17.

needs and standards in order to reduce the level of emotive discussion on more abstract issues of national identity.

Resources and Political Will

Van der Stoel subscribed to the old adage that 'an ounce of prevention is worth a pound of cure'. He also observed that 'capital invested in conflict prevention is capital well spent'.[54] He was often quick to point out that the ratio between resources devoted to conflict rehabilitation as opposed to conflict prevention is for more than an ounce to a pound. For example, after peace was established in Kosovo in the summer of 1999 he asked rhetorically: 'we are now pouring millions of Euro into South-East Europe by way of post-conflict rehabilitation. Would not a fraction of these resources and efforts, invested at an earlier stage, have helped to prevent the *malaise* that we now find ourselves in?'[55] The ratio between the amount of money spent on military resources as opposed to conflict prevention is even higher. He once observed: 'It always amazes me to think that the annual budget of my office is approximately the same as two Tomahawk cruise missiles. One E-2C Hawkeye early warning reconnaissance and command airplane costs approximately ten times the entire expenditures of my office since it opened in 1993. This helps to put things in perspective'.[56]

Another point that Van der Stoel made was that less than one percent of what OSCE States spend for defence and security annually could go a long way towards effectively preventing inter-ethnic conflict. He argued that this is a sound investment with long-term benefits that could prevent conflicts which could be costly in political, material and human terms.

> 'Investing in preventive diplomacy and minority integration pays huge dividends, A society at peace with itself is a society that can concentrate on issues of common interest, which benefit all citizens. Conversely, a divided society will be bogged down in the politics of difference rather than integrating diversity. If those differences lead to conflict, the price is high – economically,

54 Address to the Rome Meeting of the Council of Ministers for Foreign Affairs of the CSCE, Rome, 30 November 1993.

55 Speech at the Royal Institute of International Affairs, London 9 July 1999.

56 Remarks at the International Institute for Strategic Studies, London 9 July 1999.

in terms of human lives, and in terms of long-term stability. We are quick to offer assistance to people in need, either during or after a crisis. But we have to do more to prevent crises from getting to that stage at all. That requires political will, but also investment.'[57]

This point was not made in an effort to gain more resources for his office. Indeed, his budget only rose modestly from $600,000 in 1994 to $3 million in 2000 (despite considerable expansion of his activities) and he seldom appealed to central OSCE institutions in Vienna for more funds. Rather, his aim was to affect a paradigm shift in the way that people looked at conflict prevention. His argument was that investing in financial and human resources related to conflict prevention makes good political and economic sense, both within States and in the context of regional security. Because of the inter-connected nature of European security, instability in one country can have a knock-on effect on the security of others. Nipping such conflicts in the bud can not only prevent human suffering and internal instability but can also negate the need for expensive military interventions, humanitarian assistance, social support for refugees, and post-conflict rehabilitation. He therefore encouraged States to have more foresight when looking at security in the broadest sense of the word. As he once remarked: 'States must have an open eye for longer-term developments with a view to anticipating future crises and not only pay attention to already existing conflicts . . . it is never too early for a realistic assessment of worrisome developments. If we devote our attention only to the wars of today, we will have reasons to mourn again tomorrow'.[58]

However, States (especially those in post-Communist transition) sometimes could simply not afford to implement the High Commissioner's recommendations, even if the political will was there. A government may well have been aware of a problem and have had the best intentions to solve it, but it lacked the means to do so. In such cases Van der Stoel tried to match funders to projects. For example in the case of the Crimean Tatars, he identified socio-economic problems as some of the biggest challenges faced by the Tatars during resettlement. He felt that discontentment over unemployment, housing and

57 Speech in Warsaw, 6 November 2000.

58 'The Role of the High Commissioner on National Minorities in Conflict Prevention', address to a workshop on 'Agenda for Diplomacy', Skopje 18 October 1996.

insufficient infrastructural development was radicalizing the political views of the returning Crimean Tatars. He therefore organized two donor conferences to raise international support for the resettlement of the Tatars. These conferences were able to raise several million dollars. In Macedonia, Van der Stoel took a leading role in raising sufficient funds to establish the South-Eastern European University in Tetovo.

Sometimes the amounts needed were relatively limited because the problems were relatively small. As described in Chapter 3, it was at times like these that he introduced 'tension-reducing projects'. The philosophy with such projects was that timely and targeted assistance could pay big dividends in promoting inter-ethnic harmony. His view was that although the problems being addressed may have seemed minor, if they were not addressed they could develop into bigger issues that could become politicized questions of 'identity'. Furthermore, the accumulation of small problems could quickly add up to a bigger problem.

Access to and allocation of resources were recurrent problems noted by the High Commissioner. This was particularly the case of government spending on culture and education. In Slovakia, for example, the Hungarian minority protested against the limited amount of cultural subsidies available for them under the Meciar Government and the lack of transparency in the way that they were distributed. In Slovakia as well as Romania, Albania, and the former Yugoslav Republic of Macedonia, minorities complained about a lack of State support for minority education. This has also been a recurrent complaint of the Roma in a number of Central and Eastern European countries. In situations where refugee return is a central concern (for example the Crimean Tatars in Ukraine, the Meskhetian Turks in Georgia, and the Serbs in Croatia) minorities often feel that not enough has been done to provide them with housing, an equitable share of public resources and social support let alone opportunities for equitable political participation. In other cases, for example with the Albanian minority in the fYROM, Russian minorities in former Soviet republics, and the Roma, the High Commissioner has noted that inter-ethnic tensions can develop over issues of access to employment within the public service, access to governmental contracts, and an equitable share of government financed investment and development projects.[59] For people who are non-citizens but long-

59 Packer 2001, p. 9.

term residents (and usually tax payers) belonging to minorities, there may also be the question of access to social security benefits.[60] This was, for example, the case in Latvia and Estonia.

In working with OSCE Governments on these issues, Van der Stoel stressed the importance of avoiding discrimination and the *perception* of discrimination. The problems faced by minorities may be symptomatic of problems faced by a broad spectrum of society. However, socio-economic problems can take on an inter-ethnic character when the perception of inequality corresponds to inter-ethnic fault lines. This may occur in sectors of industry, strata of society, or a particular region of a country where there is a high concentration of a minority population that is also economically disadvantaged (e.g. the Russophone population in the northeast of Estonia). In such cases minorities have a tendency either to mobilize themselves against the government on the basis of ethnicity as well as socio-economic grievance, or conversely they may find themselves as the target of scapegoating when an economy is faltering.

Van der Stoel also noted the importance of investing political capital in preventing inter-ethnic conflict. OSCE States were obviously interested in preventing inter-ethnic conflict. After all, they created his office in 1992. But Van der Stoel sometimes reproached States for not showing enough foresight and generating enough political will to deal with brewing crises. He once observed that the logic of timely and effective action to avert costly crises is often not applied.

> 'I find this ironic, for in our Internet and media-driven world of rapid communications there is no shortage of information. But attention spans are short, and sometimes longer term trends are not properly analyzed. As a result, warning signs are often overlooked. Decision-makers at the highest levels are often unable – or simply fail – to draw the logical conclusions from the facts. In many cases, they are so preoccupied with the crises of the day that they do not think about the potential crises of tomorrow. When warning signs are clear, there is too often paralysis. Action is usually only in reaction to what is on the screen in front of us . . . and by then it is too late.'[61]

---

60 *Ibid.*

61 Speech at the Royal Institute of International Affairs, London, 9 July 1999.

He bemoaned the fact that 'there is sometimes the feeling that even though there is a potential danger, the clouds might drift away. In my view, we have to overcome this passive attitude. Somehow time has to be found – even on ministerial agendas – for what might be the crises of tomorrow'.[62]

This issue was raised by Michael Igantieff in an interview with Van der Stoel in October 1999. Ignatieff asked: '. . . Problems are on a politician's back burner until they turn urgent . . . until they turn violent. Isn't it simply always going to be the case that the international community will not turn to basic problems of human rights violations until they turn violent. Isn't that the essential frustration of the kind of work you try to do?' Van der Stoel responded: 'I think unfortunately yes, this has been the practice so far, but considering the consequences of conflict, is it not time that we started a serious debate on changing our ways? I really do think that there is a lot of talk about conflict prevention, but so far there has been far too little effort really to make conflict prevention work'.[63] There is clearly a need for more support for, and recognition of, quiet diplomacy in action.

62 Speech at Strausberg, 7 July 1995.

63 Interview between Van der Stoel and Micahel Ignatieff, 7 October 1999.

Part Two

SCHRANK

CHAPTER SIX

Situations

Previous chapters explained the High Commissioner's approach, his work in practice and recurrent themes and issues that he encountered. References were made to the various countries and situations that he was engaged in between the beginning of 1993 and the first part of 2001. This chapter goes into greater detail of these situations by making a review of all the situations that he was involved in. It is designed to give a thorough chronicle of his work and illustrate some of the points made in earlier chapters. It does not cover every country that he travelled to, only those that he issued recommendations on and in which he was engaged in conflict prevention. (See also the section on lobbying and contacts with kin-States in Chapter 3.) This chapter is not designed to evaluate the effectiveness of the work of Van der Stoel in the situations in which he was engaged. That challenge is left to others.

Van der Stoel and his staff did not deal simultaneuosly with all of the situations chronicled here. Nevertheless, few dossiers were closed during his term as High Commissioner. Once he became engaged in a country he usually kept the situation under constant review. Sometimes issues were on the front burner more often than not, while others simmered on the back burner and only needed occasional attention. In all cases the aim of the High Commissioner was to keep the pots from boiling over.

Capital City
City
Helsinki
Tallinn
Jõhvi
Narva
Sillamäe
Estonia
Baltic Sea
Ventspils
Liepāja
Riga
Latvia
Daugavpils
Lithuania
Vilnius
Russian Federation
Moscow
Minsk
Belarus
Warsaw
Poland
Lviv
Kyiv
Kharkov
Dneister
Ukraine
Moldova
Cluj-Napoca
Chisinau
Tiraspol
Bendery
Odessa
Romania
Comrat
Sea of Azov
Crimea
N
Bucharest
Simferopol
Black Sea
0
300 km
Sevastopol
© Dora Kemp

Estonia

Estonia was one of the first countries that the High Commissioner visited and has been one of the countries in which he has been most actively engaged during his eight years in office. His approach to developments in Estonia, as in neighbouring Latvia (described below), always took account of the political and psychological background of the long years that Estonia suffered under Soviet occupation and the bitterness caused by the policy of Sovietization. Van der Stoel was sensitive to the desire of Estonians to reassert their cultural, linguistic and national identity in the post-independence period. Nevertheless, because of the large mostly Russian-speaking minority population (close to 30% overall and over 80% in areas of the northeast), the contiguity of the Russian Federation to Estonia, the fragility of Russian–Estonian relations and the importance of Estonia living up to international standards (e.g. for accession to the European Union), the High Commissioner frequently intervened in order to caution and assist the Estonian Government on measures and legislation affecting the protection of persons belonging to national minorities.

The High Commissioner's engagement began with his trip to all three Baltic States in January 1993. His first visit to Estonia resulted in a catalogue of recommendations which aimed at reducing the existing tensions between the Estonian and non-Estonian communities. The central recommendation was for the Estonian Government to show a clear intention to reduce the number of stateless persons through naturalization. Many Russian-speakers with citizenship of the former USSR suddenly found themselves 'stateless' in independent Estonia and this created a great deal of insecurity. Van der Stoel suggested that more should be done to inform non-citizens better about the provisions of the Law on Aliens and possibilities for naturalization. He proposed to promote the learning of the Estonian language through State-financed programmes and to set the standards for the language naturalization test at a level sufficient to carry out a simple conversation.

Van der Stoel appealed to the Estonian Government to create an atmosphere more conducive to the integration of the different communities into Estonian society and cautioned that the failure to do so could undermine the stability of the country. He stressed the importance of equality based on citizenship rather than ethnicity. As in Latvia, he pointed out that it was unrealistic to expect the non-Estonian population to leave: many had been living in Estonia for a long time and/or had been born there; most of them did not want to leave; those who did contemplate leaving saw few better prospects in the Russian Federation or another CIS State. However, the problem was not one-sided. Van der Stoel observed that non-Estonians, should they be given the chance to acquire citizenship, would have to come to terms with the post-Soviet reality that they were living in an independent Estonia and that citizenship brought with it obligations (for example learning the State language) as well as rights.

Van der Stoel's initial visits and extensive contacts with the principal players helped define his role as an interested third party, established his first-hand familiarity with the situation, and developed the parties' confidence in his abilities to facilitate.[1] This basis proved essential for his success in heading off a crisis that broke out just a few months later.

On 21 June 1993 the Estonian Parliament voted overwhelmingly in favour of a Law on Aliens that was designed to formalize the 'alien' status of approximately 400,000 (mostly ethnic Russian) long-time residents of Estonia. The law provoked an outcry among the minority population, particularly in the northeast of the country which has a high concentration of non-citizen Russophones.[2] They feared that through the Law on Aliens and what they considered discriminatory legislation on education and local elections a process of expulsion had been set in motion.[3] Calls for general strikes (in part due to worsening socio-economic conditions) soon became calls for autonomy. This legislation strained relations between Estonia and the Russian Federation which were already fraught over the lack of progress on Russian troop withdrawals and over Moscow's reaction to what it claimed as grave violations of human rights in the efforts of the Estonian Government to assert Estonian cultural and linguistic identity. As

---

1 See Huber 1994, p. 12.

2 See *Ibid.*

3 Zaagman 1999, p. 27.

a result, not only was the situation within Estonia becoming increasingly polarized, but the threat of more explosive consequences could not be ruled out. On 30 June 1993 the Committee of Senior Officials took the unusual step of asking the High Commissioner to look into the situation, and for the Estonian Government to take appropriate action in response to the High Commissioner's recommendations.[4]

To head off the deepening crisis in the northeast, Van der Stoel proposed to the Estonian President Lennart Meri that he should not promulgate the Law on Aliens but submit it instead for scrutiny by the Council of Europe and the OSCE. He said that it was necessary not only to consider the law on its legal merits, but also its psychological effect on the Russian-speaking population in Estonia. The President (who had asked the OSCE Chairman-in-Office for urgent assistance[5]) was receptive to the idea and agreed to submit the law to the Council of Europe and the OSCE for an 'unbiased professional' assessment 'in order to secure domestic peace and a balanced policy essential for the reconstruction of the Republic of Estonia'.[6] A number of amendments were proposed by the experts. Parliament was reconvened at short notice and the amendments were adopted. The President also responded to the High Commissioner's suggestion to set up an organ representing the national minorities of the country by establishing a Round-table of Non-Citizens and Ethnic Minorities headed by a Presidential Plenipotentiary.

Despite the President's initiatives, the leaders of the Russian-speaking population in the province of Ida-Virumaa (in the northeast of the country) continued to demand a referendum on local autonomy. The High Commissioner, who visited the region a number of times during the height of the crisis, tried to dissuade the presidents of the City Councils of Narva and Sillamae from continuing with the referendum, and when that failed he asked them to delay the referendum until the National Court had given its ruling on whether or not the referendum was in violation of Estonian law. He was able to convince them to abide by the ruling of the National Court on the legality of the referendum. This assurance was part of a package of assurances which Van der Stoel was able to win from both sides during a hectic period of shuttle diplomacy.

---

4 22nd CSO meeting, Journal no. 2, annex 2 (30 June 1993).

5 See Zaagman 1999, p. 27.

6 Communique of the Estonian President dated 25 June 1993.

On 12 July he took the unusual step of issuing a public statement in which he listed the assurances that he had received. From the Estonian Government, these included a commitment 'to develop a relationship of friendship and co-operation with the Russian community in Estonia, expecting loyalty towards the Republic of Estonia in return', the initiation of a dialogue with minority representatives, a clarification and facilitation of naturalization requirements and procedures (including that language requirements would not exceed the ability to conduct a simple conversation in Estonian and that requirements would be even lower for persons over 60 or invalids), a categorical statement that the Government had no intention of expelling Russians from Estonia, an assurance to improve the economic situation in Northeastern Estonia, and an assurance that force would not be used to prevent the referendum on autonomy (which the Government considered as illegal).[7] Van der Stoel received assurances from representatives of the Russian community that they would play an active and constructive role in the dialogue with the Government, that they would fully respect the Constitution and territorial integrity of Estonia, and they would respect the ruling of the National Court on the legality of the referendum. (The referendum was later ruled to be unconstitutional – a decision which was respected by the minority representatives.)

During the crisis the High Commissioner maintained informal contacts with Russian officials, including Foreign Minister Andrei Kozyrev. To avoid misunderstandings (and accusations that he was taking sides) the High Commissioner was careful to inform the Estonian authorities, on this and subsequent occasions,[8] about his consultations with his Russian interlocutors. He also worked closely with the OSCE Mission to Estonia and the Swedish Foreign Ministry. The Swedes were active with regard to Estonia both because of Foreign Minister Margaretha af Ugglas' tenure as CSCE Chairperson-in-Office and because of Sweden's strong interest in regional stability.[9] A level of co-ordination was also maintained with Council of Europe officials.

Although a crisis was averted, the High Commissioner continued to follow-up on his specific recommendations and the more general process of inter-

---

7 Statement of the High Commissioner on National Minorities, Max van der Stoel, Tallin, 12 July 1993.

8 See for example his letter to Foreign Minister Riivo Sinijarv of 15 June 1995.

9 Huber 1994, pp. 13, 20–21.

ethnic integration in Estonia. After a visit in October 1993, he made a number of observations and recommendations, most of which concerned citizenship issues. For example, he recommended that (in line with the United Nations Convention on the Rights of the Child to which Estonia is a party) citizenship should be granted to children of stateless parents who had been born in Estonia after the country regained its independence. This recommendation was only implemented in 1998 following persistent efforts on the part of the High Commissioner. He reiterated the need for a more pro-active public information campaign to clarify language test requirements and application procedures for naturalization. He also recommended that the costs for naturalization and registration for aliens should be lowered. A further recommendation made in 1993 was in favour of the establishment of a National Commissioner on Ethnic and Language Questions who was supposed to act in an Ombudsman function.[10]

Many of these issues were raised again during visits in 1994. In a letter dated 9 March, Van der Stoel urged the Government to extend the deadline for applications under the Law on Aliens. The Law, which had come into force on 12 July 1993, had established a one-year period for applications for residence permits for aliens who settled in Estonia prior to 1 July 1990 and who had a registered residence in the former Estonian SSR. The registration process had taken longer than expected and had encountered administrative difficulties which risked leaving over 300,000 people unregistered. The complicated procedures, the refusal of the Estonian Government to recognize Russian 'aliens' as stateless (and to therefore grant them alien passports), a lack of clarity concerning various provisions of the law (i.e. would applicants be granted permanent or only temporary residence permits) led to bitterness and insecurity among the Russian-speaking minority and provoked threatening statements from Moscow.

Concerned about this situation, the High Commissioner urged the Chairman-in-Office and OSCE participating States to make it clear to the Estonian Government that as much as they supported Estonia in its efforts to ensure the departure of the remaining Russian troops in Estonia, they would consider it unacceptable if Estonia would refuse to take the steps necessary to address the

10 Although such an office was never established, the Legal Chancellor has some competences similar to those of an ombudsman.

concerns of the Russian minority in relation to the implementation of the Law on Aliens. The Estonian Government eventually agreed to extend the deadline by one year. Assurances were also given that residents would be issued with temporary travel documents to allow them to leave and re-enter the country and that they would enjoy social guarantees. Efforts were also made to better inform aliens on registration for work and residence permits and to improve the functioning of the Citizenship and Migration Department.

Although it sometimes made him unpopular with Estonian nationalists, Van der Stoel continued to reiterate his point on the need for integration. He tried to explain that this would not present a threat to the identity of Estonians or the integrity of the Estonian State, that it was in line with international standards that Estonia subscribed to, that it was good governance and that it was in the best security interests of the country. The latter point was a consideration in 1994 when suggestions were made that the expulsion of retired Russian military personnel was imminent. Nevertheless, some voices within Estonia and in the émigré community began to tire of Van der Stoel's frequent visits and recommendations and felt that the country was being unfairly singled out and stigmatized. This was a complaint which he would encounter in greater or lesser degrees over the next several years.

Resentment also continued over the handling of the aliens registration process. The process, in itself unpopular, was slower than expected, even with the one year extension. This created the potentially destabilizing situation wherein a large group of people would have no legal status in the country, or could even be expelled. Many ethnic Russians began registering for Russian citizenship. Whereas many Estonian officials might have thought that upon acquiring Russian citizenship these people would emigrate to Russia, polls indicated otherwise. The High Commissioner explained to the Government the potentially divisive effect that this trend could have on areas of high Russophone concentration, like Narva. He also publically encouraged non-citizens to stay in Estonia and to register for Estonian citizenship. To rectify the problem in the short term, he suggested to the Government that alien passports should be issued. This suggestion was rejected and only temporary travel documents (only valid for one journey) were introduced. This was seen by minorities as a further irritant and increased their perception that they were not welcome in Estonia.

A new law on citizenship came into force on 1 April 1995. The law stated that applicants for citizenship, apart from having to undergo a language test, would also have to pass a test on the Constitution of Estonia. After studying the tests, the High Commissioner appealed to the Government to make them easier.[11] He also criticized a Law on Public Service which made citizenship a requirement for persons wanting to join the civil service. He said that if the law were to come into force before the naturalization process was complete, it would cause considerable disruption, particularly in the northeast, as many civil servants had still not had an opportunity to clarify their status in the country. He asked that the implementation of the law be delayed in order to allow prospective citizens to take the language and Constitution exams. An amendment was made to the law to allow an additional year for non-citizens to register. This was later extended.

A new issue arose in April 1996 when the Riigikogu (Parliament) passed a Law on Local Elections on 17 April which contained provisions which restricted potential candidates on the basis of their proficiency in the Estonian language. In a letter to President Meri dated 22 April Van der Stoel pointed out how this ran contrary to the International Covenant on Civil and Political Rights of which Estonia is a party. He asked the President not to promulgate the law and to return it to the Parliament for further consideration.[12] This was done.

Still the naturalization process and issuing of aliens passports progressed only very slowly, and although many of the problems were due to the sheer number of applicants, the High Commissioner remained concerned that the efforts of the Government to facilitate integration were half-hearted. He therefore asked the Government to re-invigorate the Presidential Round-table on inter-ethnic relations and to give a high priority to enhancing the teaching of Estonian to non-Estonians to stimulate the process of integration, particularly through strengthening the Language Training Centre and swiftly adopting a Language Training Strategy. Conscious of the financial difficulties in implementing some of his recommendations, Van der Stoel tried to secure foreign assistance for Estonian language training.

Upon its ratification of the Framework Convention of the Council of Europe,

---

11 For the Estonian Government's response see the letter of Foreign Minister Siim Kallas dated 7 February 1996.

12 Letter to President Lennart Meri, President of the Republic of Estonia (22 April 1996), ref. no. 636/96.

the Estonian Government made a reservation stressing that it would apply the Convention only to citizens. The High Commissioner pointed out that some articles of the Framework Convention referred also to the rights of non-citizens and recommended that the Estonian Government drop the reservation, or at least make it clear that 'the intended reservation will not in any way change Estonia's international commitments and obligations, and that the reservation does not signify that the Government intends to restrict the existing rights of non-citizens living on its territory'.[13]

By this time the Estonian Government began to show signs of 'Van der Stoel fatigue'. Regardless of which party was in Government, there was a growing weariness of what was perceived as 'Estonia bashing'.[14] The Government argued that as soon as one issue was addressed, another was raised and that Estonia was being singled out for 'violations' that were significantly worse in other countries. Estonian officials argued that conditions of minorities in Russia (or even the Netherlands) were not being investigated while Van der Stoel paid so much attention to the Russian minority in Estonia. They once politely suggested that he should concentrate instead on the situation in Chechnya.[15] Off, and sometimes even on, the record Estonian officials complained that the bar was constantly being raised in terms of compliance with international standards. On the question of granting citizenship to children of stateless parents, the Estonian Foreign Minister once wrote, after summarizing the practice on this question in other OSCE countries, that 'it is difficult to accept singling out Estonian legislation as discriminatory. Moreover, even in countries where the legislation has been changed in the direction recommended, practice is not always consistent with your recommendations'.[16] However, the Government finally consented to

---

13 For details see letter to Siim Kallas, Minister for Foreign Affairs of the Republic of Estonia (28 October 1996), OSCE HC/1/97.

14 This criticism was not restricted to the High Commissioner. It was openly suggested that the OSCE Mission to Estonia had completed its mandate and should be either transformed or discontinued.

15 See for example the last paragraph of the letter from Acting Foreign Minister Riivo Sinijarv to the High Commissioner dated 27 November 1997. A similar argument was made in 1999 in relation to Kosovo.

16 Letter from Foreign Minister Toomas Ilves to the High Commissioner (4 June 1997), HC/8/97.

implement Van der Stoel's recommendations on this point.

In 1997 the Estonian Foreign Ministry produced a list of the High Commissioner's recommendations and announced that Estonia had now implemented 28 out of 30 of them. The High Commissioner did not comment on this statement but on 21 May 1997 he sent a lengthy letter to Foreign Minister Toomas Ilves in which he commented on the policies of the present Government, the naturalization process, and children of stateless parents. Van der Stoel assessed the general inter-ethnic situation in the country to be good. He was satisfied that a number of recommendations that he had made between April 1993 and October 1996 had been implemented by the Government. He was encouraged by a number of steps taken by the Government which showed 'its determination to pay increased attention to the interests of those residents of the country who are not Estonian citizens'.[17] For example, he expressed his satisfaction about the changes to the Law on Aliens which aimed at accelerating the process of changing temporary residence permits into permanent ones. He also welcomed the appointment of a Minister for Population and Ethnic Affairs and a public information campaign designed to inform prospective citizens about tests on the Constitution and the application procedures for citizenship. (Brochures on these subjects were issued through assistance provided by the Hague-based Foundation on Inter-Ethnic Relations.) However, he expressed concern about the fact that 14% of the population remained stateless, that the naturalization process progressed too slowly and he repeated the need for more Estonian language teaching. He said that he hoped that the proposed position of Ombudsman would be introduced and that this institution could in effect fulfil the role of the National Commissioner on Ethnic and Language Questions which was proposed in an earlier recommendation by the High Commissioner. He also reiterated the need to speed up distribution of aliens' passports. He again recommended a simplification of the constitutional test and suggested that citizenship be automatically granted to children of stateless parents.

Through the persistence of the High Commissioner and the support of OSCE participating States (particularly those in the EU), more changes were eventually introduced. The constitutional tests were made easier and in December 1998 the Riigikogu finally passed a law on stateless children.

---

17 Letter to Foreign Minister Toomas Ilves (21 May 1997), HC/8/97.

However almost immediately a new situation arose, this time concerning an amendment made by the Riigikogu to the Estonian Laws on Parliamentary Elections, Local Elections and the State Language to the effect that 'knowledge of written and spoken Estonian' would be required for all members of the Riigikogu or a local government council. In a confidential letter to President Meri dated 19 December 1998 (which somehow found its way into the media) the High Commissioner said that, in his view the proposed amendment was neither in accord with the Estonian Constitution nor with Estonia's international obligations and commitments. He also said that it 'would not constitute a constructive contribution to the national integration process'.[18] He appealed to the President not to promulgate the amendments.

This time the President did not heed the High Commissioner's recommendations. In a reply to the High Commissioner's letter he noted that 'due process is guaranteed in Estonia' and that people whose rights are infringed have recourse to the courts. He concluded by saying 'I would like to recall that there is widespread agreement both in Estonia and in the international community that the legislative framework of integration is nearly complete. I believe that you will agree with me on this matter. It is time now to concentrate all our efforts on the practical aspects of integration, to keep the process on track and to avoid false signals'.[19]

The annoyance of some Estonians with the persistence of the High Commissioner was evident in a letter sent by several members of the Estonian Parliament to the Chairman-in-Office on 28 January 1999 (in the run-up to Parliamentary elections). In it they outlined steps taken by the Government to foster integration and criticized the efforts of the High Commissioner as being 'unconsidered, political in effect' and no longer serving to defuse situations involving minority issues.

The Chairman-in-Office, in his reply to the parliamentarians, and Van der Stoel, in a private letter to President Meri, made it clear that the High Commissioner had the interests of Estonia in mind when making his recommendations and that he had long supported the need to protect, promote, and develop the use of the Estonian language. As Van der Stoel stated in a letter to Foreign

---

18 Letter from the High Commissioner to President Lennart Meri (19 December 1998).

19 Letter from President Meri to the High Commissioner (12 January 1999).

Minister Ilves in March 1999, 'in principle I support and sympathise with all efforts to strengthen the position of the Estonian language. I do feel strongly that the process of integration, which is so vital for the future of your country, will be served if more non-Estonians acquire an adequate command of the Estonian language'.[20] He nevertheless expressed reservations about amendments to the Law on Language, especially because they made an intrusion into the private sphere which went far beyond what international standards allow. He reiterated that one of the best ways of addressing the language issue was to increase efforts at teaching Estonian. The amendments to the Language Law were discussed with Estonian officials, including the President, when the High Commissioner visited Tallinn in May 1999. He encouraged the Government to ensure that implementing decrees on the law would be in compliance with international standards and noted that it would be regrettable if the matter would become an obstacle in the negotiations between Estonia and the European Commission.

The High Commissioner continued to stress the need for integration. At a seminar in Tallinn on 'Integration, Educational and Linguistic Rights' in June 1999 organized by the Foundation on Inter-Ethnic Relations, he articulated his views on integration. He said: 'successful integration means that majority and minority do not turn their back on each other, but try to know each other better and to learn about each other's culture'. He noted the importance of all people living in Estonia to realize that they have common interests. He said that 'the integration process in Estonia can be considered to be successful if persons belonging to national minorities are increasingly identifying themselves with Estonia and if the majority tries to stimulate the process by taking due account of the vital needs and interests of the minorities'.[21] He also noted that integration would mean coming to terms with the past.

In the summer of 1999 the High Commissioner's attention turned to two Language Law implementing decrees which concerned the language requirements for employment in the private and public sectors. He raised several reservations with the Estonian Government about the implementation decree

---

20 Letter to Foreign Minister Toomas Henrik Ilves (26 March 1999), HCNM.GAL/2/99.

21 Remarks by the High Commissioner at the Seminar on Integration in Estonia (11 June 1999).

concerning the private sector which he felt was overly intrusive. Furthermore, he felt that the Law on Language (1995) was itself not completely in conformity with international standards and needed amending.[22] Under international pressure, the Government decided to review the draft decree, especially their intrusion into the private sphere.

In spring 2000 discussion was reopened on the Law on Language. The proposed amendments related to a limited number of articles in the law (which had been amended as recently as February 1999). In May 2000 Estonian Foreign Minister Ilves invited a group of experts from the High Commissioner's office to discuss the issue. During the course of the consultations, the position of the High Commissioner on certain provisions related to the use of language in the private sphere was reiterated and clarified.

Soon after, the Estonian Parliament adopted amendments to the Law on Language. In a statement issued on 15 June the High Commissioner welcomed adoption of the amendments and noted that the amended Law was 'largely in conformity with Estonia's international obligations and commitments'.[23] He expressed the hope that the Cabinet of Ministers would follow the letter and spirit of the amended Law in elaborating implementing regulations and in supervising administration of the Law. His Office remained in close contact with the Estonian Government concerning the drafting of the implementation decrees. He also continued to co-operate with the Estonian authorities on matters concerning inter-ethnic integration. For example, he participated in a seminar on teacher training for education integration in Narva in August 2000. During the visit he also met with Prime Minister Laar and Foreign Minister Ilves to further discuss the implementation decrees and amendments to the election law concerning language requirements to stand for elected office. Informal discussions between experts continued on a regular basis concerning these issues.

---

22 See letter to Foreign Minister Ilves (12 July 1999).

23 Statement regarding the adoption of amendments to the Law on Language by the Estonian Parliament, 15 June 2000.

Latvia

The High Commissioner was involved in Latvia on a continuous basis from the beginning of his term in office in January 1993. Because of the country's delicate ethnic balance (approximately 45% of the population is non-Latvian) issues of citizenship, education, and language are at the centre of political debate. The High Commissioner played an important role in ensuring that these issues did not strain inter-ethnic relations and that legislation enacted to deal with questions of citizenship, language, and education were in conformity with international standards.[24]

The High Commissioner made exploratory visits to Latvia in January and April 1993. In his first report of April 1993 he said that he had no evidence of persecution of national minorities. He acknowledged the importance of preserving and strengthening Latvian identity while at the same time ensuring harmonious inter-ethnic relations. He suggested that these two goals could be best attained by adopting an open policy of dialogue and integration, with particular focus on citizenship and language issues. He stressed that such a policy would require an effort not only on the part of the Government but also on the part of the non-citizen population.

Citizenship was a particularly contentious issue because the Latvian Government had decided, soon after independence in 1991, that automatic citizenship would not be granted to all those who settled in the country during the Soviet period. As a result a considerable number of people were disenfranchised and uncertain of their status within the country. This not only had a direct bearing on inter-ethnic relations within the country, but as most of those affected by this decision were Russian, it caused tensions between Latvia and the Russian Federation.

---

24 For a further analysis of the High Commissioner's role see Zaagman 1999.

In June 1993 the High Commissioner paid his third visit to Latvia within six months. His main aim was to find out more about the views of the various political parties concerning the policies to be followed vis-à-vis the roughly 600,000 non-Latvian residents of Latvia who might have an interest in becoming citizens of the country. He urged the Government to adopt a fairly liberal naturalization policy to allow those people seeking citizenship to be able to receive it.

Van der Stoel often stressed that he understood the historical grievance of the Latvians and their concerns over the demographic situation, but he urged them to protect and promote their identity through cultural, educational, and linguistic fields rather than through a restrictive citizenship law. He noted that the non-Latvian population had rights but also duties, like loyalty to the state. However, he argued that this loyalty would be hard to win and maintain if these people were excluded from certain rights, like citizenship. He therefore urged speedy adoption of a citizenship law.

As in Estonia, the High Commissioner urged the Government to assist in the process of integration by not making citizenship tests too difficult and by helping the non-Latvians to acquire a reasonable level of knowledge of the Latvian language. Other suggestions to ease inter-ethnic tensions included granting citizenship to children born in Latvia who would otherwise be stateless and requiring only five years of residency before being eligible for naturalization.

In order to allow minorities to be involved in decisions affecting their future and in order for them to have a vehicle to air grievances, he proposed the creation of a National Commissioner on Ethnic and Language Questions and suggested that the Latvian National Minorities Department (at that time part of the Ministry of Justice) should be transformed into an independent body.

The High Commissioner made a number of recommendations on the first draft of the citizenship law in December 1993. He underlined the fact that although the Latvian State wanted to protect its identity, the Government had to bear in mind that a considerable number of non-ethnic Latvians (many of whom had been living in Latvia for many years) wanted to stay in the country and to acquire Latvian citizenship. In a letter to Foreign Minister Georg Andrejevs dated 10 December 1993, he cautioned against an overly restrictive law saying: 'To deny citizenship to hundreds of thousands of non-Latvians residing in Latvia is tantamount to refusing to grant them political rights, and this, in turn would, sooner or later, have negative repercussions on inter-ethnic relations which might even endanger the stability of your country'.[25]

He suggested that a way out would be to grant citizenship to those non-Latvians who applied for it, provided that they accepted certain conditions. These would be: acquiring a basic knowledge of the Latvian language which would be tested in the course of the naturalization process according to standardized procedures; acquiring a knowledge of the basic principles of the Latvian Constitution which would also be tested during the naturalization process; and swearing an oath of loyalty to the Republic of Latvia.

He objected to the proposal of introducing annual quotas for the naturalization process. He said that such a quota system could 'lead to considerable uncertainty amongst a large part of the population about their future status. This uncertainty, moreover, could possibly last for many years, even for persons who have been living in Latvia for a long time or have been born in Latvia, and for persons with a sincere willingness to integrate into Latvian society'.[26]

He suggested an alternative system that would speed up the naturalization process and give clear dates on which people who had been living in Latvia for a certain period of time could expect to acquire citizenship. Under his proposal, priority groups would be naturalized in 1994 and 1995; naturalization would be extended to those residents living in Latvia for 20 years in 1996, those living in Latvia for 15 years in 1997 and those living in Latvia for at least 10 years in 1998.

Van der Stoel also urged that non-citizens should be better informed about the law and corresponding decisions as well as about the practical procedures to follow in order to obtain Latvian citizenship. Furthermore, he re-emphasized the importance of involving minorities in legislative processes on issues of fundamental importance to them.

He visited Latvia several times in 1994, every time focusing on the draft law on citizenship and in particular the provisions concerning naturalization. He remained concerned about the Government-proposed quota system which would affect 'non-priority' groups. Under the proposed system, the number of citizens to be naturalized every year would be determined by the cabinet and approved by the Parliament 'taking into consideration the demographic and economic situation in the country, in order to ensure the development of Latvia

---

25 Letter to Georgs Andrejevs, Minister for Foreign Affairs of the Republic of Latvia (10 December 1993), CSCE Communication no. 8/94.

26 *Ibid.*

as a mono-community state'. This, in the view of the High Commissioner, politicized the process and failed to distinguish between citizenship and nationality.

In the summer of 1994 the Latvian Saeima (Parliament) adopted a law on citizenship which included the annual quota. Under international pressure President Guntis Ulmanis used his presidential prerogative to send the law back to parliament, stressing the need to take into account recommendations made by the High Commissioner and the Council of Europe. The quota system was eliminated from the law which was adopted in July.

During the course of this process, the High Commissioner was sensitive to the effect that inter-ethnic relations in Latvia had on bilateral relations between Latvia and Russia. In a discrete way, he sounded out Russian opinion on the issues under discussion and urged them to exercise restraint. Bilateral relations between Russia and Latvia were improved in 1994 when agreement was reached on the withdrawal of Russian troops and an agreement was signed on the 'Legal Status of the Skrunda Radar Station during its Temporary Operation and Dismantling'.

However, citizenship remained a contentious issue. Although quotas were dropped, the requirements which applicants for citizenship had to meet were made higher. Applicants had to demonstrate fluency in the Latvian language both in reading and writing; they had to be able to recite the Latvian national anthem; they had to pass a test (in Latvian) on their knowledge of the history of Latvia and their knowledge of the Latvian constitution; and they had to produce some twenty-five documents to the citizenship and immigration board. Many prospective applicants were daunted by these criteria. Others were concerned about their legal status in the country as they were no longer Soviet citizens, yet were neither Latvian nor officially 'stateless'. The Government adopted a Law on the Status of Non-Citizens in April 1995 which took into account some of the High Commissioner's recommendations.

In January 1996 the High Commissioner visited Latvia in order to assess further the naturalization process. While acknowledging the great efforts being made by the Naturalization Board, given the magnitude of their task, he expressed concern at the low rate of applications particularly among younger non-citizens. This trend was in stark contrast to polls that showed that there was a desire by many non-Latvian non-citizens to acquire citizenship. The High Commissioner suggested that the high level of requirements and an expensive fee (at that time equal to one month's minimum wage) were barriers to a higher application rate.

In a letter to Foreign Minister Valdis Birkavs in March 1996 he said that 'quite a large number of non-citizens, who show in principle an interest in integrating into Latvian society in order to get Latvian citizenship, are at present deterred from making such an effort because their perception is that they might not be able to meet the requirements'.[27] He pointed out that in Latvia, the number of registered aliens and stateless persons was far higher than in most other states of the world: more than 28% of the total population. He remarked that 'it is therefore especially important to promote their integration and to avoid a situation in which a high percentage of aliens will not be motivated to try to integrate'. He suggested that the language, history, and constitutional tests should be simplified and that the fee for receiving citizenship be lowered. He also urged that persons over the age of 65 should be exempted from taking the Latvian language test.

One of the major restrictions on the number of people applying for citizenship was the introduction of the so-called 'window system' which gave priority to those born in Latvia over those born outside Latvia. It spread the right to apply for naturalization over seven years (instead of the three proposed by the High Commissioner) during which a new window of opportunity would be opened for particular groups of prospective citizens every year.

The High Commissioner returned in October 1996 and was impressed by the establishment of a National Human Rights Office, the creation of the President's Consultative Council on Nationalities, and the introduction of a national program to increase the knowledge of Latvian in Latvia (which were in line with recommendations made earlier by the High Commissioner). However, he noted that the naturalization process was virtually stagnant. In a letter to Foreign Minister Birkavs written after his trip, he said that:

> 'it is clear that the problem confronting Latvia now is not the danger of being swamped by a great number of applicants at the same time, but the risk of the process of naturalization – an essential element of the process of integrating non-Latvians into Latvian society – moving much too slowly.

27 Letter to Valdis Birkavs, Minister for Foreign Affairs of the Republic of Latvia (14 March 1996), OSCE HC/5/96.

> I hope therefore that due consideration will be given to the abolishment of the "window" system."[28]

One of the recurring themes that the High Commissioner noted during his frequent trips to Latvia and in discussions with minority representatives was that there was a low level of public knowledge of citizenship legislation and regulations. To increase awareness about naturalization procedures, the High Commissioner asked the Foundation on Inter-Ethnic Relations to prepare a pamphlet in Latvian and Russian which would provide information about how the naturalization process works.

The High Commissioner again noted little progress on the naturalization process when he returned to Latvia in April 1997. He reiterated his view that changes in the system were needed. However it was clear that the fragility of the Government coalition made it politically inexpedient for any party to suggest changes to the Law on Citizenship. It should be borne in mind that in the post-independence period, Latvia (like Estonia) had a fairly rapid turnover of Governments, most of which felt obliged to address issues relating to national identity and inter-ethnic relations. Van der Stoel's role was therefore influential (perhaps disproportionately so) in political developments within the country.

Throughout the spring of 1997 Van der Stoel continued to focus on the citizenship issue. For example, in line with international instruments to which Latvia is a party (including the International Covenant on Civil and Political Rights, the Convention on the Rights of the Child, and the Convention on the Reduction of Statelessness), he frequently stressed the importance of providing citizenship for children born in Latvia who would otherwise be stateless.

As in Estonia, these and other issues related to minorities and citizenship were questions which the Government could not ignore as it sought accession to the European Union: proper treatment of minorities is one of the requirements of potential EU members. This, and the support of OSCE participating States, gave the High Commissioner considerable leverage in his efforts. Although it did not make him very popular (he received a steady stream of hate mail and was vilified in certain sections of the Latvian and international press), the High Commissioner's persistence paid off.

---

28 Letter to Valdis Birkavs, Minister for Foreign Affairs of the Republic of Latvia (28 October 1996), HC/2/97.

Changes were gradually made in line with the High Commissioner's recommendations. Naturalization fees were lowered, the history exams were simplified, the language tests were redesigned, and the National Programme for Latvian Language Training was intensified.

In late 1997, the High Commissioner turned his attention to a draft of a new Law on the Latvian Language. In analyzing the draft law he noted that it required the use of the State language in the private sphere of commercial activities, that all public information (including with regard to private activities) had to be in the Latvian language, and that no accommodation had been made for the use of other languages in criminal proceedings, in respect of personal and place names, in education and in contacts with public authorities. In a letter to President Ulmanis dated 10 November 1997 he said that 'the relevant provisions of the draft Law should be harmonized with the relevant provisions of international instruments, in particular the Council of Europe's Framework Convention'.[29]

On another issue related to language, the High Commissioner sent a letter to President Ulmanis on 10 February 1998 taking issue with an amendment to the Labour Code of the Republic of Latvia which would empower the State Language Inspectorate to require employers to terminate contracts of employees who do not meet language requirements as stipulated under Latvian law. The High Commissioner said that this violated freedom of expression and association (as provided in several international instruments to which Latvia is a party) and raised questions about economic liberty and discrimination in employment. On the recommendation of the High Commissioner, the President did not sign the law, but sent it back to Parliament for reconsideration.

In March and early April 1998, the High Commissioner had frequent contacts with the Prime Minister, Guntars Krasts, appealing to him to revise the Citizenship Law, to grant automatic citizenship to children of stateless parents born in independent Latvia and to abolish the so-called 'window' system. He also urged the Prime Minister to ensure that the amendment to the Labour Code and the new Law on the State Language would be in conformity with international standards. These calls were increasingly echoed by a number of OSCE States and international organizations.

---

29 Letter to Guntis Ulmanis, President of Latvia (10 November 1997).

These recommendations were made at a time of worsening bilateral relations between Latvia and the Russian Federation. Moscow's general accusations of human rights violations in Latvia were further fuelled by the dispersal of a demonstration of mainly Russian-speaking pensioners by riot police and marches by the Latvian Legion (an organization of veterans who had fought alongside the German forces in the Second World War).

In his contacts with Russian officials, Van der Stoel frequently argued that Moscow's view of the situation of Russian minorities in Latvia and Estonia was too alarmist. While criticizing some policies of the Latvian and Estonian Governments, he tried to defend Latvia and Estonia against those accusations of the Russian Government which he considered unjustified. He frequently observed that despite certain policies or isolated cases, there were no systemic violations of human rights in either country.

In this highly charged environment, Van der Stoel reminded the Latvian Government of his earlier recommendations in regard to the 'window system' and stateless children. Despite the resistance of members of the coalition, Prime Minister Krasts publicly supported Van der Stoel's recommendations. Amendments to the Citizenship Law were introduced to the Saeima in April. On 17 April the High Commissioner issued a statement in which he welcomed the decision of the Government of Latvia to support his recommendation to completely abolish the 'window' system of naturalization. He also welcomed the decision of the Government to support his recommendation to grant citizenship, without having to pass tests, to all children born in Latvia since August 21 1991, whose parents are stateless and have legally resided in Latvia for no less than five years, provided that the parents apply for such naturalization. He said that 'if the Saeima (Parliament) approves the changes in the Citizenship Law needed to implement these recommendations, a very important step towards the solution of the naturalization problem in Latvia will have been taken'.[30] He also expressed the hope that 'stateless persons who would benefit from such changes in the Law will react positively by applying for naturalization.'

Although the amendments were vigorously contested by nationalist parties, the Law on Citizenship, abolishing the 'window system' and granting citizenship to stateless children, was eventually adopted in an extraordinary session of the Latvian parliament on 22 June 1998. Van der Stoel issues a statement the

30 Press Statement by the OSCE HCNM, 17 April 1998.

next day welcoming the Saeima's decision. He noted that 'once the Law has come into force – and I hope this will be the case next week – the key elements of my recommendations regarding citizenship and naturalization will have been fulfilled'. However, several opposition parties remained staunchly opposed to the decision and began to collect signatures for a referendum on the issue. There was also an impression that Van der Stoel kept moving the goal posts. He responded to this criticism by issuing a statement on 16 July 1998 in which he clarified that his recommendations on the citizenship law had been laid down in his letter to Foriegn Minister Birkaus of 23 May 1997. These included: abolition of the 'window system'; granting of Latvian citizenship to children of stateless parents born in Latvia after August 1991 (without language testing); and simplification of the naturalization process tests. He sais that 'since I made these recommendations I have not changed my position on this subject and I do not see the need to do so in the future.'[31]

During the summer, the High Commissioner's focus shifted back to the language question. Together with a team of experts, he visited Riga in August 1998 to discuss the compatibility of the draft text of the State Language Law with international legal standards. Earlier drafts, particularly articles relating to private enterprise, had been criticized by the High Commissioner for their lack of conformity with international standards. Although a compromise text was introduced (after the involvement of a group of international experts in a meeting of the Education Committee of Parliament), this text was not adopted by the Parliament.

This disappointment was eclipsed by the unexpected news that over the summer nationalist parties, which were opposed to the abolition of the so-called 'window' system and the conferral of citizenship on stateless children, had secured the required number of signatures (over 10% of the electorate) to oblige the Government to hold a referendum on the amendments to the Citizenship Law. The referendum held on 3 October 1998 was defeated and the amendments were retained. On 5 October the High Commissioner issued a statement in which he welcomed the outcome of the referendum and said that 'by deciding to approve the amendments to the Law on Citizenship, the people of Latvia have taken an important step towards solving interethnic problems

---

31 Press statement on Latvia, 16 July 1998.

and promoting the process of integration'.[32]

Van der Stoel visited Latvia in January 1999 to discuss the draft Law on the State Language and the implementation of the Law on Education. Several opposition parties argued that it was necessary to compensate for the acceptance of amendments to the Citizenship Law by having a strong law on the State language. The High Commissioner tried to convince Latvian Government representatives that it was possible to have a meaningful language law while respecting international standards. It was agreed that a group of experts would return in February to discuss the draft text in detail. Although the suggestions of the experts were favourably received by the Government, they did not enjoy the support of the Parliament.

The law passed second reading in the Saeima on 18 March. In a letter to Foreign Minister Birkavs dated 22 March, Van der Stoel expressed dissatisfaction with a number of points. He wrote:

> 'As I am confident that your Government has no intention for Latvian law to be inconsistent with Latvia's international obligations and commitments, I draw your attention to the fact that many of the provisions of the draft State Language Law fail to distinguish between permissible regulation of use of language in the public sphere and impermissible interference in the private sphere.'[33]

He said that this interference in the private sphere was not in the pursuit of legitimate public interests under international law (i.e. it was not for the purpose of protecting national security, public order, public health, or morals, or the rights and reputations of others). He also criticized the draft Law for leaving too much to the Executive Branch of Government to decide in implementation, and for not including a regime for implementation and supervision of the law.

Foreign Minister Birkavs asked to visit the High Commissioner in order to discuss the issue further. On 12 April 1999, a meeting was held in The Hague in which the latest draft of the language law was discussed, particularly those provisions of the law about which the High Commissioner had proposed changes. During the meeting Birkavs requested Van der Stoel to provide the

32 Press Release of the OSCE HCNM, 5 October 1998, Ref. 3-98.

33 Letter to Foreign Minister Valdis Birkavs (22 March 1999).

Latvian Ministry for Foreign Affairs with further written arguments about the incompatibility of the draft law with international standards.

The High Commissioner did so through a letter in which he said: 'The current draft Law would, in various provisions and to varying degrees, violate the freedoms of expression, association and assembly, the right to privacy (including correspondence), the norms of international labour law, and the freedom of choice in private enterprise'. He pointed out that 'these interferences in the private sphere would not only be unjustified, but they would be very difficult to implement, entailing considerable disruption in a range of personal and business affairs.' Moreover, he added that

> 'aside from the general social and economic disruption which would follow adoption of the current draft Law, I believe there would be serious negative implications for Latvia in terms of attracting foreign investment, creating local conditions friendly towards business development, and eventually, also in terms of accession to the European Union which has specific requirements relating to the effective functioning of the single market.'[34]

The High Commissioner stressed that the law should be considered in the context of social transformation in Latvia. He emphasized the need for expanding the State Language Training Programme as part of a transition period to enable persons, who according to the law must use the State language, to learn it. He said: 'It seems to me that the challenge facing Latvia is to increase the knowledge and use of the Latvian language while ensuring protection of the freedom of expression and without creating practical problems for the free market or for the implementation of the law in general'.[35] The High Commissioner attached a suggested revision of the previous Saiema draft State Language Law to his letter.

These points were reiterated during a visit to Latvia on 24 and 25 May 1999. Pressure was also brought to bear by the European Commission which expressed concern about the text. However, despite showing some willingness to bring a key article of the law into line with international standards, the Latvian Government refused to accept a formulation that would lead to weaker provisions

---

34 Letter to Valdis Birkavs, Minister for Foreign Affairs of the Republic of Latvia (13 April 1999).

35 *Ibid.*

than those of the 1992 State Language Law. These developments took place against a background of a new Government crisis and on the eve of the election of a new President by the Parliament.

Although the new President, Mrs Vike-Freiberga, spoke out in support of the law soon after her inauguration, Van der Stoel appealed to her not to sign it and to send it back to the Parliament for reconsideration. She asked the High Commissioner for a more detailed explanation about which aspects of the law violate international standards. It was agreed during a telephone conversation that the High Commissioner's senior legal adviser, John Packer, would travel to Riga to explain to the Presdient the objections to the law. After extensive consultations, President Vike-Freiberga decided to send the law back to Parliament.

In August 1999 the High Commissioner visited Riga to assess progress made on the elaboration of the revised State Language Law. In order to facilitate the drafting process and to assist the parliamentarians in ensuring that the law was in line with international standards, the High Commissioner pledged his willingness to send a group of experts to assist the Standing Committee on Culture and Education which was responsible for the draft law. The experts visited Latvia in November 1999.

The law was adopted on 9 December 1999 on the eve of the EU Helsinki Summit. The High Commissioner issued a statement welcoming the adoption of the law saying that 'the Law is now essentially in conformity with Latvia's international obligations and commitments'.[36] He also said that 'I trust that the Cabinet of Ministers will follow the letter and spirit of the Law in elaborating implementing regulations, as foreseen in certain provisions of the Law, and in supervising public administration of the Law'.[37]

The High Commissioner visited Latvia again in March 2000 and agreed with the Minister of Justice that experts would be sent to assist with the elaboration of the implementating decrees foreseen in the new State Language Law.

Van der Stoel also spoke with the President about the case of a Russian-speaker living in Latvia (Mr Kononov) accused of crimes against Latvia while fighting on the side of the Soviet Union during the Second World War. Although

36 'High Commissioner welcomes State Language Law in Latvia', press release, 9 December 1999.

37 *Ibid.*

Van der Stoel can not, according to his mandate, take up individual cases, he was concerned about how the case (and possible similar ones) could affect Latvian–Russian relations. He therefore asked for clarification. He was aware from a visit to Moscow in February 2000 that the Russian Government had serious concerns about the case and what they viewed as the possibility of many more like it. Foreign Minister Ivanov even refered to the 'encouragement of Nazism' in Latvia and Estonia.

In April and June 2000 experts from the Office of the High Commissioner and the Council of Europe returned to Latvia to discuss with local experts initial and draft decrees to implement the State Language Law.

On 22 August the Cabinet of Ministers approved the implementing decrees under the State Language Law. The High Commissioner said that he viewed the regulations as being 'essentially in conformity with both the [State Language] Law and Latvia's international obligations.'[38] He noted that most of his recommendations had been accepted in the drafting process. He expressed the hope that the public administration of the implementing regulations and the Law as a whole 'will be in the spirit of an open and liberal democracy'.[39] Some minor points needed to be ironed out, for example the regulations concerning the degree of proficiency in the State language that was necessary to carry out certain jobs in the private sector. The High Commissioner recommended to the Latvian Government that the list of professions that required a regulated high level of Latvian proficiency should not be excessive. A relatively short list was eventually drawn up and adopted by the Cabinet. Advice was also provided on the remaining implementation decrees. The High Commissioner also continued to follow issues relating to the naturalization process, education reform and the integration process.

---

38 Statement regarding the adoption of regulations implementing the Latvian State Language Law, 31 August 2000.

39 *Ibid.*

Lithuania

The High Commissioner visited Lithuania as part of his first trip to the Baltic States in January 1993. During his one and only trip to Lithuania from 21 to 23 January 1993, Van der Stoel found no domestic or international tensions arising from inter-ethnic relations.

Unlike Latvia and Estonia, the population of Lithuania is relatively ethnically homogeneous. The non-Lithuanian component of the population (mostly Polish and Russian) does not exceed 20%. There were few difficulties concerning naturalization as the Government of Lithuania introduced a fairly liberal citizenship law in December 1991 by which Lithuanian citizenship was granted automatically to all permanent residents of the former SSR of Lithuania. This so-called 'zero option' solved in one stroke the citizenship problem for the country.

In a letter to Foreign Minister Povilas Gylys, dated 5 March 1993, Van der Stoel characterized inter-ethnic relations within Lithuania as 'harmonious'.[40] The few complaints that he heard (mostly from the Polish minority) concerned registration procedures for regional elections. In that connection, as in Latvia and Estonia, Van der Stoel recommended the creation of an Ombudsman's office which would have as its main task to address, in a non-judicial way, complaints concerning administrative decisions and practices.

In his reply of 16 April, Foreign Minister Gylys referred to Article 73 of the Lithuanian Constitution which says that offices of Seimas (Parliament) controllers will be established with the mandate 'to examine complaints of citizens concerning the abuses of powers by and bureaucracy of, State and local government officers (with the exception of judges). Controllers shall have the right to

---

40 Letter to Povilas Gylys, Minister for Foreign Affairs of the Republic of Lithuania (5 March 1993), CSCE Communication no. 124/93.

submit proposals to the court to dismiss guilty officers from their posts'. He said that 'the drafters of the Constitution were very impressed by Scandinavian experience of Ombudsmen activities, and this Article 73 is an attempt to reflect this experience in our presently reformed state governing system'.[41] He promised to keep the High Commissioner informed of developments relating to the legal establishment of the powers of controllers. The matter was not pursued by the High Commissioner.

41 Letter from Foreign Minister Gylys to Van der Stoel (16 April 1993), CSCE Communication no. 124/93.

Croatia

The involvement of the High Commissioner in Croatia began on the day that the General Framework Agreement for Peace in Bosnia and Herzegovina (also known as the Dayton Accords) was signed. The reason that he did not become involved earlier is that he is an instrument of conflict prevention rather than of conflict resolution.

However, Croatia was one of the few cases where Van der Stoel was involved in post-conflict rehabilitation. As he once explained, there is a fine line between where one conflict ends and another begins. In terms of inter-ethnic conflict, post-conflict rehabilitation can be considered a type of conflict prevention in the sense that 'even if violence has come to an end, very often the underlying causes which led to the conflict have not been removed. In situations in which the threshold between non-violence and violence has been crossed before, renewed armed clashes are not unlikely'.[42]

The High Commissioner flew to Zagreb on 14 December 1995, one hour after the Dayton Accords were signed. The reason for his visit was to assess inter-ethnic relations between Croats and Serbs. Relations were tense as the war had brought about considerable population dislocation in both communities as well as distrust and fear. The future status of Eastern Slavonia was also a bone of contention.

The percentage of Serbs in Croatia dropped from 12.2% in 1991 to below 3% in 1996. Most of these Serbs fled Krajina during operations 'Storm' and 'Flash' carried out by the Croatian army in the summer of 1995. On the other hand, the Serb population in Eastern Slavonia rose when Croats fled the region in 1991 and Serbs, fleeing Western Slavonia and Krajina, arrived. One of the most

---

42 Speech at the CSCE Seminar on Early Warning and Preventive Diplomacy, Warsaw 19 January 1994.

pressing post-war issues was therefore the two-way return of refugees and internally displaced persons: in particular, Croats to Eastern Slavonia and Serbs back from Eastern Slavonia, Serbia and Republika Srpska to Krajina and Western Slavonia.

During his first trips to Croatia, the High Commissioner noted substantial inter-ethnic animosities and a tendency by the Croatian Government, strongly supported by the lower levels of Government, to make the return of Serbs (particularly in the Krajina and Eastern Slavonia) as difficult as possible. He looked at a whole range of issues concerning the two-way return of refugees, studied the legal situation regarding minorities in Croatia and made a series of recommendations to the Government. These recommendations related to overcoming administrative and practical difficulties concerning housing, property rights, an amnesty law, and legislation to protect the rights of persons belonging to national minorities. He was also concerned about the security situation including demilitarization and refugee return. Generally speaking, he encouraged the Government to promote a process of inter-ethnic reconciliation.

Although his main focus was on the treatment of Serbs, Van der Stoel tried to be even-handed. He once wrote to Deputy Prime Minister and Minister for Foreign Affairs, Mate Granič: 'my interest in the return of refugees does not restrict itself to those residents of Croatia who are of Serb ethnicity but equally to the tens of thousands of Croats who had to flee during the war'.[43] He appealed to the Serb population to stay. At the same time he urged the Croatian authorities to create conditions in which Serbs would be satisfactorily integrated into Croatian society.

Refugee return and inter-ethnic reconciliation were the main priorities of the international community in Croatia and Van der Stoel often discussed the issue with international organizations involved there, particularly the United Nations Transitional Administration in Eastern Slavonia, Baranja and Western Sirmium (UNTAES) and the European Community Monitoring Mission (ECMM). An OSCE Mission to Croatia was established in April 1996 and it began its operation in July 1996.

However, the initial size of this Mission was very small and as the UNTAES mandate was due to expire in 1997, people began to look to the post-UNTAES

---

43 Letter to Mate Granič Deputy Prime Minister and Minister for Foreign Affairs of Croatia (23 August 1996), HC/11/96.

period. On 26–28 September 1996 Van der Stoel presided over a Round-table in Bizovac (Croatia) on 'Practical long-term solutions for stability in Eastern Slavonia, Baranja and Western Sirmium'. On the one hand the meeting was useful in focusing on the need for continued international efforts in assisting (and sometimes prodding) the Croatian Government concerning inter-ethnic integration in the area. On the other hand, it was useful in building confidence among the parties. The Serb representatives said that they would respect the sovereignty and territorial integrity of Croatia and at the same time were pleased that the Croats were interested in serious dialogue. A follow-up meeting was held in Trakoscan, Croatia on 11 to 13 October 1996. A number of points were further clarified and agreement was reached on specific issues which needed to be addressed in the post-UNTAES period. For example, assurances were given concerning adequate police protection and provisions were included on non-discriminatory employment and economic practices. These were important confidence-building measures. Another of the agreed points was that the Croatian Government would fully comply with the long-term monitoring of human rights in the Danube Region. This paved the way for the significant strengthening of the capabilities of the OSCE Mission to Croatia in order to effectively take over many of the functions fulfilled by UNTAES. A meeting, hosted by the High Commissioner, was held in Vienna on 4 November 1996 that helped to further define an expanded role for the OSCE in Croatia.

On 26 June 1997 the Permanent Council decided to significantly expand the capabilities of the Mission (up to 250 expatriates) and authorized it to assist with and monitor implementation of Croatian legislation and agreements entered into by the Croatian Government on: a two-way return of all refugees and displaced persons and on protection of their rights, and the protection of persons belonging to national minorities.

Obviously, the Mission's work over-lapped to a great extent with that of the High Commissioner. Both Van der Stoel and the Head of Mission stressed that the work would be mutually re-enforcing rather than overlapping, but in reality there were frictions as to areas of competence and who should take the lead role on certain issues. As a result, to a certain extent, Croatia slipped down Van der Stoel's agenda. That being said, the High Commissioner made several visits to Croatia at the request of the Mission in order to help it to raise a particular issue to a higher political level or to give expertise on specific issues relating to the protection of persons belonging to national minorities. He paid particular attention to the situation in Eastern Slavonia.

Between 1996 and 1998 the High Commissioner made a number of visits to different parts of Croatia including the Knin area, Eastern Slavonia, and Zagreb. On his trips he was repeatedly dissatisfied by the failure of the Government to create the conditions necessary for the return of Serbs from Eastern Slavonia to Krajina. In some cases he attributed the problem to a lack of proper legislation. In others, it was the failure of the Government (or often regional and local authorities[44]) to implement legislation that had been passed.

While Van der Stoel pressured the Croatian Government to introduce meaningful reforms, he also urged the Serbs to stay in Croatia. Indeed, in January 1997, at the request of the UN Administrator, Jacques Klein, Van der Stoel took the uncharacteristic step of holding a press conference in Vukovar were he appealed to the Serb population to actively participate in the upcoming local elections in particular and political life in general.

Still, his main priority was to hold the Croatian Government to its word concerning creating conditions for the 'voluntary, safe, dignified and speedy return of all displaced persons and refugees, regardless of their nationality and ethnic origin'.[45] He warned the Croatian Government that a failure to do this would reflect badly on the country and delay its closer integration into Western Europe. In a letter to Foreign Minister Granič on 2 June 1998 he said unequivocally: 'Mr Minister, you have yourself mentioned to me that the successful integration of the Danube Region constitutes a test of the credibility of Croatia. You might agree with me that the continuation, and possibly in the coming months the further increase, of the outflows of Serbs to Serbia and the Republika Srpska would constitute a failure of this integration process'.[46]

Despite his warnings the abuses continued. For example, the High Commissioner was concerned that the amnesty law was not being properly implemented.

44 Van der Stoel, in characteristic diplomatic understatement, noted in a letter to Foreign Minister Granič on 8 October 1997: 'I am of course aware that instructions to the relevant authorities have been sent in the past to ensure that government policies will be properly implemented, but I would hope that some further steps will be taken in cases where such instructions have apparently not had the desired effect'. HCNM.GAL/3/97.

45 As cited in letter to Mr Granič (4 April 1997). HC/6/97.

46 Letter to Foreign Minister Granič (2 June 1998).

The law provided that Serbs who had fought against the Croats (with the exception of war criminals) would not be punished. However, a number of Serbs (who clearly met the requirements for amnesty) were arrested and others faced harrassment and intimidation, even by Croatian police. Van der Stoel noted the importance of police monitors in the post-UNTAES environment. (The OSCE later took on the role of police monitoring in the Danube region.)

Even with the constant pressure of the international community, little was done to stem the flow of Serb refugees from Croatia, particularly Eastern Slavonia. Time and again Van der Stoel appealed to the Government to take a number of steps to reverse the tide. These steps included: a clear public warning that no violence against temporary Serbian occupants of Croat houses would be tolerated; a public assurance that the Government wants to promote equal access to employment for all ethnic groups; the introduction of measures to ensure equal access to reconstruction assistance; and a public assurance that no new indictments for war crimes would be started without the evidence being established in co-operation with the International Criminal Tribunal for Yugoslavia.[47] He was also concerned about improving dialogue between the Croat and Serb communities.

A Joint Council of Municipalities (situated in Vukovar) was established pursuant to the Erdut Agreement of November 1995 in order to facilitate dialogue. Having studied the proceedings of the Council, Van der Stoel proposed that its powers should be strengthened in order to give Serbs more input into processes that affect them. He therefore helped work out a formula between the Croat Government and Serb representatives to increase the effectiveness of this body. It was given the right to propose candidates for a number of junior minister positions, to follow the implementation of the cultural and educational autonomy and the implementation of the human rights of the Serbian minority, and to analyze the promised proportional representation of Serbs in the police and public sector. It was also given the right to make recommendations on this range of issues and to have biannual meetings with the President and/or his Chef de Cabinet.

In 1998, in an effort to increase the effectiveness of the Council, Van der Stoel requested the Foundation on Inter-Ethnic Relations to establish a capacity-building project and to attach an external consultant to the Council. Together

47 *Ibid.* and letter to Granič (28 June 1999).

with the Mission he was engaged in raising funds to support the Council's activities. The High Commissioner also helped the Council to elaborate its own fund-raising. In 1999 a Legal Aid Project was set up to offer legal aid and representation in courts and during administrative procedures for persons belonging to minorities facing legal difficulties in regard to property, employment, or in obtaining official documents and validating documents issued during the war by the Serb self-government.

Van der Stoel also facilitated dialogue by organizing a seminar in the summer of 1999 on the Oslo and Hague Recommendations. This provided a rare opportunity to bring together Government officials and minority representatives to discuss minority education and minority language use.

In order to provide returnees with affordable (often *pro bono*) legal advice on issues of citizenship, status and property rights, the High Commissioner arranged through the Foundation on Inter-Ethnic Relations to create a Legal Clinic for the Knin area. The clinic not only provides legal advice but also takes up the cases of returnees before the respective administrative bodies courts.

In all of these respects Van der Stoel was able to exert constant pressure on the Croatian Government concerning its commitments as regards persons belonging to national minorities. He was also able to offer expertise and specific projects to facilitate inter-ethnic reconciliation and integration.

The death of President Franjo Tudjman in December 1999 and the parliamentary and presidential elections in January and February 2000 changed the political climate in Croatia. This was evident to the High Commissioner during a trip to Croatia in May 2000. It was clear from meetings with President Stipe Mesic and members of the new government that they were determined to make a break with the past. Statements by the Government gave hope that progress would be quickly made on some of the issues on which the High Commissioner had previously faced considerable resistance from the Tudjman regime: elimination of the discriminatory provisions from laws concerning the status of refugees and the implementation of the Amnesty Law.

However, it soon became clear that the resistance of local and regional authorities often blocked essential reforms, particularly concerning housing and occupancy rights.

In May 2000 Van der Stoel visited the Danube Region (Eastern Slavonia, Baranja and Western Sirium). In September he traveled to an area near the Croatian border with Bosnia where many Serbs had fled during the war. On both trips it was evident that inter-ethnic tensions still simmered and that many issues (like facilitating the process of return, and questions concerning housing and employment) remained unresolved. New arrests of ethnic Serbs renewed doubts about the full implementation of the amnesty law. There was also a clear discrepancy between the willingness of the central government to tackle these issues, and the hesitancy of local officials to act. This was fresh on Van der Stoel's mind when he told an OSCE meeting in October 2000 that 'it is unacceptable that the policy of the Government to facilitate the return of Serbs to their places of origin is frequently sabotaged at the local level.'[48]

In a speech to an international conference in Zagreb in December 2000 Van der Stoel addressed the question of return saying:

> 'I would like to draw particular attention to the fact that the right of return to one's place of origin and home, both voluntarily and in conditions of safety, is of fundamental importance. The primary responsibility lies with the state of origin to create and ensure conditions of return. The right of return also has a bearing on regional peace and security since the prolonged displacement of large numbers of persons can be destabilizing. Of course, conditions of return also imply respect for all other human rights in order to integrate societies and avoid the recurrence of displacement.'[49]

Van der Stoel was concerned about a decision by the government to link repossession of property owned by Serbs to the requirement of alternative accommodation for the occupants who would have to leave. On the margins of the conference, Van der Stoel took the opportunity to discuss the latest developments concerning the Constitutional Law on Minorities and to meet with the President of Serb National Council in Croatia. In the following months he continued to assist the Croatian Government to promote inter-ethnic dialogue and to create a legal framework for the protection of minority rights in line with international standards.

48 Speech at the OSCE Human Dimension Implementation Review Meeting, Warsaw, 17 October 2000.

49 'Minority Rights, Participation and Bilateral Agreements', speech to an international seminar in Zagreb, 4 December 2000.

Czech Republic
Poland
Slovakia
Kosice
Ukraine
Vienna
Bratislava
Austria
Budapest
Hungary
Slovenia
Ljubljana
Croatia
Zagreb
Romania
Subotica
VOJVODINA
Vukovar
Novi Sad
Belgrade
Federal Republic of Yugoslavia
SERBIA
Bosnia and Herzegovina
Sarajevo
Knin
Adriatic Sea
SANJAK
Novi Pazar
MONTENEGRO
Podgorica
Pristina
KOSOVO
Bulgaria
Sofia
Tetovo
Skopje
Gostivar
former Yugoslav Republic of Macedonia
Tirana
Italy
Albania
Strait of Otranto
Gjirokastra
Saranda
Delvina
Greece
Athens
N
0
100 km
© Dora Kemp
Capital city
City

Albania

The High Commissioner was actively involved in Albania between 1993 and 1994, focusing mainly on the situation of the Greek minority. His involvement began at a time when relations between the Albanian Government and the Greek minority were deteriorating to the point of having a negative impact on relations between Albania and Greece. The High Commissioner's quiet shuttle diplomacy and confidential talks with the Albanian President, the Governments of Albania and Greece and representatives of the Greek minority resulted in an easing of tensions and the prevention of conflict. His recommendations on issues such as minority education, dialogue between the Government and the minority, restitution of, or compensation for, church property confiscated by the communist regime and the strengthening of democratic institutions in the country were widely seen as having a calming effect on the inter-ethnic situation. The implementation of his recommendations facilitated the creation of frameworks for minority rights protection to the extent that when civil unrest erupted between 1996 and 1998 it did not take on an inter-ethnic dimension.

In the summer of 1993, the High Commissioner visited both Albania and Greece to form a better understanding of the situation regarding the Greek minority in Albania and the Albanian minority in Greece. Despite protestations by Albanian President Sali Berisha that minority situations in Greece and Albania should be given equal attention, the problems of Albanians in Greece related mainly to migrant workers whereas the situation of the Greek minority in Albania was endangering inter-ethnic tensions. Van der Stoel therefore decided to focus most of his attention on the situation in Albania, particularly the southern region of the country in the districts of Gijokastra, Saranda and Delvina where the Greek minority is concentrated.

On 10 September 1993, the High Commissioner submitted a letter to the then Foreign Minster of Albania, Alfred Serreqi, which contained a number of recommendations to the Albanian Government. The recommendations dealt mainly with the need for further developing and strengthening democratic institutions, including full respect for human rights and the rule of law.

Noting that the Albanian Government had introduced a number of policies relating to national minorities, the High Commissioner stated that

> 'it is of the greatest importance that your Government will consistently carry out the policies it has outlined to me, and will ensure that the minority will be fully informed about them. Policies aimed at strengthening democratic institutions, implementation of the norms laid down in the Copenhagen Document and improvement of the educational opportunities for the Greek minority will promote interethnic harmony and thus enhance the stability of the country.'[50]

Van der Stoel also stressed the importance of reflecting constitutional provisions regarding persons belonging to national minorities in future legislation. He noted that 'continuing progress in the transition from dictatorship towards a democratic system which is now going on in Albania provides the best guarantees for the legitimate interests of the Greek community in your country'.[51]

The High Commissioner recommended that the Government should establish a special governmental office for minority questions, speed up the process of restitution, or compensation for, property of the churches which were confiscated during the communist regime. Furthermore, he urged the Government to give priority to the completion of legislation on the educational system.

In the summer and autumn of 1994 relations between Albania and Greece deteriorated when five activists of the Greek association *Omonia* were arrested. The High Commissioner closely followed the arrest and trial of the five activists and had numerous discussions with high-level representatives in Tirana and Athens in an effort to avoid a further deterioration of relations over the incident. The activists were later released, in large part due to the calming effect that the High Commissioner's involvement had on creating an environment of constructive inter-ethnic dialogue.

In October 1994, together with international experts, he paid a second visit to Albania, mainly to the south of the country, in order to make a thorough

---

50 Letter to Foreign Minister of the Republic of Albania Alfred Serreqi (10 September 1993), CSCE Communication no. 251/93.

51 *Ibid.*

study of inter-ethnic relations, particularly issues concerning the Greek minority.

The main issue which Greek representatives raised with the High Commissioner was the position of Greek language education outside so-called 'compact minority areas', especially in the cities of Gjirokastra, Saranda and Delvina. (Despite being the administrative centres of the three districts where the Greek minority was most highly concentrated, the Greek population did not make up an absolute majority of the population in these cities and the Albanian Government therefore maintained that the cities themselves could not be considered minority areas.) They wanted more possibilities for members of the Greek minority to educate their children in their mother tongue.

Having become aware of the problems, the High Commissioner tried to work out solutions which would be acceptable to all parties concerned. He suggested to Albanian President Sali Berisha that third-party involvement in the field of minority education could be beneficial, including the financing of projects aimed at supporting Greek language education. The Foundation on Inter-Ethnic Relations was charged with following up on this point, in co-operation with the Albanian Ministry of Education and the Institute for Pedagogical Research. Various projects were analyzed including improvements in teacher training, curriculum development and textbooks. Implementation of these projects had to be abandoned amid the worsening security situation in 1997.

The High Commissioner and experts who had travelled with him to Albania in October addressed the education issue in their letter to the acting Foreign Minister dated 2 November 1994. They noted that through the policies implemented by the Government, 'assimilation is actively prevented and pluralism is protected, while it is legitimate under international instruments to pursue a policy of integration into a common society'.[52] They came to the conclusion that the requirements regarding educational rights of persons belonging to national minorities as laid down in the CSCE Copenhagen Document of 1990, and other international standards, had been met by Albania. However, they noted that there was room for improvement in the education system in general and minority language education in particular.

---

52 Letter to the Foreign Minister of the Republic of Albania Mr Arian Starova (2 November 1994), Ref. 2959/94/L.

A number of recommendations were made concerning the school bus system, the opportunities for optional classes in Greek and other languages, and the minimum number of pupils required to start such classes. Another recommendation dealt with the question of the education of children from mixed marriages. The experts suggested that the parents concerned should be able freely to decide on a child's attendance of a Greek language school or of Greek optional classes, even if the child had been registered as Albanian at birth.

The recommendations covered other aspects of society which had a bearing on inter-ethnic harmony. For example, in relation to complaints by the Greek community that persons of Greek nationality had been dismissed from the Albanian army and the police force on ethnic grounds, the High Commissioner and his experts recommended that ways should be sought of increasing the number of police officers of Greek origin serving in Greek minority communities. A recommendation was also made that a programme of special training for Albanian police personnel in the field of human rights should be established.

Concerning discrimination in general, the report suggested that the Albanian Government should consider adherence to those international legal instruments which provide for complaints by individuals. The experts noted that 'even in a situation where no discrimination is actually taking place, we observe that social peace is enhanced if mechanisms exist to address such allegations'.[53]

The High Commissioner and his experts also made recommendations on the need to undertake efforts to rebuild religious communities in Albania and on the process of restitution of, or compensation for, church property confiscated during the communist period.

The main focus was, however, on education. The report described as 'an important step forward' the opening, on 1 October 1993, of a new branch of Gjirokastra University, providing four-year courses to prepare teachers in the Greek language.

A central recommendation was that the Government should, as a matter of priority, draft and adopt a Law on Education. This recommendation was implemented on 21 June 1995 with the adoption of the Law on the System of Pre-University Education. The law guarantees the equality of all citizens in the sphere of education irrespective of nationality (including the right to study and be taught in their mother tongue), and creates a legal framework for establishing

---

53 *Ibid.*

minority language public schools. The law also contains provisions on establishing private schools, including those in which instruction may be carried out in foreign languages or in which religious subjects may be taught.

The passage of this law accelerated the process of Greek–Albanian rapprochement which had started with a visit of Minister of Foreign Affairs of Greece Karolos Papoulias to Tirana in March 1995.

One year later, the President of Greece Konstandinos Stephanopoulos paid an official visit to Albania. During the visit, on 21 March 1996, the Ministers of Foreign Affairs, Alfred Serreqi and Theodoros Pangalos, signed a Treaty of Friendship, Cooperation, Good Neighbourliness and Security between Albania and Greece. President Berisha received assurances that Athens would consider legalization of the status of Albanian immigrants working in Greece. The Albanian side promised to consider possibilities for an extension of Greek language education in Albania, especially in the three southern cities of Gjirokastra, Saranda and Delvina.

On 5 August 1996, the Albanian Government took a decision to expand Greek language education. According to the decision, Greek language classes can be formed within existing Albanian schools in the three southern cities provided that there are a minimum of 20 pupils in the class. The Ministry of Education undertook measures to implement this decision in practice. In September 1996, the Government gave a positive response to an application presented by a Greek non-governmental organization to establish a private school in Tirana, which would offer courses in different languages, including Greek.

The High Commissioner's work in Albania was important in heading off a potential conflict between the Greek minority and the Albanian Government and for improving strained relations between Greece and Albania on the issue of minority rights. It was also an important contribution to the process of building democratic institutions and civil society in Albania. Although that process was derailed between 1996 and 1998, a new constitution was approved by a national referendum in November 1998. As the focus is no longer on national minority issues, but rather on strengthening the foundations of democratic government and institutions, the emphasis of OSCE involvement has shifted to the OSCE Presence in Albania which, together with organizations like the Council of Europe, plays an important role in assisting the development of civil society in Albania.

The former Yugoslav Republic of Macedonia

The High Commissioner was actively involved in the former Yugoslav Republic of Macedonia (fYROM) for the duration of his period in office. Indeed, he visited the country more than fifty times during his period as High Commissioner. Most of his activities were focused on the status of the sizeable Albanian minority which is concentrated mostly in the west of the country. He worked to defuse tensions on specific issues and to promote inter-ethnic dialogue and co-operation. This involved him in issues concerning a national census, minority language education (especially higher education), the employment of Albanians in public service, minority access to the media, local self-government, and the use of minority flags. In addition to these internal issues, the High Commissioner paid close attention to the spillover effects of the crisis in neighbouring Kosovo and how this affected inter-ethnic relations in the fYROM.

Van der Stoel began his active involvement in the former Yugoslav Republic of Macedonia in June 1993. At that time, the international position of the country was in question. Although Macedonia declared its independence in September 1991, it was not recognized by some of its neighbours (most notably Greece) and was admitted to the United Nations under its provisional name as 'the former Yugoslav Republic of Macedonia'. Bilateral and multilateral relations were complicated by the precarious regional security situation in Southeast Europe. The Government also had to contend with a complex internal political environment.

In Macedonia, inter-ethnic relations were frequently at the centre of political disputes and politics was often polarized along ethnic lines. Ethnic Albanians (who make up at least one quarter of the population) were aggrieved by what they perceived as policies that made them second-class citizens. They cited economic indicators and the preamble of the Constitution that speaks of 'Macedonia as a national state of the Macedonian people' to support their view. Meanwhile, the Macedonians, already wary of their tenuous relations with their neighbours, feared internal instability if the demands of the Albanians were met. Furthermore, they were concerned that the ideas of the Albanian community in favour of a confederation instead of the existing unitary State could lead to the break-up of the country. Preventive activity in the field of inter-ethnic relations was therefore important for promoting internal and regional security.

After his first visit in June 1993 (when he met with the highest officials of the republic and representatives of national minorities), the High Commissioner formulated a number of initial recommendations which focused on the census of the population, inter-ethnic dialogue, minority language education, participation of minorities in public affairs, non-discrimination, the role of local self-government, access to the media and citizenship. His findings and suggestions played an important role in the final formulation of the report of the CSCE Rapporteur Mission to the fYROM that paid a visit to the country the same month (and, as result of its findings, recommended that the fYROM should be an OSCE participating State).

The High Commissioner returned to the fYROM in October 1993. His impression was that the situation had deteriorated due in particular to wrangling over the question of a census and to deteriorating economic conditions. He also noted the Government's concern at the lack of consensus over the admission of the fYROM to the CSCE. He formulated a number of recommendations that he communicated to the Foreign Minister of the Republic in a letter dated 1 November 1993.

In the letter he devoted most of his remarks to the importance of holding a census under international supervision. This was particularly important to the Albanians who felt that official figures underrepresented the size of the ethnic Albanian community in the Republic and felt that a more accurate reflection of their numbers would improve their chances of getting better state support in areas like education. The High Commissioner also proposed the establishment of a pedagogical faculty for the training of teachers who would teach in the Albanian language. Furthermore he stressed the need to reinforce the competencies of the Council for Inter-Ethnic Relations (a constitutional body in which all ethnic groups in fYROM participate) in order to promote inter-ethnic harmony and, when necessary, to initiate an investigation of events triggering inter-ethnic tensions. He also recommended that staffing of Government departments, the military and police should more adequately reflect the recognized minorities. He also expressed his regret that no decisive progress had been made concerning the law on local self-government 'notwithstanding the fact that clarity about the role and competencies of local government is clearly needed'.[54] These recommendations were aimed at overcoming what he perceived as a wide gap between the Macedonian and Albanian communities. He often remarked that he was struck by the fact that the communities lived in two very separate worlds.

In January 1994 the High Commissioner again visited the Republic. The main purpose of his visit was to seek a better understanding between Greece and Macedonia in the light of continued Greek resistance to the latter's participation in the CSCE. He also closely followed developments within the ethnic Albanian parties as they jockeyed for position in the run-up to parliamentary and presidential elections. He tried to defuse the issues (particularly concerning the census and education) which threatened to polarize and destabilize the communities in Macedonia.

With financial support from the European Union and technical support from the Council of Europe, a census went ahead in June and July of 1994. Van der Stoel paid a special visit to the country during this period in order to contribute to the international supervisory efforts. The census revealed that ethnic Albanians constitute nearly 23% of the entire population, which makes them by far the largest minority. This figure is disputed by ethnic Albanians who claim that the percentage is even higher.

The High Commissioner next visited the fYROM in November 1994 after the publication of the census results and the parliamentary and presidential elections. He was again struck by the potentially destabilizing effects of economic deterioration and the fragile state of inter-ethnic relations. In a letter to the Foreign Minister dated 16 November, Van der Stoel offered a number of recommendations designed to promote inter-ethnic harmony. In line with the observations of election monitors, he suggested a number of electoral reforms. A major recommendation was that the length of time that a person would have to reside in the country before acquiring citizenship (and therefore the right to vote) should be reduced from fifteen to five years. This was in line with the practice used in many OSCE participating States.

---

54 Letter to Stevo Crvenkovski, Minister for Foreign Affairs of the former Yugoslav Republic of Macedonia (1 November 1993), CSCE Communication no. 305/93.

Concerning education, he stressed that efforts were required to increase the percentage of Albanian pupils continuing their education at the secondary school level. He also reiterated his recommendation relating to the training of Albanian teaching staff for elementary schools.

He recommended that the draft law on local self-government should be re-submitted to the newly elected parliament. He underlined the importance of articles 79–82 of the draft which contained provisions on the official use of the languages and alphabets of the country's various ethnic groups in units of local self-government where they constituted a majority or a significant part (according to the law 20%) of the population. The law was adopted in 1995.

He once again urged the Government to intensify its efforts to achieve a more balanced ethnic composition of the personnel in the various branches of the public service. He also recommended that broadcasts in the Albanian language be increased. Finally, he called for more effective use of the Council for Inter-Ethnic Relations as an instrument for inter-ethnic dialogue.

In the course of 1995, educational issues, including the question of the so-called 'Albanian University' in Tetovo, were the main focus of the High Commissioner's activities in Macedonia. The creation of this university, without previous consultation with, and the consent of, the authorities, resulted in increased tensions. On the one hand it raised the spectre of 'parallel institutions' (as in Kosovo), while on the other, the clear desire by the ethnic Albanians to have better access to higher education could not be ignored. The High Commissioner pointed out, both publicly and during conversations with the highest Macedonian officials and representatives of the Albanian minority, that international instruments recognized the right of persons belonging to national minorities to establish their own educational institutions, but that this right must be exercised within the framework of, and in conformity with, national legislation.

During a visit to Macedonia in January 1995 he urged the Government to accommodate the Albanian aspirations for a university and, at the same time, appealed to the self-proclaimed rector of Tetovo University to choose legal ways to achieve his aims. However, the issue became increasingly divisive and threatened to erupt into violence.

Tensions rose in February when an Albanian demonstrator was killed and a number of people (including policemen) were injured during an unauthorized demonstration on the occasion of the opening of the so-called Albanian

University in Tetovo on 17 February. At short notice the High Commissioner flew to Skopje to try to defuse the situation. He called for calm and dialogue in the process of searching for mutually acceptable solutions. In a public statement, made after a meeting with President Gligorov on 20 February 1995, he said that 'now is not the time for mass demonstrations, but for dialogue . . . the issues [of the university] should be discussed within the framework of preparing the new law on higher education. It cannot be enforced by illegal actions'.[55] Van der Stoel was instrumental in temporarily easing the tensions. However, he was eager to work with the Government to tackle the underlying issues which precipitated the violence.

He therefore visited the fYROM in March and again in May in order to look more closely at the contentious issue of higher education. One proposal that he made was to create a private Higher Education Center for Public Administration and Business that would offer courses in Albanian, Macedonian and English. He suggested that the Board should be made up of representatives of the Government and minorities and that the university could be financed in part by international assistance. He also looked into the question of Albanian language courses at the Pedagogical Faculties in Skopje and Bitola.

As the debate concerning higher education had led to a worsening of relations between Macedonia and Albania, the High Commissioner made a visit to both countries in July 1995 in order to get a better view of perceptions on both sides of the border. At the same time, he closely followed relations between fYROM and Greece. (A compromise between Greece and Macedonia was eventually reached. Macedonia became a full participating State in the OSCE in October 1995 under the name 'former Yugoslav Republic of Macedonia'. It was agreed that there would be further negotiations concerning the name.)

The High Commissioner visited the fYROM five more times before the end of 1996. The main focus of his visits was the Albanian language university of Tetovo. He met with representatives of the Government and the Albanian minority to constantly stress the need for dialogue and constructive solutions to the problem. In a letter to Foreign Minister Crvenkovski dated 28 April 1995 he expressed his views on the need for a compromise formula saying

'any further step towards creating a new institution of higher education must

55 Statement by the High Commissioner, 20 February 1995.

> be in accordance with the constitutional order and has to be in conformity with OSCE principles; such an institution would also have to have the purpose to contribute to inter-ethnic harmony; such an institution would have to respond to specific educational needs; and all population groups in the country ought to benefit from its creation.'[56]

On 17 and 18 December 1996, the High Commissioner chaired a round-table on the theme 'Building harmonious inter-ethnic relations in Macedonia'. The round-table, which was organized by the Foundation on Inter-Ethnic Relations, brought together leading personalities representing the Parliament, the Government, Albanian political parties, the Macedonian academic community, and local NGOs. The most relevant inter-ethnic issues facing the country were discussed, including the role of local self-government in a multi-ethnic society, minority education as a way of both preserving minority ethnic identity and strengthening the integration of the whole society and the participation of minorities in public affairs.

In March 1997, the High Commissioner visited the fYROM twice to review the latest developments in the country, including those with a direct bearing on inter-ethnic relations. He was concerned about demonstrations by Macedonian professors and students in Skopje against the Law on the Pedagogical Faculty (regarding the training of Albanian teachers in the Albanian language) and celebrations by ethnic Albanians in Tetovo and Gostivar over the victory of the Party of Democratic Prosperity of Albanians (PDP-A) in local elections. He expressed concern about rising inter-ethnic tensions and alarm at manifestations of intolerance during both events. The situation was clearly becoming more polarized. On the one hand, the PDP-A was on the verge of a campaign of civil disobedience while, on the other hand, there was a growing resistance amongst Macedonians against any further concessions to the Albanians.

The situation deteriorated in the summer when two Albanians were killed in riots in Gostivar on 9 July. The riots were the result of tensions which had been growing for several months concerning the use of flags on public buildings. For several months, the mayors of Tetovo and Gostivar had been flying the flag of the Albanian nationality (which is identical to the flag of the Republic of Albania)

---

56 Letter to Stevo Crvenkovski, Minister for Foreign Affairs of the fYROM (28 April 1995), HC/3/95.

next to the Macedonian flag on flagpoles in front of their townhalls. When this question was brought before the Constitutional Court, the Court ruled that this was a violation of the law on flags. When this decision was challenged by the municipalities of Gostivar and Tetovo, the Court confirmed the decision, ordering the municipalities to take down the Albanian flags. The flags were taken down by police in the early morning of 9 July. Rioting broke out later in the day: two Albanians were shot dead and one policeman and eight civilians were wounded.

The High Commissioner went to Gostivar immediately. He visited the scene on 10 July and met with members of the Government and the Albanian community. He stayed in the country for three more days to meet with as many interlocutors as possible. On 13 July he issued a statement in which he noted that the Mayors of Tetovo and Gostivar 'have persistently refused to implement the order of the Constitutional Court to remove the flags. Nor did they give any indication that they would change their attitude after adoption by Parliament of the new law on the use of the flags of nationalities, which restricts the use of the Albanian flag at the town halls to official State holidays'.[57] He went on to say that:

> 'In the coming period, it is in my view more important than ever before that all nationalities within the State strive to find solutions for inter-ethnic problems by rejecting ethnic hatred and intolerance and by seeking constructive and continuous dialogue, with equal rights for all ethnic groups as the guiding principle. In order to be successful, such a dialogue must be based on internationally accepted norms and standards, but it must equally be based on respect for the sovereignty and territorial integrity of the State as well as the Constitutional order and the Rule of Law.'[58]

During confidential meetings with the authorities, the High Commissioner supported a thorough parliamentary investigation into the alleged misuse of authority by the police. He also expressed himself in favour of an internationally organized training programme for the Macedonian police force. These issues

57 The flag of the Albanian nationality (which is identical to the flag of Albania) was also permitted during sport and cultural events.

58 Statement of the HCNM, 13 July 1997.

were taken up again during his visit to Skopje in late September 1997.

As always, the High Commissioner was also in close contact with representatives of the Albanian community, both moderate and hard-line.[59] In November 1997, he held consultations in The Hague with leaders of the Albanian Party for Democratic Prosperity. It was clear from the meeting that education remained one of their central concerns.

Upon the request of the High Commissioner, the Foundation on Inter-Ethnic Relations initiated a project in 1997 called the Transition Year Programme. The aim of the Programme is to provide interested Albanian secondary school students with a specialized course of preparation for university entrance examinations, thus increasing their chances of passing them successfully. Although it was initially resisted by Albanians (who felt that it directed attention away from the separate issue of a central university), statistics showed that the programme was successful in improving entrance examination results of Albanian students.

The High Commissioner followed the situation in Macedonia closely throughout 1998, particularly in the light of internal developments in neighbouring Albania and Kosovo. Although the situation beyond the borders was fragile, a dissipation of the crisis situation within Macedonia allowed the High Commissioner to work with the Government and representatives of the Albanian community on the core issues of difference, particularly education. He visited the country five times in 1998 in order to assist the parties in finding an accommodation to outstanding issues.

On 6 November 1998, the High Commissioner issued a comprehensive statement on a number of inter-ethnic issues in the fYROM. It was released soon after the completion of parliamentary elections, but before the new Government was formed. The statement was a series of recommendations on promoting inter-ethnic harmony which the High Commissioner wanted to bring to the attention of the President of the Republic, the leaders of political parties and to the general public.

In his statement, Van der Stoel stressed the importance of realizing common interests such as the maintenance of peace and stability, the promotion of economic development and the reduction of unemployment. He also said that

---

59 For example, during a visit to Macedonia in September 1997, he visited the former Mayor of Gostivar, Rufi Osmani, in prison.

ethnic groups are obliged to respect the territorial integrity of the State and the constitutional order. At the same time, he stressed the need for integrating the Albanian minority into Macedonian society. He emphasized that the essence of democracy is compromise: 'In a democratic multi-ethnic State a minority cannot impose a dictate on a majority, but neither can a majority afford to ignore the desiderata of a minority, even less so when it constitutes an important percentage of the population. In the interest of interethnic harmony and stability, both sides will have to modify some of their positions'.[60]

More concretely, on language education, the High Commissioner emphasized the need for improvement in the quality of Albanian schools at the primary and secondary levels, and for an improvement in teacher training for Albanian language teachers. He recommended the creation of a special Albanian Language State University College for teacher training. He also repeated his proposal for the creation of a private Higher Education Centre for Public Administration and Business. Other issues covered in the recommendations included taking steps to increase the number of ethnic Albanians in public services, and strengthening the role of local self-government. The High Commissioner followed up on these ideas when he visited Skopje in December 1998.

Although these views were quite positively received by the new Government (which included the Democratic Party of Albanians), the issues of education and decentralization dropped down the Government's agenda with the worsening of the situation in Kosovo. This was obvious to the High Commissioner during his visits to the fYROM in March, April and May of 1999. These visits coincided with a rising tide of refugees leaving Kosovo for Macedonia due to 'ethnic cleansing'. With more than 250,000 ethnic Albanians crossing the border into the fYROM in the spring of 1999, the inter-ethnic balance in the country was changing dramatically.

The High Commissioner was so concerned with the potential affect of the massive influx of refugees into the country that he issued a formal early warning for the first time in his six years as High Commissioner. After addressing the Permanent Council on 12 May, he issued a statement in which he said that 'the increase of the population of the fYROM of more than 10 per cent within a few weeks, resulting in a major change of the interethnic balance, is proving to be

60 Statement of the HCNM, 6 November 1998.

too big of a burden for the country'.[61] He called on increased international efforts to assist the refugees and to provide more support for the UNHCR's work in Macedonia and Albania. He also noted that 'the economic crisis in the fYROM caused by the conflict in the Balkans increases the risk of social discontent and interethnic tensions' and therefore urged donor countries to come forward with assistance.[62]

The Chairman-in-Office asked the High Commissioner to continue to follow the situation closely. On 1 June Van der Stoel flew to Skopje where he met with the Minister for Foreign Affairs, Aleksandar Dimitrov, leaders of the main political parties, and representatives of the international community in Macedonia.

On 3 June he updated the Permanent Council on the situation. He said that the potential for an acute crisis remained. He again outlined the difficulties that the Government of Macedonia was facing in coping with the refugee crisis and the danger of inter-ethnic tension as a result of the significant increase in the number of ethnic Albanians in the fYROM. He highlighted the humanitarian situation and repeated that the country's economic crisis, caused by the conflict in Kosovo, increased the risk of social discontent and inter-ethnic tensions. He reiterated his early warning and emphasized the need for the international community to share the responsibilities associated with the refugee crisis.

Shortly afterwards, the end of the military conflict in Kosovo and the withdrawal of Serb forces from the region, led to a rapid return of refugees to Kosovo. Van der Stoel visited Macedonia between 14 and 16 July. He was informed that the number of Kosovar Albanian refugees had fallen from 240,000 to 30,000. As a result, the Government was able to concentrate more on internal political developments like inter-ethnic relations, particularly in the context of higher education.

During his visit, particularly in discussions with Prime Minister Ljubco Georgievski and the chairman of the Democratic Party of Albanians (DPA), Arben Xhaferi, the High Commissioner noted a new atmosphere of constructive dialogue on the issue of an Albanian language university. The High Commissioner indicated to his interlocutors that he would remain closely engaged in helping to find a solution to this issue.

---

61 'OSCE High Commissioner on National Minorities addresses Permanent Council on Situation in the Former Yugoslav Republic of Macedonia' (12 May 1999).

62 *Ibid.*

He was true to his word. He returned in September 1999 and again in December and twice in February 2000. On his second visit in February 2000 he was accompanied by three international education experts. Discussions focused on the modalities of establishing an Albanian Language Institute of Higher Education. However these were bogged down on issues of funding, the subjects that should be taught, whether the university would be private or State-funded, and what the legal status of the university would be. The latter was particularly contentious as it was linked with the redrafting of a Law on Higher Education, including the recognition of a new institution of higher learning. The old Macedonian law on higher education (from the Yugoslav era) which was still in force did not allow for the creation of any institution with a curriculum in a language other than Macedonian or so-called 'world languages'. The High Commissioner and experts were actively involved in the preparation of the new law.

The High Commissioner paid a follow-up visit on 17 to 20 April. He presented detailed recommendations on the creation of a private Institute of Higher Education. He proposed that it should consist of two sections, one dealing with the training of teachers for the higher classes of primary schools and secondary education, and the other providing training for key positions in business management and public administration. He knew that the formula was not perfect. He noted that, 'It is a compromise. It would not win a beauty prize.'[63] Nevertheless, it was a concrete initiative which he felt could, finally, end the dispute on Albanian-language higher education which had been a source of inter-ethnic tensions for so long. He explained his views to members of the Government and the Albanian community. All interlocutors were receptive to the recommendations. Ways were also discussed for implementing the recommendations.

Throughout the spring discussions continued on the education law and the modalities of the university. The two were interlinked because the education law would create the legal basis for the private Institute of Higher Education with opportunities for the use of minority languages. Van der Stoel and the international education experts were closely involved in the preparation of the bill which was presented to the Macedonian Parliament in June. For example,

---

63 Quentin Peel, 'OSCE minorities chief aims for early action', *Financial Times*, 19 May 2000, p. 3.

a two-day meeting was held in Vienna with the Minister of Education, Mr Galev, to discuss the draft law. There was fierce opposition from both extremes: ethnic Albanian nationalists in Macedonia (including the rector of the unrecognized University in Tetovo) and some members of the archconservative Academy of Sciences and Arts in Skopje. Protests were organized against the bill and the proposed Institute. Even among those who supported the project there were wrangles about the recognition (or transfer) of credits for students who had studied at the Tetovo University, there were disagreements about the number and type of faculties for the new Institute and concerns about funding. The failure to resolve the education issue threatened to break-up the Government and risked heightening inter-ethnic tensions. As Van der Stoel said in an uncharacteristically candid interview to the *Financial Times*: 'So far, not a shot has been fired in Macedonia, but this problem has been dragging on for years. The Albanians are insisting that this year there should be some sort of solution. If nothing is done by the end of the year, the government will fall apart.'[64]

After heated debate, the Law on Higher Education was passed by the Macedonian Parliament on 25 July 2000. Article 95 stipulates that 'education at private higher education institutions may also be performed in the languages of national minority members or in world languages'. Article 198 allows for persons who attended education within various forms of civic initiatives (i.e. Tetovo University) to continue their studies at existing higher education institutions, and, after an assessment of the knowledge acquired, to request enrolment at the appropriate year of study. This opened the way for the fruition of the new project. As OSCE Chairperson-in-Office, Austrian Foreign Minister Benita Ferrero-Waldner, noted in a press release dated 26 July, the adoption of the Law on Higher Education represented 'an important measure in promoting the peaceful co-existence of different ethnic groups in the country'.[65] Observers acknowledged the personal efforts of Van der Stoel in defusing a 'potentially dangerous row'.[66] There were even rumors that the new institution would be

64 Quentin Peel, 'OSCE minorities chief aims for early action', *Financial Times*, 19 May 2000, p. 3.

65 'Chairperson-in-Office welcomes adoption of Law on Higher Education by former Yugoslav Republic of Macedonia Parliament', Press Release, Vienna, 26 July 2000.

66 See for example 'Balkan pieces', editorial in the *Financial Times*, 1 August 2000.

called the 'Max van der Stoel College'.[67]

Despite this breakthrough, Van der Stoel remained cautious. He knew that the whole process risked unraveling. There was concern that Article 198 would be challenged before the constitutional court. There were still disagreements about the number of faculties to be included in the new university and what subjects they would encompass. Under the Law on Higher Education, a tertiary institution with five faculties is considered a University. A lower number would only allow it to have the title of Institution of Higher Education. Furthermore, the Albanian experts insisted on a teacher training faculty whereas Minister Galev supported a more modest proposal limited to teaching pedagogy. Van der Stoel tried to iron out these various problems in a round of meetings with international and Macedonian experts (including ethnic Albanian representatives) in Zurich and Skopje.

In October 2000 the High Commissioner presented a business plan for the new university which had been prepared by international and local experts. The plan included modalities for the establishment of the University and outlined the funding requirements. The latter was a vital consideration because the Macedonian Government made it clear early on that it could not contribute funding to the University, at least for a few years. Van der Stoel therefore sought support from a number of potential donors including some OSCE participating States, the European Commission and the Soros Foundation.

An international Foundation was soon established to manage international funds for the new institution, to provide international expert and executive support to oversee the implementation of the project, as well as to establish appropriate legal structures for the new institution in Macedonia. Its international board met for the first time in Zurich on 29-30 November.

It was eventually agreed that the university would be made up of five faculties including law, business administration, public administration, communication and computer studies, and teacher training. Curriculum would be in Albanian and courses would also be offered in Macedonian and other European languages. The project was officially unveiled in February 2001. In the following months Van der Stoel remained closely involved in the establishment of the project.

67 See 'New Law boosts Albanian college hope', *Financial Times*, 1 August 2000, p.3 and EU Statement on the HCNM, PC.DEL/412/00, 20 July 2000.

The University was scheduled to open its doors on 1 October.

In March 2001 violence erupted in Macedonia. It was decided to continue with the University project. Nevertheless, Van der Stoel was concerned by the flare up of inter-ethnic tensions. When shooting broke out in the hills overlooking Tetovo, Van der Stoel issued a joint press release with OSCE Chairman-in-Office, Romanian Foreign Minister Mircea Geona, that noted that 'everything possible should be done' to prevent armed conflict. He pointed out that 'recently, the chances of finding solutions for inter-ethnic differences have greatly improved. It would be a tragedy if the ongoing peaceful dialogue would be replaced by armed struggle'.[68] Van der Stoel tried to facilitate that dialogue and to address the root causes of the tensions during several visits to Macedonia in the spring of 2001. In addition to the University project, Van der Stoel provided advice on a number of issues including linguistic rights, the civil structure of the state, the census, and decentralization. Macedonia remained his highest priority during his last months as High Commissioner.

68 'Violence as a threat to peace and stability in the former Yugoslav Republic of Macedonia', Press Release, 15 March 2001.

The Federal Republic of Yugoslavia including Kosovo

While Slobodan Milosevič was President, Van der Stoel's room for maneuver in the Federal Republic of Yugoslavia was extremely limited. This was due in large measure to the fact that it was difficult for him to gain access to the country. As will be described below, his main involvement was in Kosovo in his capacity as a Personal Representative of the Chairman-in-Office rather than High Commissioner.

For the most part, until the autumn of 2000, Van der Stoel could only monitor inter-ethnic relations in Yugoslavia from a distance. He closely followed relations between Belgrade and Podgorica over the status of Montenegro. He kept an eye on efforts by the Hungarian minority in Vojvodina to develop political and legal frameworks for self-government. He also followed the proposals of Bosniac representatives in Sanjak to push for greater autonomy.

In the spring of 2000 Van der Stoel decided to organize a conference in Budva, Montenegro, to which representatives of various national minorities in Serbia as well as representatives of the Serb democratic opposition were invited. The main objective of the meeting was to evaluate the current situation regarding the minority situation in Serbia, to identify potential conflict situations and to discuss the future status of Serbia in the post-Milosevic era. As well as the minority issues in Sanjak and Vojvodina, it was clear from the meeting that there were also concerns among the Bulgarian, Croatian, Albanian, and Roma communities. The meeting was useful for the High Commissioner, but also afforded the various minority representatives an opportunity to develop a network of contacts.

When Milosevic was swept aside in October 2000, things moved quickly. On 15 November the Federal Minister of National and Ethnic Communities, Mr. Rasim Ljajic, invited Van der Stoel to Belgrade. The High Commissioner responded positively on 16 November and suggested that the visit should 'follow the pattern of first visits by me to other OSCE states, which usually include an opportunity to present myself to the Head of State and the Foreign Minister and to explain my role as High Commissioner on National Minorities'.[69] The Federal Republic of Yugoslavia joined the OSCE at the Vienna Ministerial Council meeting two weeks later. A member of the High Commissioner's staff participated in the OSCE Rapporteur Mission to Belgrade on 3–5 December and the High Commissioner visited one week later, from 11–13 December.

During his December visit, the High Commissioner met with a number of high-ranking Yugoslav officials including President Kostunica, the Minister of Foreign Affairs, Goran Svilanovic, and the Minister of National and Ethnic Communities, Rasim Ljajic. At the meeting with Ljajic, a basis for future co-operation between the Ministry and the High Commissioner's Office was worked out. In a visit to Belgrade in January 2001, Van der Stoel met with other leading officials including Prime Minister Djindic and the Federal Minister of Justice, Momcilo Grubac.

The High Commissioner monitored developments in several regions of the Federal Republic of Yugoslavia. In the second half of 2000 the High Commissioner's office provided legal advice to the Montenegran authorities on a draft law on symbols, and amendments to the law on use of personal names. Van der Stoel also closely followed relations between Podgorica and Belgrade, particularly after the collapse of the Milosevič regime. He was concerned about the potentially destabilizing effect that Montenegran independence could have in the region. In a letter to the editor in the *International Herald Tribune*, published on 2 February 2001, he wrote: 'For those who think that we should not bother trying to keep Bosnia and the Federal Republic of Yugoslavia together, what is the alternative . . . and where do we draw the line? Kosovo and Montenegro are not ethnically pure, nor is the rest of Serbia. Is separation a panacea for the interest of all communities, and if so, what would a map of Europe look like?'[70] He was not only concerned about the precedent that Montenegran independence would create, but also about the fact that more Montenegrans lived outside the province than in it, Serbs owned a significant amount of land in Montenegro, Sandzak's eleven municipalities were split between Serbia and Montenegro,

69 Letter from Van der Stoel to Foreign Minister Goran Svilanovic, Minister of Foreign Affairs of the Federal Republic of Yugoslavia, 16 November 2000.

70 Max van der Stoel, 'The Multiethnic State', *International Herald Tribune*, 2 February 2001, p. 7.

and Montenegran independence could complicate inter-ethnic relations within the new state and in the region. His views on a possible solution to revising the federal structure of Yugoslavia were stated in a speech in Bled, Slovenia on 23 February 2001 when he said: 'Self-government can be flexible in terms of the division of responsibilities between the centre and the regions. Functions may be allocated asymmetrically to respond to different minority situations within the same State. This seems particularly applicable to the Federal Republic of Yugoslavia at the moment'.[71]

The High Commissioner also followed developments in Vojvodina. Van der Stoel was particularly interested in the position of the Hungarian minority (which makes up approximately 15% of the province) which advocated three levels of autonomy (personal, local and provincial). He was also curious about the relationship between the provincial authorities (who also favored greater autonomy) and the central government. During a visit to Novi Sad in January 2001 he met with representatives of the Hungarian, Croat and Slovak minorities and well as the representatives of the Provincial Assembly.

Kosovo

Mr Van der Stoel became concerned with the situation in Kosovo at the beginning of his term as High Commissioner in 1993. Being actively involved in minority situations in the former Yugoslav Republic of Macedonia and Albania, he saw the close inter-relationship between those problems and the status of Albanians in the Yugoslav province of Kosovo. He immediately realized that without substantial progress in solving the Kosovo problem there could be no lasting stability in the region.

From the beginning, the nature of the High Commissioner's involvement in Kosovo was contentious. The debate over his role epitomized the divergent viewpoints which characterized inter-ethnic tensions in Kosovo.

During a visit to Tirana in December 1993, the High Commissioner met with Professor Ibrahim Rugova, head of the Kosovo Democratic League, to discuss the situation in Kosovo and the position of the Kosovo Albanians in solving the Kosovo question. Professor Rugova said that he did not object to

71 'Minority Protection, Integration and Stability in South-Eastern Europe', speech at a conference in Bled, Slovenia, 23 February 2001.

confidential meetings with Van der Stoel, but he did not support the formal involvement of the High Commissioner on National Minorities. He stressed that the ethnic Albanian community was not a minority, but a nation. Involving the High Commissioner would be a recognition of the status of the Kosovar Albanians as a national minority within the Federal Republic of Yugoslavia (FRY); this ran counter to their stated political objective of independence for Kosovo.

The suspension of Yugoslavia from the OSCE in June 1992 and the subsequent rejection of continued Yugoslav support for the OSCE Missions in Kosovo, Sandjak and Vojvodina also complicated the High Commissioner's role.

The situation in Kosovo remained relatively neglected by the international community, even after the signing of the Dayton Accords in December 1995. Although his scope for involvement in Kosovo remained limited, Van der Stoel remained concerned. He saw the danger of the further deterioration of the situation, particularly as there was a virtual lack of structured dialogue between the central authorities and political representatives of the Kosovar Albanians.

Following the 1 September 1996 agreement on education in Kosovo signed by President Slobodan Milosevic and Professor Rugova, the High Commissioner decided, in consultation with the then Chairman-in-Office (Swiss Foreign Minister Flavio Cotti), to try to initiate more constructive dialogue between the two parties with the aim of contributing to the overall solution of the problem. During a visit to Belgrade on 27 November 1996 (as a member of the International Commission on Missing Persons in former Yugoslavia) the High Commissioner met with President Milosevic who raised no objection to Van der Stoel visiting Kosovo in his capacity as High Commissioner on National Minorities.

Immediately after returning from Belgrade, the High Commissioner initiated contacts with the political leadership of the Kosovar Albanians. He was not able, however, to establish contact with Rugova and, under the constraint of time, decided to meet instead with the 'Prime Minister of Kosovo in exile' Bujar Bukoshi. Mr Bukoshi raised no objection to the involvement of Van der Stoel, but said that it was a matter of principle with the representatives of ethnic Albanian representatives from Kosovo that he could not be involved in his capacity as OSCE High Commissioner on National Minorities.[72] He suggested

72 For more on the Kosova Albanian position see John Packer, 'The role of the High Commissioner on National Minorities in the Former Yugoslavia', *Cambridge Review of International Affairs* xii/2 (spring/summer 1999), p. 177.

that Van der Stoel be involved in a different capacity. This idea was broached with the then Chairman-in-Office, Danish Foreign Minister Niels Helveg Petersen. As a result, on 6 February 1997 Van der Stoel was appointed Personal Representative of the Chairman-in-Office for Kosovo with a mandate 'to explore the possibilities for ways and means of reducing existing tensions as well as preventing potential tensions from building up [and] to explore the possibilities for a constructive dialogue on these issues between the authorities of the FRY and representatives of Albanians in Kosovo.'

Some members of the divided political leadership of the Kosovar Albanians (including Adem Demaci and Mr Bukoshi, notwithstanding his suggestion) still declined to co-operate with Van der Stoel '. . . for as long as he continues to remain as High Commissioner on National Minorities [since t]his would constitute a direct prejudgement and compromising of the political aspiration of Kosova as expressed through the general referendum. A people that has opted for independence has no need for minority rights'. Despite these objections, Van der Stoel persevered.

However, he soon encountered another hurdle. Referring to the suspension of Yugoslavia from the OSCE, the Belgrade authorities refused to grant him a visa to visit the country. This could be attributed in part to Belgrade's reaction to the strong condemnation of the flawed municipal elections of November 1996 made by another Personal Representative of the Chairman-in-Office, former Spanish Prime Minister Felipe Gonzalez. Another reason that may have influenced Belgrade's decision not to grant Van der Stoel a visa was that unlike the initial invitation issued in November 1996, this time Van der Stoel was not coming in his capacity as High Commissioner on National Minorities. The FRY authorities saw the involvement of the High Commissioner in the Kosovo crisis as recognition of the Kosovo issue as being a minorities problem and therefore a confirmation of the status of Kosovo as a province of Yugoslavia. In other words, Milosevic initially invited the HCNM to visit Kosovo for the same reasons that the Kosovo Albanians rejected him, and then refused to invite him for the same reasons that many Kosovo Albanians would have welcomed his involvement.

Because of these circumstances, Van der Stoel decided to continue his diplomacy outside of Yugoslavia, through quiet channels and through developing contacts with important personalities relevant to the crisis. Between 8 and 12 October 1997 he organized a closed round-table meeting of selected politicians and experts in order to discuss some specific issues and to promote possible solutions. The meeting, which was held in Dürnstein, Austria, was attended by a number of Kosovar leaders and Serb experts on Kosovo. The talks were designed as a purely informal and confidential forum. After the consultations, Van der Stoel prepared an extensive confidential report to the Chairman-in-Office. The report contained an analysis of the situation in and around Kosovo, and conclusions on possible steps to be undertaken by the international community in order to prevent further escalation of what he described as 'the most dangerous problem in Europe'.

At the same time in Pristina, the Independent Union of Albanian Students was organizing peaceful demonstrations to take place on 28 and 29 October 1997, while reports of a 'Kosovo Liberation Army' were increasing in frequency. Tensions were evidently rising and Rugova was clearly losing his grip on the situation. Violence erupted on 30 December 1997 when FRY police forcefully dispersed a peaceful student demonstration. Van der Stoel publicly condemned the violence on the part of the authorities and communicated his concerns to the new Chairman-in-Office, Polish Foreign Minister Bronislaw Geremek, and through him to the Contact Group.

In early January 1998, Van der Stoel prepared another confidential report for the OSCE Chairman-in-Office on the developments in Kosovo and its possible impact on regional stability, including the situation the former Yugoslav Republic of Macedonia and in Albania. His bleak assessment was that 'there is a considerable risk that in 1998, like in previous years, there will be no or only little progress towards the solution of the issue in Kosovo' indeed 'it can certainly not be excluded that the situation will even worsen. . . . The risk of such a scenario is sufficiently great to justify an analysis of what steps could be taken to assure the Kosovo conflict will not spill over to neighbouring countries as well'.

Following a visit to Belgrade on 19 January as a member of the ICMP during which he again met with President Milosevic, Van der Stoel sought and received a visa to visit the FRY, including Kosovo, in 'a private capacity'. For pragmatic reasons and upon approval of the OSCE Troika, he took advantage of this opportunity and paid a visit to Belgrade and Pristina between 17 and 20 February 1998. He had talks with high representatives of Serbian political parties and Serbian experts in Belgrade, as well as Kosovo Albanian leading politicians and experts in Pristina, including Professor Rugova. He also held talks with political representatives of Kosovo Serbs.

But by this point it was too late. Incidents of violence became more frequent and the Kosovo region seemed on the verge of erupting.

Fearing that the level of mistrust and violence was spiralling out of control, Van der Stoel took the unusual step of immediately submitting to the Permanent Council a report of his visit to the FRY. This was, in effect, an informal early warning. In it he noted continuing disputes concerning implementation of the education agreement, tension surrounding the elections for the 'Presidency' and 'Parliament' in Kosovo, and an increasing number of violent incidents. He wrote that 'the main conclusion I have reached during my visit is that the situation has clearly deteriorated in the last few months and will continue to deteriorate unless further progress will be made towards the eventual solution of the conflict. If this does not happen, the risk of increasing violence on the part of the Kosovars, followed by even harder repression by the Serb side, is very real'.

This 'early warning' raised the alarm about an impending explosion. Just a few days later, the explosion occurred as FRY security forces cracked down with indiscriminate and disproportionate force in response to a KLA attack on 28 February 1998 against a police patrol. The character of the situation was evolving from 'tensions' to 'conflict'.

In response to the crisis, the Contact Group proposed a number of diplomatic initiatives including a new mission for Felipe Gonzales as Personal Representative of the OSCE Chairman-in-Office for all of the FRY, including Kosovo. The Chairman-in-Office responded positively as did the Permanent Council at an emergency meeting in Vienna on 11 March 1998. In a letter dated 17 March Van der Stoel asked to be released from his function as Personal Representative for Kosovo.

It is impossible to speculate as to how effective Van der Stoel could have been had he been allowed access to the FRY in 1996. The fact that the crisis developed in slow motion over a period of several years leads one, in hindsight, to think that preventive diplomacy could have played a more effective role in heading off one of the worst conflicts in Europe since the Second World War. Van der Stoel once remarked:

> 'I do not think that we, the international community, tried hard enough . . . and for a long time we followed the policy of illusions . . . that we would

> see to it that a shot would never be fired, but developments pointed in another direction. The hope that it would be possible to have a partial solution for specific Kosovar problems, that miraculously some kind of atmosphere of confidence would develop in which the basic problem of the future of Kosovo would be solved – we clung to these ideas until it was too late. In other words we ought to have tried, but we didn't try hard enough.'[73]

On another occasion he said that the seriousness of the Kosovo crisis was underestimated.

> 'For a long time, moreover, western policies were based on two illusions. The first was that Rugova, with his great prestige, would be able to keep the internal situation in Kosovo under his control. In reality, however, power was gradually slipping from his hands. First the students started to follow their own course. A bit later, disregarding Rugova's pacifist leanings, the KLA came into being. The second illusion was that the Kosovo problem could be solved by concentrating on partial solutions, regarding education, the health services, the judiciary and so on. It was anticipated that each partial breakthrough would lead to an increase of mutual confidence between the parties and that finally an atmosphere would be created in which the key question of the future status of Kosovo could be resolved by negotiations. What was overlooked was that it was virtually impossible to make progress regarding partial solutions without touching the central question of the division of powers between the central authorities in Belgrade and the Albanians in Kosovo, with Milosevic refusing to restore the autonomy the Albanians enjoyed until 1989, and the Albanians insisting on independence.'[74]

---

73 Interview between Van der Stoel and Michael Ignatieff, 7 October 1999.

74 Interview, in Zellner & Lange 1999, p. 23.

Greece

The High Commissioner's involvement with Greece was of three varieties. The first related to Greece as a kin-State, particularly to the Greek minority in Albania. The second concerned bilateral relations between Greece and its neighbours, particularly Albania and the former Yugoslav Republic of Macedonia. And the third related to the treatment of national minorities in Greece.

The situation of the Greek minority in Albania has already been discussed above (in the section on Albania). To recap, the basic disagreements which led to a deterioration of inter-ethnic relations in Albania and bilateral relations between Greece and Albania included: a number of border incidents; Albanian suspicions over the activities of Greek–Albanian organizations Omonia and the Equal Rights Party in Albania and the treatment of several of Omonia's members after they were arrested in the spring of 1994; demonstrations by the Greek minority in Albania and the treatment of protestors by Albanian police; the closure of Greek schools in Albania; the status of the Orthodox Autocephalous Church of Albania and its (mostly Greek) clergy; and the expulsion of a Greek Orthodox priest from Albania on charges of distributing nationalist propaganda and maps that gave the impression that Southern Albania (or Northern Epirus as Greek nationalists refer to it) belongs to Greece. A nationalist furor was whipped up by the Greek media and inflammatory statements were made by some members of the Greek episcopate.

Van der Stoel made several trips to Albania in 1993 and 1994 to work with the Albanian Government to address some of the complaints raised by the Greek minority. On 24 August 1993 he was invited to Athens and met the Foreign Minister and the Prime Minister. He received assurances that the Greek Government would respect the territorial integrity of Albania and not reopen the question of 'Northern Epirus' (which was added to Albania in 1913), and that senior Government officials would talk to leading figures in the Greek Orthodox church to urge them to exercise moderation.

With these assurances, he continued to press the Albanian Government on a number of issues. He monitored the trial of five members of the Greek–Albanian cultural organization Omonia in 1994, even visiting them in prison. Although it is not in his mandate to take up individual cases, he felt that it was important to be involved as the trial had become highly politicized (producing claims and counter claims about violations of human rights and the mistreatment of minorities) and could be a catalyst in worsening inter-ethnic tensions in Albania and inter-State relations between Albania and Greece. He also looked at the situation of Greek schools in Albania and came up with a number of recommendations to improve the situation in a way that was agreeable to both sides (see Albania section). His main goal during that period was to facilitate dialogue between the Greek and Albanian Governments and to suggest ways out of the main points of contention. He tried to encourage both sides to calm down nationalist hysteria, and sought the support of OSCE participating States to do the same.

Albanian President Sali Berisha maintained that the High Commissioner should also look into the plight of the Albanian minority in Greece. Although Van der Stoel, rather hesitantly, agreed to take up the point with the Greek Government, Athens effectively quashed the idea as it said that it did not recognize the existence of an Albanian minority on its territory.

During his visits and conversations with Greek officials in 1993 and 1994, Van der Stoel raised the question of the fYROM's admission to the CSCE. The Greek Government complained about what they described as the irredentist policies of Macedonian President Gligorov. Van der Stoel pursued the possibility of the Greek Government softening its position if the Government in Skopje (as it was euphemistically referred to in order to get around sensibilities concerning the name Macedonia) would provide assurances that it had no territorial ambitions, would respect existing borders and would not interfere in the internal affairs of other States. No immediate breakthrough was reached, but with continued international pressure a compromise was eventually agreed upon and the fYROM was welcomed as an OSCE participating State in October 1995.

Van der Stoel also followed minority issues in Greece, particularly issues concerning the ethnic (Slav) Macedonians and the Turkish (Muslim) minority in Greek Macedonia and Western Thrace. The Greek Government denies the existence of minorities on its territory with the exception of the 'Muslim' minority which is protected under the 1923 Lausanne Treaty. Turks are lumped together with Pomaks (Slavs of the Muslim religion) as the 'Muslim minority' while past Governments have explicitly argued that a Macedonian minority does not exist in Greece. The High Commissioner's office received a steady stream of complaints and appeals from minorities in Greece concerning education, representation in public service, use of language, alleged forced assimilation, economic underdevelopment, citizenship, property, difficulties with travel and visas, cultural expression and exchanges with kin-communities on the other side of the Greek border (either in Turkey or the fYROM).

Van der Stoel brought up some of these points during a visit to Athens in October 1998. Whereas he had frequently encountered resistance to discussions on minority issues with Greek interlocators, he found a receptive ear in Greek Foreign Minister George Papandreou. Papandreou had known, and highly respected, Van der Stoel for many years since Van der Stoel (as Rapporteur for the Council of Europe) had supported his grandfather who was put under house arrest during the time of the Greek colonels junta in 1967–74 and, like his father who was in exile, had been an outspoken critic of the military regime. Among the issues discussed were the possibility of abrogating Article 19 of the Greek Citizenship Law by which Greek citizenship could be, and was, withdrawn from persons who resided outside Greece and failed to renew their passports and/or return to Greece. (This article was abolished later in the year.) He also raised the question of travel restrictions on non-ethnic Greeks born in Greece and on non-Greek citizens who used to live in Greece who tried to visit or return to the country. The situation in Western Thrace and the status of the Turkish minority there was also discussed, as was the Law passed in 1990 that granted the State wide-ranging powers in appointing the mufti, the community's religious leader who also serves as an Islamic judge in civil matters.

Although no substantive policy changes were made, the points raised by the High Commissioner found some resonance in remarks made by Foreign Minister Papandreou in a magazine interview in July 1999.[74] His remarks, including the sentence 'If they ['Muslims'] do not question the borders, I do not care if one is called Muslim, Turk, Bulgarian or Pomak', touched off a storm of controversy in Greece over questions of minority recognition, self-determination and the connotations of the OSCE Copenhagen Document.

---

74 Papandreou was interviewed in a magazine called *Klik* on 26 July, 1999.

Van der Stoel entered the debate after he was asked by the Greek section of the BBC World Service for a comment on the situation. In a statement issued on 23 August he tried to clear up the confusion surrounding the way that the Copenhagen Document was being interpreted by sections of the Greek media and political élite. He reminded the Greek authorities and public at large that

> 'The Copenhagen Document commits governments *inter alia* to provide persons belonging to national minorities the right freely to express, preserve and develop (individually as well as in community with other members of their group) their ethnic, cultural, linguistic and religious identity and to maintain and develop their culture in all aspects, to profess and practice their religion, and to establish and maintain organizations and associations.'[75]

In order to clarify the issue to self-determination, he explained that the right of self-determination relates to the status of territory but allowing minorities to freely express, preserve and develop their ethnic, cultural, linguistic and religious identity is something completely different. He stressed that 'the rights or persons belonging to national minorities to express, preserve and develop their identity is to be exercised within the existing boundaries of the State'.[76] This was a reiteration of his oft-stated position on the compatibility of self-determination and the territorial integrity of States, in other words 'internal' self-determination. He noted that the Copenhagen Document mentions territorial autonomy as an option but not as an obligation. At the same time, he noted that there was a common misunderstanding that minorities would have to be formally recognized by the State in order to enjoy the rights mentioned in the Copenhagen Document. He quoted paragraph 31 which provides as follows: 'persons belonging to national minorities have the right to exercise fully and effectively their human rights and fundamental freedoms without any discrimination and in full equality before the law'. He noted that the same principles of non-discrimination and equality also apply pursuant to Article 14 of the European Convention on Human Rights.[77] Reference was made to the fact that Greek law obliges an association of persons belonging to a national minority to be registered if it is to acquire

75 Statement of 23 August 1999, OSCE doc. HCNM.GAL/6/99.

76 *Ibid.*

77 *Ibid.*

legal personality 'for purposes of enjoying one of their enumerated rights'. But, he pointed out, 'the requirements for registration cannot be different from those for associations not composed of persons belonging to national minorities' for this would constitute a violation of the principle of non-discrimination. Discriminatory too would be the fact that a group is refused registration on the grounds that it is an association of persons belonging to a national minority.[78] This was a veiled reference to the Government's decision to ban an ethnic (Slav) Macedonian association called 'Home of Macedonian Civilization', a decision that was condemned by the European Court for Human Rights in a judgement of 10 July 1998.

Also in the statement of 23 August 1999, the High Commissioner addressed confusion about the relationship between the Treaty of Lausanne of 1923 and the Copenhagen Document. He said that although the former dealt with the religious rights of the 'Muslim minority' in Greece, the latter had relevance in the sense that 'within the wider religious group, there are smaller groups with an ethnic or linguistic identity of their own, such as Turks, Roma and Pomaks to which the provisions of the Copenhagen Document do apply'.[79]

The High Commissioner followed this up with a visit to Athens on 8 October 1999. Building on the more open position of Mr Papandreou and the rapprochement between Greece and Turkey which followed a series of serious earthquakes in the region, he wanted to reaffirm his views on the possibility of integrating diversity and to support voices of moderation and liberalism within the Greek Government. In his meetings he stressed to representatives of the minority communities that they should give public assurances that they would always respect the territorial integrity of Greece. Soon thereafter they gave exactly such public assurances. To Government officials, particularly Mr Papandreou, he stressed the need for fully implementing the chapter of the Copenhagen Document on national minorities and urged them to ratify the Council of Europe Framework Convention for the Protection of National Minorities without an overly restrictive interpretative declaration or reservation limiting its scope of application. These were small yet progressive steps in loosening up what, to that point, had been a very rigid position of the Government towards minorities within Greece.

---

78 *Ibid.*

79 *Ibid.*

Turkey

Although many Kurdish groups and international human rights NGOs repeatedly appealed to the High Commissioner to become involved in the Kurdish issue, this question fell outside the scope of his mandate. As he explained in a letter of July 1993 to Lord Avebury, Chairman of the Parliamentary Human Rights Group of the House of Lords, in response to the latter's request for information on the High Commissioner's potential role:

> 'What I have said . . . is that in the perception of the Turkish Government the PKK [Kurdish Worker's Party] is performing organized acts of terrorism, and that, as a consequence, the Turkish Government would strongly oppose my involvement in this question. It is also clear that, without the active co-operation on the part of the Turkish Government, I would not be able to play a useful role. . . . My mandate [also] precludes me from dealing with situations in which armed conflict has already broken out.'[80]

It is worth recalling, as Van der Stoel often did, that under paragraph 5b of his mandate 'The High Commissioner will not consider national minority issues in situations involving organized acts of terrorism'. Furthermore, under paragraph 25 'The High Commissioner will not communicate with and will not acknowledge communications from any person or organization which practices or publically condones terrorism or violence'. (It is no coincidence that Turkey was one of the States that pushed for these limitations to be included in the High Commissioner's mandate when it was discussed in 1992.) Finally, as Van der Stoel noted in his letter to Lord Avebury, the High Commissioner is an instrument of conflict prevention rather than crisis management.

There were, however, issues beyond the Kurdish crisis which the High

80 Letter to Lord Avebury, 19 July 1993.

Commissioner was interested in discussing with Turkish authorities. The Turkish Government has clear views on who is and who is not considered a minority. In an interpretative statement made after the agreement on the High Commissioner's mandate in December 1992, the Turkish delegation to the OSCE reiterated a statement that had been made at the Copenhagen and Moscow Meetings on the Human Dimension to the effect that according to the Turkish constitutional system, 'the word "minorities" encompasses only groups of persons defined and recognized as such on the basis of multilateral or bilateral instruments to which Turkey is a party'.[81] Van der Stoel was interested in probing this interpretation and entering into a dialogue with the Turkish authorities, much as he had done in Greece, to explain international standards relating to the protection of the rights of persons belonging to national minorities. He felt that a more open discussion on minority questions could have a bearing on a number of important security issues including Cyprus, Turkish–Greek relations, Turkey's eventual accession to the European Union and, of course, the Kurdish crisis.

Although it was clear to Van der Stoel that these issues (and his possible involvement in them) were considered taboo by Ankara, he sought a window of opportunity to make his views known. The opportunity came in April 2000 when he participated in a seminar hosted by the OSCE Parliamentary Assembly in Antalya. With relations between Greece and Turkey improving and inter-ethnic violence within the country subsiding, he felt the time was ripe to make some subtle remarks and cautious overtures to the Turkish authorities. In his speech he explained the merits of integrating diversity. He said that it is 'a matter of foresight and some courage that political leaders take steps to enter into a certain dialogue and commit themselves to find solutions for existing problems'. He went on: 'For those who are prepared to take such steps, it is also essential that they remain realistic and, respecting each other's rights and common interests, seek solutions within the framework of the State'.[82] He

81 Text of the Turkish interpretive statement CSCE Journal no. 50, 22nd plenary. The statement goes on: 'This is without prejudice to the constitutional principle that all citizens are equal before the law, enjoy the same rights and have the same obligations without discrimination, regardless of their sex, religion, race or ethnic origin'.

82 'The Protection of Minorities in the OSCE Region', address by Van der Stoel at a seminar of the OSCE Parliamentary Assembly, Antalya, 12 April 2000.

explained the possibility of maintaining the territorial integrity of the State while respecting minority rights. He reminded his audience of international standards, like the International Covenant on Civil and Political Rights, which provides that persons belonging to minorities 'shall not be denied the right, in community with the other members of their group, to enjoy their own culture, to profess their own religion, or to use their own language'. He said that 'guarantees of fundamental rights and freedoms such as speech, the press, association and assembly, without discrimination and exercised under the rule of law, are irreplaceable'. He also warned that 'their suppression not only inhibits integration and development, but undermines confidence in the State both among the citizenry and other States'. In a similar vein he said: 'I am aware of the fear that support for such a degree of diversity within the State will lead to its disintegration. I am convinced that those who argue along these lines are wrong. A minority that has the opportunity to fully develop its identity is more likely to remain loyal to the State than a minority which is denied its identity'. All of this highlighted the need to protect and promote minority rights and integrate diversity in an effort to build peace, justice, stability and democracy. With a nod to Turkey's future he remarked that protection of minority rights 'is an expression of the fundamental values of European morality and [standards relating to minority rights protection] are pillars of the contemporary European social and political order. For a State to be European in this sense, it is simply expected and required that it respects these standards'.[83]

Van der Stoel tried to follow up this presentation with a more comprehensive analysis of minority rights in Turkey. In a letter to Foreign Minister Ismail Cem of Turkey, dated 6 June 2000, he expressed his interest in carrying out a mission to Turkey to collect information regarding minorities' issues. He stressed that, in compliance with article 5c of his mandate, it was not his intention 'to get involved in those aspects of the situation of the minorities which are related to organized acts of terrorism'. Rather, he emphasized, his mission would concentrate on 'collecting information regarding the implementation of the constitutional principle of your country that all citizens are equal before the law, enjoy the same rights and have the same obligations without discrimination,

83 All from *Ibid.*

regardless *inter alia* of race or ethnic origin'.[84] He also made it clear that he wanted to restrict his contacts in Turkey to Foreign Minister Cem and the minister of human rights.

Van der Stoel's overtures were rebuffed by the Turkish Government. In an unequivocal response to Van der Stoel's letter of 6 June, Foreign Minster Cem said that he did not agree with the High Commissioner's stated intention to conduct a mission in Turkey. Reminding the High Commissioner that his mandate was to deal with 'early warning' and tensions involving national minorities, he said that 'There is no situation in Turkey warranting early warning or which may be described as tension in the sense of the mandate of the High Commissioner on National Minorities'.[85]

To further explain his position, Foreign Minister Cem repeated his Government's position that 'according to the Turkish legal system the word "minorities" encompasses only groups of persons defined and recognized as such on the basis of multilateral or bilateral instruments to which Turkey is a signatory party'. He noted that 'the status of minorities in Turkey has been defined by the 1923 Treaty of Lausanne according to which there are only non-muslim minorities in Turkey'. He noted that 'no muslim Turkish citizen can be defined as belonging to any sort of minority'.[86] In short, the argument was that there are few national minorities in Turkey and those that exist do not face any sort of problems that would necessitate the High Commissioner's involvement. It was clear that the High Commissioner was not welcome.

Van der Stoel repeated his desire to visit Turkey in a letter dated 27 July. In order to clarify any misunderstandings about his intentions, he repeated his wish to only use the trip to collect information. He noted that, according to his mandate, 'collecting information does not in any way oblige the High Commissioner to issue an early warning later.' He pointed out that during his seven and a half years as High Commissioner he had only once issued an early warning. As to Cem's assessment that there was no situation in Turkey that warranted

84 Letter from Van der Stoel to Minister of Foreign Affairs of the Republic of Turkey, 6 June 2000.

85 Letter from Minister of Foreign Affairs of the Republic of Turkey, 14 June 2000.

86 *Ibid.* See also the interpretative statements made at the Copenhagen Meeting 1990 and the Helsinki Summit 1992.

the High Commissioner's involvement, Van der Stoel pointedly noted that paragraph 3 of his mandate leaves it to the High Commissioner to exercise his judgment as to whether or not a situation falls within his mandate. He pointed out: 'To this end, the mandate envisages in paragraph 11c visits by the High Commissioner to enable direct contacts with *inter alia* government leaders in order precisely to clarify positions of policy and law. Such visits have become an ordinary part of my work'.[87] He also repeated his preference for quiet diplomacy. He asked the Government to reconsider its position.

Foreign Minister Cem replied, but did not change his position. In a letter dated 15 September he reiterated his view that 'there is no situation in Turkey that falls within your mandate'.[88] He also repeated the assertion that based on the Treaty of Lausanne 'there are only non-Moslem minorities in Turkey'.[89] In other words, there was no point in Van der Stoel pursuing the matter.

This was the first time in the eight year history of the High Commissioner's office that he had been refused access to a participating State. According to paragraph 28 of the High Commissioner's mandate, if a State 'does not allow the High Commissioner to enter the country and to travel and communicate freely, the High Commissioner will so inform the CSO [Committee of Senior Officials]'. As most of the CSO's functions have been replaced by the Permanent Council, Van der Stoel sent a letter to the Chairwoman of the Council to explain his interpretation of the situation. The points that he raised were as much a defence of his mandate as a justification for why he wanted to visit Turkey. As to Foreign Minister Cem's assertion that he did not agree with the High Commissioner's stated intention to conduct a mission in Turkey, Van der Stoel recalled the principle of the Moscow Document (1991) that says 'the commitments undertaken in the field of the human dimension of the CSCE are matters of direct and legitimate concern to all participating states and do not belong exclusively to the internal affairs of the state concerned'. He also reemphasized the spirit and letter of paragraph 3 of the HCNM mandate that leaves it to the

---

87 Letter from Van der Stoel to Minister of Foreign Affairs of the Republic of Turkey, 27 July 2000.

88 Letter from Ismail Cem, Minister of Foreign Affairs of the Republic of Turkey, to the HCNM, 15 September 2000.

89 *Ibid.*

judgement of the High Commissioner (and nobody else) whether he should get involved in a specific situation in an OSCE state. He pointed out that 'if it would be left to any government unilaterally to determine whether or not a situation exists which falls within the mandate of the HCNM, the effectiveness of the institution of the HCNM would be seriously undermined and the broader OSCE principle of 'co-operative security' would be a setback'.[90] Van der Stoel added: 'so far I have merely sought a meeting with Minister Cem to begin a very specific and limited dialogue . . . I remain hopeful that ways can still be found to have a dialogue with the Turkish Government'. He stressed that 'the dialogue would be focused on the constitutional principle in Turkey that all citizens are equal before the law and enjoy the same rights and obligations regardless of race or ethnic origin. That makes it even more difficult for me to understand the refusal for a dialogue on this issue. Even more so because article 39 of the 1923 Treaty of Lausanne, to which the government attaches decisive importance, also contains important provisions regarding equal treatment of all Turkish nationals'.[91]

The issue of Turkey and the High Commissioner's role was raised during a Permanent Council meeting on 12 October 2000. The High Commissioner received full support from influential States (including the European Union and the United States). OSCE participating States also welcomed the announcement, made at the meeting, that Van der Stoel would meet with Cem during the OSCE Ministerial in Vienna in late November. At that meeting on 27 November it was agreed that dialogue should continue, beginning with an exchange of letters.

---

90 Letter from Van der Stoel to Ambassador Jutta Stefan-Bastl, Chairperson of the Permanent Council, 3 October 2000.

91 *Ibid.*

Ukraine

The High Commissioner's involvement in Ukraine centred around three main issues; the status of Crimea within Ukraine, the resettlement of Crimean Tatars, and relations between the Russian minority and Ukrainian majority.

Around 22% of the population of Ukraine is ethnic Russian. Most Russophones are concentrated in the eastern industrial areas of Ukraine (the Donbas region) and in Crimea where they constitute around 70% of the population. In the USSR, the Crimean peninsula used to belong to Russia until it was given by Nikita Khruschev to the Ukrainian SSR as a gift in 1954 in recognition of the so-called 300 years of friendly union between the Russian and Ukrainian people.

On 1 December 1991, a referendum was held that gave overwhelming support to declaring Ukraine an independent State. Just over half of the population of Crimea also voted in favour.[92] A degree of political authority was granted to Crimea by Ukraine (which declared its independence on 1 December 1991), but this did not go far enough for the Crimean Parliament which adopted an 'Act on State Independence' on 5 May 1992 and introduced a new constitution the next day declaring the Republic of Crimea as a sovereign State. The Crimean declaration called for relations between the States of Crimea and Ukraine to be recognized by a treaty, it called for separate Crimean citizenship, the election of a President of Crimea, and the acknowledgement that Sevastopol would remain under Crimean control. A referendum on independence was announced for August 1992. This was considered a provocation by the Ukrainian parliament which annulled the independence decree. However, in an effort to reach a compromise, a law was passed in June 1992 outlining a division of power between

92 See John Packer, 'Autonomy within the OSCE: the case of Crimea', in Markku Suksi (ed.), *Autonomy: Applications and Implications* (Dordecht: Kluwer Law International, 1998), p. 302.

the central Government and the Crimean authorities. The Crimean leaders agreed to cancel the referendum and the immediate crisis was overcome. Nevertheless, the relationship remained undefined as the law on division of powers was not enforced.

The High Commissioner walked into this volatile environment when he visited Ukraine on the invitation of the Government in February 1994.[93] Although he noted that there were no significant ethnic tensions between the Ukrainians and Russians,[94] the potential for instability was very real. In Western Ukraine, nationalist feelings ran high, and in Crimea positions were becoming increasingly polarized – support grew for leaders who favoured a weakening of ties with Ukraine and a closer union with Russia. As the economic situation across the country deteriorated, there was a fear that many Russians in the eastern industrial cities (many of whom had voted for Ukrainian independence in 1991) would follow the example of Russians in Crimea and seek ways of establishing closer ties with Russia. The economic and political issues were complicated by strategic factors in Ukraine's relations with neighbouring Russia, particularly the ownership of the Black Sea Fleet, the status of Sevastopol and the division of assets and costs.[95]

Another major issue affecting the stability of the country and inter-ethnic relations was the status of the Crimean Tatars who had been deported to Central Asia by Stalin in 1944. By the early 1990s close to 250,000 had returned and many others tried to follow, but they experienced difficulties in leaving Central Asia and had problems in resettling in Ukraine. For example, Uzbekistan did not allow the Tatars to take any property with them, and when they arrived in Crimea they usually landed up living in miserable conditions with very little support and limited political representation. Their dissatisfaction grew at their increasing marginalization within Ukrainian society. The Ukrainian Government, because of the overall decline in the economy, was not able to provide

93 One may speculate that the Ukrainian Government was eager to involve the OSCE in order to limit the possibility of direct Russian involvement.

94 See letter to Ukrainian Foreign Minister Anatoly Zlenko dated 15 May 1994, CSCE Communication no. 23/94.

95 These issues were resolved on 31 May 1997 with the signing of a Basic Treaty of Friendship and Co-operation between Russia and Ukraine.

them with better employment opportunities and living conditions. This created a potentially explosive minority problem on a peninsula which itself was the subject of tensions between Simferopol and Kyiv and between Ukraine and the Russian Federation. All of the issues noted above (each with its own complications) 'were inter-linked such that the whole "Crimean question" constituted a matrix featuring wide-spread multifarious tensions and significant volatility'.[96]

In tackling these issues, Van der Stoel had the full support of the Ukrainian Government. At the same time, his early contacts with Crimean leaders and representatives of the Crimean Tatars made him better aware of their perspectives and were instrumental in demonstrating his role as an 'interested' third party.[97] His early observations were that the root of many of the problems were economic and therefore Ukraine needed international support, that participating States should insist on the need for the territorial integrity of Ukraine,[98] that an early settlement of the tensions between Russia and Ukraine concerning the Black Sea Fleet and Crimean naval bases was essential, that the plight of the Crimean Tatars required greater attention (particularly humanitarian assistance) and that inter-ethnic relations in Ukraine should be closely monitored in order to detect a worsening of any of these situations. He made several follow-up trips to Ukraine (including Crimea) in 1994.

In eastern Ukraine the steady worsening of the economy raised discontent with the Government. This manifested itself in strikes and social discontent, but also by a growing tendency of the Russian minority to reconsider the merits of having voted for an independent Ukraine in 1991. At the same time, relations between Crimea and Ukraine worsened as the President of the Crimean Republic, Yuri Meshkov, consolidated his grip on power and pushed for greater

---

96 Packer 1998, p. 301.

97 The visits to Crimea were particularly important to dispel any doubts that the Crimean representatives may have had that because Van der Stoel had been invited by the Ukrainian Government he may have been susceptible to defending Kyiv's interests.

98 In February 1994 an agreement was signed between Ukraine, the Russian Federation and the United States in which the parties reaffirmed their commitment, in accordance with the CSCE Final Act, to respect the independence, sovereignty and existing borders of CSCE-participating States, and recognized that changes to the borders could only be made by peaceful and consenual means.

autonomy. One of his main aims was to have greater freedom to develop the economic potential of the peninsula. He also wanted a free hand in privatization. Although Meshkov cultivated close links with Russia, the impression of the High Commissioner was that he sought maximum independence from Ukraine rather than union with Russia. The key was therefore to find an arrangement whereby the territorial integrity of Ukraine could be maintained while providing for substantial autonomy for Crimea, especially in the economic field.

The High Commissioner had to juggle many balls at the same time. In Donetsk, in eastern Ukraine, the Russian population expressed concern about the State's efforts to restore the Ukrainian language. For example, Ukrainian became a compulsory subject in the curriculum of Russian schools. Van der Stoel cautioned the Government that although he understood the desire to increase teaching of the Ukrainian language, it was important to reassure Russian-speakers that those who had not had an opportunity to learn Ukrainian in schools would not suffer negative consequences in employment, nor should they fear a process of forced 'Ukrainianization'.[99]

As there were many issues to be addressed he suggested that a team of constitutional and economic experts be sent to Ukraine who could investigate the issues in dispute and provide some suggestions for solutions. This offer was accepted by the Ukrainian Government. The formal decision to send experts to Ukraine was made by the Committee of Senior Officials on 15 June 1994. Their mandate, as given by the CSO, was 'to facilitate the dialogue between the central government and the Crimean authorities concerning the autonomous status of the Republic of Crimea within Ukraine and, in particular, to formulate specific recommendations towards the solution of existing problems with due regard to the fundamental principles of the constitution of Ukraine'.[100]

The three experts (specialists on economic and constitutional issues) visited Ukraine in August 1994. Around the same time, the Permanent Committee (later Permanent Council) approved the mandate of the OSCE Mission to Ukraine with headquarters in Ķyiv and a branch office in Simferopol. Part of the Mission's early tasks were to support the work of the High Commissioner

---

99 See letter to Ukrainian Foreign Minister Anatoly Zlenko (15 May 1994), CSCE Communication no. 23/94.

100 27 CSO/ Journal no.3 Annex 2, 15 June 1994.

and the team of experts. During their trip to Ukraine in August, the experts experienced logistical difficulties in visiting Crimea and therefore were not able to gather very much information on the situation there. They therefore decided to make a return visit in October and made a final trip in December. The High Commissioner took into consideration their advice when carrying out his own on-going quiet diplomacy.[101]

Relations between Kyiv and Simferopol worsened in the spring of 1994 when, in May, the Verkhovna Rada (Parliament) of the Republic of Crimea adopted a law 'On Renewal of the Constitutional Basis of Statehood of the Republic of Crimea'. The Crimean Parliament later declared that all Ukrainian State property in Crimea belonged to Crimea. Kyiv's stance hardened. On 17 March 1995 the Ukrainian Parliament abolished Crimea's Constitution of May 1992 and replaced it with a 'Ukrainian Law on the Autonomous Republic of Crimea' while President Kuchma issued a decree on 31 March 1995 subordinating the Crimean Government directly to the control of the central Government of Ukraine.[102] Criminal charges were brought against President Meshkov. Despite the High Commissioner's appeals to both sides to exercise restraint, the Crimean Parliament announced on 25 April 1995 its intention to hold a referendum asking the Crimean population whether they supported reinstatement of the 1992 Crimean Constitution.[103] The situation seemed to be coming to a head.

The High Commissioner stepped up his efforts to avert a crisis. From 11 to 14 May 1995 he organized a round-table in Locarno, Switzerland which was attended by high-level Ukrainian and Crimean representatives. The meeting provided an important forum for open, face-to-face communication in a confidential setting and led to a breakthrough on a number of substantive points. After the meeting the High Commissioner wrote a letter to Ukrainian Foreign Minister Hennady Udovenko which contained a number of comments and recommendations. On the most immediate crisis, he urged the Parliament of the Autonomous Republic of Crimea not to proceed with its plan to submit to a referendum the Crimean Constitution which was abolished by the Ukrainian parliament. At the same time, he said that 'it would not bring the solution of

101 Packer 1998, p. 308.

102 Packer 1998, pp. 308–9.

103 Packer 1998, p. 309.

the existing problems any nearer if the Crimean Parliament were dissolved'.[104] Regarding constitutional differences, the High Commissioner stressed the importance of respecting the sovereignty and territorial integrity of Ukraine and the fundamental principles of the Ukrainian constitution. Echoing the view of many participants of the round-table, he expressed support for the 'law of Ukraine on the demarcation of powers between organs of state power of Ukraine and the Republic of Crimea' which was agreed to in June 1992 but which had not entered into force. On the question of the Crimean Tatars, he noted the fact that many Crimean Tatars who had returned to Ukraine still did not have citizenship and therefore would not be able to vote. He said that he hoped ways could be found of solving this problem in a short period of time in order to ensure appropriate representation of Tatars in local government. Pending the setting up of a Constitutional Court, the High Commissioner recommended that the Parliaments of Ukraine and the Autonomous Republic of Crimea create an organ of conciliation with the task of suggesting solutions to differences arising in the course of dialogue about relevant legislation. The High Commissioner asked the Foreign Minister to pass these comments and recommendations on to the Ukrainian and Crimean Parliaments.[105] This was done.

Indeed, many of the recommendations made at the Locarno round-table were acted upon with a positive effect. Most notably, the Ukrainian Parliament refrained from dissolving the Crimean Parliament, and the Crimean Parliament dropped its plans for a referendum on the Crimean Constitution of May 1992. Moreover, both sides accepted the recommendation to use the law on demarcation of powers between Ukraine and Crimea as the basis for their negotiations. A new 'Constitution of the Autonomous Republic of Crimea' – taking into account many of the points raised by the High Commissioner – was adopted on 1 November 1995.

A complicating factor in all of these discussions was the position of the Crimean Tatars. They were not in favour of autonomy for Crimea. They also resented the fact that that the new constitution failed to include guaranteed representation for the Crimean Tatar community. Many Tatars boycotted the

---

104 Letter to Hennady Udovenko Minister for Foreign Affairs of Ukraine 15 May 1995, HC/4/95.

105 *Ibid.*

vote on the Crimean Constitution and some went on a hunger strike.[106] Above and beyond politics, their plight continued to be miserable. Their political isolation and growing disillusionment caused increased radicalization, particularly among young Tatars. Concerned about the potential destabilizing effects that this situation could have in its own right, not to mention the potential complications it raised for the larger Crimean issue, the High Commissioner tried to mobilize assistance for the Crimean Tatars and to address some of the problems that they faced during resettlement. He organized a round-table in Yalta on 20–22 September 1995 on 'Reintegration of Deported Peoples in Crimea'. The main goal of the round-table was to identify the immediate and longer-term needs for the reintegration of the deported peoples as well as the relevant legislative, political and economic mechanisms to meet those needs.[107] As a follow-up, a donor conference on the deported peoples of Crimea was held in Geneva on 2 April 1996 to encourage participants to make substantial contributions to assist the Ukrainian Government in meeting the needs of the returning peoples, particularly the Crimean Tatars.

But funding was not the only issue. The High Commissioner suggested that the inter-ministerial committee set up to assist in the process of integrating returnees should be turned into a permanent high-level committee with the task of making recommendations on issues of resettlement, land allocation and the creation of more employment opportunities for returnees. He also suggested that it study ways and means of ensuring a more orderly return process for those Crimean Tatars in Uzbekistan and other States in Central Asia who wanted to come to Crimea. Two other issues regarding the Crimean Tatars that he thought required urgent attention were the acquisition of Ukrainian citizenship for returnees, and the problem of fixed representation of Crimean Tatars in the Parliament of the Autonomous Republic of Crimea. On the former point he advocated granting citizenship to all persons who could demonstrate that they were descendents of people deported during the Second World War, provided that they renounced the citizenship of the State that they left. On the latter

106 For more see Packer 1998, p. 310.

107 See *The Role of the High Commissioner on National Minorities in OSCE Conflict Prevention: an Introduction* (The Hague: The Foundation on Inter-Ethnic Relations, 1997), p. 76.

point he recommended the continuation of a fixed 10% quota system. The status of the Mejlis (the supreme representative college of the Crimean Tatars) was also an issue.[108] The High Commissioner suggested that it be given specific responsibilities regarding the revival and development of Tatar culture and Tatar schools, and funding to carry out these tasks. He also suggested it be given the power to appoint Tatar representatives to the high-level committee (noted above).

While in Ukraine for the round-table in September 1995 he also visited Kyiv and Simferopol to discuss a number of questions regarding the Crimean Constitution. Particular attention was paid to the division of powers. He suggested that defense, the armed forces and foreign policy should remain the exclusive competence of the State organs of the Ukraine (pursuant to international practise) while the Autonomous Republic of Crimea (ARC), taking into account the Ukrainian legal order, should have the right to conclude international agreements regarding commercial and cultural questions, and that it would have the right to open trade offices abroad. He said that 'Ukraine might commit itself to consult with the ARC before concluding treaties of special relevance for Crimea' while Crimean representatives could be included in official Ukrainian delegations to other States.[109] Suggestions were also made on citizenship, the division of revenues and property and the status of Sevastopol.

To continue the momentum for the implementation of these recommendations, the High Commissioner organized a round-table in Noordwijk, in the Netherlands, from 14 to 17 March 1996. Members of the Government of Ukraine, the representative of the President in the Autonomous Republic of Crimea and leading members of the Government and the Parliament of the Autonomous Republic of Crimea took part. It was apparent to the High Commissioner that although there were still disagreements, differences had narrowed considerably. On the basis of the discussions, Van der Stoel made a number of recommendations. In a letter to Foreign Minister Udovenko dated 19 March 1996, he said

108 The Mejlis is roughly equivalent to a council whereas there is also a Kurultai which is a pan-Tatar parliament. The role of these bodies in deciding Tatar-related issues in Ukraine was complicated by the fact that they are extra-territorial (representing all Tatars).

109 Letter to Foreign Minister of Ukraine Hennady Udovenko (12 October 1995), HC/10/95.

that 'it would be desirable to adopt as quickly as possible a law of Ukraine on the approval of the Constitution of the Autonomous Republic of Crimea, which would approve the coming into force of the Constitution of the Autonomous Republic of Crimea with the exception of those articles which are still in dispute'. At the same time he suggested (through the Foreign Minister to the Crimean representatives) that references to 'Republic of Crimea' and 'citizens of Crimea' be replaced by the terms 'the Autonomous Republic of Crimea' and 'citizens of Ukraine residing in Crimea' respectively. A number of legal suggestions were also provided, and he urged that remaining differences be addressed and resolved as soon as possible.[110] On 4 April 1996 the Ukrainian Parliament adopted a new 'Law on the Autonomous Republic of Crimea' whereby it approved the vast majority of the articles of the new Crimean Constitution – leaving aside some twenty articles or parts thereof from a total of 136 articles.[111]

Van der Stoel continued to be engaged in the process in an effort to iron out remaining differences. He proved a valuable instrument for ensuring that dialogue continued, he got both sides to moderate their positions and to reach agreement on a number of Constitutional articles which had formerly been contested. The issue of internal citizenship was dropped, and a compromise formula on the language issue was reached that allowed for the equal status of Ukrainian and Russian in official communications, with a slightly lower status for Crimean Tatar. Agreement on these points created a more constructive environment for dealing with a number of underlying economic and financial issues. The Constitution of Ukraine was eventually adopted by Parliament on 28 June 1996 by which the Autonomous Republic of Crimea became officially entrenched in Chapter X.[112] Agreement on the constitutional status of Crimea

---

110 Letter to Foreign Minister of Ukraine Hennady Udovenko (19 March 1996), HC/7/96.

111 Packer 1998, p. 311. As Packer (the then legal adviser of the High Commissioner) points out, notable among the provisions which were not approved were those bearing the signs of statehood including provisions on official symbols (that is, the Crimean flag, emblem and hymn), an internal 'citizenship', and the status of Sevastopol.

112 However, as Packer notes, 'the specific nature and content of the 'autonomy' remained open to question', p. 311. This was rectified to some extent through a new law (largely based on the previous model) was adopted and approved in full by both Parliaments in 1998.

and the improvement of relations between Russia and Ukraine (which culminated in an agreement on the Black Sea Fleet and Sevastopol as well as a Treaty of Friendship) significantly reduced the threat of inter-ethnic conflict on the Crimean peninsula.

With relations between Kyiv and Simferopol improving, the High Commissioner focused more of his attention on the plight of the Crimean Tatars. After a donors conference in Geneva, Van der Stoel tried to continue to draw the attention of the international community to the humanitarian crisis of the Tatars. He was also concerned about increased inter-ethnic tensions between Tatars and Russians – in some areas both sides had formed paramilitary units. For its part, Kyiv worried about the legal and political ramifications of the Tatars being recognized as an indigenous people and also feared the appeal of Muslim fundamentalism to young, disgruntled Tatars. The moderate Crimean Tatar leaders – conscious of the increasing popularity of the radicals – began to increase their demands. The large number of Crimean Tatars who had difficulties getting Ukrainian citizenship was one of the major sources of discontent. The High Commissioner supported provisions in a new draft law on citizenship which facilitated this process enormously. He repeated the suggestion made several years earlier that applicants should be granted Ukrainian citizenship immediately upon renouncing citizenship of another country, thereby eliminating a period of statelessness. At the same time he also worked with the United Nations High Commissioner for Refugees to lobby the Uzbek Government to facilitate the procedure regarding the relinquishing of citizenship and to abolish the fee of US$100 which each person had to pay in order to obtain the required certification. Part of the problem stemmed from the fact that many Crimean Tatars were unaware of the processes necessary for acquiring citizenship. The High Commissioner therefore suggested an intensive public information campaign to clarify the issues. He also encouraged the Ukrainian Government to develop a formula to ensure the Crimean Tatars a number of seats in the Crimean Parliament which roughly corresponded to the proportion of Tatars in Crimea. Another recommendation that he made was the need for constitutional guarantees for the free development, use and protection of the Russian language and the languages of other minorities in Crimea. Most of these recommendations were positively acted upon, with the exception of the guarantee of parliamentary representation. Dissatisfaction over this issue risked causing further radicalization of the Tatars. Demonstrations turned increasingly violent. Chechen flags were waved at Tatar street demonstrations in an ominous warning of a potential secessionist movement. As the atmosphere became increasingly heated, the High Commissioner stayed in regular contact with the Tatar leadership and the Representative of the President in Crimea in order to encourage both sides to exercise restraint. The issue was resolved to some extent when the Mejlis (the unofficial Tatar parliament) was granted advisory status to the President of Ukraine by a Presidential decree in 1999.

Still, the High Commissioner remained concerned about the urgent need for houses, schools and hospitals for the Tatars and their high level of unemployment. A meeting of experts was organized by the High Commissioner in Kyiv on 5 and 6 November 1997 to look at ways of attracting further international assistance for addressing the needs of deported people in Crimea. During the meeting, problems were identified, projects were proposed and some targetted funding was secured. A donor conference was held in Kyiv on 25 and 26 June 1998 at which US$6 million was pledged. Although this was short of the desired mark, the meeting nevertheless served to create greater awareness of the situation. Education was identified by the High Commissioner, with the assistance of international experts, as an area where more attention was necessary. Tatar settlements were often widely dispersed and/or away from urban areas. Tatar children often could not get to schools or faced difficulties in integrating into mainstream schools. To address this problem the High Commissioner encouraged the development of so-called 'home schools'. Under the system (which is run by the United Nations Development Programme), a volunteer from a local community is given a certain amount of money to enlarge or renovate his or her home in exchange for providing space for mixed classes. Two or three local teachers are contacted to teach the classes (thereby also supporting local employment) according to a curriculum approved by the Ukrainian and Crimean Ministries of Education. Classes are taught in Crimean Tatar, Ukrainian and Russian. The pilot project, which began in 1998, has proved successful and is being copied in a growing number of settlements.

While concentrating mostly on the Crimean Tatars, the High Commissioner still closely followed developments in Crimea. On a trip to the region in April 1999 he noted that there were still tensions between the Ukrainian and Russian communities over education and language issues. Russian nationalists in Crimea campaigned against what they regarded as 'Ukrainianization' despite the fact that they constitute 70% of the population and the position of the Russian language was undisputed. He therefore decided to hold a seminar in Odessa in September 1999 on linguistic and educational rights. Russian, Romanian and Hungarian minorities were invited together with Ukrainian and Crimean government representatives.

A few months after this seminar, the High Commissioner received requests from the Russian Government to investigate the situation of Russian language education in Ukraine, and from the Ukrainian Government to make a similar investigation of Ukrainian language education in the Russian Federation. He received assurances from both Governments that he would enjoy their full support in these activities.

He began with a visit to Ukraine, with two international experts, from 19 to 26 June 2000. In order to get an impression of the situation in various regions of Ukraine they visited Kharkov, Lviv, Odessa, Simferopol, and Kyiv. In each city they met with representatives of Russian organizations and with local and regional authorities. The High Commissioner was particularly interested in investigating complaints by the Russian authorities that Russian language schools in Ukraine were being closed down.

Meanwhile Van der Stoel was alarmed about developments in Western Ukraine, particularly in Lviv and the Lviv region. In the summer of 2000 inter-ethnic tensions ran high following the death of a well-known Ukrainian composer who was beaten to death by two Russians in a drunken brawl after singing Ukrainian songs in a bar that was playing Russian music. Graffiti and pamphlets bluntly encouraged Russians to leave and supporters of the so-called National Social Party organized a march in which they paraded in Nazi-style uniforms and gave the Nazi salute. The Lviv city authorities exacerbated the situation by proposing that the city council adopt an ordinance forbidding the playing of so-called 'low quality' (Russian pop) music. The district council decided to put a levy of 50% on printed material from outside Ukraine.

In an effort to calm down the situation, the High Commissioner urged the Minister for Foreign Affairs, Boris Tarasyuk, to issue a statement. This was done. In a statement issued after Van der Stoel's visit, the Government of Ukraine repeated its commitment to implement article 10 of the Constitution of Ukraine which guarantees the free development, use and protection of Russian and other languages of national minorities in Ukraine, and article 53, paragraph 4 of the Constitution, which guarantees, in accordance with the law, citizens belonging to national minorities the right to receive instruction in the native language, or to study the native language in State and communal educational establishments and through national cultural societies. The statement also noted that Ukraine will fully implement the provisions of the law of minorities and the Framework Convention of the Council of Europe, to which Ukraine is a Party.

Still concerned about the situation in Lviv, the High Commissioner returned two weeks later. As well as looking further into the language and education questions, he urged the authorities not to implement the ordinances forbidding foreign 'vulgar music' and imposing fees on foreign printed material.

The second phase of the visits relating to the language education report took place at the end of August. Visits were made to Moscow, St. Petersburg and Tyumen (in Siberia). In Moscow, the High Commissioner met with governmental officials as well as representatives of Ukrainian organizations in Krasnador, Ekaterinburg and Moscow Oblast.

In December 2000 the High Commissioner made a further trip to Ukraine to make some final clarifications concerning the educational system for minorities. During his visit to Kyiv he attended a donors conference for projects related to the resettlement of Crimean Tatars and other formerly deported peoples in Crimea. This was an issue that he had been following for some time and one which he felt was vital for improving inter-ethnic relations.

Van der Stoel issued his report on minority language education, with recommendations, to the Ukrainian and Russian governments in January 2001. Also in January, the High Commissioner's office hosted a delegation from Ukraine to discuss the Draft Law on Development and Use of Languages in Ukraine. After the meeting, a note on selected issues arising from the draft law were sent to the Chairman of the Committee on Culture of Ukrainian Parliament.

Moldova

The High Commissioner first visited Moldova, at the request of the Permanent Committee (now Council) and on the invitation of the Moldovan Government, from 7 to 10 December 1994 with a view to gaining an impression of the state of inter-ethnic relations in the Republic. After meeting in Chisinau with the President, leading members of the Government and Parliament as well as representatives of the national minorities, Van der Stoel travelled to the southwest of the country, to the region inhabited by the Gagauz. The Gagauz are an ethnically Turkish people of Orthodox Christian faith of whom approximately 155,000 live in Moldova. At the time of the High Commissioner's visit, a Law on Gagauz Autonomy was awaiting its second reading in the Moldovan Parliament. This law, which was adopted by Parliament on 30 December 1994, gave the Gagauz extensive cultural and economic autonomy in the region where they are concentrated. The High Commissioner expressed particular interest in the law since, although the Gagauz make up a majority of the local population, they are only a plurality or even a minority in many of the villages on the periphery of the region, and substantial numbers of Moldovans, Bulgarians and Ukrainians also live there. During his visit to the regional capital, Comrat, the High Commissioner met with Gagauz leaders and leaders of regional political parties.

The High Commissioner also travelled to Tiraspol, on the left bank of the Dniester river. The eastern part of Moldova (also referred to as Transdniestria) has a large Russian-speaking population: taken together, ethnic Russians and Ukrainians outnumber Moldovans in the region. Conflict around the Dniester river (separating Transdniestria, which is contiguous to Ukraine, from the rest of Moldova) was sparked off in 1990 over a number of issues including what some authorities in Tiraspol described as 'Romanian nationalism' (e.g. the Language Act of 1989 making Moldovan the State language) and, on the other hand, what Chisinau saw as secessionist tendencies in Transdniestria, especially after the declaration of a 'Dniestr Autonomous Socialist Republic' in September

1990 and then independence of the 'Dniestr Molodova Republic' in 1991. Bloody clashes broke out between Moldovan Government troops and the Dniestr Republic National Guard (supported by Cossacks and the 14th Soviet Army which was based in Tiraspol). Although the violence eventually subsided, the situation remained a stalemate. Relations between Chisinau and Tiraspol remained tense over the status of Transdniestria, the presence of Russian troops there, and other issues like language and education. For example, Transdniestrian authorities insisted that Moldovan should be written in Cyrillic characters in the 'Dniestr Moldova Republic': Moldovan written in the Latin script was Romanian and therefore considered a foreign language. This touched off a so-called 'school war' in the autumn of 1993. Teachers and officials who opposed the use of the Cyrillic alphabet were removed from their positions. This was one of the main issues that the High Commissioner investigated during his visit of 1994. He met with local authorities and leaders of national minorities in Tiraspol and the neighbouring city of Bendery. He talked with the 'President' and 'Chairman of the Supreme Soviet' about the possibilities for a solution to the Transdniestrian crisis. He also visited Moldovan-language schools in the region, where he spoke with teachers and parents anxious for their children to study the Moldovan language in the Latin script, rather than the Cyrillic alphabet mandated by the Transdniestrian authorities. (During a visit to one of the schools he ran into General Alexander Lebed who was then commander of the 14th Army.) The High Commissioner appealed to the Transdniestrian authorities to show flexibility on this controversial issue and to ensure that it was resolved to the satisfaction of all persons concerned and in full accordance with international norms. This was not done. As a follow-up to the visit, at the request of the chairman of the Permanent Parliamentary Mission on Human Rights and National Minorities, the High Commissioner submitted several comments on a law concerning national minorities which was due to be discussed by the Moldovan Parliament in January 1995. In his letter to the Chairman, he urged that the adoption of the law would be based on consultations with and effective participation of persons belonging to national minorities. The law was never adopted.

The High Commissioner's overall assessment of the situation was rather bleak. This may help to explain why five years passed before he again became engaged in Moldova. In July 1999, the OSCE Mission to Moldova informed the High Commissioner that the Moldovan Government was in the process of amending a law on commercial advertising that would make the Romanian language (or Moldovan, the two being practically the same) obligatory in all advertising. The Mission was concerned that this could lead to a deterioration of relations between the Russophone and Moldovan-speaking communities. In a letter to Moldovan Minister for Foreign Affairs Nicolae Tabacaru dated 2 November 1999 the High Commissioner noted that although he appreciated that the promotion of the Moldovan language on the territory of the Republic should be supported, he felt obliged to point out some aspects of the draft law which were contrary to Moldova's international obligations. As was the case in similar situations in Latvia and Estonia, the High Commissioner pointed out the difference between regulation of language use in the private and public spheres. He said that 'by imposing the mandatory use of the State language in private advertising, the amendment contradicts the freedom of expression'.[113] He therefore recommended that the Moldovan Government withdraw the draft law from consideration of the Parliament. At the same time he said that he would support the Government's efforts to strengthen the position of the State Language. He said that 'projects of this nature go to the heart of issues which often become the sources of inter-ethnic tension and even violent conflict. In our efforts to thaw the "frozen" conflicts in Moldova, one can not afford to overlook issues of language, education and minority rights'.[114]

On 31 March 2000 the Foreign Minister of Moldova responded to Van der Stoel's letter of 2 November 1999 and rebuffed the High Commissioner's criticism saying that the draft Law on Advertisement 'does not contradict the international obligations of the Republic of Moldova'. The Foreign Minister noted the importance of protecting the Moldovan language after years of Tsarist and Soviet assimilation. At the same time he welcomed the High Commissioner to visit Moldova at his convienience.

Van der Stoel took up Tabacaru's invitation and visited Moldova on 17 May 2000. He met with the Foreign Minister, minority representatives as well as Government and State officials dealing with language and education issues. In his meeting with Tabacaru, Van der Stoel took the opportunity to reiterate his

---

113 Letter from the High Commissioner to Foreign Minister of the Republic of Moldova, Nicolae Tabacaru (2 November 1999).

114 Letter to Ambassador Jan Kubis, Secretary General of the OSCE (28 February 2000).

reservations concerning the draft Law on advertising.

The next day he co-hosted a seminar on the linguistic and educational rights of national minorities. In his speech he outlined his views on the situation in Moldova. He said that further steps needed to be taken to protect the rights of persons belonging to national minorities. He warned, for example, of over regulation by the State in the private sphere concerning the use of minority languages. This was an issue in Moldova because of attempts by the Government to curb the use of Russian in private enterprises and the media. At the same time, he sympathized with the Government's efforts to strengthen the State language. As he had noted in similar situations in Latvia and Estonia, 'the strengthening of the State language does not have to come at the expense of the linguistic and educational rights of national minorities and vice versa'.[115] He also used the occasion to again express his concerns about the difficulties encountered by Moldvan children in Transdniestria to learn the Moldovan language using the Latin script. He called on the Transdniestrian authorities to put an end to this practice. In reference to the harassment faced by the few schools teaching Moldovan in eastern Moldova, he also cautioned that 'authorities should not hinder the enjoyment of the rights of citizens to education in their mother tongue by imposing unduly and burdensome legal and administrative requirements regulating the establishment and management of educational institutions, whether private or public'.[116]

To follow up on his point that the strengthening of the State language and the protection of minority rights could be complementary, the High Commissioner took a two-track approach. On the one hand, he continued to make recommendations to the Government concerning the importance of finding solutions to minority issues in line with international standards. At the same time, his Office initiated a language training project in Moldova.

In line with his views on the importance of integrating diversity, the High Commissioner also suggested to the Moldovan Government that it elaborate a comprehensive integration strategy. In a letter to Foreign Minister Tabacaru dated 31 May 2000 he suggested that this strategy could include language training, training of public officials, harmonizing various aspects of minority-

115 'The Linguistic and Education Rights of National Minorities and their Application in Moldova', key-note speech by Max van der Stoel, Chisinau, 18 May 2000.

116 *Ibid.*

related legislation, and looking at the media as a tool of social integration. He noted that 'such a strategy could facilitate inter-ethnic integration in Moldova while strengthening the State language, ensuring a proper legal framework for the protection of minority rights, and sending a positive signal concerning Moldova's commitment to implement the relevant international standards'.[117]

Van der Stoel was back in Moldova in September. This visit prepared the ground for the teacher training programme (which became operational a few months later with the assistance of experts from Estonia, Romania and Moldova). The purpose of the programme was to improve techniques for teaching Moldovan, particularly as a second language in schools with a high percentage of minorities. During his visit, the High Commissioner also went to Transdniestria. He visited two schools which continue to teach Moldovan in the Latin script despite the efforts of the Transdniestrian authorities to impose the Cyrillic script. He also met with Igor Smirnov, 'President' of the 'Dniestr Moldavian Republic', and urged him to adopt a more lenient attitude towards the seven schools teaching in the Latin script.

Following up his visit to Moldova, the High Commissioner sent a letter to Foreign Minister Tabacaru in which he reiterated 'the need to promote the State language without impinging on the rights of minorities'.[118] Although proposed amendments to the law on advertising (that Van der Stoel had expressed serious reservation about) had been dropped, he was concerned about restrictive measures in the Law on Audio-Visual Broadcasting. He felt that certain provisions infringed upon the right to freedom of expression. This was particularly in connection to a stipulation that at least 65% of all broadcasts (even on private stations) had to be in the State language. He encouraged the Parliament to amend this article of the Law. This was done, but not in a way that was in line with international standards.

In the following months the High Commissioner maintained his position on the need for protecting the linguistic rights of minorities while at the same time seeking to improve the quality of teacher training in the State language. This was in line with his view that there could be a compatibility between the

117 Letter from Van der Stoel to Nicolae Tabacaru, Foreign Minister of the Republic of Moldova, 31 May 2000.

118 Letter to Nicolae Tabacaru, Foreign Minister of the Republic of Moldova (22 September 2000).

use of the majority and minority languages that created opportunities without restricting usage.

Romania

The High Commissioner's involvement in Romania mainly concerned the Hungarian minority and its desire to have education at the tertiary level in Hungarian.

In 1993 Van der Stoel visited Romania twice, in June and August. He travelled to Bucharest and then to Transylvania where the Hungarian minority is most highly concentrated. He met with Government officials and representatives of the Hungarian, German and Roma minorities.

In a letter to Romanian Foreign Minister Teodor Melescanu on 9 September 1993 he observed that 'if moderation and reasonableness prevail and extreme nationalism is rejected on both sides, there seem to be no insuperable barriers to constructive solutions'.[119] He made a number of recommendations to work towards that end. He encouraged the Government and minority representatives to make full use of the Council for National Minorities, he suggested that the Government should draft minority and education laws, he recommended that extensive powers be given to the Advocate of the People (like an ombudsman), and he urged the Government to support the Roma in job training and education and to take strong action against discrimination.

In August 1994 the High Commissioner visited Hungary and Romania as tensions were mounting between the Government and the Hungarian Democratic Federation of Romania (UDMR), particularly over education and language issues. On the one hand he tried to dissuade the UDMR from mounting a civil disobedience campaign in opposition to the proposed Law on Education, while on the other he proposed to the Government a number of amendments.

The High Commissioner returned to Bucharest in February 1995 at a time

---

119 Letter to Teodor Melescanu, Minister for Foreign Affairs of Romania (9 September 1993), CSCE Communication no. 253/93.

when the relationship between the Romanian Government and UDMR remained fractious: the Government was strengthening its relations with nationalist parties, while the UDMR placed increasing emphasis on ethnic-based regional autonomy. The difficulties were compounded by the lack of progress on the adoption of a Law on Minorities, controversy over the draft Law on Education and extremist statements from high-level individuals from both communities. The High Commissioner spoke to all concerned parties on these issues and also discussed progress on concluding a treaty on good neighbourliness, friendship and co-operation between Romania and Hungary, including provisions on the protection of minorities.

He returned to Romania in August 1995, mainly to evaluate the Law on Education which was adopted on 29 June 1995. After reviewing the legislation and meeting with Romanian officials, the High Commissioner made a public statement in which he said that the Law on Education allows 'a considerable amount of flexibility' in its implementation.[120] At the same time he reminded the Government of its commitments to protect minority education rights pursuant to international standards that Romania subscribed to. He made public a number of clarifications and explanations which he had received from the Government. These included: the possibility for the establishment of schools with teaching in the language of national minorities; the choice of parents to decide on the type of schooling or classes for their children; the fact that creating Romanian language classes would have no adverse financial consequences for minority schools and classes; the fact that the law allows for the existence of private denominational schools; the assurance that experts from national minorities would have an input into the writing of history textbooks; and that although public university education in minority languages would continue to be restricted to teacher training and the cultural/artistic field, possibilities now existed for additional private university education also in other fields. He also recommended that socio-economic subjects be added to those that could already be studied in the minority language at public universities and that minority language education at vocational schools should be improved.

The High Commissioner was invited to Romania by the Prime Minister in January 1996 to study the implementation of the law. During his visit he met

120 Statement of the OSCE HCNM on the occasion of his mission to Romania on 28–31 August 1995, 1 September 1995, ref. HC/6/95.

with the headmasters and teachers of eight minority schools, representatives of the Hungarian Teachers' Association as well as Government representatives and members of the UDMR. He subsequently recommended that the passing of regulations on the implementation of the law be speeded up in an effort to avoid confusion, and that consideration should be given to the possibility of revising the law to overcome unforeseen weaknesses and deficiencies.

In the summer of 1996, the High Commissioner made a number of visits to Romania and Hungary to discuss matters relating to the conclusion of a bilateral Treaty on Friendship and Cooperation between these two countries. Since both Romania and Hungary are the kin-State to a minority living in the other country (although the relative proportion of Hungarians in Romania is significantly higher), the issue of national minorities played an important role in the drafting of the Treaty. The High Commissioner suggested that the minority provisions be based on the international commitments which both countries had undertaken, such as the OSCE Copenhagen Document. After the Treaty was signed, in August 1996, Romanian Minister of Foreign Affairs Melescanu stated that the activities of the High Commissioner had the effect of a 'catalyst' on the conclusion of the negotiations. Both the Romanian and Hungarian Governments thanked the High Commissioner for his mediation efforts.

The High Commissioner returned to Romania at the beginning of April 1997. He was encouraged by the signing of the Treaty, the creation of a Department for the Protection of Ethnic Minorities, and the fact that for the first time representatives of the Hungarian minority held posts as Ministers or State Secretaries in the Government which was elected in November 1996. He saw these as important factors in the improvement of relations between Hungary and Romania and between the Romanian majority and the Hungarian minority. He was also encouraged by promises contained in the Government programme that would eliminate the grievances of the Hungarian minority concerning the education law.

However, those promises were not lived up to in the eyes of the UDMR. Emergency Ordinance no. 38 1997 which amended the 1995 Law on Education did not go far enough, in the opinion of the Hungarian minority, towards ensuring possibility for study in the mother tongue at the tertiary level. Efforts to amend the Ordinance were turned down by the Education Commission of the Chamber of Deputies.

At the same time, some positive steps were being taken at Babes-Bolyai

University in Cluj-Napoca towards the development of study programmes in Hungarian and German. The High Commissioner visited the University in February 1998. He urged the Government to support the University's multicultural approach. He also recommended more decentralization in the system of tertiary education in general.

Aware of the fact that revisions to the Law on Education were being discussed, he encouraged the Government not to include a provision in the revised Law that would exclude the possibility of a State-funded university with education in a minority language. He suggested that the possibility for the creation of such institutions should be left to a decision of a commission that would analyze whether the preservation of the cultural identity of a minority would require such an institution and what subjects it should teach. In his recommendations he also raised a few points about curriculum, particularly the teaching of Romanian history.

While in Romania, the High Commissioner hosted a two-day round-table in Snagov, near Bucharest, on 7 and 8 February 1998 which looked at questions related to tertiary education in minority languages in Romania.

That issue boiled up again later in the year. In August the UDMR threatened to leave the Government by the end of September if no agreement was reached on the possibility of tertiary education. A Commission was established to study the feasibility of a Hungarian language State university. The emphasis of the Committee's work soon shifted to initiating procedures to establish a possible Multicultural Hungarian- and German-Language State University, the so-called Petőfi-Schiller University. In a letter to the President of Romania dated 9 September 1998, Van der Stoel said that such a compromise solution 'would be widely welcomed by the international community as an innovative formula for solving a difficult and complicated inter-ethnic problem'.[121] He warned the President that 'if the UDMR and its coalition partners would be unable to continue their co-operation, this might lead to a worsening of inter-ethnic relations and to a setback for the international prestige of your country'.[122] The prestige of Romania was a key factor at this time as the country was lobbying hard for EU accession and NATO membership.

---

121 Letter to Emil Constantinescu, President of Romania (9 September 1998), ref. 1127/98. See also his statement on Petőfi-Schiller issued in October 1998, ref. HCNM 4–98.

122 Letter to President Constantinescu (9 September 1998).

However the debate over Petöfi-Schiller split the Commission along ethnic lines (the Romanians refused to sign the Committee report) and the legality of such an institution was challenged (successfully) by two opposition parties as being unconstitutional. This decision was reversed in 1999. Van der Stoel remained frustrated at the lack of progress on this issue.

The issue remained contentious and delayed the adoption of a new Law on Education until June 1999. The High Commissioner visited Romania from 15 to 18 June in order to familiarize himself with the latest developments concerning tertiary education and to act as a catalyst in resolving the issue. Coincidentally, on 15 June, the day that he visited the Chamber of Deputies, the law was passed. In a press briefing the next day, the High Commissioner praised the Parliament's decision and encouraged the Senate to also give its approval to the law. This was done, with an amendment, on 30 June. The law expanded the possibilities for teaching in minority languages and created the possibility for the establishment of multicultural institutions of higher education. Article 123 (1) stated that 'At state higher education establishments it is possible to organize, according to the law, upon request, groups, sections, colleges and departments with teaching in the languages of ethnic minorities . . . Upon request and under the law it is possible to set up multicultural higher education establishments'.[123] However, each new establishment would be created through a special law and the languages of teaching in these institutions would also be defined through a special law.

This created some legal space in which to expand the possibilities for minority education at the University level. However, it was clear to the High Commissioner that there was no majority within the Romanian Parliament for taking full advantage of the law to the extent hoped for by the Hungarian representatives. He therefore concentrated his efforts on further developing minority education at existing institutions. On 17 and 18 June he visited Babes-Bolyai University (BBU) in Cluj together with an international education expert. Babes-Bolyai University has been the focus of considerable debate in connection with minority education and multiculturalism. At the University, they met with the rector, vice-rectors and members of the faculty in order to better assess the programme of study and the impact that a law on minority education would

123 Law no. 151, 30 July 1999, Article 123 (1).

have on the future of the University, particularly as regards the Hungarian 'line' of study. In a press conference on 18 June Van der Stoel stressed that the main emphasis, after adoption of the law, should be on implementation in order 'to put wind in the sails' of the idea of multi-culturalism.

In the summer of 1999 his office developed an outline for a project for assisting the University in taking advantage of the opportunities afforded by the adoption of the Law on Education. Three international education experts visited BBU several times during the winter of 1999/2000 and submitted their recommendations to the rector, Andrei Marga, (who was also the Minister of Education) on 17 February 2000. The report recommended that the University should more clearly articulate its mission statement concerning multi-culturalism (including the development of a strategy for its implementation), it should revise its decision-making structures to make them more transparent, accountable and representative (particularly taking into account the desire of the Hungarian minority to have more say over decisions affecting them), it should adapt its curriculum to reflect the multi-cultural character of the University, and introduce measures to have the staff more accurately refect the University's commitment to excellence and multiculturalism.[124]

These recommendations did not go far enough for the UDMR and some Hungarian professors who stuck to their position on the need for separate Hungarian faculties within the University – and ultimately a State-funded Hungarian University. Bearing this in mind (and the fact that 2000 was an election year in Romania and views could again become polarized) Van der Stoel urged Mr Marga to implement reforms that would expand the possibilities for education in the minority mother tongues at BBU. In a letter dated 30 March 2000 he stressed the importance of introducing courses in Hungarian in the faculties of law and economics and revising the University Charter. He put particular emphasis on the need for changing the decision-making structures to allow the Hungarian minority 'additonal guarantees that its interests will be adequately safeguarded'.[125]

124 'Recommendations on Expanding the Concept of Multi-culturalism at the Babes-Bolyai University, Cluj-Napoca, Romania', attached to a letter addressed to Andrei Marga, Rector of BBU and Minister of Education, 17 February 2000.

125 Letter to Andrei Marga (30 March 2000), ref. 11/00.

These proposals, particularly the revision of the Charter, were discussed by a special committee set up by the Rector and their proposals were submitted to the University Senate in May 2000.

On trips to Bucharest in mid-May and early July 2000 the High Commissioner met with Minister Marga to keep abreast of developments in the Senate. On 8 July the Senate of Babes-Bolyai University approved a revised University Charter that included most of the recommendations made by the High Commissioner and international experts on expanding the concept of multiculturalism at BBU. There were no votes against: the Hungarian professors in the Senate abstained. Although this still did not satisfy the wish of the Hungarians to have their own state-sponsored University (or at least separate faculties), it provided for increased opportunities for members of minority communities to have tertiary education in their mother tongue and gave them a considerable degree of administrative control over decisions that affect them. This progress, and the importance of multi-cultural education, were discussed during a seminar held at BBU on 7 October 2000 on 'Integrating Diversity in Higher Education: Lessons from Romania'.

The elections of November/December 2000 changed the political landscape in Romania. In the early months of 2001, the High Commissioner monitored how these changes affected inter-ethnic relations. A significant development was the passage of a law on public administration in January 2001 that allowed for the official use of minority languages in communities make up at least 20% of the population. As well as minority-related issues, the High Commissioner had regular contacts with Romanian officials in the context of Romania's Chairmanship of the OSCE in 2001.

Hungary

When starting his work in 1993, the High Commissioner was faced with complaints from Hungary about the treatment of the Hungarian minority in Slovakia and from Slovakia regarding the situation of the Slovak minority in Hungary. A confidence-building measure in the form of outside third-party involvement on a regular basis seemed to be necessary. The High Commissioner therefore recommended the establishment of a team of minority rights specialists who would assist him in analyzing the situation of the Hungarians in Slovakia and the Slovaks in Hungary in the light of the general policies towards minorities of each of the Governments concerned.

The team (consisting of three experts) was established and made two visits per year to both countries until May 1996 (see also the section on Slovakia). During its visits, the Team met with Government officials, representatives of national minorities, members of relevant parliamentary commissions, academics, NGOs and individuals. After each visit, the Team reported to the High Commissioner who then decided whether, and in what form, recommendations would be communicated to the Government involved.

The first visit of the Team to Hungary took place in the second half of September 1993. The focus of discussions was the Hungarian Government's minority policy. The Team discussed the new Act on the Rights of National and Ethnic Minorities (which had been passed by the Parliament on 7 July 1993) and the possible problems which could arise from implementing it, for example the functioning of minority self-governments and the level of financial support necessary to implement the Act. The Team also registered the reactions of the Slovak minority to the Act. The High Commissioner followed up by making a number of recommendations to the Hungarian Government which were designed to enhance the effectiveness of implementing the Act. He put particular emphasis on those provisions of the Act which concerned language education.

During the second and third visits, which took place in February and November of 1994, discussions concentrated on the further implementation of the Minorities Act, the question of minority representation in Parliament, minorities' self-government, the use of Slovak as a language of instruction in schools and the establishment of a minority ombudsman.

The fourth visit took place in early June 1995. The Team concentrated on the functioning of the local Slovak minority self-governments and the Slovak national self-governing body established earlier in the year (as a result of the election of self-governing bodies in addition to minority councils in elections in December 1994). In a letter to Hungarian Minister for Foreign Affairs Laszlo Kovacs (who was also the OSCE Chairman-in-Office at the time), dated 24 August 1995, the High Commissioner wrote that 'undoubtedly, the system of local minority self-government reflects an original and innovative approach to the problem of ensuring the various minorities the optimal chances for protection of their interests and developing their identity'.[126] However, he noted that two further steps could be taken to ensure better effectiveness of the system. He said that the minority self-government bodies should be given a more solid financial basis and that interaction between different levels of government should be made less complicated.

In the same letter, which took into account the observations of the expert team, the High Commissioner called on the Hungarian Government to increase its efforts to strengthen the linguistic identity of the Slovak minority in Hungary. He also reiterated his concerns about the parliamentary representation of ethnic minorities and urged the Government to elect a parliamentary commissioner for minority affairs. The latter point was solved, indeed there is now an Office for National and Ethnic Minorities and three Ombudsmen. However, the former point remained unresolved. The High Commissioner often returned to this issue because Hungarian legislation had guaranteed the right of national minorities to be represented in the National Assembly.

Visits in the autumn of 1995 and the spring of 1996 were also devoted to these subjects. In February 1996 the High Commissioner sent a letter to Foreign Minister Kovacs in which he welcomed progress made on a number of initiatives designed to protect the rights of persons belonging to national minorities and

---

126 Letter to Laszlo Kovacs, Minister for Foreign Affairs of the Republic of Hungary (24 August 1995), HC/8/95.

to strengthen the identity of the various national minorities. He noted in particular the appointment of a Parliamentary Commissioner for Minority Rights, the establishment of the Public Foundation for National and Ethnic Minorities, the creation of the Hungarian-Slovak Experts Committee and the proposal to create a Minority Interest Mediation Council (consisting of delegates of the national minority self-governing bodies and the minorities that had not formed such bodies together with representatives of the Government). He also praised the establishment of minority self-government, although he again brought up the need for further financial and legal steps to improve the system.

However, he described as 'critical' the situation of the Slovak language in the education system.[127] He recommended the elaboration of a comprehensive programme aimed at improving the position of the Slovak language in the school system.

After the last visit of the team of experts to Hungary in May 1996, the High Commissioner wrote a letter to Foreign Minister Kovacs in which he reviewed a number of subjects which the experts had followed and also made a number of recommendations. These concerned the rights of minorities, the system of their participation in the national parliament, education issues, provisions for minority languages and self-government, support for Hungarians abroad and the use of the term 'Hungarian nation'.[128]

He also put forward his views on autonomy (with a veiled reference to Hungarians in Slovakia) by noting that 'it is important to keep in mind that persons belonging to national minorities can exercise their right, as recognized by international norms and standards, not to be assimilated against their will and their right to see their identity respected and ensured without keeping themselves isolated from the majority'.[129] He referred to the Preamble of the Treaty on Good Neighbourliness and Friendly Cooperation between the Republic of Hungary and the Slovak Republic (signed on 19 March 1995) which, while stressing the responsibility of the signatories for granting protection to

---

127 Letter to Laszlo Kovacs, Minister for Foreign Affairs of the Republic of Hungary (26 February 1996), HC/8/96.

128 Letter to Laszlo Kovacs, Minister for Foreign Affairs of the Republic of Hungary (13 August 1996), HC/13/96.

129 *Ibid.*

and promoting preservation and deepening of the national or ethnic, cultural, religious and linguistic identity of the minorities living within their respective territories, also recognizes that persons belonging to national minorities form an integral part of the society and of the State of the Contracting Party on whose territory they live.

The Slovak minority in Hungary was not the only issue on which the High Commissioner made recommendations to the Hungarian Government. During negotiations between Hungary and Romania on the text of a Treaty on Friendship, Co-operation and Good Neighbourliness in 1995 and 1996, the High Commissioner proposed a number of ideas to the Hungarian and Romanian Foreign Ministers. He persuaded both sides not to have a separate treaty on minorities. He was also instrumental in overcoming a major difference of opinion between the parties on how to refer to Recommendation 1201 (1993) of the Parliamentary Assembly of the Council of Europe, so as to ensure the protection of the rights of persons belonging to national minorities without granting collective rights or territorial autonomy on the basis of ethnicity.[130] The Prime Minster of Hungary, Gyula Horn, and the Foreign Minister of Romania, Nicolae Vacaroiu, signed the Basic Treaty on 16 September 1996 in Timisoara, Romania.

In 1997 the High Commissioner followed up on a number of issues relating to the protection of persons belonging to national minorities in Hungary. He called on the Government to speed up the preparation of a draft law on direct representation of national minorities in Parliament in time for the 1998 parliamentary elections. He also raised the issues of adequate air time for public radio and television broadcasts in the Slovak language, state funding for minority self-government and proper training in the Slovak language.

In March 1998 the High Commissioner expressed his dissatisfaction with the pace of drafting a law allowing for the direct representation of minorities in the Hungarian National Assembly. In a letter dated 2 March he reminded Foreign Minister Kovacs that on the basis of Article 68 of the Constitution of Hungary (1990), Article 20(1) of the Act on the Rights of National and Ethnic Minorities of 1993 provides that 'minorities have the right to be represented in the National Assembly in a manner determined by a separate law'. Van der Stoel said that it would be 'highly regrettable' if the direct representation of the minorities in the National Assembly would only be realized during the election of 2002 and

130 See Van der Stoel 1999b, p. 77.

urged the Government to search for a solution immediately after the 1998 elections, if not before.[131] This Government introduced legislation to this effect, but the draft law failed to win enough support in Parliament.

In September 1998 the High Commissioner travelled to Hungary and met with the new Government to discuss its views regarding minority issues, both in Hungary and its policy regarding Hungarian minorities in Slovakia and Romania. He also met the Chairman of the Slovak Self-Government Council and other representatives of the Slovak minority.

He returned to Hungary in July 1999 to discuss the position of the Hungarian Government concerning the Hungarian minority in Slovakia (particularly in regard to the use of minority languages), Romania (particularly in regard to tertiary education), and Vojvodina. The High Commissioner was especially interested to learn about how the protection of national minorities in Romania and Slovakia affected Hungary's bilateral relations with those two countries. He also wanted to familiarize himself with the reasons behind Hungary's strong support for three levels of autonomy for Vojvodina (personal self-government, territorial self-government and autonomy for the province of Vojvodina). He expressed his opinion to the Hungarian Government that this issue could only be solved in a post-Milosevic Federal Republic of Yugoslavia, but emphasized the need to re-open the OSCE Mission to Vojvodina. At the same time he said that Belgrade would probably not support such an initiative until it was readmitted to the OSCE.[132]

The Law on the Use of Minority Languages, passed in Slovakia on 10 July 1999, did not meet the expectations of the Hungarian minority. In a letter to the High Commissioner dated 26 July, the Minister for Foreign Affairs of Hungary, Mr Janos Martonyi, encouraged the High Commissioner to 'urge and to assist the Government of Slovakia to take further concrete steps with a view to better ensuring the specific rights of national minorities to use their language both orally and in its written form, in private and in public life'.[133]

131 Letter to Laszlo Kovacs, Minister for Foreign Affairs of the Republic of Hungary (2 March 1998), HCNM.GAL/2/98.

132 Yugoslavia was suspended from the OSCE in June 1992.

133 Letter from Minister for Foreign Affairs of Hungary, Mr Janos Martonyi (26 July 1999).

The High Commissioner had already promised representatives of the Hungarian Coalition Party (SMK) in Slovakia that he would take such action. He followed up on these issues when he visited Slovakia in the autumn of 1999 (see below).

The situation of 'Hungarians abroad' (particularly in the Federal Republic of Yugoslavia, Slovakia and Romania) was again discussed in visits by the High Commissioner to Budapest in November 1999 and September 2000. So too was the question of the representation of minorities in the Hungarian Parliament which had remained unsolved since 1993. Throughout 2000 he kept abreast of developments of an *ad hoc* committee of the Parliamentary Commission on Human Rights, Minority and Religious Issues that was tasked with drafting this Act, amending the 1993 Act and preparing a new Act on the election of local and national minority self-governments. He also monitored the Hungarian Government's Roma policy. His main focus, however, remained the position of Hungary towards ethnic Hungarians in neighbouring States and the effects that this had on bilateral relations.

Slovakia

As noted above, the High Commissioner visited Hungary and the newly independent Slovak Republic from 14 to 20 February 1993. At that time bilateral relations between the two countries were significantly affected by national minority issues, particularly in regard to the erosion of minority rights as they existed in the former Czechoslovakia. Indeed relations between Hungary and Slovakia and between the Slovak Government and the Hungarian minority were strained throughout the duration of Prime Minister Vladimir Mečiar's term in office. On a number of occasions disputes arose over issues such as the position of the Hungarian language schools, the use of minority languages in official communications, the registration of names in their Hungarian version, the use of Hungarian place names on road signs, the amount and dispersal of State funding for minority cultural projects, and the possibility of having school certificates issued in both the official and the minority languages.

The High Commissioner felt that it was important to become involved in Slovakia in order to avoid a deterioration of the relationship between the Slovak Government and the sizeable Hungarian minority (according to the 1991 census amounting to 10.8% of the population) and between Hungary and the Slovak Republic.

In order to address the situation, Van der Stoel suggested the regular use of an outside advisory element and recommended the establishment of an independent team of experts to assist him. Hungary and Slovakia agreed and the team was established for an initial duration of two years (elapsing on 31 May 1995). The team's task was to study, based on OSCE principles and commitments, both the situation of the Hungarian minority in Slovakia and the situation of the Slovak minority in Hungary in the light of the general policies towards minorities of each of the Governments concerned. In 1995 the team's mandate was extended by a further year after which Slovakia stated that the team had fulfilled its task. There was therefore no agreement on further extension.

In its their visits to Slovakia and Hungary, the High Commissioner (together with the experts) had extensive discussions with Governmental officials in Bratislava, and with representatives of the Slovak and Hungarian communities in southern Slovakia. Many of the meetings were devoted to planned legislative reforms which included: administrative reform and its possible consequences for the Hungarian minority; alternative education, i.e. the creation of new schools with both Hungarian and Slovak languages as languages of instruction; the law on the State language; the debate on a law on minority languages; teacher training; and the Government's cultural policy. Discussions also focused on the implementation of existing or recently adopted legislation.

For the High Commissioner, creating proper frameworks for discussing inter-ethnic relations was an important factor for encouraging transparency and building confidence. In a letter to Mr Eduard Kukan, Minister for Foreign Affairs of the Slovak Republic, dated 20 June 1994, the High Commissioner stressed that 'the creation and development of instruments of dialogue and the promotion of public discussion as part of the evolving structure of democratic institutions are an essential factor in a living democracy'.[134]

The High Commissioner closely followed cultural policy and the funding of minority activities. When contributions for minority cultural activities (particularly the Hungarian minority) were reduced in 1995, he urged the Government to reverse this trend in the future in order to allow for adequate protection and creation of conditions for the promotion of the cultural identity of national minorities. He also called for greater transparency in the distribution of funds and suggested that minorities be adequately represented in organs which decide on cultural subsidies. This call was repeated in 1996 and 1997.

In June 1995 the High Commissioner met with Slovak parliamentarians to encourage them to ratify the basic treaty concluded in March 1995 between Hungary and Slovakia. He hoped that this step would not only improve bilateral relations, but would also relax tensions between the Slovak majority and the Hungarian minority in Slovakia. However, tensions persisted in a number of matters.

Linguistic questions were among the main points to which the High Commissioner drew the Slovak Government's attention. He made recommendations

134 Letter to Eduard Kukan, Minister for Foreign Affairs of the Slovak Republic (20 June 1994), CSCE Communication no.36/94.

on the draft law on State language of the Slovak Republic and when it was adopted (on 15 November 1995) he encouraged rapid adoption of a law on minority languages as a counter-balance to avoid having a legal vacuum in issues like the use of minority languages in official communications. The High Commissioner also addressed the question of 'alternative education' in linguistically mixed territories. The aim of this government programme was to introduce 'alternative', bilingual schools or classes in addition to the existing Hungarian and Slovak schools. The programme, which was voluntary, was met with considerable resistance from the Hungarian community. The High Commissioner received the assurance of the Slovak Government that it would respect the free choice of parents concerning their children's participation in the scheme. In this and other linguistic issues Van der Stoel stressed to members of the Slovak Government and the Hungarian minority the need to strike an overall balance between the interest of the State in ensuring the position of the State language and the need to ensure the protection of minority languages. This view was stated most explicitly in a letter to Foreign Minister Juraj Schenk on 13 August 1996 when the High Commissioner wrote: 'It is my firm belief that only on the basis of respect by the State for the identity of the minority on the one hand, and of the willingness of the minority to consider itself an integral part of the State they are living in on the other, can harmonious inter-ethnic relations develop'.[135]

He also encouraged the Government to enact administrative reform (particularly as regards local self-government) that would create effective frameworks for protecting national identity within the State structure and which would also bring Slovak legislation in line with European and international norms and standards. For example, he recommended giving more responsibilities to the municipalities on issues like the running of schools.

In 1995 and 1996 there was considerable discussion in Slovakia and Hungary about territorial autonomy on an ethnic basis. In a letter to Foreign Minister Schenk on 26 February 1996, the High Commissioner wrote that the norms and political commitments enshrined in Recommendation 1201 (1993) of the Parliamentary Assembly of the Council of Europe (particularly Article 11) 'cannot be interpreted as imposing a legal obligation on Slovakia to introduce territorial

135 Letter to Juraj Schenk, Minister for Foreign Affairs of the Slovak Republic (13 August 1996), HC/12/96.

autonomy on an ethnic basis'.[136] At the same time, he recommended that the Government not make propaganda for advocating such an autonomy a punishable act. After closely studying the possible repercussions of proposed amendments to Slovakia's penal code (which aimed at protecting the State and which were meant to introduce penalties for those who spread false information abroad about the State), the High Commissioner asked the Government to review its position on the issue. The Slovak President, Michal Kovac, sent the amendments back to Parliament for reconsideration.

The High Commissioner's involvement in Slovakia did not end with the conclusion of the mandate of the team of experts in the spring of 1996; he continued to closely monitor developments in the country. He visited Slovakia in April 1997 and was increasingly alarmed by a number of the Mečiar Government's policies. These included its suggestions that ethnic Hungarians would be excluded from teaching the Slovak language, geography and history, the dismissal of headmasters for seemingly political reasons, and the decision to only issue school certificates in the State language. The Government also had yet to provide satisfactory provisions for persons belonging to national minorities to use their language in official communications.

On 9 and 10 March 1998 a joint delegation of the High Commissioner's office, the Council of Europe and the European Commission visited Slovakia to discuss Slovak legislation on the use of minority languages in the light of Slovakia's international commitments. In a joint statement following a series of meetings, the delegation noted that 'whilst the Slovak Constitution provides for protection for minorities, a situation of legal uncertainty exists regarding the use of minority languages'. Steps for overcoming this uncertainty were suggested and a number of issues related to the compatibility of Slovak legislation with international standards were discussed.

In 1998, the High Commissioner expressed serious concerns about a draft law on local elections which he said violated 'a number of international principles and specific standards concerning free elections and individual human rights'.[137] He criticized it for fixing electoral representation along ethnic lines warning

136 Letter to Juraj Schenk, Minister for Foreign Affairs of the Slovak Republic (26 February 1996), HC/4/96.

137 Letter to Zdenka Kramplova, Minister of Foreign Affairs of the Slovak Republic (29 May 1998), HCNM.GAL/5/98.

that it would leave voters with a choice between ethnicities rather than political candidates. He also took issue with the proposed bill to impose the concept of the so-called alternative school (see above). The latter legislation was thrown out while the former was adopted without the amendments which the High Commissioner had described as being necessary 'to ensure the Law would be in conformity with international standards accepted by Slovakia'.[138] On this and other occasions the High Commissioner cautioned the Government that compliance with international principles and standards was an important condition for developing closer integration into the European and international communities. Van der Stoel's constant insistence on respect for human rights made him something of a nemesis for Mečiar. His criticisms of the Mečiar Government were influential in shaping the opinion of the OSCE community towards Slovakia. One could argue that Van der Stoel's constant criticisms of the Mečiar regime effectively highlighted the extent to which Meciar was out of step with international standards and therefore re-enforced Slovakia's isolation from Western Europe.

Just after the elections of September 1998 (which Mečiar lost), Van der Stoel met with a number of Slovak political leaders in Hainburg (close to the Austrian–Slovak border). To his interlocutors (including Mikulas Dzurinda who later became Prime Minister and Rudolf Schuster who later became President) the High Commissioner mentioned specific concerns about the minority policy of the previous Mečiar Government and made a number of recommendations concerning national minority issues.

When the new Government, which included Hungarian minority representatives, was formed later in October 1998 it immediately started to implement some of the High Commissioner's recommendations. The Law on Local Elections was abolished, school certificates in both the State and minority languages were reintroduced and the Government committed itself to introducing a new law on minority languages. This law was eventually approved in July 1999, but only after considerable debate within the coalition.

The interpretation of the Hungarian Coalition Party (SMK) concerning what should be contained in the law on minority languages was substantively different from the view held by the other coalition parties. Whereas the SMK wanted a

138 Letter to Zdenka Kramplova, Minister of Foreign Affairs of the Slovak Republic (24 July 1998), *Ibid.*

certain complementarity with the State Language Law, the other coalition parties wanted to concentrate mainly on the use of minority languages in official communications. Frustration mounted as a draft by one side was met by a counter draft by the other. The High Commissioner repeatedly urged the Dzurinda Government to give priority to the preparation of the law, pointing out that this was very much in the interest of Slovakia because not only would it help improve inter-ethnic relations, but it would help to open the door for negotiations on accession of Slovakia to the European Union.

Towards the end of April 1999, the High Commissioner telephoned Prime Minister Dzurinda to express his disappointment that there was still no draft of the law available for the analysis of international experts. During the conversation it was agreed that a joint group of international experts from the OSCE, the Council of Europe, and the European Commission would come to Bratislava on 29 April.

During the group's visit, it was evident that there was still no common Government draft. In order to add his voice to the discussions, the High Commissioner travelled to Bratislava at short notice and met with the Ministers responsible for drafting the law.

Written recommendations on the Government draft (the draft approved by three of the four coalition parties but not the SMK) were sent by the High Commissioner to the Prime Minister in a letter dated 14 May. In the letter, he stressed the need for achieving complementarity between the regulation of the State language and minority languages. On the question of the use of minority languages in official contacts with public authorities, the High Commissioner welcomed the Government's willingness to restore the right of persons belonging to national minorities to use their own language with public authorities in those regions where they constitute at least 20% of the population. However, he expressed the need to resolve issues concerning the use of minority languages in general. He said that 'legal certainty and public confidence would be served by including in the Law on the Use of Minority Languages expressed principles applicable to relevant law or expressed cross references to various relevant provisions or a combination of both'. This was done, mostly through the inclusion of references. For the sake of legal certainly, the High Commissioner also suggested including an article in the law that would explain the relationship between the law on minority languages and the law on State language, although, as he noted in his letter, 'I do realise that some of these provisions are clarified for the purposes of public administration and judicial consideration by virtue of the principles of *lex specialis* and *lex posterior derogat priori*'.[139]

These and other issues were addressed in a meeting hosted by the High Commissioner in The Hague on 14 June. At the meeting, representatives of the High Commissioner's Office, the European Commission and the Council of Europe met with a Slovak Government delegation led by Mr Knazko, Minister of Culture, and Mr Figel, State Secretary in the Prime Minister's Office. The representatives of the three organizations commented on the law with a view to clarifying the specific rights of persons belonging to national minorities to use their languages and to enhancing legal certainty about those entitlements, in accordance with the Slovak Constitution and relevant international standards.

Most of the comments of the international experts were regarded favourably by the Slovak delegation and incorporated into a new draft of the Law which was discussed at the beginning of July. However, there was still a lack of consensus between the SMK and its other coalition partners to the point where a rift was opening within the coalition. Meanwhile, opposition parties gathered names for a petition against the proposed law on minority languages.

After lengthy, and often heated, discussions, the Law on the Use of National Minority Languages was adopted by the Slovak Parliament on 10 July. The SMK voted against the law.

On 16 July, the Chairman of the National Council of the Slovak Republic Foreign Affairs Committee, Peter Weiss, sent a letter to the High Commissioner explaining the final outcome of the law and the reasons behind various amendments. He concluded by thanking the High Commissioner for his political work and his help and suggestions 'by which you contributed to the elaboration of the government's law proposal and its adoption. Policy is the art of the possible. Not all problems are solved but extremists both on one side or the other side did not succeed. This is the most important fact.'[140]

Although the High Commissioner regarded the law as an important step forward, he was disappointed by the Government's decision to remove a provision in the draft which expressly clarified the *lex specialis* character of the

---

139 Letter to Miklus Dzurinda, Prime Minister of the Slovak Republic (14 May 1999).

140 Letter from Peter Weiss, Chairman of the National Council of the Slovak Republic Foreign Affairs Committee, to HCNM Max van der Stoel (16 July 1999).

law and other laws regulating the use of minority languages. (He later received written assurances from the Government that this principle would be respected.) He was also sensitive to the SMK's reservations about the law. As a result, in a press release issued on 19 July he was careful to put particular emphasis on those provisions of the law relating to the use of minority languages in official communications. He said that 'as a result of the new Law, persons belonging to national minorities will be able to use their language in communications with public administrative organs and organs of local self-administration in those municipalities where the minority constitutes at least twenty per cent of the population'. He commented that this not only 'restored an established practice which was eliminated under the previous Government, but it brings Slovakia's law in this matter back into conformity with the Slovak Constitution, applicable international standards and specific recommendations from relevant international institutions, including my own office'. He said that he considered the 'solution of the question of the use of minority languages in official communications to be a step forward which follows previous decisions of the Government in the field of inter-ethnic relations, for example with regard to the use of bilingual school certificates and improvements in the policy of cultural subsidies'.[141]

However, the High Commissioner felt that certain further steps would be necessary in the future. He concluded his press release by saying: 'I hope that the Government will move without delay to settle other still unresolved inter-ethnic issues'.[142]

To explain their objections to the law and their views on inter-ethnic relations in Slovakia, three members of the SMK including Mr Bela Bugar, Chairman of the SMK, and Mr Miklos Duray, Honorary Chairman of the SMK visited the High Commissioner in The Hague on 22 July.

One of the 'unresolved inter-ethnic issues' was education. When the Dzurinda Government came to power in October 1998, the High Commissioner encouraged the Prime Minister to enact a number of reforms. Some reforms were carried out almost immediately. However, other issues remained unresolved. Therefore, the High Commissioner decided to hold a round-table on education

141 'High Commissioner Welcomes Restoration of Use of Minority Languages in Official Communications in Slovakia', OSCE HCNM Press Release 19 July 1999.

142 *Ibid.*

in Casta Papiernica on 23 and 24 September. This seminar allowed for discussion of a number of issues concerning minority education.

One of the most pressing minority-related education issues concerned teacher training for teachers in minority schools. The Government Programme of 1998 pledged that the Government would 'guarantee the improvement of the educational level of citizens belonging to minorities to the nation-wide average and solve the problem of preparation of teachers for schools with teaching languages of minorities, theologians, and cultural and educational staff in minority languages by creating an appropriate institutional level within existing universities'. By the autumn of 2000, the SMK was frustrated that this promise had not yet been kept. It called for the creation of a separate Hungarian faculty at Constantine the Philosopher University in Nitra which has a long tradition of teacher training. The High Commissioner visited the University at the end of October 2000. He also discussed the issue with Government ministers and Hungarian representatives. He decided to send education experts to Nitra in January 2001 to see what could be done to address the needs of the Hungarian community.

The teacher training issue was one of a number of issues that the SMK said needed to be addressed before it would give its support for the Constitutional amendments which were needed to bring Slovakia closer to EU accession. The others included ratification of the European Charter on Minority and Regional Languages, and land reform. Public administration reform – particularly the fate of two mostly Hungarian counties in the south of Slovakia – was also an issue on which the SMK sought compromise from its coalition partners. The High Commissioner discussed these issues, and the Government's policy towards the Roma, with a range of ministers during his October 2000 visit. He returned to Bratislava in June 2000 for a regional seminar on the Roma

The deadlock on constitutional reform was broken in early 2001. In January 2001 the High Commissioner, together with two international education experts, visited Constantine the Philosopher University in Nitra to see what steps could be taken to improve teacher training for minorities, particularly prospective Hungarian teachers. Soon after, the government gave its support to the creation of a separate faculty to provide instruction in Hungarian. It was then up to the University to decide how this recommendation would be implemented. In February, Slovakia signed the European Charter on Regional and Minority Languages. Compromise was also reached on land reform. SMK deputies therefore supported the constitutional amendments which were passed in late February 2001.

Roma

The plight of Europe's Roma population presented the High Commissioner with a dilemma. The Roma are clearly a minority in many OSCE States and face considerable hardship, but does their situation present a threat to security? As the High Commissioner is an instrument of early warning who is mandated to intervene in situations that have the potential to develop into conflict in the OSCE area, should he deal with Roma-related issues?

Whatever the arguments for and against, it was clear by the early 1990s that something had to be done to address the plight of the Roma in the OSCE area. At a meeting of the Committee of Senior Officials in late April 1993 the High Commissioner was requested by the Chairman-in-Office to 'study the social, economic and humanitarian problems relating to the Roma population in some participating States and the relevance of these problems to the Mandate of the High Commissioner and to report thereon to the Committee of Senior Officials through the Chairman-in-Office'. This request (itself unusual as the High Commissioner was seldom requested by the Chairman-in-Office to look at a particular issue) was phrased in such a way that it implied that the Roma did not fit conveniently into the High Commissioner's mandate; note the reference to the importance of looking not only at the Roma issue, but also the relevance to his mandate.

The report submitted in September 1993 and its findings and recommendations were discussed at the first Human Dimension Implementation Meeting in Warsaw which took place from 27 September to 15 October 1993. It noted that

> 'currently, due to complex factors including discrimination against them, the vast majority of Roma could be regarded as occupying an extremely vulnerable position in the societies, economies, and political systems of the region. This overall condition manifests itself in widespread and acute poverty,

> unemployment, illiteracy, lack of formal education, substandard housing, and other problems among the Roma. Furthermore, persistent anti-Roma prejudice has also found renewed expression in the collective 'scape-goating' of the Roma for the ills of society-at-large and has served as the backdrop for numerous attacks against Roma and their property in recent years.'[143]

He noted that in many cases, this was contributing to the migration of Roma. The problem of persistent discrimination and racism against the Roma was especially highlighted.

Having issued his report, Van der Stoel was hesitant to carry on as the main CSCE instrument for dealing with Roma issues. He clearly stated that 'the High Commissioner should become involved in only those situations that meet the criteria of the mandate'.[144] His recommendations were therefore directed not at what he could do, but at what should be done by the OSCE and its participating States.

To start with, he stressed that the participating States should reaffirm all OSCE commitments relevant to the situation of the Roma, implement civil, political, economic, social, and cultural rights and strengthen democratic institutions and the rule of law. He noted that policies that are introduced 'should be initiated on the basis of objective analysis of community needs, designed in consultation with the affected population, and implemented with their participation'.[145] He called for humane policies and procedures on such issues as political asylum and refugee provisions. He also recommended that citizenship laws should be devised and implemented in a reasonable fashion. More specifically, he suggested that Roma issues should be a standard topic of consideration at OSCE Human Dimension meetings, that resources available in the Human Dimension relevant to Roma-related affairs should be enhanced ('most logically through the Office for Democratic Institutions and Human Rights')[146] and that a point of contact for Roma issues should be established

143 Roma (Gypsies) in the CSCE Area: Report of the High Commissioner on National Minorities, Meeting of the Committee of Senior Officials, 21–23 September 1993, Executive Summary.

144 *Ibid.*, p. 13.

145 *Ibid.*, p. 14.

146 *Ibid.*, p. 15.

within the ODIHR. He encouraged more study on Roma-related issues and stressed the importance of complementarity and co-ordination of efforts among international organizations dealing with the Roma.

As a follow-up to the report, a high-level seminar on the Roma was organized on 20–23 September 1994 by the ODIHR and the office of the High Commissioner, in co-operation with the Council of Europe. It involved government officials, multilateral institutions, and non-governmental organizations including those of the Roma themselves. Later that year, in line with the High Commissioner's recommendations, a Contact Point on Roman and Sinti issues was established within the ODIHR. The decision, taken at the Budapest Review Conference of November 1994, mandated the Contact Point to serve as a clearing-house for information and expertise on Roma-related issues and to facilitate contacts on Roma issues between participating States, international institutions, and non-governmental organizations. In December 1998 the Oslo Ministerial Council decided to enhance the capabiliy of the OSCE regarding Roma and Sinti issues by strengthening the Contact Point through the appointment of an Adviser on Roma and Sinti Issues.

Although the main emphasis on Roma and Sinti issues was therefore with the ODIHR, the High Commissioner continued to follow Roma issues in several countries that he was engaged with. For example, during some visits to Slovakia, Hungary and Romania he came into contact with Roma representatives, visited Roma settlements and discussed the plight of the Roma with Government officials. As time passed, he noted little improvement in their situation. In 1999 he therefore felt that the situation of the Roma and Sinti merited fuller study and analysis. Financial support from the United States Government enabled the High Commissioner to engage Professor Diane Orentlicher of the Washington College of Law at the American University to assist with the research and preparation of a report on the Roma in the OSCE area. The report was prepared throughout 1999.

Although the report was not issued until April 2000, Van der Stoel's views and recommendations on the Roma issue were already clear by the autumn of 1999. At a Supplementary Human Dimension Meeting on Roma and Sinti Issues held in Vienna on 6 September 1999, he delivered a keynote speech in which he said that 'the plight of the Roma is something that we should all be concerned with, not only in the context of the protection of persons belonging to national minorities or the human dimension, but because it is a matter that affects us all as Europeans'. In his outspoken remarks, the High Commissioner said that 'for too long the Roma issue has been swept under the carpet'. He listed some of the common problems: intolerance, mutual distrust, poor housing, exclusion, unemployment, education and systemic discrimination. He also noted the symptoms: racist attacks and segregation, Roma asylum seekers, horrendous living conditions, extreme poverty, and disproportionately high rates of illiteracy and ill-health including infant mortality. He said that

> 'images of a mother and child begging in the streets, of families reduced to living on garbage dumps, or Roma houses being burnt down by angry mobs do not tell the whole story, but they stay with us because of their poignancy. Such images seem like they should be from another time or place. But they occur – here and now . . . in "modern" Europe, a Europe that prides itself on being a civilized continent based on common principles, particularly respect for human rights.'

He concluded by making a number of recommendations and saying that it is time 'to overcome the barriers that still divide us and build bridges instead of walls'.[147]

Van der Stoel was aware that the problem was not a simplistic one. He noted that 'the problem is multi-faceted and the challenges confronting Roma communities and OSCE Governments are complex. Furthermore, because of the rich diversity among Roma, it is not wise to make generalizations'. However, one point which he felt that he could make plainly and unequivocally was that 'discrimination and exclusion are fundamental features of the Roma experience'.[148]

This theme was the centre-piece of the *Report on the Situation of Roma and Sinti in the OSCE Area* issued in April 2000. In the introduction he warned that 'ten years after the Iron Curtain fell, Europe is at risk of being divided by new walls. Front and center among those persons being left outside Europe's

147 Address to the Supplementary Human Dimension Meeting on Roma and Sinti Issues, Vienna, 6 September 1999. The reference to 'walls' was meant to allude, in part, to the controversial wall built round an apartment block of Roma in Usti and Labem in the north of the Czech Republic.

148 *Ibid.*

new security and prosperity are the Roma'.[149]

The 170-page report comprehensively examined four main themes: discrimination and violence; education; living conditions; and political participation. In each section it reminded States of the international standards, outlined the problems, and offered recommendations.

The section on discrimination and racial violence tackled the question of discrimination in employment, public services and the administration of justice, racial violence (private, collective and by police), and the problem of racial stereotyping. A number of issues on combatting discrimination and racial violence were raised including the need for political leadership, proper legislation, training of public officials, conflict-management mechanisms by and between police and Roma communities, and specialized State bodies to combat discrimination. Other ideas included making available legal aid, developing codes for foreign investors, looking into the use of ethnic data, and using the media to discourage racial stereotyping and to promote greater public understanding of Romani culture.

On education, the report outlined the problem of illiteracy, school attendance and performance. The problem of racially-segregated schools and classes was raised, as was the problem of exclusion from enrollment. Furthermore, the High Commissioner noted that 'perhaps no legally-sanctioned practice affecting Roma is more pernicious than the phenomenon of channelling Roma children to "special schools" – schools for the mentally disabled'.[150] To combat these difficulties, the report highlighted various programmes aimed at improving Romani education. Among these are multi-cultural curricula and training, Romani schools, Romani teachers' assistants and mediators, pre-school and kindergarten classes, and extra-curricular support programmes.

The section on living conditions focused on conditions of housing and health care, especially discrimination against Roma with regard to access to and enjoyment of housing and health, and including the particular needs and situation of women. The cases of sedentary and nomadic Roma were examined, as were the issues of Roma relocation, and the exclusion of Roma families from municipalities.

---

149 *Report on the Situation of Roma and Sinti in the OSCE Area*, OSCE High Commissioner on National Minorities, April 2000.

150 *Ibid.*, p. 74.

The section on political participation noted that

> 'policies and laws aimed at improving the situation of Roma will no doubt fail without the active participation of Roma in the identification and analysis of specific problems, the design and elaboration of programs and projects and, ultimately, their implementation. This means that, in accordance with OSCE standards, Roma must enjoy some form of effective participation in the political decision-making process.'[151]

Several ways of involving Roma in government were raised and particular case studies were given as examples. Among the general conclusions made were that the Roma should be involved at an early stage in decisions that affect them, they should have meaningful (and not token) participation, participatory mechanisms should be inclusive and transparent, and Roma representatives should be involved in the implementation and evaluation of programmes aimed at improving the conditions of Romani communities. Citizenship issues were also addressed.

The High Commissioner concluded the report with a number of specific recommendations. Among these were the enhancement of the mandate of the OSCE Contact Point on Roma and Sinti Issues. As with the 1993 report, his conclusion was that although he was aware of the issues confronting the Roma, he was not the best person to deal with them. As he said in the report:

> 'While concerns relating to Roma may and sometimes do fall within the mandate of the HCNM, Romani communities experience a complex set of problems which are beyond the competency of the High Commissioner to address. These are matters falling squarely within the human dimension of OSCE commitments and require long-term programmatic assistance, monitoring and financial support. Adequate support should be given to ODIHR to carry out its functions in this important European matter.'[152]

Nevertheless, the High Commissioner could not simply walk away from the issue. In June 2000 a seminar was held in Bratislava where the recommendations of the Roma report were the main focus of discussion. The idea was to get

---

151 *Ibid.*, p. 128.

152 *Ibid.*, p. 10.

States with significant Roma populations to discuss the recommendations and to facilitate an exchange of views on putting the High Commissioner's recommendations into practice. This was obviously in the interests of the various Roma communities, but also for a growing number of OSCE-participating States that were looking for ways to deal more progressively and satisfactorily with Roma-related issues.

Georgia

The High Commissioner first visited Georgia on 23–25 June 1997 on the invitation of the Government of Georgia. He was fully briefed on the frozen conflict over Abkhazia by representatives of the Georgian Government, the OSCE Mission to Georgia and other representatives of the international community in Georgia. He was particularly interested in issues relating to the status of Abkhazia and the return of the approximately 250,000 Georgian internally displaced persons (IDPs) who fled Abkhazia in 1992/93. Although the Georgian Government was eager to have him involved in finding a settlement to the Abkhaz conflict, Van der Stoel felt that there was little added value to his involvement as a number of international actors (most notably the United Nations and to a lesser extent the OSCE Mission to Georgia) were already engaged in seeking a peaceful solution to the conflict. However, he recommended to the Chairman-in-Office that the OSCE stick to the clear line taken during the December 1996 Lisbon Summit[153] and to maintain regular contacts with the United Nations.

Van der Stoel returned to Georgia one year later in June 1998 following a crisis in the Gali district (the southernmost district of Abkhazia which has a high concentration of ethnic Georgians). The crisis (the worst in several years) unleashed a new wave of internally displaced persons and reopened festering wounds between Georgia and the Abkhaz separatists. Although a cease-fire was agreed in May, the underlying problems of the status of Abkhazia and the IDPs crisis remained unresolved. President Shevardnadze sought guarantees of the

153 The 1996 Lisbon Document expresses unequivocal support for the 'sovereignty and territorial integrity of Georgia within its recognized borders'. It also condemned '"ethnic cleansing" resulting in mass destruction and forcible expulsion of the predominantly Georgian population of Abkhazia'.

territorial integrity of Georgia, yet was willing to discuss a significant amount of autonomy for Abkhazia. At the same time, he expressed concern to the High Commissioner about the affects of the crisis in the context of worsening regional security (especially in Chechnya and Dagestan) and the overall security of the country, including relations with South Ossetia. The High Commissioner welcomed the decision of the President not to impose a military solution to the problem in Abkhazia. A planned trip by the High Commissioner to Sukhumi to meet the Abkhazian leader Vladislav Ardzinba (as suggested by the UN representative to Georgia) was postponed at the last minute. The meeting was rescheduled for August.

On 10 August the High Commissioner visited Sukhumi and had two long talks with Mr Ardzinba. Whereas Van der Stoel emphasized the importance that the OSCE attached to the territorial integrity of Georgia and the inviolability of its borders, Mr Ardzinba emphasized the right to self-determination. Van der Stoel explained that the implementation of the right to self-determination can take many forms and could have an internal and not just an external dimension. In this connection he referred to the Helsinki principles which refer to the need to respect the territorial integrity of states. His impression after the two meetings was that Mr Ardzinba was determined to stick to the idea of Abkhazia as an independent and sovereign state, despite international rejection of this concept. The gap between the Georgian and Abkhazian bargaining positions was very wide. Georgia insisted on the concept of a single state with an asymmetrical federal structure including Abkhazia, Adjaria and South Ossetia. It was willing to allow Abkhazia a wide degree of autonomy and a virtual veto right on Georgian legislation which affects Abkhazian interests (on the condition that Georgian internally displaced persons would be allowed to return to Abkhazia). Mr Ardzinba talked about two independent states which would enter into negotiations on a number of common institutions. The threat of military action to break the deadlock grew as Georgian nationalist forces rallied around the cause of the IDPs. The situation was complicated by other security threats in the region and sometimes turbulent Russian–Georgian relations (including over the issue of Russian bases). The High Commissioner urged the Government not to support the provocative actions of para-military forces. On several occasions Georgian officials expressed frustration to Van der Stoel at the division of roles between the UN and OSCE (where the UN takes a leading role in Abkhazia and the OSCE in South Ossetia) and at Russia's attitude towards the Abkhaz conflict. The High Commissioner urged the members of the UN's 'Geneva process'[154] (especially its Western members) to take a more active role in finding a settlement to the conflict.

The High Commissioner took a much more pro-active role on a different inter-ethnic issue relating to Georgia, namely the situation of the Meshketian Turks. The Meshketian Turks are a group of Muslim Georgians (Meskhs) who were deported in their tens of thousands, mostly from the Meskheti-Javakheti region of Georgia to Central Asia in 1944. Unlike many other entire nations that were deported by Stalin, very few Meshketian Turks have managed to return to their homeland. Most of those who settled around the Fergana Valley fled when violence erupted there in 1989/90. They then faced difficulties when trying to integrate into the Russian Federation, particularly in Krasnador Krai. They encountered difficulties with their legal status, lived in poor conditions and became the target of discrimination and racism. In the view of the High Commissioner, the situation was gradually becoming one that could lead to inter-ethnic tensions.

A meeting on the situation of the Meskhetian Turks was held in The Hague between 7 and 10 September 1998. It was co-sponsored by the Open Society's Forced Migration Projects, the High Commissioner's office and the UNHCR and was attended by governmental officials from Russia, Azerbaijan and Georgia, as well as Meshketian Turk representatives and international experts. The main goals of the meeting were to exchange first-hand information on the situation of the Meskhetian Turks, to promote dialogue and understanding among the parties involved, to discuss the problems faced by the Meskhetian Turks and possible solutions, to attract international attention to the problem, and to establish a follow-up framework of activities. Among the main issues discussed were human rights, repatriation and local integration. A final document was issued in which one of the conclusions was that the principles enshrined in the Program of Action adopted at the 1996 CIS Conference should serve as the framework for addressing the Meskhetian Turk issue. It is worth noting that one of the conditions of Georgia's acceptance to the Council of Europe was the improvement of the situation of the Meshketian Turks.

154 A negotitiating mechanism which brought together the parties as well as 'friends of the UN Secretary General regarding Georgia'; Russia, the USA, France, the United Kingdom, Germany and the head of the OSCE Mission as an observer.

A second meeting on the issue was held in Vienna on 15–17 March 1999. The aim of the meeting was to advance the identification of practical steps to improve the situation of the Meskhetian Turks. Many specific proposals and commitments were made by the Governments of Azerbaijan, Georgia and the Russian Federation.

In 2000 the High Commissioner's attention shifted to another minority situation in Georgia, namely that in Samtskhe-Javakheti. This region, created in 1995 and located in the south-west of the country, borders Armenia and Turkey and has a significant ethnic Armenian minority. Disagreements over economic, cultural (mostly linguistic and educational), and self-government issues often strained relations between the region and the central government in Tbilisi. There were even some violent clashes between Georgians and Armenians living in the region. Following the model used in Kazakhstan and Kyrgyzstan, the High Commissioner's office, in close co-operation with the Georgian government, set up a monitoring network to report on the political, social and economic situation and their impact on inter-ethnic relations and relations between the regional minority and the central government.

Kazakhstan

The High Commissioner paid his first visit to Kazakhstan from 18 to 25 April 1994. He was particularly interested in the problem of a large number of Germans and Russians leaving the country, partly because of poor economic conditions and also because of what many feared as a 'Kazakhization' of society at the expense of these minorities. He noted tensions between Kazakhs (who made up approximately 43% of the population) and Russians (who made up approximately 36%[155]). In the north and east of the country, where Russians make up the majority of the population, the bitterness of the Russians was particularly acute. Some groups, including some Cossack leaders, even called for the transfer of these areas to Russia.

After his visit, the High Commissioner sent a letter to Foreign Minister Kanat B. Saudabayev in which he made a number of observations and recommendations. He stressed the need for the development of democratic institutions, especially an independent judicial system and free elections. He urged the Government not to develop the Kazakh language at the expense of other languages, particularly Russian. Concerning disputes over hiring practises on the basis of ethnicity, the High Commissioner suggested that an independent study group composed of representatives from various ethnic groups analyze the issue and a special board be set up to deal with complaints of job discrimination and discrimination in higher education. He said that these and other steps might convince ethnic groups who had been leaving Kazakhstan to stay. The High Commissioner stressed that in order to maintain inter-ethnic harmony in Kazakhstan 'no ethnic group must strive for domination; persons of each ethnic group must have the conviction that there is equality amongst them, and that

155 It is worth noting that this percentage steadily fell after the independence of Kazakhstan.

nobody will be condemned to second-hand citizenship because he or she belongs to a specific ethnic group'.[156]

The Kazakh Government introduced measures to stem the tide of emigrants by concluding two treaties with Russia that provided virtually automatic Russian citizenship for Russians wanting to leave. (These treaties were not ratified by the Duma.) The hope was that Russians in Kazakhstan, in the knowledge that Russian citizenship would be available should the need arise, would opt to stay in Kazakhstan for a few years to see how the economic and political situation in the country would develop. To assuage fears of 'Kazakhization' constitutional amendments were introduced that stressed inclusive citizenship rather than ethnicity and raised the status of the Russian language to an official language.

When Van der Stoel visited Kazakhstan in October 1995 he expressed concern about the problem of the Cossacks. He suggested to address the issue in a round-table. During his visit the High Commissioner also took an interest in the work of the Assembly of the Peoples of Kazakhstan, a consultative body that met for the first time in March 1995. In the course of the next few years, the High Commissioner's office developed a close working relationship with the Assembly.

In February 1996 a seminar was held on the theme 'Building harmonious inter-ethnic relations in the Newly Independent States – the instance of Kazakhstan'. The seminar was co-organized by the High Commissioner, the Foundation on Inter-Ethnic Relations, the Administration of the President of Kazakhstan and the Foreign Ministry. Discussion centred on four themes: the relevance of international legal norms for domestic policy-making on minority issues and inter-ethnic relations; the development and implementation of language policy in a multi-lingual state; the role of state bodies in local level minority affairs; and the need for effective dialogue between minority representatives and state authorities.

In early September 1996 Van der Stoel visited those border areas of Kazakhstan where the percentage of ethnic Russians is particularly high. With the assistance of a plane provided by the Swiss Government, he flew to Ust-Kamenogorsk in the East, Petropavlovsk in the North, and Uralsk in the West. In every town he met with regional authorities and then held separate conversations, without

156 Letter to Kanat B. Saudabayev, Minister for Foreign Affairs of Kazakhstan (29 April 1994), CSCE Communication no. 26/94.

Government officials present, with representatives of various ethnic groups. His assessment was that the situation was stable, although – mainly because of economic difficulties – susceptible to populist manipulation. Van der Stoel made a special effort to find out more about the Cossack movement and spoke to some of its leaders. Many of them made it clear that they accepted the reality of the new state of Kazakhstan, but wanted to be able to protect their traditions and to have a special status within the country. Radical Cossacks, on the other hand, insisted that the Russians in the predominantly Russian areas of Kazakhstan should be able to decide by referendum whether their region ought to be part of Russia or not.

In order to facilitate dialogue on inter-ethnic issues in Kazakhstan – particularly on the Cossack issue – the High Commissioner organized a round-table hosted by the Swiss Government in Locarno on 8 and 9 December 1996 entitled 'Kazakhstan: Builiding a coherent multicultural and multiethnic society on the eve of the 21st century'. In attendance from Kazakhstan were representatives of the Presidential Administration, Parliament, the Cabinet of Ministers, ministries and government agencies, representatives of local authorities, the Assembly of Peoples of Kazakhstan (APK), leaders of regional assemblies of the APK, national-cultural centres and public associations and Archbishop Aleksiy of Almaty and Semipalatinsk. International experts were also present. The meeting presented a rare chance for dialogue on a wide range of inter-ethnic issues. It was suggested that the APK and its regional branches be developed and that a permanent system for monitoring inter-ethnic processes be established. Representatives also highlighted the need for the early adoption and implementation of the Law on Languages and the need for promoting more understanding of relevant legislation regarding minority rights. Other themes included the balance of rights and obligations of the state and the minorities and the improvement of legislation regulating inter-ethnic relations; ways to promote inter-ethnic harmony in Kazakhstan; and the need for fostering mechanisms for inter-ethnic and minority–majority dialogue. Issues relating to the country's Cossack movements were also raised. A common formula was agreed upon which has subsequently formed the basis for co-operation between the parties. Subsequently relations between the Kazakh authorities and the various Cossack authorities improved.

When the High Commissioner visited Kazakhstan in early June 1997 he tried to impress upon the Government the need for invigorating the work of the Assembly of the Peoples of Kazakhstan. He reached agreement with the Government on a proposal made at the Locarno round-table to establish a research and information centre attached to the Assembly. The aim was that through the instruments of surveys and polls conducted by the centre, a much clearer picture would emerge of the various ethnic groups regarding both governmental policies and their relationship with other ethnic groups. Agreement was also reached on the organization of training courses on international minority rights standards for deputy-governors who are charged with the responsibility for inter-ethnic relations in the various oblasts of the country. He attended a training course for such officials (organized by the Foundation on Inter-Ethnic Relations) when he visited Almaty in December 1997.

In a brief trip to Almaty in March 1999 the High Commissioner raised the issue of creating an independent Ombudsman for Human and Ethnic Rights. He followed this up with a letter on 30 April 1999 in which he and the Director of the OSCE's Office for Democratic Institutions and Human Rights sent a joint letter to President Nazarbaev recommending the creation of the independent Ombudsman.

The High Commissioner returned to Kazakhstan in late October as part of his trip to four of the five Central Asian republics. His visit came in the wake of critical remarks by the ODIHR concerning the parliamentary elections. Although this overshadowed his visit, the main focus of his discussions was on increased co-operation with the Assembly of the Peoples of Kazakhstan. The High Commissioner's office, together with the Foundation on Inter-Ethnic Relations (FIER), worked with the Assembly in co-organizing a number of conferences. Together they also set up a network of monitors in various regions of the country who report on a regular basis on inter-ethnic developments. During the visit the Assembly, the FIER and the High Commissioner's office organized a discussion on the draft law on the state language. It was designed to assuage fears by the Russian minority that their interests would be threatened by the strengthening of the state language.

In April 2000 the High Commissioner's office organized another seminar. This time the topic was the Lund Recommendations on the Effective Participation of Minorities in Public Life and their application to Kazakhstan. The High Commissioner also familiarized himself with the latest developments concerning the monitoring project carried out in co-operation with the Assembly of the Peoples of Kazakhstan.

As a follow-up to the seminars, in June 2000 the High Commissioner hosted a working visit by the leadership of the Assembly of the Peoples of Kazakhstan and the Ministry of Culture, Information and National Accord in order to discuss the legislative and administrative aspects of promoting better participation of minorities in public life.

A few months later, in October, the High Commissioner returned to Kazakhstan and met with a number of high-ranking officials including the Prime Minister, the Foreign Minister and the Minister for Information. The main topic of discussion was the threat to security posed by religious extremism. This theme was also the main focus of an international seminar in Almaty from 26 to 28 October organized by the Assembly of the Peoples of Kazakhstan, under the auspices of the High Commissioner's office. At the conclusion of the seminar, a statement was issued in which the participants noted that:

> '[guaranteeing the principle of freedom of religion] means the right to practice one's religion free from governmental interference. It also means that people have the right to interpret the basic tenets of their religion in a way that they consider appropriate, free from governmental interference.
>
> At the same time, freedom of religion does not signify absolute freedom. No religious group has the right to use violence in order to undermine or overthrow the existing political order, even though members of such a group might consider it their religious duty to do this. The state has the right to defend itself against such attempts and to impose severe punishment on religious extremists who commit acts of terrorism and violence. However, the state must take the utmost care to ensure that only the real culprits are prosecuted. It would be a major mistake to prosecute people simply because they deviate from the dominant or traditional interpretation of a religion. The use of excessive force leads to state extremism. Recent history shows that this merely strengthens support for extremist groups by those unjustly repressed. Thus, such measures should be excluded from the tool-box of anti-terrorist and anti-extremist policies.
>
> It is clear that current efforts by religious extremists to undermine the political structure in some Central Asian states are receiving support from outside the region. It is therefore of prime importance that concerted political and diplomatic efforts be applied in order to bring an end to this practice. On the other hand, there is a need to analyze carefully the methods the

> extremists are using in their efforts to mobilize support from the local population. There are clear indications that they are targeting those in difficult social and economic circumstances, notably young and unemployed people who have little hope of finding work, luring them with false promises of a better life after the revolution. Thus, the securing of peace and stability in Central Asia also has a clear economic dimension. Economic and social progress could perhaps provide the most effective barrier against extremist efforts to destabilize the region. There was always a strong case for extensive economic assistance to Central Asian states. In the light of the recent developments the need for this has even become more evident.'

In the following months, the High Commissioner, with the assistance of the monitoring network, continued to monitor the impact of religious extremism on inter-ethnic relations. Furthermore, as had been the case over the past few years, he followed developments in north Kazakhstan where there is a sizeable Russian population, and in the south of the country particularly around the Fergana valley.

Kyrgyzstan

As in Kazakhstan, the newly independent State of Kyrgyzstan faced the problem of a large exodus of Russians (and Germans). In order to help the Kyrgyz Government to find ways of stemming the tide, the High Commissioner suggested that a formula (on the Kakzakh model) be introduced that would create greater legal flexibility in regard to citizenship for Russians moving to and from Kyrgyzstan. Such a formula was adopted and President Askar Akaev went even further by proposing to Parliament that Russian be given the status of an official language.

During Van der Stoel's first visit to Kyrgyzstan on 22 to 24 April 1994 President Akaev proposed that a seminar be convened on inter-ethnic relations. A seminar on 'inter-ethnic relations and regional co-operation' took place in Bishkek on 16 to 19 May 1995. The main focus of the discussions was on the importance of inter-ethnic dialogue. In addition to attending the seminar, the High Commissioner also met with President Akaev and other leading Government and parliamentary officials.

Following the seminar, the High Commissioner sent a letter to the Foreign Minister containing a number of recommendations. He said that he was struck by 'the determination of President Akaev and of the Government to respect fully the OSCE norms and principles regarding persons belonging to national minorities and to spare no effort to remove sources of inter-ethnic tensions'.[157] In that respect he was encouraged by the creation of the Assembly of the People of Kyrgyzstan (APK). However, he felt that the Assembly 'had not yet reached its full potential'. Although lack of funding was part of the problem, Van der Stoel's remarks were a euphemism for the fact that the Assembly did not play a significant role in addressing acute inter-ethnic problems. He therefore proposed

157 Letter to Mrs Roza Otunbaeva, Minister for Foreign Affairs of the Republic of Kyrgyzstan (7 August 1995), HC/7/95.

a number of steps to give the minorities more opportunities to voice their concerns and demands. His main recommendation was to set up an Executive Council within the Assembly composed of representatives of the various National Cultural Centers and representatives of various Ministries which have competences which affect the interests of the various minorities in Kyrgyzstan.[158] He said that the intensification of the work of the Assembly was justified based on the fact that there were only 15 members of the 105 seat parliament who were persons belonging to national minorities in a country where national minorities constitute more than 40% of the population.

In his letter Van der Stoel also emphasized the need for research and monitoring of possible sources of inter-ethnic conflict. Since 1996, a monitoring network has been created and has provided regular reports to the High Commissioner and the Kyrgyz authorities on inter-ethnic relations in southern Kyrgyzstan.

This information was particularly important as the Kyrgyz authorities became increasingly concerned about inter-ethnic relations around Osh (in the south of Kyrgyzstan), which is mainly inhabited by ethnic Uzbeks. In 1990 Osh was the site of serious inter-ethnic clashes that led to the deaths of hundreds of people. Because of the high concentration of Uzbeks in the region, the threat of Islamic fundamentalism, and the fact that the Osh region is separated by a mountain range from the rest of Kyrgyzstan, the Kyrgyz Government worried about the possibility of the Uzbek minority pushing for autonomy. The High Commissioner familiarized himself with the latest developments in the Osh region when he visited Kyrgyzstan in October 1995. During that visit he also sought to ensure that his proposals regarding the Assembly of the People of Kyrgyzstan were not only formally accepted but also implemented.

In April 1996 he visited Osh and Djalal-Abad to meet with local officials. During his visit the High Commissioner registered considerable distrust between the Krygyz and Uzbek communities. He noted that there were totally insufficient channels of communication between the Kyrgyz authorities in the south and the various ethnic groups especially the Uzbeks. He also observed that deteriorating socio-economic conditions coupled with political marginalization were increasing the appeal of Islamic fundamentalism. (The number of mosques in the south mushroomed in the mid 1990s.) On his visit to Bishkek he shared

158 For more details see *ibid.*

his concerns with the Kyrgyz authorities.

When the High Commissioner returned in September 1996 he was encouraged by the more meaningful role that had been given to the APK. He was also appreciative of the work being carried out by the experts of the Peace Research Centre. Their work was instrumental in tracking developments in the south of the country where Van der Stoel remained concerned about inter-ethnic tensions. For example, one issue brought to his attention during the visit was the under-representation of Uzbekis in the Kyrgyz civil service and local administration including law enforcement agencies. Following the High Commissioner's recommendations, the President issued a decree aimed at rectifying the problem. Another important issue was the need for developing education opportunities in minority languages and having new textbooks in Uzbeki schools. New books were provided with the assistance of the Foundation on Inter-Ethnic Relations. In June 1997 the Foundation also assisted the Assembly of the Peoples of Kyrgyzstan to organize a workshop on inter-ethnic tolerance in Osh.

On a visit to Bishkek in December 1997, the High Commissioner proposed that a training course be organized for high officials on how to deal with sensitive ethnic issues. This proposal was favourably received by the President.

The High Commissioner returned to Kyrgyzstan in June 1998 to take part in a seminar on 'managing inter-ethnic relations' organized, on his request, by the Foundation on Inter-Ethnic Relations. The aim was to provide governors of various regions of Kyrgyzstan with a better insight into ways of handling inter-ethnic relations. During the visit he had a meeting with President Akaev where the issue of Islamic fundamentalism was discussed, particularly in the context of inter-ethnic relations in the Fergana valley.

In a visit to Bishkek in March 1999 the High Commissioner met again with the President. At the meeting it was agreed that Kyrgyzstan would initiate the process of establishing a new independent national institution for the protection and promotion of human rights, including rights of persons belonging to national minorities. The working title of the institution used is 'ombudsperson'. The High Commissioner also took part in the celebration of the fifth anniversary of the Assembly of the People of Kyrgyzstan. Later in private discussions with the President the High Commissioner expressed his concerns about the continuing inter-ethnic tensions in the south of the country.

The High Commissioner returned to this theme in a visit to Kyrgyzstan in

October 1999. He spoke with President Akaev about the recent incursion of Uzbeki gangs into Kyrgyzstan and the threat of radical Islamic fundamentalism. Remarks that Van der Stoel made to a Dutch television crew accompanying him on his visit were later made public to the effect that the High Commissioner warned of the threat of Islamic fundamentalism in Central Asia from Afghanistan and Uzbekistan.[159]

In April 2000 the High Commissioner visited Osh in southern Kyrgyzstan to get a better idea of the conditions contributing to a rise in religious extremism. He saw first-hand the poor economic conditions in the region which led to high unemployment, poverty and growing dissatisfaction among the population, particularly young males.

While in the capital Bishkek, Van der Stoel continued an ongoing dialogue with President Akaev on the need for respecting human rights and the rule of law. Having built up a rapport with the President, Van der Stoel was able to speak privately in a very open and frank way about the reaction of the OSCE-community towards recent developments in Kyrgyzstan, particularly regarding irregularities during the parliamentary elections. Like other OSCE institutions, the High Commissioner stressed the need to respect OSCE commitments and to maintain national unity in the fight against terrorism and extremism.

On a trip to Central Asia in October 2000, Van der Stoel again visited Osh in the south of the country. He remained concerned about lingering tensions between the Uzbek and Kyrgyz communities and how discontent was being channeled into religious extremism, especially among unemployed youth. The potential threat that this posed to security continued to be monitored by the network of contacts set up under the auspices of the High Commissioner's office.

---

159 'Van der Stoel warnt vor Fundamentalismus', *Frankfurter Allgemeine Zeitung*, 23 November 1999.

Uzbekistan

The High Commissioner also kept an eye on developments in Uzbekistan. He visited Uzbekistan in June 1998, mostly to look at the effect of Islamic fundamentalism on inter-ethnic relations. The High Commissioner stressed the need for making progress in the human rights field in order to solidify the foundations of civil society and provide democratization. Uzbek officials expressed concerns about the rise of extremism and Islamic fundmentalism, particularly in the Fergana valley, and about the spill-over effects of developments in Tajikistan and Afghanistan.

This theme was reiterated by Uzbek President Karimov during a visit by Van der Stoel to Tashkent in October 1999. He warned that the threat of religious extremism was being ignored by the OSCE. The President noted the difficulty that he faced in trying to live up to OSCE standards while combatting these destabilizing tendencies. It was clear to the High Commissioner that there was difference of opinion between President Karimov and President Akaev of Kyrgyzstan on how this threat should be addressed. President Akaev supported dialogue with people who might deviate from traditional Islam. He considered that they did not necessarily constitute an immediate threat to the State whereas Karimov was more suspect of those who did not respect traditional Islam.

Russian Federation
Petropavlovsk
Ust-Kamenogorsk
Astana
Uralsk
Kazakhstan
Caspian Sea
Almaty
Bishkek
Kyrgyzstan
Uzbekistan
Tashkent
China
Osh
Turkmenistan
Tajikistan
Dushanbe
Ashgabad
Iran
Afghanistan
N
0
800 km
Capital City
City
© Dora Kemp

Tajikistan

The High Commissioner visited Tajikistan twice, once in October 1999 and once in October 2000. During his visits he met with senior Tajik officials, members of the opposition and representatives of minorities. He was particularly interested in the effect that poverty, religious extremism and the danger of destabilization from neighboring Afghanistan and the Ferghana Valley could have on inter-ethnic relations. He noted that there were few minority-related problems, but that the general political and economic climate could adversely affect inter-ethnic relations. This was particularly the case concerning the country's sizeable Uzbek minority (that makes up 20–25% of the population) which is concentrated in the south of the country.

PART THREE

Extracts from the Document of the Copenhagen Meeting of the Conference on the Human Dimension of the CSCE, 1990

(Introduction)

The representatives of the participating States of the Conference on Security and Co-operation in Europe (CSCE), Austria, Belgium, Bulgaria, Canada, Cyprus, Czechoslovakia, Denmark, Finland, France, the German Democratic Republic, the Federal Republic of Germany, Greece, the Holy See, Hungary, Iceland, Ireland, Italy, Liechtenstein, Luxembourg, Malta, Monaco, the Netherlands, Norway, Poland, Portugal, Romania, San Marino, Spain, Sweden, Switzerland, Turkey, the Union of Soviet Socialist Republics, the United Kingdom, the United States of America and Yugoslavia, met in Copenhagen from 5 to 29 June 1990, in accordance with the provisions relating to the Conference on the Human Dimension of the CSCE contained in the Concluding Document of the Vienna Follow-up Meeting of the CSCE.

The representative of Albania attended the Copenhagen Meeting as observer.

The first Meeting of the Conference was held in Paris from 30 May to 23 June 1989.

The Copenhagen Meeting was opened and closed by the Minister for Foreign Affairs of Denmark.

The formal opening of the Copenhagen Meeting was attended by Her Majesty the Queen of Denmark and His Royal Highness the Prince Consort.

Opening statements were made by Ministers and Deputy Ministers of the participating States.

At a special meeting of the Ministers for Foreign Affairs of the participating States of the CSCE on 5 June 1990, convened on the invitation of the Minister for Foreign Affairs of Denmark, it was agreed to convene a Preparatory

Committee in Vienna on 10 July 1990 to prepare a Summit Meeting in Paris of their Heads of State or Government.

IV

(30) The participating States recognize that the questions relating to national minorities can only be satisfactorily resolved in a democratic political framework based on the rule of law, with a functioning independent judiciary. This framework guarantees full respect for human rights and fundamental freedoms, equal rights and status for all citizens, the free expression of all their legitimate interests and aspirations, political pluralism, social tolerance and the implementation of legal rules that place effective restraints on the abuse of governmental power.

They also recognize the important role of non-governmental organizations, including political parties, trade unions, human rights organizations and religious groups, in the promotion of tolerance, cultural diversity and the resolution of questions relating to national minorities.

They further reaffirm that respect for the rights of persons belonging to national minorities as part of universally recognized human rights is an essential factor for peace, justice, stability and democracy in the participating States.

(31) Persons belonging to national minorities have the right to exercise fully and effectively their human rights and fundamental freedoms without any discrimination and in full equality before the law.

The participating States will adopt, where necessary, special measures for the purpose of ensuring to persons belonging to national minorities full equality with the other citizens in the exercise and enjoyment of human rights and fundamental freedoms.

(32) To belong to a national minority is a matter of a person's individual choice and no disadvantage may arise from the exercise of such choice.

Persons belonging to national minorities have the right freely to express, preserve and develop their ethnic, cultural, linguistic or religious identity and to maintain and develop their culture in all its aspects, free of any attempts at assimilation against their will. In particular, they have the right

(32.1) — to use freely their mother tongue in private as well as in public;

(32.2) — to establish and maintain their own educational, cultural and religious institutions, organizations or associations, which can seek voluntary financial and other contributions as well as public assistance, in conformity with national legislation;

(32.3) — to profess and practise their religion, including the acquisition, possession and use of religious materials, and to conduct religious educational activities in their mother tongue;

(32.4) — to establish and maintain unimpeded contacts among themselves within their country as well as contacts across frontiers with citizens of other States with whom they share a common ethnic or national origin, cultural heritage or religious beliefs;

(32.5) — to disseminate, have access to and exchange information in their mother tongue;

(32.6) — to establish and maintain organizations or associations within their country and to participate in international non-governmental organizations.

Persons belonging to national minorities can exercise and enjoy their rights individually as well as in community with other members of their group. No disadvantage may arise for a person belonging to a national minority on account of the exercise or non-exercise of any such rights.

(33) The participating States will protect the ethnic, cultural, linguistic and religious identity of national minorities on their territory and create conditions for the promotion of that identity. They will take the necessary measures to that effect after due consultations, including contacts with organizations or associations of such minorities, in accordance with the decision-making procedures of each State.

Any such measures will be in conformity with the principles of equality and non-discrimination with respect to the other citizens of the participating State concerned.

(34) The participating States will endeavour to ensure that persons belonging to national minorities, notwithstanding the need to learn the official

language or languages of the State concerned, have adequate opportunities for instruction of their mother tongue or in their mother tongue, as well as, wherever possible and necessary, for its use before public authorities, in conformity with applicable national legislation.

In the context of the teaching of history and culture in educational establishments, they will also take account of the history and culture of national minorities.

(35) The participating States will respect the right of persons belonging to national minorities to effective participation in public affairs, including participation in the affairs relating to the protection and promotion of the identity of such minorities.

The participating States note the efforts undertaken to protect and create conditions for the promotion of the ethnic, cultural, linguistic and religious identity of certain national minorities by establishing, as one of the possible means to achieve these aims, appropriate local or autonomous administrations corresponding to the specific historical and territorial circumstances of such minorities and in accordance with the policies of the State concerned.

(36) The participating States recognize the particular importance of increasing constructive co-operation among themselves on questions relating to national minorities. Such co-operation seeks to promote mutual understanding and confidence, friendly and good-neighbourly relations, international peace, security and justice.

Every participating State will promote a climate of mutual respect, understanding, co-operation and solidarity among all persons living on its territory, without distinction as to ethnic or national origin or religion, and will encourage the solution of problems through dialogue based on the principles of the rule of law.

(37) None of these commitments may be interpreted as implying any right to engage in any activity or perform any action in contravention of the purposes and principles of the Charter of the United Nations, other obligations under international law or the provisions of the Final Act, including the principle of territorial integrity of States.

(38) The participating States, in their efforts to protect and promote the rights

of persons belonging to national minorities, will fully respect their undertakings under existing human rights conventions and other relevant international instruments and consider adhering to the relevant conventions, if they have not yet done so, including those providing for a right of complaint by individuals.

(39) The participating States will co-operate closely in the competent international organizations to which they belong, including the United Nations and, as appropriate, the Council of Europe, bearing in mind their ongoing work with respect to questions relating to national minorities.

They will consider convening a meeting of experts for a thorough discussion of the issue of national minorities.

(40) The participating States clearly and unequivocally condemn totalitarianism, racial and ethnic hatred, anti-semitism, xenophobia and discrimination against anyone as well as persecution on religious and ideological grounds. In this context, they also recognize the particular problems of Roma (gypsies).

They declare their firm intention to intensify the efforts to combat these phenomena in all their forms and therefore will

(40.1) — take effective measures, including the adoption, in conformity with their constitutional systems and their international obligations, of such laws as may be necessary, to provide protection against any acts that constitute incitement to violence against persons or groups based on national, racial, ethnic or religious discrimination, hostility or hatred, including anti-semitism;

(40.2) — commit themselves to take appropriate and proportionate measures to protect persons or groups who may be subject to threats or acts of discrimination, hostility or violence as a result of their racial, ethnic, cultural, linguistic or religious identity, and to protect their property;

(40.3) — take effective measures, in conformity with their constitutional systems, at the national, regional and local levels to promote understanding and tolerance, particularly in the fields of education, culture and information;

(40.4) — endeavour to ensure that the objectives of education include special attention to the problem of racial prejudice and hatred and to the development of respect for different civilizations and cultures;

(40.5) — recognize the right of the individual to effective remedies and endeavour to recognize, in conformity with national legislation, the right of interested persons and groups to initiate and support complaints against acts of discrimination, including racist and xenophobic acts;

(40.6) — consider adhering, if they have not yet done so, to the international instruments which address the problem of discrimination and ensure full compliance with the obligations therein, including those relating to the submission of periodic reports;

(40.7) — consider, also, accepting those international mechanisms which allow States and individuals to bring communications relating to discrimination before international bodies.

ANNEX 2

Report of the CSCE Meeting of Experts on National Minorities, Geneva 1991

The representatives of Albania, Austria, Belgium, Bulgaria, Canada, Cyprus, the Czech and Slovak Federal Republic, Denmark, Finland, France, Germany, Greece, the Holy See, Hungary, Iceland, Ireland, Italy, Liechtenstein, Luxembourg, Malta, Monaco, the Netherlands-European Community, Norway, Poland, Portugal, Romania, San Marino, Spain, Sweden, Switzerland, Turkey, the Union of Soviet Socialist Republics, the United Kingdom, the United States of America and Yugoslavia met in Geneva from 1 to 19 July 1991 in accordance with the relevant provisions of the Charter of Paris for a New Europe.

An opening address to the Meeting was delivered by H.E. Rene Felber, Federal Councillor, Head of the Federal Department of Foreign Affairs of Switzerland, on behalf of the host country. Opening statements were made by H.E. Catharina Dales, Minister of the Interior of the Netherlands on behalf of the Netherlands-European Community, and by Heads of Delegation of the participating States. Contributions to the Meeting were made by Ms. Catherine Lalumiere, Secretary General of the Council of Europe, and Mr. Jan Martenson, Under-Secretary-General in charge of the United Nations Centre for Human Rights in Geneva. The State Secretary for Foreign Affairs of the host country, Mr. Klaus Jacobi, delivered a closing address to the Meeting.

In accordance with the relevant provisions of the Charter of Paris, the representatives of the participating States had a thorough discussion on the issues of national minorities and of the rights of persons belonging to them that reflected the diversity of situations and of the legal, historical, political and economic backgrounds. They had an exchange of views on practical experience with national minorities, in particular on national legislation, democratic institutions, international instruments and other possible forms of co-operation.

Views were expressed on the implementation of the relevant CSCE commitments, and the representatives of the participating States also considered the scope for the improvement of relevant standards. They also considered new measures aimed at improving the implementation of the aforementioned commitments.

A number of proposals were submitted for consideration by the Meeting and, following their deliberations, the representatives of the participating States adopted this Report.

The text of the Report of the Geneva Meeting of Experts on National Minorities will be published in each participating State, which will disseminate it and make it known as widely as possible.

The representatives of the participating States note that the Council will take into account the summing up of the Meeting, in accordance with the Charter of Paris for a New Europe.

I.

Recognizing that their observance and full exercise of human rights and fundamental freedoms, including those of persons belonging to national minorities, are the foundation of the New Europe,

Reaffirming their deep conviction that friendly relations among their peoples, as well as peace, justice, stability and democracy, require that the ethnic, cultural, linguistic and religious identity of national minorities be protected, and conditions for the promotion of that identity be created,

Convinced that, in States with national minorities, democracy requires that all persons, including those belonging to national minorities, enjoy full and effective equality of rights and fundamental freedoms and benefit from the rule of law and democratic institutions,

Aware of the diversity of situations and constitutional systems in their countries, and therefore recognizing that various approaches to the implementation of CSCE commitments regarding national minorities are appropriate,

Mindful of the importance of exerting efforts to address national minorities issues, particularly in areas where democratic institutions are being consolidated and questions relating to national minorities are of special concern,

Aware that national minorities form an integral part of the society of the States in which they live and that they are a factor of enrichment of each respective State and society,

Confirming the need to respect and implement fully and fairly their undertakings in the field of human rights and fundamental freedoms as set forth in the international instruments by which they may be bound,

Reaffirming their strong determination to respect and apply, to their full extent, all their commitments relating to national minorities and persons belonging to them in the Helsinki Final Act, the Madrid Concluding Document and the Vienna Concluding Document, the Document of the Copenhagen Meeting of the Conference on the Human Dimension of the CSCE, the Document of the Cracow Symposium on the Cultural Heritage as well as the Charter of Paris for a New Europe, the participating States present below the summary of their conclusions.

The representatives of the participating States took as the fundamental basis of their work the commitments undertaken by them with respect to national minorities as contained in the relevant adopted CSCE documents, in particular those in the Charter of Paris for a New Europe and the Document of the Copenhagen Meeting of the Conference on the Human Dimension of the CSCE, which they fully reaffirmed.

II.

The participating States stress the continued importance of a thorough review of implementation of their CSCE commitments relating to persons belonging to national minorities.

They emphasize that human rights and fundamental freedoms are the basis for the protection and promotion of rights of persons belonging to national minorities. They further recognize that questions relating to national minorities can only be satisfactorily resolved in a democratic political framework based on the rule of law, with a functioning independent judiciary. This framework guarantees full respect for human rights and fundamental freedoms, equal rights and status for all citizens, including persons belonging to national minorities, the free expression of all their legitimate interests and aspirations, political pluralism, social tolerance and the implementation of legal rules that place effective restraints on the abuse of governmental power.

Issues concerning national minorities, as well as compliance with international obligations and commitments concerning the rights of persons belonging to them, are matters of legitimate international concern and consequently do not constitute exclusively an internal affair of the respective State.

They note that not all ethnic, cultural, linguistic or religious differences necessarily lead to the creation of national minorities.

III.

Respecting the right of persons belonging to national minorities to effective participation in public affairs, the participating States consider that when issues relating to the situation of national minorities are discussed within their countries, they themselves should have the effective opportunity to be involved, in accordance with the decision-making procedures of each State. They further consider that appropriate democratic participation of persons belonging to national minorities or their representatives in decision-making or consultative bodies constitutes an important element of effective participation in public affairs.

They consider that special efforts must be made to resolve specific problems in a constructive manner and through dialogue by means of negotiations and consultations with a view to improving the situation of persons belonging to national minorities. They recognize that the promotion of dialogue between States, and between States and persons belonging to national minorities, will be most successful when there is a free flow of information and ideas between all parties. They encourage unilateral, bilateral and multilateral efforts by governments to explore avenues for enhancing the effectiveness of their implementation of CSCE commitments relating to national minorities.

The participating States further consider that respect for human rights and fundamental freedoms must be accorded on a non-discriminatory basis throughout society. In areas inhabited mainly by persons belonging to a national minority, the human rights and fundamental freedoms of persons belonging to that minority, of persons belonging to the majority population of the respective State, and of persons belonging to other national minorities residing in these areas will be equally protected.

They reconfirm that persons belonging to national minorities have the right freely to express, preserve and develop their ethnic, cultural, linguistic or religious identity and to maintain and develop their culture in all its aspects, free of any attempts at assimilation against their will.

They will permit the competent authorities to inform the Office for Free Elections of all scheduled public elections on their territories, including those held below national level. The participating States will consider favourably, to the extent permitted by law, the presence of observers at elections held below the national level, including in areas inhabited by national minorities, and will endeavour to facilitate their access.

IV.

The participating States will create conditions for persons belonging to national minorities to have equal opportunity to be effectively involved in the public life, economic activities, and building of their societies.

In accordance with paragraph 31 of the Copenhagen Document, the participating States will take the necessary measures to prevent discrimination against individuals, particularly in respect of employment, housing and education, on the grounds of belonging or not belonging to a national minority. In that context, they will make provision, if they have not yet done so, for effective recourse to redress for individuals who have experienced discriminatory treatment on the grounds of their belonging or not belonging to a national minority, including by making available to individual victims of discrimination a broad array of administrative and judicial remedies.

The participating States are convinced that the preservation of the values and of the cultural heritage of national minorities requires the involvement of persons belonging to such minorities and that tolerance and respect for different cultures are of paramount importance in this regard. Accordingly, they confirm the importance of refraining from hindering the production of cultural materials concerning national minorities, including by persons belonging to them.

The participating States affirm that persons belonging to a national minority will enjoy the same rights and have the same duties of citizenship as the rest of the population.

The participating States reconfirm the importance of adopting, where necessary, special measures for the purpose of ensuring to persons belonging to national minorities full equality with the other citizens in the exercise and enjoyment of human rights and fundamental freedoms. They further recall the need to take the necessary measures to protect the ethnic, cultural, linguistic and religious identity of national minorities on their territory and create conditions for the promotion of that identity; any such measures will be in conformity with the principles of equality and non-discrimination with respect to the other citizens of the participating State concerned.

They recognize that such measures, which take into account, *inter alia*, historical and territorial circumstances of national minorities, are particularly important in areas where democratic institutions are being consolidated and national minorities issues are of special concern.

Aware of the diversity and varying constitutional systems among them, which make no single approach necessarily generally applicable, the participating States note with interest that positive results have been obtained by some of them in an appropriate democratic manner by, *inter alia*:

- advisory and decision-making bodies in which minorities are represented, in particular with regard to education, culture and religion;
- elected bodies and assemblies of national minority affairs;
- local and autonomous administration, as well as autonomy on a territorial basis, including the existence of consultative, legislative and executive bodies chosen through free and periodic elections;
- self-administration by a national minority of aspects concerning its identity in situations where autonomy on a territorial basis does not apply;
- decentralized or local forms of government;
- bilateral and multilateral agreements and other arrangements regarding national minorities;
- for persons belonging to national minorities, provision of adequate types and levels of education in their mother tongue with due regard to the number, geographic settlement patterns and cultural traditions of national minorities;
- funding the teaching of minority languages to the general public, as well as the inclusion of minority languages in teacher-training institutions, in particular in regions inhabited by persons belonging to national minorities;

- in cases where instruction in a particular subject is not provided in their territory in the minority language at all levels, taking the necessary measures to find means of recognizing diplomas issued abroad for a course of study completed in that language;
- creation of government research agencies to review legislation and disseminate information related to equal rights and non-discrimination;
- provision of financial and technical assistance to persons belonging to national minorities who so wish to exercise their right to establish and maintain their own educational, cultural and religious institutions, organizations and associations;
- governmental assistance for addressing local difficulties relating to discriminatory practices (e.g. a citizens relations service);
- encouragement of grassroots community relations efforts between minority communities, between majority and minority communities, and between neighbouring communities sharing borders, aimed at helping to prevent local tensions from arising and address conflicts peacefully should they arise; and
- encouragement of the establishment of permanent mixed commissions, either inter-State or regional, to facilitate continuing dialogue between the border regions concerned.

The participating States are of the view that these or other approaches, individually or in combination, could be helpful in improving the situation of national minorities on their territories.

V.

The participating States respect the right of persons belonging to national minorities to exercise and enjoy their rights alone or in community with others, to establish and maintain organizations and associations within their country, and to participate in international non-governmental organizations.

The participating States reaffirm, and will not hinder the exercise of, the right of persons belonging to national minorities to establish and maintain their own educational, cultural and religious institutions, organizations and associations.

In this regard, they recognize the major and vital role that individuals, non-governmental organizations, and religious and other groups play in fostering cross-cultural understanding and improving relations at all levels of society, as well as across international frontiers.

They believe that the first-hand observations and experience of such organizations, groups, and individuals can be of great value in promoting the implementation of CSCE commitments relating to persons belonging to national minorities. They therefore will encourage and not hinder the work of such organizations, groups and individuals and welcome their contributions in this area.

VI.

The participating States, concerned by the proliferation of acts of racial, ethnic and religious hatred, anti-semitism, xenophobia and discrimination, stress their determination to condemn, on a continuing basis, such acts against anyone.

In this context, they reaffirm their recognition of the particular problems of Roma (gypsies). They are ready to undertake effective measures in order to achieve full equality of opportunity between persons belonging to Roma ordinarily resident in their State and the rest of the resident population. They will also encourage research and studies regarding Roma and the particular problems they face.

They will take effective measures to promote tolerance, understanding, equality of opportunity and good relations between individuals of different origins within their country.

Further, the participating States will take effective measures, including the adoption, in conformity with their constitutional law and their international obligations, if they have not already done so, of laws that would prohibit acts that constitute incitement to violence based on national, racial, ethnic or religious discrimination, hostility or hatred, including anti-semitism, and policies to enforce such laws.

Moreover, in order to heighten public awareness of prejudice and hatred, to improve enforcement of laws against hate-related crime and otherwise to further efforts to address hatred and prejudice in society, they will make efforts to collect, publish on a regular basis, and make available to the public, data about crimes on their respective territories that are based on prejudice as to race, ethnic identity or religion, including the guidelines used for the collection of such data. These data should not contain any personal information.

They will consult and exchange views and information at the international level, including at future meetings of the CSCE, on crimes that manifest evidence of prejudice and hate.

VII.

Convinced that the protection of the rights of persons belonging to national minorities necessitates free flow of information and exchange of ideas, the participating States emphasize the importance of communication between persons belonging to national minorities without interference by public authorities and regardless of frontiers. The exercise of such rights may be subject only to such restrictions as are prescribed by law and are consistent with international standards. They reaffirm that no one belonging to a national minority, simply by virtue of belonging to such a minority, will be subject to penal or administrative sanctions for having had contacts within or outside his/her own country.

In access to the media, they will not discriminate against anyone based on ethnic, cultural, linguistic or religious grounds. They will make information available that will assist the electronic mass media in taking into account, in their programmes, the ethnic, cultural, linguistic and religious identity of national minorities.

They reaffirm that establishment and maintenance of unimpeded contacts among persons belonging to a national minority, as well as contacts across frontiers by persons belonging to a national minority with persons with whom they share a common ethnic or national origin, cultural heritage or religious belief, contributes to mutual understanding and promotes good-neighbourly relations.

They therefore encourage transfrontier co-operation arrangements on a national, regional and local level, *inter alia*, on local border crossings, the preservation of and visits to cultural and historical monuments and sites, tourism, the improvement of traffic, the economy, youth exchange, the protection of the environment and the establishment of regional commissions.

They will also encourage the creation of informal working arrangements (e.g. workshops, committees both within and between the participating States) where national minorities live, to discuss issues of, exchange experience on, and present proposals on, issues related to national minorities.

With a view to improving their information about the actual situation of national minorities, the participating States will, on a voluntary basis distribute, through the CSCE Secretariat, information to other participating States about the situation of national minorities in their respective territories, as well as statements of national policy in that respect.

The participating States will deposit with the CSCE Secretariat copies of the contributions made in the Plenary of the CSCE Meeting of Experts on National Minorities which they wish to be available to the public.

VIII.

The participating States welcome the positive contribution made by the representatives of the United Nations and the Council of Europe to the proceedings of the Geneva Meeting of Experts on National Minorities. They note that the work and activities of these organizations will be of continuing relevance to the CSCE's consideration of national minorities issues.

The participating States note that appropriate CSCE mechanisms may be of relevance in addressing questions relating to national minorities. Further, they recommend that the third Meeting of the Conference on the Human Dimension of the CSCE consider expanding the Human Dimension Mechanism. They will promote the involvement of individuals in the protection of their rights, including the rights of persons belonging to national minorities.

Finally, the representatives of the participating States request the Executive Secretary of the Meeting to transmit this Report to the third Meeting of the Conference on the Human Dimension of the CSCE.

The representatives of the participating States express their profound gratitude to the people and Government of Switzerland for the excellent organization of the Geneva Meeting and the warm hospitality extended to the delegations that participated in the Meeting.

Geneva, 19 July 1991

ANNEX 3

CSCE High Commissioner on National Minorities CSCE Helsinki Document 1992

(1) The participating States decide to establish a High Commissioner on National Minorities.

Mandate

(2) The High Commissioner will act under the aegis of the CSO and will thus be an instrument of conflict prevention at the earliest possible stage.

(3) The High Commissioner will provide 'early warning' and, as appropriate, 'early action' at the earliest possible stage in regard to tensions involving national minority issues which have not yet developed beyond an early warning stage, but, in the judgement of the High Commissioner, have the potential to develop into a conflict within the CSCE area, affecting peace, stability or relations between participating States, requiring the attention of and action by the Council or the CSO.

(4) Within the mandate, based on CSCE principles and commitments, the High Commissioner will work in confidence and will act independently of all parties directly involved in the tensions.

(5a) The High Commissioner will consider national minority issues occurring in the State of which the High Commissioner is a national or a resident, or involving a national minority to which the High Commissioner belongs, only if all parties directly involved agree, including the State concerned.

(5b) The High Commissioner will not consider national minority issues in situations involving organized acts of terrorism.

(5c) Nor will the High Commissioner consider violations of CSCE commitments with regard to an individual person belonging to a national minority.

(6) In considering a situation, the High Commissioner will take fully into account the availability of democratic means and international instruments to respond to it, and their utilization by the parties involved.

(7) When a particular national minority issue has been brought to the attention of the CSO, the involvement of the High Commissioner will require a request and a specific mandate from the CSO.

Profile, appointment, support

(8) The High Commissioner will be an eminent international personality with long-standing relevant experience from whom an impartial performance of the function may be expected.

(9) The High Commissioner will be appointed by the Council by consensus upon the recommendation of the CSO for a period of three years, which may be extended for one further term of three years only.

(10) The High Commissioner will draw upon the facilities of the ODIHR in Warsaw, and in particular upon the information relevant to all aspects of national minority questions available at the ODIHR.

Early warning

(11) The High Commissioner will:

(11a) collect and receive information regarding national minority issues from sources described below (see Supplement paragraphs (23)-(25));

(11b) assess at the earliest possible stage the role of the parties directly concerned, the nature of the tensions and recent developments therein and, where possible, the potential consequences for peace and stability within the CSCE area;

(11c) to this end, be able to pay a visit, in accordance with paragraph (17) and Supplement paragraphs (27)-(30), to any participating State and communicate in person, subject to the provisions of paragraph (25), with parties directly concerned to obtain first-hand information about the situation of national minorities.

(12) The High Commissioner may during a visit to a participating State, while obtaining first-hand information from all parties directly involved, discuss the questions with the parties, and where appropriate promote dialogue, confidence and co-operation between them.

Provision of early warning

(13) If, on the basis of exchanges of communications and contacts with relevant parties, the High Commissioner concludes that there is a prima facie risk of potential conflict (as set out in paragraph (3)) he/she may issue an early warning, which will be communicated promptly by the Chairman-in-Office to the CSO.

(14) The Chairman-in-Office will include this early warning in the agenda for the next meeting of the CSO. If a State believes that such an early warning merits prompt consultation, it may initiate the procedure set out in Annex 2 of the Summary of Conclusions of the Berlin Meeting of the Council ('Emergency Mechanism').

(15) The High Commissioner will explain to the CSO the reasons for issuing the early warning.

Early action

(16) The High Commissioner may recommend that he/she be authorized to enter into further contact and closer consultations with the parties concerned with a view to possible solutions, according to a mandate to be decided by the CSO. The CSO may decide accordingly.

Accountability

(17) The High Commissioner will consult the Chairman-in-Office prior to a departure for a participating State to address a tension involving national minorities. The Chairman-in-Office will consult, in confidence, the participating State(s) concerned and may consult more widely.

(18) After a visit to a participating State, the High Commissioner will provide strictly confidential reports to the Chairman-in-Office on the findings and progress of the High Commissioner's involvement in a particular question.

(19) After termination of the involvement of the High Commissioner in a particular issue, the High Commissioner will report to the Chairman-in-Office on the findings, results and conclusions. Within a period of one month, the Chairman-in-Office will consult, in confidence, on the findings, results and conclusions the participating State(s) concerned and may consult more widely. Thereafter the report, together with possible comments, will be transmitted to the CSO.

(20) Should the High Commissioner conclude that the situation is escalating into a conflict, or if the High Commissioner deems that the scope for action by the High Commissioner is exhausted, the High Commissioner shall, through the Chairman-in-Office, so inform the CSO.

(21) Should the CSO become involved in a particular issue, the High Commissioner will provide information and, on request, advice to the CSO, or to any other institution or organization which the CSO may invite, in accordance with the provisions of Chapter III of this document, to take action with regard to the tensions or conflict.

(22) The High Commissioner, if so requested by the CSO and with due regard to the requirement of confidentiality in his/her mandate, will provide information about his/her activities at CSCE implementation meetings on Human Dimension issues.

Supplement

Sources of information about national minority issues

(23) The High Commissioner may:

(23a) collect and receive information regarding the situation of national minorities and the role of parties involved therein from any source, including the media and non-governmental organizations with the exception referred to in paragraph (25);

(23b) receive specific reports from parties directly involved regarding developments concerning national minority issues. These may include reports on violations of CSCE commitments with respect to national minorities as well as other violations in the context of national minority issues.

(24) Such specific reports to the High Commissioner should meet the following requirements:

- they should be in writing, addressed to the High Commissioner as such and signed with full names and addresses;
- they should contain a factual account of the developments which are relevant to the situation of persons belonging to national minorities and the role of the parties involved therein, and which have taken place recently, in principle not more than 12 months previously. The reports should contain information which can be sufficiently substantiated.

(25) The High Commissioner will not communicate with and will not acknowledge communications from any person or organization which practises or publicly condones terrorism or violence.

Parties directly concerned

(26) Parties directly concerned in tensions who can provide specific reports to the High Commissioner and with whom the High Commissioner will seek to communicate in person during a visit to a participating State are the following:

(26a) governments of participating States, including, if appropriate, regional and local authorities in areas in which national minorities reside;

(26b) representatives of associations, non-governmental organizations, religious and other groups of national minorities directly concerned and in the area of tension, which are authorized by the persons belonging to those national minorities to represent them.

Conditions for travel by the High Commissioner

(27) Prior to an intended visit, the High Commissioner will submit to the participating State concerned specific information regarding the intended purpose of that visit. Within two weeks the State(s) concerned will consult with the High Commissioner on the objectives of the visit, which may include the promotion of dialogue, confidence and co-operation between the parties. After entry the State concerned will facilitate free travel and communication of the High Commissioner subject to the provisions of paragraph (25) above.

(28) If the State concerned does not allow the High Commissioner to enter the country and to travel and communicate freely, the High Commissioner will so inform the CSO.

(29) In the course of such a visit, subject to the provision of paragraph (25) the High Commissioner may consult the parties involved, and may receive information in confidence from any individual, group or organization directly concerned on questions the High Commissioner is addressing. The High Commissioner will respect the confidential nature of the information.

(30) The participating States will refrain from taking any action against persons, organizations or institutions on account of their contact with the High Commissioner.

High Commissioner and involvement of experts

(31) The High Commissioner may decide to request assistance from not more than three experts with relevant expertise in specific matters on which brief, specialized investigation and advice are required.

(32) If the High Commissioner decides to call on experts, the High Commissioner will set a clearly defined mandate and time-frame for the activities of the experts.

(33) Experts will only visit a participating State at the same time as the High Commissioner. Their mandate will be an integral part of the mandate of the High Commissioner and the same conditions for travel will apply.

(34) The advice and recommendations requested from the experts will be submitted in confidence to the High Commissioner, who will be responsible for the activities and for the reports of the experts and who will decide whether and in what form the advice and recommendations will be communicated to the parties concerned. They will be non-binding. If the High Commissioner decides to make the advice and recommendations available, the State(s) concerned will be given the opportunity to comment.

(35) The experts will be selected by the High Commissioner with the assistance of the ODIHR from the resource list established at the ODIHR as laid down in the Document of the Moscow Meeting.

(36) The experts will not include nationals or residents of the participating State concerned, or any person appointed by the State concerned, or any expert against whom the participating State has previously entered reservations. The experts will not include the participating State's own nationals or residents or any of the persons it appointed to the resource list, or more than one national or resident of any particular State.

Budget

(37) A separate budget will be determined at the ODIHR, which will provide, as appropriate, logistical support for travel and communication. The budget will be funded by the participating States according to the established CSCE scale of distribution. Details will be worked out by the Financial Committee and approved by the CSO.

Introduction

In its Helsinki Decisions of July 1992, the Organization for Security and Cooperation in Europe (OSCE) established the position of High Commissioner on National Minorities to be 'an instrument of conflict prevention at the earliest possible stage'. This mandate was created largely in reaction to the situation in the former Yugoslavia which some feared would be repeated elsewhere in Europe, especially among the countries in transition to democracy, and could undermine the promise of peace and prosperity as envisaged in the Charter of Paris for a New Europe adopted by the Heads of State and Government in November 1990.

On 1 January 1993, Mr. Max van der Stoel took up his duties as the first OSCE High Commissioner on National Minorities (HCNM). Drawing on his considerable personal experience as a former Member of Parliament, Foreign Minister of The Netherlands, Permanent Representative to the United Nations, and long-time human rights advocate, Mr. van der Stoel turned his attention to the many disputes between minorities and central authorities in Europe which had the potential, in his view, to escalate. Acting quietly through diplomatic means, the HCNM has become involved in over a dozen States, including Albania, Croatia, Estonia, Hungary, Kazakstan, Kyrgyzstan, Latvia, the Former Yugoslav Republic of Macedonia, Romania, Slovakia and Ukraine. His involvement has focused primarily on those situations involving persons belonging to national/ethnic groups who constitute the numerical majority in one State but the numerical minority in another State, thus engaging the interest of governmental authorities in each State and constituting a potential source of inter-State tension if not conflict. Indeed, such tensions have defined much of European history.

In addressing the substance of tensions involving national minorities, the HCNM approaches the issues as an independent, impartial and cooperative actor. While the HCNM is not a supervisory mechanism, he employs the international standards to which each State has agreed as his principal framework of analysis and the foundation of his specific recommendations. In this relation, it is important to recall the commitments undertaken by all OSCE participating States, in particular those of the 1990 Copenhagen Document of the Conference on the Human Dimension which, in Part IV, articulates detailed obligations relating to national minorities. It is also important to note that all OSCE States are bound by United Nations obligations relating to human rights, including minority rights, and that the great majority of OSCE States are also bound by the standards of the Council of Europe.

After almost four years of intense activity, the HCNM has been able to identify certain recurrent issues and themes which have become the subject of his attention in a number of States in which he is involved. Minority education, in particular minority language education, is a high priority among these since, as the HCNM has recently stated, 'It is clear that education is an extremely important element for the preservation and the deepening of the identity of persons belonging to a national minority.' With this in mind, the HCNM requested, in the autumn of 1995, the Foundation on Inter-Ethnic Relations to consult a small group of internationally recognized experts with a view to receiving their recommendations on an appropriate and coherent application of minority education rights in the OSCE region.

The Foundation on Inter-Ethnic Relations – a non-governmental organization established in 1993 to carry out specialized activities in support of the HCNM – facilitated a series of consultations of experts from various pertinent disciplines, including two meetings in The Hague. Among the experts consulted were, on the one hand, jurists specializing on international law and, on the other hand, linguists and educationalists specializing on the situations and needs of minorities. Specifically the experts were: A.G. Boyd Robertson, Senior Lecturer in Gaelic, University of Strathclyde (United Kingdom); Dr. Pieter van Dijk, Member of the State Council (the Netherlands); Dr. Asbjørn Eide, Director of the Norwegian Institute of Human Rights (Norway); Professor Rein Müllerson, Chair of International Law, King's College (United Kingdom); Professor Allan Rosas, Åbo Akademi University (Finland); Dr. Tove Skutnabb-Kangas, Associate Professor, Department of Languages and Culture, Roskilde University (Denmark); Professor György Szépe, Department of Language Sciences, University Janus Pannonius (Hungary); Professor Patrick Thornberry, Department of Law, Keele University (United Kingdom); Mr. Jenne van der Velde, Senior Curriculum Adviser, National Institute for Curriculum Development (the Netherlands).

In so far as existing standards of minority rights are part of human rights, the starting point of the consultations was to presume compliance by States with all other human rights obligations including, in particular, freedom from discrimination. It was also presumed that the ultimate object of all human rights is the full and free development of the individual human personality in conditions of equality. Consequently, it was presumed that civil society should be open and fluid and, therefore, integrate all persons, including those belonging to national minorities.

The resultant Recommendations Regarding the Education Rights of National Minorities attempt to clarify in relatively straight-forward language the content of minority education rights generally applicable in the situations in which the HCNM is involved. In addition, the standards have been interpreted in such a way as to ensure their coherence in application. The Recommendations are divided into eight sub-headings which respond to the educational issues which arise in practice. A more detailed explanation of the Recommendations is provided in an accompanying Explanatory Note wherein express reference to the relevant international standards is to be found.

The Hague Recommendations Regarding the Education Rights of National Minorities, 1996

The spirit of international instruments

1) The right of persons belonging to national minorities to maintain their identity can only be fully realised if they acquire a proper knowledge of their mother tongue during the educational process. At the same time, persons belonging to national minorities have a responsibility to integrate into the wider national society through the acquisition of a proper knowledge of the State language.

2) In applying international instruments which may benefit persons belonging to national minorities, States should consistently adhere to the fundamental principles of equality and non-discrimination.

3) It should be borne in mind that the relevant international obligations and commitments constitute international minimum standards. It would be contrary to their spirit and intent to interpret these obligations and commitments in a restrictive manner.

Measures and resources

4) States should approach minority education rights in a proactive manner. Where required, special measures should be adopted by States to actively implement minority language education rights to the maximum of their available resources, individually and through international assistance and cooperation, especially economic and technical.

Decentralization and participation

5) States should create conditions enabling institutions which are representative of members of the national minorities in question to participate, in

a meaningful way, in the development and implementation of policies and programmes related to minority education.

6) States should endow regional and local authorities with appropriate competences concerning minority education thereby also facilitating the participation of minorities in the process of policy formulation at a regional and\or local level.

7) States should adopt measures to encourage parental involvement and choice in the educational system at a local level, including in the field of minority language education.

Public and private institutions

8) In accordance with international law, persons belonging to national minorities, like others, have the right to establish and manage their own private educational institutions in conformity with domestic law. These institutions may include schools teaching in the minority language.

9) Given the right of persons belonging to national minorities to establish and manage their own educational institutions, States may not hinder the enjoyment of this right by imposing unduly burdensome legal and administrative requirements regulating the establishment and management of these institutions.

10) Private minority language educational institutions are entitled to seek their own sources of funding without any hindrance or discrimination from the State budget, international sources and the private sector.

Minority education at primary and secondary levels

11) The first years of education are of pivotal importance in a child's development. Educational research suggests that the medium of teaching at *pre-school* and *kindergarten* levels should ideally be the child's language. Wherever possible, States should create conditions enabling parents to avail themselves of this option.

12) Research also indicates that in *primary school*, the curriculum should ideally be taught in the minority language. The minority language should be

taught as a subject on a regular basis. The official State language should also be taught as a subject on a regular basis preferably by bilingual teachers who have a good understanding of the children's cultural and linguistic background. Towards the end of this period, a few practical or non-theoretical subjects should be taught through the medium of the State language. Wherever possible, States should create conditions enabling parents to avail themselves of this option.

13) In *secondary school*, a substantial part of the curriculum should be taught through the medium of the minority language. The minority language should be taught as a subject on a regular basis. The State language should also be taught as a subject on a regular basis, preferably by bilingual teachers who have a good understanding of the children's cultural and linguistic background. Throughout this period, the number of subjects taught in the State language, should gradually be increased. Research findings suggest that the more gradual the increase, the better for the child.

14) The maintenance of the primary and secondary levels of minority language education depends a great deal on the availability of teachers trained in all disciplines in the mother tongue. Therefore, ensuing from their obligation to provide adequate opportunities for minority language education, States should provide adequate facilities for the appropriate training of teachers and should facilitate access to such training.

Minority education in vocational schools

15) Vocational training in the minority language should be made accessible in specific subjects when persons belonging to the national minority in question have expressed a desire for it, when they have demonstrated the need for it and when their numerical strength justifies it.

16) The curriculum of vocational schools providing training in the mother tongue should be devised in a way which ensures that, upon completion of these programmes, students are able to practice their occupation both in the minority and the State language.

Minority education at tertiary level

17) Persons belonging to national minorities should have access to tertiary education in their own language when they have demonstrated the need for it and when their numerical strength justifies it. Minority language tertiary education can legitimately be made available to national minorities by establishing the required facilities within existing educational structures provided these can adequately serve the needs of the national minority in question. Persons belonging to national minorities may also seek ways and means to establish their own educational institutions at the tertiary level.

18) In situations where a national minority has, in recent history, maintained and controlled its own institutions of higher learning, this fact should be recognised in determining future patterns of provision.

Curriculum development

19) In view of the importance and value that international instruments attach to intercultural education and the highlighting of minority histories, cultures and traditions, State educational authorities should ensure that the general compulsory curriculum includes the teaching of the histories, cultures and traditions of their respective national minorities. Encouraging members of the majority to learn the languages of the national minorities living within the State would contribute to the strengthening of tolerance and multiculturalism within the State.

20) The curriculum content related to minorities should be developed with the active participation of bodies representative of the minorities in question.

21) States should facilitate the establishment of centres for minority language education curriculum development and assessment. These centres could be linked to existing institutions providing these can adequately facilitate the achievement of the curriculum related objectives.

Explanatory Note to the Hague Recommendations Regarding the Education Rights of National Minorities

General introduction

The Universal Declaration of Human Rights of 1948 broke new ground in that it was the first international instrument to declare education to be a human right.

Article 26 of the Declaration refers to elementary education as compulsory. It engages States to make technical and professional education generally available and higher education accessible on the basis of merit. It also makes clear that the objective of education should be the full development of the human personality and the strengthening of respect for human rights and fundamental freedoms. Article 26 goes on to say that education shall promote understanding, tolerance and friendship among nations, racial or religious groups and contribute to the maintenance of peace. It also makes clear that parents have a prior right to choose the kind of education that shall be given to their children. The provisions of article 26 are reiterated with greater strength in the context of treaty law and in greater detail in article 13 of the **International Covenant on Economic, Social and Cultural Rights**.

Article 26 sets the tone of openness and inclusiveness for the subsequent international instruments which have emerged over time and have confirmed and further elaborated the right to education both generally and with reference to minorities specifically.

- Article 27 of the **International Covenant on Civil and Political Rights**.
- Article 30 of the **Convention on the Rights of the Child**.

The above mentioned articles guarantee the right of minorities to use their language in community with other members of their group. The articles below, for their part, provide guarantees relating to the possibility for national minorities of learning their mother tongue or learning in their mother tongue.

• Article 5 of the **UNESCO Convention Against Discrimination in Education.**

• Paragraph 34 of the **Document of the Copenhagen Meeting of the Conference on the Human Dimension of the CSCE.**

• Article 4 of the **UN Declaration on the Rights of Persons Belonging to National or Ethnic, Religious and Linguistic Minorities.**

• Article 14 of the **Framework Convention for the Protection of National Minorities.**

To varying degrees, all of these instruments declare the right of minorities to maintain their collective identity through the medium of their mother tongue. This right is exercised, above all, through education. These same instruments, however, underline that the right to maintain the collective identity through the minority language must be balanced by the responsibility to integrate and participate in the wider national society. Such integration requires the acquisition of a sound knowledge of both that society and the State language(s). The promotion of tolerance and pluralism is also an important component of this dynamic.

The international human rights instruments that make reference to minority language education remain somewhat vague and general. They make no specific reference to degrees of access nor do they stipulate which levels of mother tongue education should be made available to minorities and by what means. Such concepts as 'adequate opportunities' to be taught in the minority language or to receive instruction in this language, as outlined in article 14 of the Council of Europe's **Framework Convention for the Protection of National Minorities,** should be considered in the light of other elements. These include the necessity of beneficial conditions facilitating the preservation, maintenance and development of language and culture as outlined in article 5 of the same Convention or the requirement to take the necessary measures to protect the ethnic, cultural, linguistic and religious identity of national minorities as stipulated in paragraph 33 of the **Document of the Copenhagen Meeting of the Conference on the Human Dimension of the CSCE.**

Irrespective of the level of access which may be afforded by States, it should not be established in an arbitrary fashion. States are required to give due consideration to the needs of national minorities as these are consistently expressed and demonstrated by the communities in question.

For their part, national minorities should ensure that their demands are reasonable. They should give due consideration to such legitimate factors as their own numerical strength, their demographic density in any given region (or regions), as well as their capacity to contribute to the durability of these services and facilities over time.

The spirit of international instruments

Over the years there has been an evolution in the manner in which the rights of minorities have been formulated in international standards. Such passive formulae as '. . . persons belonging to minorities shall not be denied the right . . .' as expressed in the **International Covenant on Civil and Political Rights** (1966) have given way to a more positive, proactive approach such as '. . . States will protect the ethnic, cultural, linguistic and religious identity of national minorities . . .' as contained in the **Document of the Copenhagen Meeting of the Conference on the Human Dimension of the CSCE** (1990). This progressive change of approach would indicate that a restrictive or minimalistic interpretation of the instruments is not in line with the spirit in which they have been formulated.

In addition, the level of access must be established in conformity with the underlying principles of equality and non-discrimination as these are formulated in articles 1 of **The Charter of the United Nations** and in article 2 of **The Universal Declaration of Human Rights** and as reiterated in most international instruments. Consideration must also be given to the conditions specific to each State.

Measures and resources

OSCE States are encouraged to approach the issue of minority rights in a proactive manner, i.e. in the spirit of article 31 of the **Copenhagen Document** which encourages them to adopt special measures to ensure full equality for members of national minorities. In this same sense, article 33 of the **Copenhagen Document** requires States to protect the ethnic, cultural, linguistic and religious identity of national minorities living in their territory and to create conditions for the *promotion* of that identity.

In some cases OSCE States are faced with serious fiscal limitations which could legitimately hamper their capacity to implement education policies and programmes for the benefit of national minorities. Although some rights must be implemented immediately States should strive to achieve, progressively, the full realization of minority language education rights to the maximum of their available resources, including through international assistance and cooperation in the spirit of article 2 of the **International Covenant on Economic, Social and Cultural Rights.**

Decentralization and participation

Article 15 of the **Framework Convention for the Protection of National Minorities**, paragraph 30 of the **Document of the Copenhagen Meeting of the Conference on the Human Dimension of the CSCE** and article 3 of the **UN Declaration on the Rights of Persons Belonging to National or Ethnic, Religious and Linguistic Minorities** all underline the necessity for national minorities to participate in the decision-making process, especially in cases when the issues being considered affect them directly.

Effective participation in the decision-making process, especially as it affects minorities, is an essential component of the democratic process.

The active involvement of parents at local and regional levels, as well as the effective participation of institutions representing national minorities in the educational process (including the process of curriculum development as it relates to minorities), should be facilitated by States in the spirit of paragraph 35 of the **Copenhagen Document** which stresses the importance of effective participation of members of national minorities in public affairs including in the affairs relating to the protection and promotion of their own identity.

Public and private institutions

Article 27 of the **International Covenant on Civil and Political Rights** refers to the right of minorities to use their language in community with other members of their group. Article 13 of the **International Covenant on Economic, Social and Cultural Rights** guarantees the right of parents to choose for their children schools other than those established by public authorities. It also guarantees the right of individuals and bodies to establish and manage alternative educational institutions as long as these conform to minimum educational standards as laid down by the State. Article 13 of the **Framework Convention for the Protection of National Minorities** refers to the right of minorities to establish and manage their own educational institutions, although the State has no obligation to fund these institutions. Paragraph 32 of the **Copenhagen Document** imposes no obligation on the State to fund these institutions, but it does stipulate that these institutions may 'seek public assistance from the State in conformity with national legislation'.

The right of national minorities to establish and manage their own institutions, including educational ones, is well grounded in international law and must be recognized as such. Although the State has the right to oversee this process from an administrative perspective and in conformity with its own legislation, it must not prevent the enjoyment of this right by imposing unreasonable administrative requirements which might render it practically impossible for national minorities to establish their own educational institutions.

Although there is no formal obligation for States to fund these private establishments, these institutions should not be prevented from seeking resources from all domestic and international sources.

Minority education at primary and secondary levels

International instruments relating to minority language education declare that minorities not only have the right to maintain their identity through the medium of their mother tongue but that they also have the right to integrate into and participate in the wider national society by learning the State language.

In view of the above, the attainment of multilingualism by the national minorities of OSCE States can be seen as a most effective way of meeting the objectives of the international instruments relating to the protection of national minorities as well as to their integration. The recommendations relating to primary and secondary schooling are meant to serve as a guide in the development of minority language education policy and in the provision of related programmes.

The approach proposed is suggested by educational research and constitutes a realistic interpretation of relevant international norms.

The effectiveness of this approach depends on a number of factors. First there is the extent to which this approach strengthens the weaker minority mother tongue by using it as the medium for teaching. Another factor is the extent to which bilingual teachers are involved in the entire process.

Yet another factor to be considered is the extent to which both the minority and the State language are taught as subjects throughout the 12 years of schooling and finally the extent to which both languages are used as a medium of education in an optimal way in different phases of the child's education.

This approach strives to create the space that is required for the weaker minority language to thrive. It is in marked contrast with other approaches whose objective is to teach the minority language or even to carry out minimum instruction in the minority language only with a view to facilitating an early transition to teaching exclusively in the State language.

Submersion-type approaches whereby the curriculum is taught exclusively through the medium of the State language and minority children are entirely integrated into classes with children of the majority are not in line with international standards. Likewise, this applies to segregated schools in which the entire curriculum is taught exclusively through the medium of the minority mother tongue, throughout the entire educational process and where the majority language is not taught at all or only to a minimal extent.

Minority education in vocational schools

The right of persons belonging to national minorities to learn their mother tongue or to receive instruction in their mother tongue as formulated in paragraph 34 of the **Copenhagen Document** should imply the right to vocational training in the mother tongue in specific subjects. In the spirit of equality and non-discrimination, OSCE States should ensure access to such training where the desire for it is made evident and the numbers justify it.

On the other hand, the capacity of the State to plan and control its economic and educational policies should not be diminished. The ability of graduates of minority language vocational training schools also to function professionally in the State language, would be an advantage. It would enable them to work both in the region in which the minority in question is concentrated as well as anywhere else in the State. At a time of transition to the market economy which presupposes the unfettered movement of goods, services and labour, such a limitation can make it difficult for the State to facilitate opportunities for employment and overall economic development. Therefore, vocational training in the mother tongue of national minorities should ensure that the students concerned also acquire appropriate training in the State language(s).

Minority education at tertiary education

As in the previous case, the right to learn their mother tongue or to receive instruction in the mother tongue as formulated in paragraph 34 of the **Copenhagen Document** could infer the right of national minorities to tertiary education in their mother tongue. In this case again the principles of equal access and non-discrimination must be taken into consideration, as well as the needs of the community and the usual numerical justification. In the absence of government funding, the freedom of minorities to establish their own institutions of higher learning should not be restricted.

Paragraph 33 of the **Copenhagen Document** stresses the importance of the State not only protecting the identity of minorities but promoting it as well. In view of the above, States should consider the possibility of making tertiary education in the minority language available where the need has been demonstrated and the numerical strength of the minority justifies it. In this context tertiary education in the mother tongue should not be restricted to teacher training.

This having been established, the fiscal limitations faced particularly by States in transition to market economies must be taken into consideration. The provision of tertiary education in the minority language is not synonymous with the establishment of parallel infrastructures. Moreover the entrenchment of parallel educational institutions at university level could contribute to the isolation of the minority from the majority. Article 26 of the **Universal Declaration of Human Rights** stresses that the objective of education is the promotion of understanding, tolerance and friendship among nations, racial and religious groups. In this spirit, and with integration in mind, the intellectual and cultural development of majorities and minorities should not take place in isolation.

Curriculum development

Since the end of the Second World War an ever growing number of international instruments have placed increasing emphasis on the objectives of education. According to these instruments education is required not only to provide strictly academic or technical training but it is also required to inculcate such values as tolerance, pluralism, anti-racism and international and inter-communal harmony. Such requirements evidently put a special onus on States that have national minorities within their borders. In these States, the issue of inter-group\inter-ethnic cohabitation and harmony is also of vital importance to their internal stability. Such cohabitation and harmony is also an important factor in the preservation of regional peace and security.

Article 4 of the **UN Declaration on the Rights of Persons Belonging to National or Ethnic, Religious and Linguistic Minorities** requires States to 'encourage knowledge of the history, traditions, language and culture of the minorities existing within their territory'. Article 12 of the **Framework Convention for the Protection of National Minorities** requires States to 'foster knowledge of the culture, history, language and religion of their national minorities'.

Paragraph 34 of the **Document of the Copenhagen Meeting of the Conference on the Human Dimension of the CSCE** refers to the requirement that, in the school curriculum, States 'will also take account of the history and culture of national minorities'.

These requirements make it incumbent upon States to make room in the school curriculum for the teaching of the history and traditions of the various national minorities living within their borders. This can be achieved in a unilateral manner by the State authorities without due regard to the participation of the minorities in question. Such an approach, however, is not advisable and could be detrimental.

Article 15 of the **Framework Convention for the Protection of National Minorities**, paragraph 30 of the **Document of the Copenhagen Meeting of the Conference on the Human Dimension of the CSCE** and article 3 of the **UN Declaration on the Rights of Persons Belonging to National or Ethnic, Religious and Linguistic Minorities** all underline the necessity for national minorities to participate in the decision-making process especially in cases when the issues being considered affect them directly.

The emergence of centres for minority language educational curriculum development would therefore facilitate this dual process and ensure its quality and professionalism.

Final remarks

The subject of minority education rights is a sensitive issue in a number of participating States of the OSCE. At the same time the educational process has the potential to effectively facilitate and strengthen mutual respect and understanding between the various communities within participating States.

In view of the delicate nature of this issue at the present time, and in view of the somewhat vague and general nature of the standards contained in the various international human rights instruments, the elaboration of a series of recommendations may contribute to creating a better understanding of, and approach to issues of minority education rights. The Hague Recommendations are not intended to be comprehensive. They are meant to serve as a general framework which can assist States in the process of minority education policy development.

The Oslo Recommendations Regarding the Linguistic Rights of National Minorities & Explanatory Note February 1998

Introduction

In its Helsinki Decisions of July 1992, the Organization for Security and Co-operation in Europe (OSCE) established the position of High Commissioner on National Minorities to be 'an instrument of conflict prevention at the earliest possible stage'. This mandate was created largely in reaction to the situation in the former Yugoslavia which some feared would be repeated elsewhere in Europe, especially among the countries in transition to democracy, and could undermine the promise of peace and prosperity as envisaged in the Charter of Paris for a New Europe adopted by the Heads of State and Government in November 1990.

On 1 January 1993, Mr. Max van der Stoel took up his duties as the first OSCE High Commissioner on National Minorities (HCNM). Drawing on his considerable personal experience as a former Member of Parliament and Foreign Minister of The Netherlands, Permanent Representative to the United Nations, and long-time human rights advocate, Mr. Van der Stoel turned his attention to the many disputes between minorities and central authorities in Europe which had the potential, in his view, to escalate. Acting quietly through diplomatic means, the HCNM has become involved in the following States: Albania, Croatia, Estonia, Hungary, Kazakstan, Kyrgyzstan, Latvia, the Former Yugoslav Republic of Macedonia, Romania, Slovakia and Ukraine. His involvement has focused primarily on those situations involving persons belonging to national/ethnic groups who constitute the numerical majority in one State but the numerical minority in another (usually neighbouring) State, thus engaging the interest of governmental authorities in each State and constituting a potential source of inter-State tension if not conflict. Indeed, such tensions have defined much of European history.

In addressing the substance of tensions involving national minorities, the

HCNM approaches the issues as an independent, impartial and cooperative actor. While the HCNM is not a supervisory mechanism, he employs the international standards to which each State has agreed as his principal framework of analysis and the foundation of his specific recommendations. In this relation, it is important to recall the commitments undertaken by all OSCE participating States, in particular those of the 1990 Copenhagen Document of the Conference on the Human Dimension which, in Part IV, articulates detailed obligations relating to national minorities. It is also important to note that all OSCE States are bound by United Nations obligations relating to human rights, including minority rights, and that the great majority of OSCE States are also bound by the standards of the Council of Europe.

After five years of intense activity, the HCNM has been able to identify certain recurrent issues and themes which have become the subject of his attention in a number of States in which he is involved. The linguistic rights of national minorities, i.e. the right of persons belonging to national minorities to use their language in the private and public spheres, is such an issue. International human rights instruments refer to this right in a number of different contexts. On the one hand, language is a personal matter closely connected with identity. On the other hand, language is an essential tool of social organisation which in many situations becomes a matter of public interest. Certainly, the use of language bears on numerous aspects of a State's functioning. In a democratic State committed to human rights, the accommodation of existing diversity thus becomes an important matter of policy and law. Failure to achieve the appropriate balance may be the source of inter-ethnic tensions.

It is with this in mind that, in the summer of 1996, the HCNM requested the Foundation on Inter-Ethnic Relations to consult a small group of internationally recognised experts with a view to receiving their recommendations on an appropriate and coherent application of the linguistic rights of persons belonging to national minorities in the OSCE region. A similar request from the HCNM had previously resulted in the elaboration of **The Hague Recommendations Regarding the Education Rights of National Minorities and Explanatory Report.***

---

* Copies of The Hague Recommendations Regarding the Education Rights of National Minorities and Explanatory Report (October 1996) are available in several languages from the Foundation on Inter-Ethnic Relations.

Insofar as The Hague Recommendations address comprehensively the use of the language or languages of national minorities in the field of education, it was decided to exclude this issue from consideration of the experts.

The Foundation on Inter-Ethnic Relations – a non-governmental organisation established in 1993 to carry out specialised activities in support of the HCNM – facilitated a series of consultations of experts from various pertinent disciplines, including two meetings in Oslo and one in The Hague. Among the experts consulted were jurists specialising in international law, as well as linguists, advocates and policy analysts specialising in the situations and needs of minorities. Specifically, the experts were:

> Professor Gudmundur Alfredsson, Co-Director, Raoul Wallenberg Institute (Sweden); Professor Asbjørn Eide, Senior Fellow, Norwegian Institute of Human Rights (Norway); Ms. Angelita Kamenska, Senior Researcher, Latvian Centre for Human Rights and Ethnic Studies (Latvia); Mr. Dónall Ó Riagáin, Secretary General, European Bureau of Lesser Used Languages (Ireland); Ms. Beate Slydal, Adviser, Norwegian Forum for the Freedom of Expression (Norway); Dr. Miquel Strubell, Director, Institute of Catalan Sociolinguistics, Government of Catalonia (Spain); Professor György Szepe, Department of Language Sciences at Janus Panonius University (Hungary); Professor Patrick Thornberry, Department of Law, Keele University (United Kingdom); Dr. Fernand de Varennes, Director of the Asia-Pacific Centre for Human Rights and the Prevention of Ethnic Conflict (Australia); Professor Bruno de Witte, Faculty of Law, University of Maastricht (The Netherlands); Mr. Jean-Marie Woehrling, Institut de droit local alsacien-mosellan (France).

Insofar as existing standards of minority rights are part of human rights, the starting point for the consultations was to presume compliance by States with all other human rights obligations including, in particular, equality and freedom from discrimination, freedom of expression, freedom of assembly and of association, as well as all the rights and freedoms of persons belonging to national minorities.

It was also presumed that the ultimate object of all human rights is the full and free development of the individual human personality in conditions of equality. Consequently, it was presumed that civil society should be open and fluid and, therefore, integrate all persons, including those belonging to national minorities. Insofar as the use of language is also a fundamentally communicative matter, the essential social dimension of the human experience was also fully presumed.

The resultant Oslo Recommendations Regarding the Linguistic Rights of National Minorities attempt to clarify, in relatively straight-forward language, the content of minority language rights generally applicable in the situations in which the HCNM is involved. In addition, the standards have been interpreted in such a way as to ensure their coherence in application. The Recommendations are divided into sub-headings which respond to the language related issues which arise in practice. A more detailed explanation of the Recommendations is provided in an accompanying Explanatory Note wherein express reference to the relevant international standards is to be found. It is intended that each Recommendation is read in conjunction with the specifically relevant paragraphs of the Explanatory Note.

It is hoped that these Recommendations will provide a useful reference for the development of State policies and laws which will contribute to an effective implementation of the language rights of persons belonging to national minorities, especially in the public sphere.

Although these Recommendations refer to the use of language by persons belonging to national minorities, it is to be noted that the thrust of these Recommendations and the international instruments from which they derive could potentially apply to other types of minorities. The Recommendations which follow below are meant to clarify the existing body of rights. They are not meant to restrict the human rights of any person or groups of persons.

The Oslo Recommendations Regarding the Linguistic Rights of National Minorities

Names

1) Persons belonging to national minorities have the right to use their personal names in their own language according to their own traditions and linguistic systems. These shall be given official recognition and be used by the public authorities.

2) Similarly, private entities such as cultural associations and business enterprises established by persons belonging to national minorities shall enjoy the same right with regard to their names.

3) In areas inhabited by significant numbers of persons belonging to a national minority and when there is sufficient demand, public authorities shall make provision for the display, also in the minority language, of local names, street names and other topographical indications intended for the public.

Religion

4) In professing and practicing his or her own religion individually or in community with others, every person shall be entitled to use the language(s) of his or her choice.

5) For those religious ceremonies or acts pertaining also to civil status and which have legal effect within the State concerned, the State may require that certificates and documents pertaining to such status be produced also in the official language or languages of the State. The State may require that registers pertaining to civil status be kept by the religious authorities also in the official language or languages of the State.

Community Life and NGOs

6) All persons, including persons belonging to national minorities, have the right to establish and manage their own non-governmental organisations, associations and institutions. These entities may use the language(s) of their choosing. The State may not discriminate against these entities on the basis of language nor shall it unduly restrict the right of these entities to seek sources of funding from the State budget, international sources or the private sector.

7) If the State actively supports activities in, among others, the social, cultural and sports spheres, an equitable share of the total resources made available by the State shall go to support those similar activities undertaken by persons belonging to national minorities. State financial support for activities which take place in the language(s) of persons belonging to national minorities in such spheres shall be granted on a non-discriminatory basis.

The Media

8) Persons belonging to national minorities have the right to establish and maintain their own minority language media. State regulation of the broadcast media shall be based on objective and non-discriminatory criteria and shall not be used to restrict enjoyment of minority rights.

9) Persons belonging to national minorities should have access to broadcast time in their own language on publicly funded media. At national, regional and local levels the amount and quality of time allocated to broadcasting in the language of a given minority should be commensurate with the numerical size and concentration of the national minority and appropriate to its situation and needs.

10) The independent nature of the programming of public and private media in the language(s) of national minorities shall be safeguarded. Public media editorial boards overseeing the content and orientation of programming should be independent and should include persons belonging to national minorities serving in their independent capacity.

11) Access to media originating from abroad shall not be unduly restricted.

Such access should not justify a diminution of broadcast time allocated to the minority in the publicly funded media of the State of residence of the minorities concerned.

Economic Life

12) All persons, including persons belonging to national minorities, have the right to operate private enterprises in the language or languages of their choice. The State may require the additional use of the official language or languages of the State only where a legitimate public interest can be demonstrated, such as interests relating to the protection of workers or consumers, or in dealings between the enterprise and governmental authorities.

Administrative Authorities and Public Services

13) In regions and localities where persons belonging to a national minority are present in significant numbers and where the desire for it has been expressed, persons belonging to this national minority shall have the right to acquire civil documents and certificates both in the official language or languages of the State and in the language of the national minority in question from regional and/or local public institutions. Similarly regional and/or local public institutions shall keep the appropriate civil registers also in the language of the national minority.

14) Persons belonging to national minorities shall have adequate possibilities to use their language in communications with administrative authorities especially in regions and localities where they have expressed a desire for it and where they are present in significant numbers. Similarly, administrative authorities shall, wherever possible, ensure that public services are provided also in the language of the national minority. To this end, they shall adopt appropriate recruitment and/or training policies and programmes.

15) In regions and localities where persons belonging to a national minority are present in significant numbers, the State shall take measures to ensure that elected members of regional and local governmental bodies can use

also the language of the national minority during activities relating to these bodies.

Independent National Institutions

16) States in which persons belonging to national minorities live should ensure that these persons have, in addition to appropriate judicial recourses, access to independent national institutions, such as ombudspersons or human rights commissions, in cases where they feel that their linguistic rights have been violated.

The Judicial Authorities

17) All persons, including persons belonging to a national minority, have the right to be informed promptly, in a language they understand, of the reasons for their arrest and/or detention and of the nature and cause of any accusation against them, and to defend themselves in this language, if necessary with the free assistance of an interpreter, before trial, during trial and on appeal.

18) In regions and localities where persons belonging to a national minority are present in significant numbers and where the desire for it has been expressed, persons belonging to this minority should have the right to express themselves in their own language in judicial proceedings, if necessary with the free assistance of an interpreter and/or translator.

19) In those regions and localities in which persons belonging to a national minority live in significant numbers and where the desire for it has been expressed, States should give due consideration to the feasibility of conducting all judicial proceedings affecting such persons in the language of the minority.

Deprivation of Liberty

20) The director of a penal institution and other personnel of the institution shall be able to speak the language or languages of the greatest number of prisoners, or a language understood by the greatest number of them.

Recruitment and/or training programmes should be directed towards this end. Whenever necessary, the services of an interpreter shall be used.

21) Detained persons belonging to national minorities shall have the right to use the language of their choice in communications with inmates as well as with others. Authorities shall, wherever possible, adopt measures to enable prisoners to communicate in their own language both orally and in personal correspondence, within the limitations prescribed by law. In this relation, a detained or imprisoned person should, in general, be kept in a place of detention or imprisonment near his or her usual place of residence.

Explanatory Note to the Oslo Recommendations Regarding the Linguistic Rights of National Minorities

General Introduction

Article 1 of the **Universal Declaration of Human Rights** refers to the innate dignity of all human beings as the fundamental concept underlying all human rights standards. Article 1 of the **Declaration** states 'All human beings are born free and equal in dignity and rights . . .' The importance of this article cannot be overestimated. Not only does it relate to human rights generally, it also provides one of the foundations for the linguistic rights of persons belonging to national minorities. Equality in dignity and rights presupposes respect for the individual's identity as a human being. Language is one of the most fundamental components of human identity. Hence, respect for a person's dignity is intimately connected with respect for the person's identity and consequently for the person's language.

In this context, the **International Covenant on Civil and Political Rights** is of considerable importance. Article 2 of the **Covenant** requires States to ensure that the human rights of all individuals within their territory and subject to their jurisdiction will be ensured and respected 'without distinction of any kind such as . . . language . . .' Article 19 of the **Covenant** guarantees freedom of expression which, as it is formulated in the **Covenant**, not only guarantees the right to impart or receive information and ideas of all sorts, regardless of frontiers, but also guarantees the right to do so in the medium or language of one's choice. The imparting and receiving of information also suggests people acting in community. In this context, Articles 21 and 22 of the **Covenant** guaranteeing the freedoms of peaceful assembly and association may be especially relevant.

Similarly, in Europe the freedom of expression stipulated in Article 10 of the **European Convention for the Protection of Human Rights and Fundamental Freedoms** shall be, according to Article 14 of the same convention, 'secured without discrimination on any ground such as . . . language . . .' With expressed reference to both the **Universal Declaration of Human Rights** and the **European Convention for the Protection of Human Rights and Fundamental Freedoms,** the Council of Europe's **Declaration on Freedom of Expression and Information** affirms 'that the freedom of expression and information is necessary for the social, economic, cultural and political development of every human being, and constitutes a condition for the harmonious progress of social and cultural groups, nations and the international community'. In this connection, the freedoms of peaceful assembly and association as guaranteed by Article 11 of the **European Convention for the Protection of Human Rights and Fundamental Freedoms** are important.

Within the context of the Organization for Security and Cooperation in Europe (OSCE), the same fundamental ideas of freedom of expression, assembly and association are enumerated in paragraphs 9.1-9.3 of the **Document of the Copenhagen Meeting of the Conference on the Human Dimension.**

In the **Charter of Paris for a New Europe**, the Heads of State and Government of the OSCE participating States 'affirm that, without discrimination, every individual has the right to: . . . freedom of expression, freedom of association and peaceful assembly, . . .'

Article 27 of the **International Covenant on Civil and Political Rights** is another key provision which has direct bearing on the linguistic rights of national minorities. It affirms that 'persons belonging to . . . minorities shall not be denied the right, in community with the other members of their group, to . . . use their own language'.

Similarly, Article 2(1) of the **UN Declaration on the Rights of Persons Belonging to National or Ethnic, Religious and Linguistic Minorities** proclaims the right of persons belonging to national minorities to 'use their own language, in private and in public, freely and without interference or any form of discrimination'. Article 10(1) of the Council of Europe's **Framework Convention for the Protection of National Minorities** stipulates that States will recognise the right of persons belonging to national minorities 'to use freely and without interference his or her minority language, in private and in public, orally and in writing.'

Although the instruments refer to the use of minority languages in public and in private, these same instruments do not precisely delimit the 'public' as opposed to the 'private' spheres. Indeed the spheres may overlap. This may well be the case, for example, when individuals acting alone or in community with others seek to establish their own private media or schools. What might begin as a private initiative may become the subject of legitimate public interest. Such an interest may give rise to some public regulation.

The use of minority languages 'in public and in private' by persons belonging to national minorities cannot be considered without making reference to education. Education issues as they relate to the languages of national minorities are treated in detail in The Hague Recommendations Regarding the Education Rights of National Minorities which were developed for the benefit of the OSCE High Commissioner on National Minorities by The Foundation on Inter-Ethnic Relations in collaboration with experts of international repute in the fields of both international human rights and education. The Hague Recommendations were developed with a view to facilitating a clearer understanding of the international instruments pertaining to the rights of persons belonging to national minorities in this area which is of such vital importance to the maintenance and development of the identity of persons belonging to national minorities.

International human rights instruments stipulate that human rights are universal and that they must be enjoyed equally and without discrimination. Most human rights, however, are not absolute. The instruments do foresee a limited number of situations in which States would be justified in restricting the application of certain rights. The restrictions permitted by international human rights law can be invoked in life-threatening emergencies and in situations which pose a threat to the rights and freedoms of others, or in situations which threaten public morals, public health, national security and the general welfare in a democratic society*. In human rights law, restrictions on freedoms are to be interpreted restrictively.

The rights of persons belonging to national minorities to use their language(s) in public and in private as set forth and elaborated in The Oslo Recommendations Regarding the Linguistic Rights of National Minorities must be seen in a balanced context of full participation in the wider society. The Recommendations do not propose an isolationist approach, but rather one which encourages a

* The above mentioned limitations are included, e.g., in the following provisions:

Art. 30 Universal Declaration of Human Rights

Art. 19(3) International Covenant on Civil and Political Rights

Art. 10(2) European Convention for the Protection of Human Rights and Fundamental Freedoms

balance between the right of persons belonging to national minorities to maintain and develop their own identity, culture and language and the necessity of ensuring that they are able to integrate into the wider society as full and equal members. From this perspective, such integration is unlikely to take place without a sound knowledge of the official language(s) of the State. The prescription for such education is implied in Articles 13 and 14 of the **International Covenant on Economic, Social and Cultural Rights** and Articles 28 and 29 of the **Convention on the Rights of the Child** which confer a right to education and oblige the State to make education compulsory. At the same time, Article 14(3) of the **Framework Convention for the Protection of National Minorities** provides that the teaching of a minority language 'shall be implemented without prejudice to the learning of the official language or the teaching in this language.'

Names

1) Article 11(1) of the **Framework Convention for the Protection of National Minorities** stipulates that persons belonging to national minorities have the right to use their first name, their patronym and their surname in their own language. This right, the enjoyment of which is fundamental to one's personal identity, should be applied in light of the circumstances particular to each State. For example, public authorities would be justified in using the script of the official language or languages of the State to record the names of persons belonging to national minorities in their phonetic form. However this must be done in accordance with the language system and tradition of the national minority in question. In view of this very basic right relating closely to both the language and the identity of individuals, persons who have been forced by public authorities to give up their original or ancestral name(s) or whose name(s) have been changed against their will should be entitled to revert to them without having to incur any expenses.

2) Names are an important element of corporate identity as well, especially in the context of persons belonging to national minorities acting 'in community'. Article 2(1) of the **UN Declaration on the Rights of Persons Belonging to National or Ethnic, Religious and Linguistic Minorities** proclaims the right of persons belonging to national minorities to 'use their own language, in private and in public, freely and without

interference or any form of discrimination'. Article 10(1) of the **Framework Convention for the Protection of National Minorities** stipulates that States will recognise the right of persons belonging to national minorities to 'use freely and without interference his or her minority language, in private and in public, orally and in writing.' Article 27 of the **International Covenant on Civil and Political Rights** declares that 'persons belonging to . . . minorities shall not be denied the right, in community with other members of their group . . . to use their own language'. A person's right to use his or her language in public, in community with others and without any interference or any form of discrimination is a strong indication that legal entities such as institutions, associations, organisations or business enterprises established and run by persons belonging to national minorities enjoy the right to adopt the name of their choice in their minority language. Such a corporate name should be recognised by the public authorities and used in accordance with the given community's language system and traditions.

3) Article 11(3) of the **Framework Convention** states that 'in areas traditionally inhabited by substantial numbers of persons belonging to a national minority, the Parties shall endeavour . . . to display traditional local names, street names and other topographical indications intended for the public also in the minority language when there is sufficient demand for such indications'. Refusal to recognise the validity of historic denominations of the kind described can constitute an attempt to revise history and to assimilate minorities, thus constituting a serious threat to the identity of persons belonging to minorities.

Religion

4) Article 27 of the **International Covenant on Civil and Political Rights** affirms that 'In those States in which ethnic, religious or linguistic minorities exist, persons belonging to such minorities shall not be denied the right, in community with the other members of their group . . . to profess and practice their own religion, or to use their own language.' Article 3(1) of the **UN Declaration on the Rights of Persons Belonging to National or Ethnic, Religious and Linguistic Minorities** stipulates that 'Persons belonging to minorities may exercise their rights . . .

individually as well as in community with other members of their group, without any discrimination.'

Religious belief and its practice 'in community' is an area of great importance to many persons belonging to national minorities. In this context it is worth noting that the right to one's own religion is unlimited and guaranteed by Article 18(1) of the **International Covenant on Civil and Political Rights** and Article 9(1) of the **European Convention for the Protection of Human Rights and Fundamental Freedoms.** However, the freedom to manifest one's religion and beliefs, including public worship, is subject to a number of limitations listed in subsidiary paragraphs of the same articles. These limitations must be prescribed by law and relate to the protection of public safety, order, health, morals and the protection of the fundamental rights and freedoms of others. They must be reasonable and proportional to the end sought, and States may not invoke them with a view to stifling the legitimate spiritual, linguistic or cultural aspirations of persons belonging to national minorities.

In minority contexts, the practice of religion is often especially closely related to the preservation of cultural and linguistic identity. The right to use a minority language in public worship is as inherent as the right to establish religious institutions and the right to public worship itself. Hence, public authorities may not impose any undue restrictions on public worship nor on the use of any language in public worship, be it the mother tongue of the national minority in question or the liturgical language used by that community.

5) Religious acts such as wedding ceremonies or funerals may also constitute legal civil acts determining civil status in certain countries. In such cases, public interest must be taken into consideration. Keeping in mind the principle that administrative considerations should not prevent the enjoyment of human rights, public authorities should not impose any linguistic restrictions on religious communities. This should apply equally to any administrative functions which religious communities assume and which may overlap with civil jurisdiction. The State may, however, require the religious community to record legal civil acts for which it has authority also in the official language or languages of the State so that the State may perform its legitimate regulatory and administrative tasks.

Community Life and NGOs

6) The collective life of persons belonging to national minorities, their acting 'in community' as stated by the international instruments, finds its expression in numerous activities and areas of endeavour. Not least of these is the life of their non-governmental organisations, associations and institutions whose existence is usually vital for the maintenance and development of their identity and is generally seen as beneficial and conducive to the development of civil society and democratic values within States.

Articles 21 and 22 of the **International Covenant on Civil and Political Rights** and Article 11 of the **European Convention for the Protection of Human Rights and Fundamental Freedoms** guarantee the right of persons to peaceful assembly and the freedom of association. The right of persons to act 'in community' with other members of their group – their right to establish and manage their own non-governmental organisations, associations and institutions – is one of the hallmarks of an open and democratic society. Article 27 of that same **Covenant** affirms that 'Persons belonging to . . . minorities shall not be denied the right, in community with the other members of their group, to . . . use their own language'. As a rule, therefore, public authorities should not be involved in the internal affairs of such entities 'acting in community', nor may they impose any limits on them, other than those permitted under international law. Article 17(2) of the **Framework Convention for the Protection of National Minorities** similarly engages States 'not to interfere with the right of persons belonging to national minorities to participate in the activities of non-governmental organisations, both at the national and international levels'.

Article 2(1) of the **International Covenant on Civil and Political Rights** stipulates that each State undertakes 'to ensure to all individuals within its territory and subject to its jurisdiction the rights recognised in the present **Covenant**, without distinction of any kind such as . . . language'. In line with this standard, States may not discriminate against NGOs on the basis of language nor impose any undue language requirements on them. This having been said, public authorities may require that such organisations, associations and institutions conform to the requirements of domestic law on the basis of a legitimate public interest, including the use of the official language(s) of the State in situations requiring interface with public bodies.

With regard to resources, paragraph 32.2 of the **Copenhagen Document** states that persons belonging to national minorities have the right 'to establish and maintain their own educational, cultural and religious institutions, organisations or associations, which can seek voluntary financial and other contributions as well as public assistance, in conformity with national legislation.' Accordingly, States should not prevent these entities from seeking financial resources from the State budget and from public international sources as well as from the private sector.

7) With regard to State financing of non-governmental activities in, among others, the social, cultural or sports fields, application of the principles of equality and non-discrimination requires that the public authorities provide an appropriate share of funding to similar activities taking place in the language of the national minorities living within their borders. In this context, Article 2(1) of the **International Covenant on Civil and Political Rights** stresses not only that there will be no distinction based on language in the treatment of individuals, but stipulates in Article 2(2) that States are required to 'take the necessary steps . . . to adopt such legislative or other measures as may be necessary to give effect to the rights recognised in the . . . Covenant'. Furthermore, Article 2(2) of the **International Covenant on the Elimination of Racial Discrimination,** (which seeks to eliminate any distinction, exclusion, restriction, or preference based on race, colour, descent, or national or ethnic origin) stipulates that 'States Parties shall, when the circumstances so warrant, take, in the social, economic, cultural and other fields, special and concrete measures to ensure the adequate development and protection of certain racial groups or individuals belonging to them, for the purpose of guaranteeing them the full and equal enjoyment of human rights and fundamental freedoms . . .' Insofar as language is often a defining criterion of ethnicity as protected by the aforementioned convention, minority language communities may also be entitled to the benefits of such 'special and concrete measures'.

At the European level, paragraph 31 of the **Copenhagen Document** stipulates that 'States will adopt, where necessary, special measures for the purpose of ensuring to persons belonging to national minorities full equality with the other citizens in the exercise and enjoyment of human rights and fundamental freedoms'. Paragraph 2 of Article 4 of the **Framework Convention for the Protection of National Minorities** obligates the States Parties 'to adopt, where necessary, adequate measures in order to promote, in all areas of economic, social, political and cultural life, full and effective equality between persons belonging to a national minority and those belonging to the majority'; paragraph 3 of the same Article further specifies that such 'measures adopted in accordance with paragraph 2 shall not be considered to be an act of discrimination.' Moreover, Article 7(2) of the **European Charter for Regional or Minority Languages** stipulates that 'the adoption of special measures in favour of regional or minority languages aimed at promoting equality between the users of the languages and the rest of the population or which take account of their specific conditions is not considered to be an act of discrimination against the users of more widely used languages.' In this context, therefore, public authorities should provide an equitable share of resources from the State budget to the activities of persons belonging to national minorities in, among others, the social, cultural and sports related fields. Such support can be made available through subsidies, public benefits and tax exemptions.

The Media

8) Article 19 of the **International Covenant on Civil and Political Rights**, which guarantees the right to hold opinions as well as the right to express them, is a fundamental point of reference regarding the role and place of media in democratic societies. While Article 19(1) provides that 'everyone shall have the right to hold opinions without interference', Article 19(2) proceeds to guarantee to everyone the freedom 'to seek, receive and impart information and ideas of all kinds, regardless of frontiers, either orally, in writing or in print, in the form of art, or through the media of his choice.' Article 10 of the **European Convention for the Protection of Human Rights and Fundamental Freedoms** guarantees the right to freedom of expression in a similar way. The member States of the Council of Europe reiterated in Article I of the **Declaration on the Freedom of Expression and Information** 'their firm attachment to the principles of freedom of

expression and information as a basic element of democratic and pluralist society'. On this basis, States declared in the same instrument that 'in the field of information and mass media they seek to achieve . . . d. The existence of a wide variety of independent and autonomous media, permitting the reflection of diversity of ideas and opinions'.

Article 9(1) of the **Framework Convention for the Protection of National Minorities** states clearly that persons belonging to national minorities are free 'to hold opinions and to receive and impart information and ideas in the minority language, without interference by public authorities and regardless of frontiers . . .' Further on, the same provision engages States to 'ensure, within the framework of their legal systems, that persons belonging to a national minority are not discriminated against in their access to the media.' Article 9(3) of the **Framework Convention** stipulates that States 'shall not hinder the creation and the use of printed media by persons belonging to national minorities.' The same provision requires that 'in the legal framework of sound radio and television broadcasting, [States] shall ensure, as far as possible . . . that persons belonging to national minorities are granted the possibility of creating and using their own media.' It is also to be noted that media may constitute entities of the kind foreseen in *inter alia*, paragraph 32.2 of the **Copenhagen Document** which provides for the right of persons belonging to national minorities to 'establish and maintain their own educational, cultural and religious institutions, organisations or associations . . .' Even though the media are not cited expressly in this standard, the media often plays a fundamental role in the promotion and preservation of language, culture and identity.

Although there can be no doubt that persons belonging to national minorities have the right to establish and maintain private media, it is also true that this right is subject to the limitations provided by international law as well as such legitimate requirements of the State regarding the regulation of the media. Article 9(2) of the **Framework Convention** makes this very clear by underlining that the freedom of expression referred to in article 9(1) of the **Convention** 'shall not prevent Parties from requiring the licensing, without discrimination and based on objective criteria, of sound radio and television broadcasting, or cinema enterprises.' Regulatory requirements, where justified and necessary, may not be used to undermine the enjoyment of the right.

9) The issue of access to publicly funded media is closely linked with the concept of freedom of expression. Article 9(1) of the **Framework Convention** stipulates that the freedom of expression of persons belonging to national minorities includes the freedom to impart information and ideas in the minority language, without interference by public authorities, and goes on to say that 'members of minorities shall not be discriminated against in their access to the media.' Article 9(4) of the **Framework Convention** stipulates that 'Parties shall adopt adequate measures in order to facilitate access to the media for persons belonging to national minorities.' This implies that a national minority consisting of a substantial number of members should be given access to its fair share of broadcast time, on public radio and/or television, with the numerical size of the minority in question having a bearing on its share of broadcast time.

Numerical strength and concentration, however, cannot be seen as the only criteria when judging the amount of broadcast time to be allocated to any given national minority. In the case of smaller communities, consideration must be given to the viable minimum of time and resources without which a smaller minority would not meaningfully be able to avail itself of the media.

Moreover, the quality of the time allotted to minority programming is an issue that needs to be approached in a reasonable, non-discriminatory manner. The time-slots allotted to minority language programming should be such as to ensure that persons belonging to a national minority can enjoy programming in their language in a meaningful way. Hence, public authorities should ensure that this programming is transmitted at reasonable times of the day.

10) In an open and democratic society the content of media programming should not be unduly censored by the public authorities. The freedom of expression as guaranteed by Article 19(1) of the **International Covenant on Civil and Political Rights** and Article 10(1) of the **European Convention for the Protection of Human Rights and Fundamental Freedoms** is important in this regard. Any restrictions which might be imposed by the public authorities must be in line with Article 19(3) of the **Covenant** which stipulates that these restrictions 'shall only be such as

are provided by law and are necessary a) For the respect of the rights and reputations of others, b) For the protection of national security or of public order (*ordre public*), or of public health and morals.' Article 10(2) of the **European Convention for the Protection of Human Rights and Fundamental Freedoms** stipulates almost identical restrictions on any interference by public authorities with the enjoyment of freedom of expression.

Mechanisms should be put in place to ensure that the public media programming developed by or on behalf of national minorities reflects the interests and desires of the community's members and is seen by them as independent. In this context, the participation of persons belonging to national minorities (acting in their private capacity) in the editorial process would go a long way in ensuring that the independent nature of the media would be preserved and that it would be responsive to the needs of the communities to be served.

In line with the principle of equality and non-discrimination, the composition of public institutions should be reflective of the populations they are designed to serve. This also applies to public media. Article 15 of the **Framework Convention** engages States to 'create the conditions necessary for the effective participation of persons belonging to national minorities in cultural, social and economic life and in public affairs, in particular those affecting them.' Article 2 of **International Labour Organisation Convention No. 111 Concerning Discrimination in Respect of Employment and Occupation** is more explicit in committing States to 'pursue a national policy designed to promote . . . equality of opportunity and treatment in respect of employment and occupation, with a view to eliminating any discrimination in respect thereof.' The non-discriminatory hiring of persons belonging to national minorities to work in the media will contribute to the representativity and objectivity of the media.

11) In keeping with the spirit of Articles 19(2) of the **International Covenant on Civil and Political Rights** and Article 9(1) of the **Framework Convention for the Protection of National Minorities** and of the principle of non-discrimination, access to programming in the language of persons belonging to a national minority, transmitted from another State or from

the 'kin-State', should not justify a diminution of programme time allotted to the minority on the public media of the State in which its members live.

Transfrontier access to information and media networks is a fundamental element of the right to information which, in the context of accelerated technological progress, is of growing importance. Consequently, when cable licensing is involved, for example, it is not legitimate for a State to refuse to license television or radio stations based in a kin-State when the desire for access to these stations has been clearly expressed by the national minority concerned. This right applies not only to cable media but also to electronic information networks in the language of the national minority.

As a general matter, the member States of the Council of Europe resolved in Article III(c) of the **Declaration on the Freedom of Expression and Information** 'to promote the free flow of information, thus contributing to international understanding, a better knowledge of convictions and traditions, respect for the diversity of opinions and the mutual enrichment of cultures'. In relation to media contacts across frontiers, States should conform their policies to the spirit of this provision.

Economic Life

12) International instruments make little reference to the rights of persons belonging to national minorities in the field of economic activity. International instruments do, however, refer to the right of persons belonging to national minorities to use their language in public and in private, freely and without any form of discrimination, orally and in writing, individually and with others. Article 19(2) of the **International Covenant on Civil and Political Rights** and Article 10(1) of the **European Convention for the Protection of Human Rights and Fundamental Freedoms** guarantee freedom of expression with respect not only to ideas and opinions which may be transmitted to others (i.e. the content of communications), but also to language as a medium of communication. These rights, coupled with the right to equality and non-discrimination, imply the right of persons belonging to national minorities to run their businesses in the language of their choice. In view of the importance to private entrepreneurs

to be able to communicate effectively with their clientele and to pursue their initiatives in fair conditions, there should be no undue restrictions on their free choice of language.

Article 11(2) of the **Framework Convention** stipulates that 'every person belonging to a national minority has the right to display in his or her minority language, signs, inscriptions and other information of a private nature visible to the public.' In the **Framework Convention** the expression 'of a private nature' refers to all that is not official. Hence, the State may not impose any restrictions on the choice of language in the administration of private business enterprises.

Notwithstanding the above, the State may require that the official language or languages of the State be accommodated in those sectors of economic activity which affect the enjoyment of the rights of others or require exchange and communication with public bodies. This follows from the permissible restrictions on freedom of expression as stipulated in Article 19(3) of the **International Covenant on Civil and Political Rights** and Article 10(2) of the **European Convention for the Protection of Human Rights and Fundamental Freedoms.** While the limited permissible restrictions expressed in the aforementioned articles could justify restrictions on the content of communications, they would never justify restrictions on the use of a language as a medium of communication. However, protection of the rights and freedoms of others and the limited requirements of public administration may well justify specific prescriptions for the additional use of the official language or languages of the State. This would apply to sectors of activity such as workplace health and safety, consumer protection, labour relations, taxation, financial reporting, State health and unemployment insurance and transportation, depending on the circumstances. On the basis of a legitimate public interest, the State could, in addition to the use of any other language, also require that the official language or languages of the State be accommodated in such business activities as public signage and labelling – as expressly stated in paragraph 60 of the **Explanatory Report to the Framework Convention for the Protection of National Minorities.** In sum, the State could never prohibit the use of a language, but it could, on the basis of a legitimate public interest, prescribe the additional use of the official language or languages of the State.

In keeping with the logic of legitimate public interest, any requirement(s) for the use of language which may be prescribed by the State must be proportional to the public interest to be served. The proportionality of any requirement is to be determined by the extent to which it is necessary. Accordingly, for example, in the public interest of workplace health and safety, the State could require private factories to post safety notices in the official language or languages of the State in addition to the chosen language(s) of the enterprise. Similarly, in the interest of accurate public administration in relation to taxation, the State could require that administrative forms be submitted in the official language or languages of the State and that, in the case of an audit by the public authorities, relevant records be made available also in the official language or languages of the State; the latter eventuality would not require that private enterprise maintain all records in the official language or languages of the State, but only that the burden of possible translation rests with the private enterprise. This is without prejudice to the possible entitlement of persons belonging to national minorities to use their language(s) in communications with administrative authorities as foreseen in Article 10(2) of the **Framework Convention for the Protection of National Minorities.**

Administrative Authorities and Public Services

13/ OSCE Participating States are committed to taking measures which will
14/ contribute to creating a dynamic environment, conducive not only to
15) the maintenance of the identity of persons belonging to national minorities (including their language) but also to their development and promotion. As a consequence, these States have undertaken to respect 'the right of persons belonging to national minorities to effective participation in public affairs' as outlined in paragraph 35 of the **Copenhagen Document**. Article 10(2) of the **Framework Convention for the Protection of National Minorities** expressly requires States to 'make possible the use of minority languages in communications with administrative authorities.' Paragraph 35 of the **Copenhagen Document** also makes reference to the possibility of creating an environment that would be conducive to the participation of national minorities in public affairs, in their own language, by establishing 'appropriate local or autonomous administrations corresponding

to the specific historical and territorial circumstances of minorities in accordance with the policies of the State concerned'. Article 15 of the **Framework Convention** engages States to 'create the conditions necessary for the effective participation of persons belonging to national minorities in cultural, social and economic life and in public affairs, in particular those affecting them.' These provisions engage public authorities to enable persons belonging to national minorities to deal with local authorities in their language or to receive civil certificates and attestations in their own language. In line with the principles of equality and non-discrimination, these provisions also imply a dynamic participatory relationship wherein the language of the minority may be a full-fledged vehicle of communication in local political life and in the interface between citizens and public authorities including in the provision of public services.

The ethnic representativity of administrative institutions and agencies designed to serve the population is usually reflective of a pluralistic, open and non-discriminatory society. In order to counter the effects of past or existing discrimination within the system, Article 2 of **International Labour Organisation Convention No. 111 Concerning Discrimination in Respect of Employment and Occupation** requires States to 'pursue a national policy designed to promote . . . equality of opportunity and treatment in respect of employment and occupation, with a view to eliminating any discrimination in respect thereof.'

When designing and implementing programmes and services intended to serve the public, it is reasonable to expect that governments committed to the principles outlined above should take into consideration the expressed desires of persons belonging to national minorities as well as the principle of numerical justification. Where the need is expressed and the numbers are significant, equity requires that taxpayers belonging to national minorities have access to services also in their own language. This is particularly so in the case of health and social services which affect the quality of peoples' lives in an immediate and fundamental manner.

In line with the principles of equality and non-discrimination, administrative authorities are expected to deal with persons belonging to national minorities in an inclusive and equitable manner. States must recognise the demographic realities of the regions under their jurisdiction. Above all, States should not seek to avoid their obligations by changing the demographic reality of a region. Specifically Article 16 of the **Framework Convention** engages States to refrain from measures which might arbitrarily alter the proportion of the population in areas inhabited by persons belonging to national minorities with the objective of restricting the rights of these minorities. Such measures could consist of arbitrary expropriations, evictions, expulsions as well as the arbitrary redrawing of administrative borders and census manipulation.

Independent National Institutions

16) Human rights acquire real meaning for their intended beneficiaries when the public authorities of the State establish mechanisms to ensure that the rights guaranteed in international conventions and declarations, or in domestic legislation, are effectively implemented and protected. As a complement to judicial procedures, independent national institutions usually provide quicker and less expensive recourses and are as such more accessible.

Discrimination as referred to in the **Convention on the Elimination of Racial Discrimination** is not defined according to criteria relating strictly to race. Article 1(1) of the **Convention** stipulates that the concept of racial discrimination shall mean 'any distinction, exclusion, restriction or preference based on race, colour, descent or national or ethnic origin which has the purpose or effect of nullifying or impairing the recognition, enjoyment or exercise, on an equal footing, of human rights and fundamental freedoms in the political, economic, social, cultural or any other field of public life.' Article 6 of the **Convention** declares that 'State Parties shall assure to everyone within their jurisdiction effective protection and remedies, through the competent national tribunals and other State institutions against any acts of racial discrimination which violate his human rights and fundamental freedoms contrary to this Convention . . .' In this context, the establishment by States of independent national institutions that can act as mechanisms of redress and compensation, such as the institution of ombudsperson or a human rights commission is a measure of a given State's democratic and pluralistic nature. Accordingly, and with reference to **United Nations resolution 48/134 of 20 December 1993**, the Council of Europe has encouraged, in **Committee**

of Ministers Recommendation No. R(97)14 of 30 September 1997, the establishment of 'national human rights institutions, in particular human rights commissions which are pluralist in their membership, ombudsmen or comparable institutions.' Such mechanisms of redress should be made available also to persons belonging to national minorities who consider that their linguistic and other rights have been violated.

Judicial Authorities

17/ 18) International law requires public authorities to ensure that all persons who are arrested, accused and tried be informed of the charges against them and of all other proceedings in a language they understand. If need be, an interpreter must be made available to them free of charge. This standard of due process of law is universal in its application and does not relate to the linguistic rights of national minorities as such. Rather, the underlying principles are those of equality and non-discrimination before the law. Respect for these principles is particularly vital in relation to criminal charges and proceedings. As a consequence, Article 14(3)(a) of the **International Covenant on Civil and Political Rights** requires that everyone charged with a criminal offense shall 'be informed promptly and in detail in a language which he understands of the nature and cause of the charge against him'. Article 6(3)(a) of the **European Convention for the Protection of Human Rights and Fundamental Freedoms** stipulates the same requirement in almost identical language. In addition, Article 5(2) of the aforementioned convention stipulates the same requirement in relation to arrest. Furthermore, Article 14(3) of the **International Covenant on Civil and Political Rights** stipulates the entitlement of everyone 'in full equality' . . . '(e) to examine, or have examined, the witnesses against him and to obtain the attendance and examination of witnesses on his behalf under the same conditions as witnesses against him'. In this connection, Article 14(3)(f) of the **International Covenant on Civil and Political Rights** and Article 6(3)(e) of the **European Convention for the Protection of Human Rights and Fundamental Freedoms** guarantee the right of everyone 'to have the free assistance of an interpreter if he cannot understand or speak the language used in court.' While these guarantees concerning expressly the use of language are prescribed specifically in relation to criminal procedures, it follows from the fundamental guarantee of equality before courts and tribunals, as stipulated in the first sentence of Article 14(1) of the **International Covenant on Civil and Political Rights**, that legal proceedings of all kinds are to be considered more perfectly fair to the extent that the conditions are more strictly equal. This determination, which applies equally with respect to the choice of language for proceedings as a whole, should guide States in the development of their policies concerning the equal and effective administration of justice.

More generally, Article 7(1) of the **European Charter for Regional or Minority Languages** declares that States shall base their policies, legislation and practice on such objectives and principles as 'the recognition of the regional or minority languages as an expression of cultural wealth . . .' and 'the need for resolute action to promote regional or minority languages in order to safeguard them'. Article 7(4) of the **European Charter** stipulates that 'in determining their policy with regard to regional and minority languages, . . . Parties shall take into consideration the needs and wishes expressed by the groups which use such languages.' Moreover, Article 15 of the **Framework Convention** engages States to 'create the conditions necessary for the effective participation of persons belonging to national minorities in cultural, social and economic life and in public affairs, in particular those affecting them.' If one considers the above-mentioned standards while taking into consideration the importance, in democratic societies, of effective access to justice, it is reasonable to expect that States should, so far as possible, ensure the right of persons belonging to national minorities to express themselves in their language in all stages of judicial proceedings (whether criminal, civil or administrative) while respecting the rights of others and maintaining the integrity of the processes, including through instances of appeal.

19) Insofar as access to justice is vital to the enjoyment of human rights, the degree to which one may participate directly and easily in available procedures is an important measure of such access. The availability of judicial procedures functioning in the language(s) of persons belonging to national minorities, therefore, renders access to justice more direct and easy for such persons.

On this basis, Article 9 of the **European Charter for Regional or Minority Languages** provides that, to the extent feasible and pursuant to the request of one of the affected parties, all judicial proceedings should be conducted in the regional or minority language. The Parliamentary Assembly of the Council of Europe, has come to the same conclusion in Article 7(3) of its **Recommendation 1201** which provides that 'In regions in which substantial numbers of a national minority are settled, the persons belonging to a national minority shall have the right to use their mother tongue in their contacts with the administrative authorities and in proceedings before the courts and legal authorities.' Accordingly, States should adopt appropriate recruitment and training policies for the judiciary.

Deprivation of Liberty

20) Rule 51, paragraphs 1 and 2, of the **United Nations Standard Minimum Rules for the Treatment of Prisoners** as well as Rule 60, paragraphs 1 and 2 of the **European Prison Rules of the Council of Europe** stress the importance of the right of the incarcerated to be understood by the prison administration as well as the importance for the prison administration to be understood by the inmate population. These provisions do not relate to minority rights as such. However, taken into consideration along with the expressed desire of affected populations, their numerical strength and the principle of equality and non-discrimination, the aforementioned provisions are even more compelling in regions or localities where persons belonging to national minorities are present in significant numbers.

21) Rule 37 of the **United Nations Standard Minimum Rules for the Treatment of Prisoners** as well as Article 43(1) of the **European Prison Rules of the Council of Europe** uphold the right of prisoners to communicate with their families, reputable friends and persons or representatives of outside organisations. In view of the importance of such human rights as freedom of expression and the right to use one's language in public and in private, it is incumbent upon authorities to respect these rights within the limitations prescribed by law even in penitentiary institutions. As a rule, prisoners should be able to communicate in their own language both orally with other inmates and with visitors and also

in personal correspondence. Nevertheless, certain human rights and freedoms of persons detained for criminal acts may legitimately be restricted or suspended for reasons of public security in conformity with the limitations prescribed by the international instruments. As a practical matter, enjoyment of the linguistic rights of detained persons may be best facilitated by their detention in a place where their language is usually spoken.

ANNEX 6

The Lund Recommendations on the Effective Participation of National Minorities in Public Life & Explanatory Note September 1999

Contents

III. Self-Governance
  A. Non-Territorial Arrangements
  B. Territorial Arrangements

IV. Guarantees
  A. Constitutional and Legal Safeguards
  B. Remedies

Introduction

In its Helsinki Decisions of July 1992, the Organization for Security and Co-operation in Europe (OSCE) established the position of High Commissioner on National Minorities to be 'an instrument of conflict prevention at the earliest possible stage'. This mandate was created largely in reaction to the situation in the former Yugoslavia which some feared would be repeated elsewhere in Europe, especially among the countries in transition to democracy, and could undermine the promise of peace and prosperity as envisaged in the Charter of Paris for a New Europe adopted by the Heads of State and Government in November 1990.

On 1 January 1993, Mr. Max van der Stoel took up his duties as the first OSCE High Commissioner on National Minorities (HCNM). Drawing on his considerable personal experience as a former Member of Parliament, Foreign Minister of The Netherlands, Permanent Representative to the United Nations, and long-time human rights advocate, Mr. van der Stoel turned his attention to the many disputes between minorities and central authorities in Europe which had the potential, in his view, to escalate. Acting quietly through diplomatic means, the HCNM has become involved in over a dozen States, including Albania, Croatia, Estonia, Hungary, Kazakstan, Kyrgyzstan, Latvia, the Former Yugoslav Republic of Macedonia, Romania, Slovakia and Ukraine. His involvement has focused primarily on those situations involving persons belonging to national/ethnic groups who constitute the numerical majority in one State but the numerical minority in another State, thus engaging the interest of governmental authorities in each State and constituting a potential source of inter-State tension if not conflict. Indeed, such tensions have defined much of

European history.

In addressing the substance of tensions involving national minorities, the HCNM approaches the issues as an independent, impartial and cooperative actor. While the HCNM is not a supervisory mechanism, he employs the international standards to which each State has agreed as his principal framework of analysis and the foundation of his specific recommendations. In this relation, it is important to recall the commitments undertaken by all OSCE participating States, in particular those of the 1990 Copenhagen Document of the Conference on the Human Dimension which, in Part IV, articulates detailed standards relating to national minorities. All OSCE States are also bound by United Nations obligations relating to human rights, including minority rights, and the great majority of OSCE States are further bound by the standards of the Council of Europe.

Through the course of more than six years of intense activity, the HCNM has identified certain recurrent issues and themes which have become the subject of his attention in a number of States in which he is involved. Among these are issues of minority education and use of minority languages, in particular as matters of great importance for the maintenance and development of the identity of persons belonging to national minorities. With a view to achieving an appropriate and coherent application of relevant minority rights in the OSCE area, the HCNM requested the Foundation on Inter-Ethnic Relations – a non-governmental organization established in 1993 to carry out specialized activities in support of the HCNM – to bring together two groups of internationally recognized independent experts to elaborate two sets of recommendations: **The Hague Recommendations regarding the Education Rights of National Minorities** (1996) and the **Oslo Recommendations regarding the Linguistic Rights of National Minorities** (1998). Both sets of recommendations have subsequently served as references for policy- and law-makers in a number of States. The recommendations are available (in several languages) from the Foundation on Inter-Ethnic Relations free of charge.

A third recurrent theme which has arisen in a number of situations in which the HCNM has been involved is that of forms of effective participation of national minorities in the governance of States. In order to gain a sense of the views and experiences of OSCE participating States on this issue and to allow States to share their experiences with each other, the HCNM and the OSCE's Office for Democratic Institutions and Human Rights convened a conference of all OSCE States and relevant international organisations entitled 'Governance and Participation: Integrating Diversity', which was hosted by the Swiss Confederation in Locarno from 18 to 20 October 1998. The Chairman's Statement issued at the end of the conference summarized the themes of the meeting and noted the desirability of 'concrete follow-up activities, including the further elaboration of the various concepts and mechanisms of good governance with the effective participation of minorities, leading to integration of diversity within the State.' To this end, the HCNM called upon the Foundation on Inter-Ethnic Relations, in co-operation with the Raoul Wallenberg Institute of Human Rights and Humanitarian Law, to bring together a group of internationally recognized independent experts to elaborate recommendations and outline alternatives, in line with the relevant international standards.

The result of the above initiative is **The Lund Recommendations on the Effective Participation of National Minorities in Public Life** – named after the Swedish city in which the experts last met and completed the recommendations. Among the experts were jurists specializing in relevant international law, political scientists specializing in constitutional orders and election systems, and sociologists specializing in minority issues. Specifically, under the Chairmanship of the Director of the Raoul Wallenberg Institute, Professor Gudmundur Alfredsson, the experts were:

> Professor Gudmundur Alfredsson (Icelandic), Director of the Raoul Wallenberg Institute of Human Rights and Humanitarian Law, Lund University; Professor Vernon Bogdanor (British), Professor of Government, Oxford University; Professor Vojin Dimitrijevič (Yugoslavian), Director of the Belgrade Centre for Human Rights; Dr. Asbjørn Eide (Norwegian), Senior Fellow at the Norwegian Institute of Human Rights; Professor Yash Ghai (Kenyan), Sir YK Pao Professor of Public Law, University of Hong Kong; Professor Hurst Hannum (American), Professor of International Law, Fletcher School of Law and Diplomacy, Tufts University; Mr. Peter Harris (South African), Senior Executive to the International Institute for Democracy and Electoral Assistance; Dr. Hans-Joachim Heintze (German), Director of the Institut für Friedenssicherungsrecht und Humanitäres Völkerrecht, Ruhr-Universität Bochum; Professor Ruth Lapidoth (Israeli), Professor of International Law and Chairman of the Academic Committee of the Institute for European Studies, The Hebrew University of Jerusalem; Professor Rein

Müllerson (Estonian), Chair of International Law, King's College, University of London; Dr. Sarlotta Pufflerova (Slovak), Director, Foundation Citizen and Minority/Minority Rights Group; Professor Steven Ratner (American), Professor of International Law, University of Texas; Dr. Andrew Reynolds (British), Assistant Professor of Government, University of Notre Dame; Mr. Miquel Strubell (Spanish and British), Director of the Institute of Catalan Socio-Linguistics, Generalitat de Catalunya; Professor Markku Suksi (Finnish), Professor of Public Law, Åbo Akademi University; Professor Danilo Türk (Slovene), Professor of International Law, Ljubljana University; Dr. Fernand de Varennes (Canadian), Senior Lecturer in Law and Director of the Asia-Pacific Centre for Human Rights and the Prevention of Ethnic Conflict, Murdoch University; Professor Roman Wieruszewski (Polish), Director of the Poznan Human Rights Centre, Polish Academy of Sciences.

Insofar as existing standards of minority rights are part of human rights, the starting point of the consultations among the experts was to presume compliance by States with all other human rights obligations including, in particular, freedom from discrimination. It was also presumed that the ultimate object of all human rights is the full and free development of the individual human personality in conditions of equality. Consequently, it was presumed that civil society should be open and fluid and, therefore, integrate all persons, including those belonging to national minorities. Moreover, insofar as the objective of good and democratic governance is to serve the needs and interests of the whole population, it was presumed that all governments seek to ensure the maximum opportunities for contributions from those affected by public decision-making.

The purpose of the Lund Recommendations, like The Hague and Oslo Recommendations before them, is to encourage and facilitate the adoption by States of specific measures to alleviate tensions related to national minorities and thus to serve the ultimate conflict prevention goal of the HCNM. The Lund Recommendations on the Effective Participation of National Minorities in Public Life attempt to clarify in relatively straight-forward language and build upon the content of minority rights and other standards generally applicable in the situations in which the HCNM is involved. The standards have been interpreted specifically to ensure the coherence of their application in open and democratic States. The Recommendations are divided into four sub-headings which group the twenty-four recommendations into general principles, participation in decision-making, self-governance, and ways of guaranteeing such effective participation in public life. The basic conceptual division within the Lund Recommendations follows two prongs: participation in governance of the State as a whole, and self-governance over certain local or internal affairs. A wide variety of arrangements are possible and known. In several recommendations, alternatives are suggested. All recommendations are to be interpreted in accordance with the General Principles in Part I. A more detailed explanation of each recommendation is provided in an accompanying Explanatory Note wherein express reference to the relevant international standards is found.

The Lund Recommendations on the Effective Participation of National Minorities in Public Life

I. General Principles

1) Effective participation of national minorities in public life is an essential component of a peaceful and democratic society. Experience in Europe and elsewhere has shown that, in order to promote such participation, governments often need to establish specific arrangements for national minorities. These Recommendations aim to facilitate the inclusion of minorities within the State and enable minorities to maintain their own identity and characteristics, thereby promoting the good governance and integrity of the State.

2) These Recommendations build upon fundamental principles and rules of international law, such as respect for human dignity, equal rights, and nondiscrimination, as they affect the rights of national minorities to participate in public life and to enjoy other political rights. States have a duty to respect internationally recognized human rights and the rule of law, which allow for the full development of civil society in conditions of tolerance, peace, and prosperity.

3) When specific institutions are established to ensure the effective participation of minorities in public life, which can include the exercise of authority or responsibility by such institutions, they must respect the human rights of all those affected.

4) Individuals identify themselves in numerous ways in addition to their identity as members of a national minority. The decision as to whether an individual is a member of a minority, the majority, or neither rests with that individual and shall not be imposed upon her or him. Moreover, no person shall suffer any disadvantage as a result of such a choice or refusal to choose.

5) When creating institutions and procedures in accordance with these Recommendations, both substance and process are important. Governmental authorities and minorities should pursue an inclusive, transparent, and accountable process of consultation in order to maintain a climate of confidence. The State should encourage the public media to foster intercultural understanding and address the concerns of minorities.

II. Participation in Decision-Making

A. Arrangements at the Level of the Central Government

6) States should ensure that opportunities exist for minorities to have an effective voice at the level of the central government, including through special arrangements as necessary. These may include, depending upon the circumstances:

- special representation of national minorities, for example, through a reserved number of seats in one or both chambers of parliament or in parliamentary committees; and other forms of guaranteed participation in the legislative process;
- formal or informal understandings for allocating to members of national minorities cabinet positions, seats on the supreme or constitutional court or lower courts, and positions on nominated advisory bodies or other high-level organs;
- mechanisms to ensure that minority interests are considered within relevant ministries, through, e.g., personnel addressing minority concerns or issuance of standing directives; and
- special measures for minority participation in the civil service as well as the provision of public services in the language of the national minority.

B. Elections

7) Experience in Europe and elsewhere demonstrates the importance of the electoral process for facilitating the participation of minorities in the political sphere. States shall guarantee the right of persons belonging to national minorities to take part in the conduct of public affairs, including through the rights to vote and stand for office without discrimination.

8) The regulation of the formation and activity of political parties shall comply with the international law principle of freedom of association. This principle includes the freedom to establish political parties based on communal identities as well as those not identified exclusively with the interests of a specific community.

9) The electoral system should facilitate minority representation and influence.

   - Where minorities are concentrated territorially, single-member districts may provide sufficient minority representation.
   - Proportional representation systems, where a political party's share in the national vote is reflected in its share of the legislative seats, may assist in the representation of minorities.
   - Some forms of preference voting, where voters rank candidates in order of choice, may facilitate minority representation and promote inter-communal cooperation.
   - Lower numerical thresholds for representation in the legislature may enhance the inclusion of national minorities in governance.

10) The geographic boundaries of electoral districts should facilitate the equitable representation of national minorities.

C. Arrangements at the Regional and Local Levels

11) States should adopt measures to promote participation of national minorities at the regional and local levels such as those mentioned above regarding the level of the central government (paragraphs 6-10) The structures and decision-making processes of regional and local authorities should be made transparent and accessible in order to encourage the participation of minorities.

D. Advisory and Consultative Bodies

12) States should establish advisory or consultative bodies within appropriate institutional frameworks to serve as channels for dialogue between governmental authorities and national minorities. Such bodies might also include special purpose committees for addressing such issues as housing, land, education, language, and culture. The composition of such bodies should reflect their purpose and contribute to more effective communication and advancement of minority interests.

13) These bodies should be able to raise issues with decisionmakers, prepare recommendations, formulate legislative and other proposals, monitor developments and provide views on proposed governmental decisions that may directly or indirectly affect minorities. Governmental authorities should consult these bodies regularly regarding minority-related legislation and administrative measures in order to contribute to the satisfaction of minority concerns and to the building of confidence. The effective functioning of these bodies will require that they have adequate resources.

III. Self-Governance

14) Effective participation of minorities in public life may call for non-territorial or territorial arrangements of self-governance or a combination thereof. States should devote adequate resources to such arrangements.

15) It is essential to the success of such arrangements that governmental authorities and minorities recognize the need for central and uniform decisions in some areas of governance together with the advantages of diversity in others.

- Functions that are generally exercised by the central authorities include defense, foreign affairs, immigration and customs, macroeconomic policy, and monetary affairs.
- Other functions, such as those identified below, may be managed by minorities or territorial administrations or shared with the central authorities.
- Functions may be allocated asymmetrically to respond to different minority situations within the same State.

16) Institutions of self-governance, whether non-territorial or territorial, must be based on democratic principles to ensure that they genuinely reflect the views of the affected population.

A. Non-Territorial Arrangements

17) Non-territorial forms of governance are useful for the maintenance and development of the identity and culture of national minorities.

18) The issues most susceptible to regulation by these arrangements include education, culture, use of minority language, religion, and other matters crucial to the identity and way of life of national minorities.
   - Individuals and groups have the right to choose to use their names in the minority language and obtain official recognition of their names.
   - Taking into account the responsibility of the governmental authorities to set educational standards, minority institutions can determine curricula for teaching of their minority languages, cultures, or both.
   - Minorities can determine and enjoy their own symbols and other forms of cultural expression.

B. Territorial Arrangements

19) All democracies have arrangements for governance at different territorial levels. Experience in Europe and elsewhere shows the value of shifting certain legislative and executive functions from the central to the regional level, beyond the mere decentralization of central government administration from the capital to regional or local offices. Drawing on the principle of subsidiarity, States should favourably consider such territorial devolution of powers, including specific functions of self-government, particularly where it would improve the opportunities of minorities to exercise authority over matters affecting them.

20) Appropriate local, regional, or autonomous administrations that correspond to the specific historical and territorial circumstances of national minorities may undertake a number of functions in order to respond more effectively to the concerns of these minorities.
   - Functions over which such administrations have successfully assumed primary or significant authority include education, culture, use of

minority language, environment, local planning, natural resources, economic development, local policing functions, and housing, health, and other social services.

- Functions shared by central and regional authorities include taxation, administration of justice, tourism, and transport.

21) Local, regional, and autonomous authorities must respect and ensure the human rights of all persons, including the rights of any minorities within their jurisdiction.

IV. Guarantees

A. Constitutional and Legal Safeguards

22) Self-governance arrangements should be established by law and generally not be subject to change in the same manner as ordinary legislation. Arrangements for promoting participation of minorities in decision-making may be determined by law or other appropriate means.
   - Arrangements adopted as constitutional provisions are normally subject to a higher threshold of legislative or popular consent for their adoption and amendment.
   - Changes to self-governance arrangements established by legislation often require approval by a qualified majority of the legislature, autonomous bodies or bodies representing national minorities, or both.
   - Periodic review of arrangements for self-governance and minority participation in decision-making can provide useful opportunities to determine whether such arrangements should be amended in the light of experience and changed circumstances.

23) The possibility of provisional or step-by-step arrangements that allow for the testing and development of new forms of participation may be considered. These arrangements can be established through legislation or informal means with a defined time period, subject to extension, alteration, or termination depending upon the success achieved.

B. Remedies

24) Effective participation of national minorities in public life requires established channels of consultation for the prevention of conflicts and

dispute resolution, as well as the possibility of *ad hoc* or alternative mechanisms when necessary. Such methods include:

- judicial resolution of conflicts, such as judicial review of legislation or administrative actions, which requires that the State possess an independent, accessible, and impartial judiciary whose decisions are respected; and
- additional dispute resolution mechanisms, such as negotiation, fact finding, mediation, arbitration, an ombudsman for national minorities, and special commissions, which can serve as focal points and mechanisms for the resolution of grievances about governance issues.

Explanatory Note to the Lund Recommendations on the Effective Participation of National Minorities in Public Life

I. General Principles

1) Both the **Charter of the United Nations** (hereafter the 'UN Charter') and the foundational documents of the CSCE/OSCE seek to maintain and strengthen international peace and security through the development of friendly and co-operative relations between equally sovereign States respecting human rights, including the rights of persons belonging to minorities. Indeed, history shows that failure to respect human rights, including minority rights, can undermine stability within the State and negatively affect relations between States, thus endangering international peace and security.

Beginning with Principle VII of the decalogue of the 1975 **Helsinki Final Act**, the OSCE participating States have emphasised the fundamental link between respecting the legitimate interests of persons belonging to national minorities and the maintenance of peace and stability. This link has been reiterated in subsequent basic documents such as the 1983 **Concluding Document of Madrid** (Principle 15), the 1989 **Concluding Document of Vienna** (Principles 18 and 19), and the 1990 **Charter of Paris for a New Europe**, in addition to subsequent Summit Documents, e.g. the 1992 **Helsinki Document** (Part IV, paragraph 24) and the 1996 **Lisbon Document** (Part I, **Lisbon Declaration on a Common and Comprehensive Security Model for Europe for the Twenty-First Century**, paragraph 2). At the level of the United Nations, the link between protection and promotion of minority rights and maintenance of peace and stability is expressed, inter alia, in the preamble to the 1992 **UN Declaration on the Rights of Persons Belonging to National or Ethnic, Religious and Linguistic Minorities** (hereafter the 'UN Declaration on Minorities'). Moreover, following adoption of the **Charter of Paris for a New Europe**, all OSCE participating States are committed to democratic governance.

Full opportunities for the equal enjoyment of the human rights of persons belonging to minorities entails their effective participation in decision-making processes, especially with regard to those decisions specially affecting them. While situations vary greatly and ordinary democratic processes may be adequate to respond to the needs and aspirations of minorities, experience also shows that special measures are often required to facilitate the effective participation of minorities in decision-making. The following international standards commit States to take such action in such situations: according to paragraph 35 of the 1990 **Document of the Copenhagen Meeting on the Human Dimension** (hereafter the 'Copenhagen Document'), OSCE participating States 'will respect the right of persons belonging to national minorities to effective participation in public affairs, including participation in the affairs relating to the protection and promotion of the identity of such minorities'; according to Article 2, paragraphs 2 and 3, of the 1992 **UN Declaration on Minorities**, '[p]ersons belonging to minorities have the right to participate effectively in [...] public life' and 'the right to participate effectively in decisions on the national and, where appropriate, regional level concerning the minority to which they belong or the regions in which they live'; and, according to Article 15 of the Council of Europe's 1994 **Framework Convention for the Protection of National Minorities** (hereafter the 'Framework Convention'), States Parties 'shall create the conditions necessary for the effective participation of persons belonging to national minorities in cultural, social and economic life and in public affairs, in particular those affecting them.'

The creation of opportunities for effective participation takes for granted that such participation will be voluntary. Indeed, the underlying notion of social and political integration is distinguished from processes and outcomes which constitute coerced assimilation, as cautioned in Article 5 of the **Framework Convention**. Only through voluntary processes may the pursuit of the legitimate interests of persons belonging to minorities be a peaceful process which offers the prospect of optimal outcomes in public policy- and law-making. Such inclusive, participatory processes thus serve the objective of good governance by responding to the interests of the whole population – weaving all interests into the fabric of public life and ultimately strengthening the integrity of the State. The international standards referring to effective participation of minorities in public life underscore the fact that they do not imply any right to engage in activities contrary to the purposes and principles of the United Nations, OSCE or Council of Europe, including sovereign equality, territorial integrity and political independence of States (see paragraph 37 of the **Copenhagen Document**, Article 8(4) of the **UN Declaration on Minorities**, and the preamble of the **Framework Convention**).

2) In the spirit of paragraph 25 of Part VI of the 1992 **Helsinki Document**, these recommendations build upon the relevant commitments insofar as they offer OSCE participating States 'further avenues for more effective implementation of their CSCE commitments, including those related to the protection and the creation of conditions for the promotion of the ethnic, cultural, linguistic and religious identity of national minorities'.

Article 1(3) of the **UN Charter** specifies that one of the purposes of the organisation is 'To achieve international co-operation in solving international problems of an economic, social, cultural, or humanitarian character, and in promoting and encouraging respect for human rights and for fundamental freedoms for all without distinction as to race, sex, language, or religion' – which is further specified in Article 55(c) as including 'universal respect for, and observance of, human rights and fundamental freedoms for all without distinction as to race, sex, language, or religion.' The **Charter** is based upon the intimate relationship between respect for human rights and international peace and security, and the fundamental value of human dignity is further expressed in Article 1 of the 1948 **Universal Declaration of Human Rights** and the preambles of the 1966 **International Covenant on Civil and Political Rights**, the 1966 **International Covenant on Economic, Social and Cultural Rights**, and the 1965 **International Convention on the Elimination of All Forms of Racial Discrimination**. Such dignity is equally inherent in all human beings and accompanied by equal and inalienable rights.

Following from the premise of equal dignity and inalienable rights is the principle of non-discrimination as expressed in virtually all international human rights instruments, including notably Article 2 of the **Universal Declaration of Human Rights**, Articles 2 and 26 of the **Inter-**

national Covenant on Civil and Political Rights, and Article 2 of the **International Covenant on Economic, Social and Cultural Rights.** Article 1 of the **International Convention on the Elimination of All Forms of Racial Discrimination** makes clear that this instrument prohibits discrimination also on the basis of 'descent, or national or ethnic origin'. Article 14 of the 1950 **European Convention for the Protection of Human Rights and Fundamental Freedoms** (hereafter the 'European Convention on Human Rights') also expressly extends the principle of non-discrimination to cover grounds of 'national or social origin, [or] association with a national minority', whenever the rights and freedoms guaranteed by the convention are engaged. Indeed, the constitutions of most OSCE participating States incorporate these affirmations and principles.

Insofar as persons belonging to national minorities are entitled to the right to effective participation in public life, they are to enjoy this right without discrimination, as expressed in paragraph 31 of the **Copenhagen Document**, Article 4 of the **Framework Convention**, and Article 4(1) of the **UN Declaration on Minorities**. However, according to Article 4(2) of the **Framework Convention**, concern for equal dignity extends beyond the principle of non-discrimination towards 'full and effective equality between persons belonging to a national minority and those belonging to the majority' for which States should 'adopt, where necessary, adequate measures . . . in all areas of . . . political . . . life' in respect of which 'they shall take due account of the specific conditions of the persons belonging to national minorities.'

The connection made in the recommendation between respect for human rights and the development of civil society reflects the call for an 'effective political democracy' which, according to the Preamble of the **European Convention on Human Rights**, is intimately related to justice and peace in the world. OSCE participating States have further affirmed in the **Charter of Paris for a New Europe** that democratic governance, including respect for human rights, is the basis for prosperity.

3) When specific institutions are established to ensure the effective participation of national minorities in public life, this must not be at the expense of others' rights. All human rights must be respected at all times, including by such institutions which may be delegated authority by the State.

According to paragraph 33 of the **Copenhagen Document**, when participating States take measures necessary for the protection of the identity of persons belonging to national minorities, 'Any such measures will be in conformity with the principles of equality and non-discrimination with respect to the other citizens of the participating State concerned.' The **Copenhagen Document** further stipulates at paragraph 38 that OSCE 'participating States, in their efforts to protect and promote the rights of persons belonging to national minorities, will fully respect their undertakings under existing human rights conventions and other relevant international instruments'. The **Framework Convention** has a similar stipulation in Article 20: 'In the exercise of the rights and freedoms flowing from the principles enshrined in the present framework Convention, any person belonging to a national minority shall respect the national legislation and the rights of others, in particular those of persons belonging to the majority or to other national minorities.' This addresses in particular the case of 'minorities within minorities', especially in the territorial context (see recommendations 16 and 21 below). This would also include respect for the human rights of women, including freedom from discrimination in relation to 'the political and public life of the country' as stipulated at Article 7 of the 1979 **Convention on the Elimination of All Forms of Discrimination against Women**.

4) The principle of self-identification of persons belonging to minorities is based on several fundamental commitments. Paragraph 32 of the **Copenhagen Document** specifies that 'To belong to a national minority is a matter of a person's individual choice and no disadvantage may arise from the exercise of such choice'. Article 3(1) of the **Framework Convention** provides similarly that 'Every person belonging to a national minority shall have the right freely to choose to be treated or not to be treated as such and no disadvantage shall result from this choice or from the exercise of the rights which are connected to that choice.' Article 3(2) of the **UN Declaration on Minorities** includes the same prohibition against any disadvantage resulting 'for any person belonging to a minority as the consequence of the exercise or non-exercise of the rights set forth in the present Declaration.'

An individual's freedom to identify oneself as one chooses is necessary to ensure respect for individual autonomy and liberty. An individual may possess several identities that are relevant not only for private life, but also in the sphere of public life. Indeed, in open societies with increasing movements of persons and ideas, many individuals have multiple identities which are coinciding, coexisting or layered (in an hierarchical or non-hierarchical fashion), reflecting their various associations. Certainly, identities are not based solely on ethnicity, nor are they uniform within the same community; they may be held by different members in varying shades and degrees. Depending upon the specific matters at issue, different identities may be more or less salient. As a consequence, the same person might identify herself or himself in different ways for different purposes, depending upon the salience of the identification and arrangement for her or him. For example, in some States a person may choose a certain language for submission on tax forms, yet identify herself or himself differently in a local community for other purposes.

5) In the framework of democracy, the process of decision-making is as important as the substance of decisions made. Since good governance is not only of the people but also for the people, its processes should always be inclusive of those concerned, transparent for all to see and judge, and accountable to those affected. Only such processes will inspire and maintain public confidence. Inclusive processes may comprise consultation, polling, referenda, negotiation and even the specific consent of those directly affected. Decisions resulting from such processes are likely to inspire voluntary compliance. In situations where the views of the public authorities and the affected community may differ substantially, good governance may suggest using the services of a third party to assist in finding the most satisfactory arrangement.

In relation specifically to national minorities, paragraph 33 of the **Copenhagen Document** commits OSCE participating States to take measures to 'protect the ethnic, cultural, linguistic and religious identity of national minorities on their territory and create conditions for the promotion of that identity [. . .] after due consultations, including contacts with organizations or associations of such minorities'. In Part VI, paragraph 26, of the **Helsinki Document**, OSCE participating States further committed themselves to 'address national minority issues in a constructive manner, by peaceful means and through dialogue among all parties concerned on the basis of CSCE principles and commitments'. In connection with 'all parties concerned', paragraph 30 of the **Copenhagen Document** recognizes 'the important role of non-governmental organizations, including political parties, trade unions, human rights organizations and religious groups, in the promotion of tolerance, cultural diversity and the resolution of questions relating to national minorities.'

Inclusive processes require conditions of tolerance. A social and political climate of mutual respect and equality needs to be assured by law and also taught as a social ethic shared by the whole population. The media have a special role in this regard. Article 6(1) of the **Framework Convention** provides that 'the Parties shall encourage a spirit of tolerance and intercultural dialogue and take effective measures to promote mutual respect and understanding and co-operation among all persons living on their territory, irrespective of those persons' ethnic, cultural, linguistic or religious identity, in particular in the fields of education, culture and the media.' In particular, States should act to stop the public use of derogatory or pejorative names and terms and should take steps to counteract negative stereotypes. Ideally, the representatives of the affected community should participate in the choice and design of any steps taken to overcome such problems.

II. Participation in Decision-Making

A. Arrangements at the Level of the Central Government

6) Building upon paragraph 35 of the **Copenhagen Document**, paragraph 1 of Part III of the 1991 **Report of the CSCE (Geneva) Meeting of Experts on National Minorities** underlines that 'when issues relating to the situation of national minorities are discussed within their countries, they themselves should have the effective opportunity to be involved . . . [and] that [such] democratic participation of persons belonging to national minorities or their representatives in decision-making or consultative bodies constitutes an important element of effective participation in public affairs.' Paragraph 24 of Part VI of the **Helsinki Document** committed OSCE participating States to 'intensify in this context their efforts to

ensure the free exercise by persons belonging to national minorities, individually or in community with others, of their human rights and fundamental freedoms, including the right to participate fully, in accordance with the democratic decision-making procedures of each State, in the political, economic, social, and cultural life of their countries including through democratic participation in decision-making and consultative bodies at the national, regional, and local level, *inter alia*, through political parties and associations.'

The essence of participation is involvement, both in terms of the opportunity to make substantive contributions to decision-making processes and in terms of the effect of those contributions. The notion of good governance includes the premise that simple majoritarian decision-making is not always sufficient. In terms of the structure of the State, various forms of decentralization may be appropriate to assure the maximum relevance and accountability of decision-making processes for those affected, both at the level of the State and at sub-State levels. This may be accomplished through various ways in a unitary State or in federal and confederal systems. Minority representation in decision-making bodies may be assured through reserved seats (by way of quotas, promotions or other measures), while other forms of participation include assured membership in relevant committees, with or without voting rights. Representation on executive, judicial, administrative and other bodies may be assured through similar means, whether by formal requirement or by customary practice. Special bodies may also be established to accommodate minority concerns. Meaningful opportunities to exercise all minority rights require specific steps to be taken in the public service, including ensuring 'equal access to public service' as articulated in Article 5(c) of the **International Convention on the Elimination of All Forms of Racial Discrimination.**

B. Elections

7) Representative government through free, fair and periodic elections is the hallmark of contemporary democracy. The fundamental objective is, in the words of Article 21(3) of the **Universal Declaration of Human Rights**, that 'The will of the people shall be the basis of the authority of government'. This basic standard is articulated in universal and European

treaties, namely Article 25 of the **International Covenant on Civil and Political Rights** and Article 3 of Protocol I additional to the **European Convention on Human Rights.** For OSCE participating States, paragraphs 5 and 6 of the **Copenhagen Document** specify that, 'among those elements of justice which are essential to the full expression of the inherent dignity and of the equal and inalienable rights of all human beings', 'the will of the people, freely and fairly expressed through periodic and genuine elections, is the basis of the authority and legitimacy of all government'.

While States have considerable latitude in choosing the specific manner in which to comply with these obligations, they must do so without discrimination and should aim for as much representativeness as possible. Indeed, within the context of the United Nations, the Human Rights Committee has explained in paragraph 12 of its **General Comment 25** on Article 25 (57th Session 1996) that 'Freedom of expression, assembly and association are essential conditions for the effective exercise of the right to vote and must be fully protected. [. . .] Information and materials about voting should be available in minority languages.' Moreover, paragraph 5 of **General Comment 25** clarifies that 'The conduct of public affairs [. . .] is a broad concept which relates to the exercise of political power, in particular the exercise of legislative, executive and administrative powers. It covers all aspects of public administration, and the formulation and implementation of policy at international, national, regional and local levels.'

Insofar as no electoral system is neutral from the perspective of varying views and interests, States should adopt the system which would result in the most representative government in their specific situation. This is especially important for persons belonging to national minorities who might otherwise not have adequate representation.

8) In principle, democracies should not interfere with the way in which people organize themselves politically – as long as their means are peaceful and respectful of the rights of others. Essentially, this is a matter of freedom of association, as articulated in a wide variety of international instruments including: Article 20 of the **Universal Declaration of Human Rights**; Article 22 of the **International Covenant on Civil and Political Rights**; Article 11 of the **European Convention on Human Rights**; and paragraph

6 of the **Copenhagen Document**. Freedom of association has also been guaranteed specifically for persons belonging to national minorities under paragraph 32.6 of the **Copenhagen Document** and Article 7 of the **Framework Convention.** More specifically, paragraph 24 of Part VI of the **Helsinki Document** commits OSCE participating States 'to ensure the free exercise by persons belonging to national minorities, individually or in community with others, of their human rights and fundamental freedoms, including the right to participate fully, [. . .] in the political [. . .] life of their countries including [. . .] through political parties and associations.'

While full respect for equal rights and non-discrimination will reduce or eliminate the demand and need for political parties formed on the basis of ethnic ties, in some situations such communal parties may be the only hope for effective representation of specific interests and, thus, for effective participation. Of course, parties may be formed on other bases, e.g. regional interests. Ideally, parties should be open and should cut across narrow ethnic issues; thus, mainstream parties should seek to include members of minorities to reduce the need or desire for ethnic parties. The choice of electoral system may be important in this regard. In any event, no political party or other association may incite racial hatred, which is prohibited by Article 20 of the **International Covenant on Civil and Political Rights** and Article 4 of the **Convention on the Elimination of All Forms of Racial Discrimination.**

9) The electoral system may provide for the selection of both the legislature and other bodies and institutions, including individual officials. While single member constituencies may provide sufficient representation for minorities, depending upon how the constituencies are drawn and the concentration of minority communities, proportional representation might help guarantee such minority representation. Various forms of proportional representation are practised in OSCE participating States, including the following: 'preference voting', whereby voters rank candidates in order of choice; 'open list systems', whereby electors can express a preference for a candidate within a party list, as well as voting for the party; '*panachage*', whereby electors can vote for more than one candidate across different party lines; and '*cumulation*', whereby voters

can cast more than one vote for a preferred candidate. Thresholds should not be so high as to hamper minority representation.

10) In drawing the boundaries of electoral districts, the concerns and interests of national minorities should be taken into account with a view to assuring their representation in decision-making bodies. The notion of 'equity' means that no one should be prejudiced by the chosen method and that all concerns and interests should be given fair consideration. Ideally, boundaries should be determined by an independent and impartial body to ensure, among other concerns, respect for minority rights. This is often accomplished in OSCE participating States by means of standing, professional electoral commissions.

In any event, States should not alter electoral boundaries, or otherwise alter the proportions of the population in a district, for the purpose of diluting or excluding minority representation. This is expressly prohibited by Article 16 of the **Framework Convention**, while Article 5 of the **European Charter of Local Self-Government** stipulates that 'Changes in local authority boundaries shall not be made without prior consultation of the local communities concerned, possibly by means of a referendum where this is permitted by statute' (see recommendation 19 regarding territorial arrangements).

C. Arrangements at the Regional and Local Levels

11) This Recommendation applies to all levels of government below the central authorities (e.g. provinces, departments, districts, prefectures, municipalities, cities and towns, whether units within a unitary State or constituent units of a federal State, including autonomous regions and other authorities). The consistent enjoyment of all human rights by everyone equally means that the entitlements enjoyed at the level of the central government should be enjoyed throughout the structures below. However, the criteria used to create structures at the regional and local level may be different from those used at the level of the central government. Structures may also be established asymmetrically, with variation according to differing needs and expressed desires.

D. Advisory and Consultative Bodies

12) Paragraph 24 of Part VI of the **Helsinki Document** commits OSCE participating States 'to ensure the free exercise by persons belonging to national minorities, individually or in community with others, of their human rights and fundamental freedoms, including the right to participate fully [. . .] in the political [. . .] life of their countries including through democratic participation in [. . .] consultative bodies at the national, regional, and local level'. Such bodies can be standing or ad hoc, part of or attached to the legislative or executive branch or independent therefrom. Committees attached to parliamentary bodies, such as minority round tables, are known in several OSCE participating States. They can and do function at all levels of government, including self-government arrangements. In order to be effective, these bodies should be composed of minority representatives and others who can offer special expertise, provided with adequate resources, and given serious attention by decisionmakers. Aside from advice and counsel, such bodies can constitute a useful intermediary institution between decisionmakers and minority groups. They can also stimulate action at the level of government and among minority communities. Such bodies may also perform specific tasks related to the implementation of programs, e.g. in the field of education. In addition, special purpose committees may hold particular significance for certain minorities who should be represented therein.

13) The possibilities for constructive use of such bodies vary with the situations. However, in all cases, good governance requires positive steps on the part of the authorities to engage established advisory and consultative bodies, to refer to them as needs may arise and to invite their in-put. An open and inclusive approach on the part of the authorities vis-à-vis these bodies and their members will contribute to better decisions and to greater confidence of the wider society.

III. Self-Governance

14) The term 'self-governance' implies a measure of control by a community over matters affecting it. The choice of the term 'governance' does not necessarily imply exclusive jurisdiction. In addition, it may subsume

administrative authority, management, and specified legislative and judicial jurisdiction. The State may achieve this through delegation or devolution, or, in the case of a federation, an initial division of constituent powers. Among OSCE participating States, 'self-governance' arrangements are variously referred to as delegations of autonomy, self-government, and home rule. In no case is this to include any ethnic criterion for territorial arrangements.

In paragraph 35 of the **Copenhagen Document**, OSCE participating States have noted 'the efforts undertaken to protect and create conditions for the promotion of the ethnic, cultural, linguistic and religious identity of certain national minorities by establishing, as one of the possible means to achieve these aims, appropriate local or autonomous administrations corresponding to the specific historical and territorial circumstances of such minorities and in accordance with the policies of the State concerned.' Following upon this, the **Report of the CSCE (Geneva) Meeting of Experts on National Minorities** noted in paragraph 7 of Part IV 'that positive results have been obtained by some [participating States] in an appropriate democratic manner by, *inter alia*: [. . .] local and autonomous administration, as well as autonomy on a territorial basis, including the existence of consultative, legislative and executive bodies chosen through free and periodic elections; self-administration by a national minority of aspects concerning its identity in situations where autonomy on a territorial basis does not apply; decentralized or local forms of government; [. . .] provision of financial and technical assistance to persons belonging to national minorities who so wish to exercise their right to establish and maintain their own educational, cultural and religious institutions, organizations and associations [. . .]'. Of a more general nature, the Preamble to the **European Charter of Local Self-Government** stresses 'the principles of democracy and the decentralisation of power' as a contribution to 'the safeguarding and reinforcement of local self-government in the different European countries'. In this last connection, the **European Charter of Local Self-Government** provides in Article 9 for the entitlement of adequate financial resources for the exercise of such decentralized authorities.

15) Insofar as the State holds responsibility in certain fields affecting the whole

State, it must assure their regulation through the central authorities of the State. These typically include: defense, which is essential to maintain the territorial integrity of the State; macroeconomic policy, which is important insofar as the central government serves as a sort of equalizer between economically disparate regions; and the classical affairs of diplomacy. Insofar as other fields may have important national implications, these too must be regulated at least to some degree by the central authorities. Regulation in these fields may also be shared, including with specially affected territorial units or minority groups (see recommendations 18 and 20). Such sharing of regulatory authority must nevertheless be consistent with human rights standards and be managed in a practical and coordinated manner.

One field which is well-established as being shared on either a territorial or a non-territorial basis, or both, and holds special importance both for the State as a whole and also for minority groups, is education. Article 5.1 of the **UNESCO Convention against Discrimination in Education** spells out in some detail how such sharing in this field should be achieved: 'The States Parties to this Convention agree that: [. . .]

(b) It is essential to respect the liberty of parents and, where applicable, of legal guardians, firstly to choose for their children institutions other than those maintained by the public authorities but conforming to such minimum educational standards as may be laid down or approved by the competent authorities and, secondly, to ensure in a manner consistent with the procedures followed in the State for the application of its legislation, the religious and moral education of the children in conformity with their own convictions; and no person or group of persons should be compelled to receive religious instruction inconsistent with his or their conviction;

(c) It is essential to recognize the right of members of national minorities to carry on their own educational activities, including the maintenance of schools and, depending on the educational policy of each State, the use or the teaching of their own language, provided however: (i) That this right is not exercised in a manner which prevents the members of these minorities from understanding the culture and language of the community as a whole and from participating in its activities, or which prejudices national sovereignty; (ii) That the standard of education is not lower than the general standard laid down or approved by the competent authorities; and (iii) That attendance at such schools is optional.'

16) The principle of democratic governance, as articulated in Article 21 of **the Universal Declaration of Human Rights**, Article 25 of the **International Covenant on Civil and Political Rights**, Article 3 of Protocol I to the **European Convention on Human Rights** and in OSCE standards is applicable at all levels and for all elements of governance. When institutions of self-governance are needed or desirable, the equal enjoyment by everyone of their rights requires application of the principle of democracy within these institutions.

A. Non-Territorial Arrangements

17) This section addresses non-territorial autonomy – often referred to as 'personal' or 'cultural autonomy' – which is most likely to be useful when a group is geographically dispersed. Such divisions of authority, including control over specific subject-matter, may take place at the level of the State or within territorial arrangements. In all cases, respect for the human rights of others must be assured. Moreover, such arrangements should be assured adequate financial resources to enable performance of their public functions and should result from inclusive processes (see Recommendation 5).

18) This is not an exhaustive list of possible functions. Much will depend upon the situation, including especially the needs and expressed desires of the minority. In different situations, different subjects will be of greater or lesser interest to minorities, and decisions in these fields will affect them to varying degrees. Some fields may be shared. One area of special concern for minorities is control over their own names, both for representative institutions and individual members, as provided in Article 11(1) of the **Framework Convention**. With regard to religion, the Recommendation does not advocate governmental interference in religious matters other than in relation to those powers (e.g. concerning personal civil status) delegated to religious authorities. This Recommendation also does not intend that minority institutions should control the media –

although persons belonging to minorities should have the possibility to create and use their own media, as guaranteed by Article 9(3) of the **Framework Convention**. Of course, culture has many aspects extending to fields such as welfare, housing and child care; the State should take into account minority interests in governance in these fields.

B. Territorial Arrangements

19) There is a general trend in European States towards devolution of authority and implementation of the principle of subsidiarity, such that decisions are taken as close as possible to, and by, those most directly concerned and affected. Article 4(3) of the **European Charter of Local Self-Government** expresses this objective as follows: 'Public responsibilities shall generally be exercised, in preference, by those authorities which are closest to the citizen. Allocation of responsibility to another authority should weigh up the extent and nature of the task and requirements of efficiency and economy.' Territorial self-government can help preserve the unity of States while increasing the level of participation and involvement of minorities by giving them a greater role in a level of government that reflects their population concentration. Federations may also accomplish this objective, as may particular autonomy arrangements within unitary States or federations. It is also possible to have mixed administrations. As noted in recommendation 15, arrangements need not be uniform across the State, but may vary according to needs and expressed desires.

20) Autonomous authorities must possess real power to make decisions at the legislative, executive or judicial levels. Authority within the State may be divided among central, regional and local authorities and also among functions. Paragraph 35 of the **Copenhagen Document** notes the alternatives of 'appropriate local or autonomous administrations corresponding to the specific historical and territorial circumstances'. This makes clear that there need not be uniformity within the State. Experience shows that powers can be divided even with respect to fields of public authority traditionally exercised by central government, including devolved powers of justice (both substantive and procedural) and powers over traditional economies. At a minimum, affected populations should be systematically

involved in the exercise of such authority. At the same time, the central government must retain powers to ensure justice and equality of opportunities across the State.

21) Where powers may be devolved on a territorial basis to improve the effective participation of minorities, these powers must be exercised with due account for the minorities within these jurisdictions. Administrative and executive authorities must be accountable to the whole population of the territory. This follows from paragraph 5.2 of the **Copenhagen Document** which commits OSCE participating States to assure at all levels and for all persons 'a form of government that is representative in character, in which the executive is accountable to the elected legislature or the electorate'.

IV. Guarantees

A. Constitutional and Legal Safeguards

22) This section addresses the issue of 'entrenchment', that is, solidifying arrangements in law. Very detailed legal arrangements may be useful in some cases, while frameworks may be sufficient in other cases. In all cases, as noted in recommendation 5, arrangements should result from open processes. However, once concluded, stability is required in order to assure some security for those affected, especially persons belonging to national minorities. Articles 2 and 4 of the **European Charter of Local Self-Government** express a preference for constitutional arrangements. To achieve the desired balance between stability and flexibility, it may be useful to specify some reconsideration at fixed intervals, thereby depoliticizing the process of change in advance and making the review process less adversarial.

23) This Recommendation differs from Recommendation 22 insofar as it encourages the testing of new and innovative regimes, rather than specifying terms for alteration of existing arrangements. Responsible authorities may wish to follow different approaches in different situations among central authorities and minority representatives. Without compromising final positions, such an approach may yield good experiences, not least through the processes of innovation and implementation.

B. Remedies

24) In paragraph 30 of the **Copenhagen Document**, OSCE participating States 'recognize that the questions relating to national minorities can only be satisfactorily resolved in a democratic political framework based on the rule of law, with a functioning independent judiciary.' The idea of effective remedies is also provided in Article 2(3) of the **International Covenant on Civil and Political Rights**, while 'a judicial remedy' is specified in Article 11 of the **European Charter of Local Self-Government.**

Judicial review can be performed by constitutional courts and, in effect, by relevant international human rights bodies. Non-judicial mechanisms and institutions, such as national commissions, ombudspersons, inter-ethnic or 'race' relations boards, etc., may also play critical roles, as envisaged by paragraph 27 of the **Copenhagen Document**, Article 14(2) of the **International Convention on the Elimination of All Forms of Racial Discrimination**, and paragraph 36 of the **Vienna Declaration and Programme of Action** adopted by the World Conference on Human Rights in 1993.

Bibliography

Bloed, Arie (ed.), 1993. *The Conference on Security and Co-operation in Europe: Analysis and Basic Documents, 1972–1993*. Dordecht: Kluwer International Publishers.

Bloed, Arie (ed.), 1994. *The Challenges of Change: the Helsinki Summit of the CSCE and its Aftermath*. Dordecht: Martinus Nijhoff Publishers.

Bloed, Arie & Pieter van Dijk (eds.), 1999. *Protection of Minority Rights Through Bilateral Treaties: the Case of Central and Eastern Europe*. The Hague: Kluwer Law International.

Chigas, Diana, 1994. 'Bridging the gap between theory and practice: the CSCE High Commissioner on National Minorities', *Helsinki Monitor* 5(3): 27–41.

Chigas, Diana, with Elizabeth McClintock & Christophe Kamp, 1996. 'Preventive diplomacy and the Organization for Security and Co-operation in Europe: creating incentives for dialogue and co-operation', in *Preventing Conflict in the Post-Communist World: Mobilizing International and Regional Organizations*, eds. Abram Chayes & Antonia Handler Chayes: 25–97. Washington: Brookings Institution.

Cohen, Jonathan, 1998a. *Conflict Prevention Instruments in the Organization for Security and Co-operation in Europe: an Assessment of Capacities*. London: Netherlands Institute of International Relations.

Cohen, Jonathan, 1998b. 'Zusammenarbeit im Bereich der Konkliktprävention: Die Stiftung für Interethnische Beziehungen un der Hohe Kommissar für Nationale Minderheiten der OSZE – eine Fallstudie', in *Friedenspolitik der Zivilgesellschaft*: 207–24. Münster: agenda Verlag.

Conflict Management Group/Harvard Negotiation Project, 1993. 'Early Warning and Preventive Action in the CSCE: Defining the Role of the High Commissioner on National Minorities', Report of the CSCE Devising Session, 19 October 1992 (Cambridge, MA).

Conflict Management Group, 1994. 'Methods and strategies in conflict prevention', Report of an Expert Consultation in Connection with the Activities of the CSCE High Commissioner on National Minorities, 2–3 December 1993, *Working Paper Series* (Cambridge, MA).

The Economist, 1999. 'Max van der Stoel, minority man', 352(8136) (11–17 September): 36.

Foundation on Inter-Ethnic Relations, 1997. *The Role of the High Commissioner on National Minorities in OSCE Conflict Prevention: an Introduction.* The Hague.

——, 1996. *The Hague Recommendations Regarding the Education Rights of National Minorities and Explanatory Note.* The Hague (October).

——, 1998. *The Oslo Recommendations Regarding the Linguistic Rights of National Minorities and Explanatory Note.* The Hague (February).

——, 1999. *The Lund Recommendations on the Effective Participation of National Minorities in Public Life and Explanatory Note.* The Hague (June).

Gal, Klinga, 1999. *Bilateral Agreements in Central and Eastern Europe: a New Inter-State Framework for Minority Protection?* (European Centre for Minority Rights Working Paper no. 4.) Flensburg (May).

Ghebali, Victor-Yves, 1996. *L'OSCE dans l'Europe post-communiste, 1990–1996: Vers une identité paneuropéenne de sécurité.* Brussels: Bruylant.

Huber, Konrad, 1993. 'The CSCE and ethnic conflict in the East', *RFE/RL Research Report* 2(31): 30–36.

Huber, Konrad, 1994. 'Averting inter-ethnic conflict: an analysis of the CSCE High Commissioner on National Minorities in Estonia, January–July 1993', *Working Paper Series* 1(2) (The Carter Center of Emory University: Atlanta 1994).

Huber, Konrad & Susanna Terstal, with Christophe Kamp, 1994. 'The functioning of the CSCE High Commissioner on National Minorities', *New Community* 20(3) (April): 502–8.

Ignatieff, Michael, 1993. *Blood and Belonging: Journeys into the New Nationalism.* London: BBC Books, Chatto & Windus.

Kemp, Walter A., 1996. *The OSCE in a New Context.* (Discussion Paper no. 64.) London: Royal Institute of International Affairs.

Kemp, Walter A., 1999a. *Nationalism and Communism in Eastern Europe and the Soviet Union: a Basic Contradiction?* London: Macmillan.

Kemp, Walter A., 1999b. 'Ever heard of the OSCE?', *Helsinki Monitor* 10(1): 37–42.

Packer, John, 'The OSCE High Commissioner on National Minorities', Contribution to the *Liber Amicorum* for Jacob Müller.

Packer, John, 1993. 'On the definition of minorities', in *The Protection of Ethnic and Linguistic Minorities in Europe*, by J. Packer & K. Myntti: 23–65. Turku-Åbo: Institute for Human Rights, Åbo Akademi University.

Packer, John, 1996a. 'Conflict prevention by the OAU: the relevance of the OSCE High Commissioner on National Minorities', *African Yearbook of International Law* 4.

Packer, John, 1996b. 'On the content of minority rights', in *Do We Need Minority Rights? Conceptual Issues*, ed. J. Räikkä. The Hague: Martinus Nijhoff: 121–78.

Packer, John, 1997. 'Problems in defining minorities', in *Minority and Group Rights Towards the New Millenium*, eds. D. Fortrell & B. Bowring: 223–273. The Hague: Kluwer Law International.

Packer, John, 1998. 'Autonomy within the OSCE: the case of Crimea', in *Autonomy: Applications and Implications*, ed. M. Suksi: 295–316. The Hague: Kluwer Law International.

Packer, John, 1999a. 'The role of the OSCE High Commissioner on National Minorities in the Former Yugoslavia', *Cambridge Review on International Affairs* xii/2 (spring/summer): 169–84.

Packer, John, 1999b. 'Problems in defining minorities, in *Minority and Group Rights in the New Millennium*, eds. D. Fottrell & B. Bowring. The Hague: Kluwer Law International: 223–74.

Packer, John, 2000. 'The Origin and Nature of the Lund Recommendations on the Effective Participation of National Minorities in Public Life', *Helsinki Monitor* II(4): 29–45.

Packer, John, 2001. 'The OSCE High Commissioner on National Minorities', in *Human Rights Monitoring Procedures: A Textbook on How to Petition and Lobby International Organisations*; Festschrift für Jakob Müller, eds. G. Alfredsson, G. Melander & B Ramcharan. The Hague: Kluwer Law International: 632–647.

Peel, Quentin, 2000. 'OSCE minorities chief aims for early action', *Financial Times* 19 May: 3.

Ratner, Steven, 2000. 'Does International Law Matter in Preventing Ethnic Conflict?', *New York University Journal of International Law and Politics* 32(3): 591–698.

Simonsen, Sven Gunnar (ed.), 1997. *Conflicts in the OSCE Area.* Oslo: International Peace Research Institute.

Suksi, Markku (ed.), 1998. *Autonomy: Applications and Implications.* The Hague: Kluwer Law International.

Thornberry, Patrick, 1992. *International Law and Rights of Minorities.* Oxford: Clarendon and Oxford University Press.

Van der Stoel, Max, 1996. 'Peace and justice, power and principle: from Nuremburg to the Hague', *The Finnish Yearbook of International Law* VII: 334–40.

Van der Stoel, Max, 1997. 'Minorities in transition', *War Report* 48 (January/February): 14–17.

Van der Stoel, Max, 1999a. 'Reflections on the role of the OSCE High Commissioner on National Minorities as an instrument of conflict prevention', *OSZE Jahrbuch*, Baden-Baden: Nomos: 429–442.

Van der Stoel, Max, 1999b. 'The role of the OSCE High Commissioner on National Minorities in conflict prevention', in *Herding Cats: Multiparty Mediation in a Complex World*, eds. Chester A. Crocker, Fen Osler Hampson & Pamela Aall: 65–83. Washington (DC): United States Institute for Peace.

Vassilev, Stefan, 1999. 'The HCNM approach to conflict prevention', *Helsinki Monitor* 10(3): 45–58.

Zaagman, Rob, 1994. 'The CSCE High Commissioner on National Minorities: an analysis of the mandate and the institutional context', in *The Challenges of Change: the Helsinki Summit of the CSCE and its Aftermath*, ed. A. Bloed: 113–75. Dordrecht: Martinus Nijhoff.

Zaagman, Rob, 1999. *Conflict Prevention in the Baltic States: the OSCE High Commissioner on National Minorities in Estonia, Latvia and Lithuania.* (European Centre for Minority Issues Monograph 1.) Flensburg: ECMI.

Zaagman, Rob & Hannie Zaal, 1994. 'The CSCE High Commissioner on National Minorities: prehistory and negotiations', in *The Challenges of Change: the Helsinki Summit of the CSCE and its Aftermath*, ed. A. Bloed: 95–111. Dordrecht: Martinus Nijhoff.

Zaal, H., 1992. 'The CSCE High Commissioner on National Minorities', *Helsinki Monitor* 3(4): 33–7.

Zellner, Wolfgang & Falk Lange (eds.), 1999. *Peace and Stability through Human and Minority Rights: Speeches by the OSCE High Commissioner on National Minorities.* Baden-Baden: Nomos.

Selected Speeches by the High Commissioner

15 December 1992 – Acceptance Speech to the Stockholm Meeting of the Council of Ministers of Foreign Affairs of the CSCE, Stockholm, Sweden.

3 March 1993 – Speech in Acceptance of a Honorary Doctorate, Prague, The Czech Republic.

6 March 1993 – 'International Response to Ethnic Conflicts: Focusing on Prevention', Address by Max van der Stoel, CSCE High Commissioner on National Minorities to the Closing Banquet of the Martin Ennals Memorial Symposium on Self-Determination, Co-sponsored by the College of Law, University of Saskatchewan, and International Alert, Saskatoon, Saskatchewan, Canada.

24 May 1993 – 'Case Studies National Minority Issues: Positive Results', Keynote Address to the CSCE Human Dimension Seminar, Warsaw, Poland.

25 June 1993 – 'International Response to Ethnic Conflicts: Focusing on Prevention', Keynote Address to the Fourth International PIOOM Symposium: 'Ethnic Conflicts and Human Rights Violations in Europe', Leiden, The Netherlands.

8 July 1993 – 'Early Response to Ethnic Conflicts: Focusing on Prevention', Address to the Parliamentary Assembly of the CSCE, Helsinki, Finland.

28–29 September 1993 – Intervention at the CSCE Human Dimension Implementation Meeting, Warsaw, Poland.

30 November 1993 – Address to the Rome Meeting of the Council of Ministers for Foreign Affairs of the CSCE, Rome, Italy.

19 January 1994 – Keynote Speech to the CSCE Seminar on Early Warning and Preventive Diplomacy, Warsaw, Poland.

27–28 January 1994 – 'Preventive Diplomacy in Situations of Ethnic Tensions: the Role of the CSCE High Commissioner on National Minorities', Remarks at seminars of the Friedrich Ebert Stiftung and the Federal Academy for Security Policy, Bonn, Germany.

24 March 1994 – 'Political Order, Human Rights and Development'. Introduction to a seminar on 'Conflict and Development: Causes, Effects and Remedies' at the Netherlands Institute of International Relations, the Hague.

6 July 1994 – 'Preventing Conflict and Building Peace: the CSCE and Conflict Prevention in Europe', Address to the Meeting of the Third Committee of the CSCE Parliamentary Assembly, Vienna, Austria.

19 September 1994 – 'Controlling Ethnic Tensions: the Experience of the CSCE High Commissioner on National Minorities', Remarks at the Annual Conference of the European Research Centre on Migration and Ethnic Relations (ERCOMER), Utrecht University, Utrecht, The Netherlands.

20 September 1994 – Introductory Remarks at the CSCE Human Dimension Seminar 'Roma in the CSCE Region', Warsaw, Poland.

4 July 1995 – 'The Role of the High Commissioner on National Minorities in OSCE Conflict Prevention', Address to the Meeting of the Third Committee of the OSCE Parliamentary Assembly, Ottawa, Canada.

1 September 1995 – Statement by the High Commissioner on National Minorities on the Occasion of his Mission to Romania on 28–31 August 1995.

2 October 1995 – 'Report of Mr Max van der Stoel, the OSCE High Commissioner on National Minorities', OSCE Implementation Meeting on Human Dimension Issues, Warsaw, Poland.

14 June 1996 – 'Peace and Justice, Power and Principle: From Nuremberg to the Hague', Statement to the Seminar on 'Punishing War Crimes in the Former Yugoslavia: a Critical Juncture for the International Community', Institute for Human Rights, Åbo Akademi University, Åbo/Turku, Finland.

5 July 1996 – Speech of the High Commissioner on National Minorities to the Parliamentary Assembly, Stockholm, Sweden.

30 September 1996 – 'The Role of the OSCE in Conflict Prevention', Address to the Royal Institute for International Relations, Brussels, Belgium.

18 October 1996 – 'The Role of the High Commissioner on National Minorities in Conflict Prevention'. Address to a workshop on 'An Agenda for Diplomacy', Skopje, former Yugoslav Republic of Macedonia.

4 November 1996 – Report by Mr Max van der Stoel, OSCE High Commissioner on National Minorities, OSCE Review Meeting, Vienna, Austria.

17 March 1997 – 'Democracy and Human Rights: On the Work of the OSCE High Commissioner on National Minorities', Speech at the Institute for Peace Research and Security Policy at the University of Hamburg, Germany.

10 April 1997, 'The OSCE and Conflict Prevention: the Role of the High

Commissioner on National Minorities' at the European Centre for Minority Studies, Flensburg, Germany.

16 June 1997 – Speech at a Forum on Conflict Prevention, Bonn, Germany.

17 June 1997 – Michael Akehurst Memorial Lecture, Keele University, UK.

20 November 1997 – Speech at the OSCE Human Dimension Implementation Meeting, Warsaw, Poland.

18 March 1998 – Speech at the Bruno Kreisky Forum, Vienna, Austria.

18 October 1998 – 'The Role and Importance of Integrating Diversity', Address to the Conference on 'Governance and Participation: Integrating Diversity', Locarno, Switzerland.

28 October 1998 – Address at the OSCE Human Dimension Implementation Meeting, Warsaw, Poland.

9 July 1999 – 'Early Warning and Early Action: Preventing Inter-Ethnic Conflict', Speech to the Royal Institute of International Affairs.

6 September 1999 – Address to the Supplementary Human Dimension Meeting on Roma and Sinti Issues, Vienna, Austria.

20 September 1999 – Speech at the OSCE Review Conference, Vienna, Austria.

19 October 1999 – 'Human Rights, the Prevention of Conflict and the International Protection of Minorities: a Contemporary Paradigm for Contemporary Challenges', Speech at the London School of Economics and Political Science, London, UK.

24 November 1999 – Address to Pazmany Peter Catholic University, Faculty of Law, Budapest.

10 December 1999 – Address at the International Conference on Human Rights of the Visegrad 4 Countries, Bratislava.

16 March 2000 – 'Integrating Diversity in a Multi-Ethnic Region: Promoting Peace and Security in South-Eastern Europe', Portoroz, Slovenia.

12 April 2000 – 'The Protection of Minorities in the OSCE Region', Address to a OSCE Parliamentary Assembly Seminar, Antalya, Turkey.

18 May 2000 – 'The Linguistic and Education Rights of National Minorities and their Application in Moldova', Chisinau, Moldova.

For more of the High Commissioner's speeches, see the HCNM section of the OSCE website at www.osce.org.

OSCE Documents

Conference on Security and Co-operation in Europe, Final Act, Helsinki 1975.

Document of the Copenhagen Meeting of the Conference on the Human Dimension of the CSCE, 1990.

Charter of Paris for a New Europe, Paris 1990.

Document of the Moscow Meeting of the Conference on the Human Dimension of the CSCE, Moscow 1991.

Report of the CSCE Meeting of Experts on National Minorities, Geneva 1991.

CSCE Helsinki Document 1992: The Challenges of Change.

Summary of Conclusions of the Third Meeting of the Council of the Stockholm Council Meeting, 1992.

HCNM Reports

Roma (Gypsies) in the CSCE Region, Report of the HCNM at the Meeting of the Committee of Senior Officials, 21 September 1993.

Report on Linguistic Rights of Persons Belonging to National Minorities in the OSCE Area, OSCE HCNM, March 1999.

Report on the Situation of Roma and Sinti in the OSCE Area, OSCE HCNM, March 2000.

www.ingramcontent.com/pod-product-compliance
Ingram Content Group UK Ltd.
Pitfield, Milton Keynes, MK11 3LW, UK
UKHW022208051026
15624UKWH00001B/62

9 789041 116512